PARTISAN REVIEW

The 50th Anniversary Edition

Edited by

WILLIAM PHILLIPS

PARTISAN REVIEW

William Phillips, EDITOR

Edith Kurzweil, EXECUTIVE EDITOR

ASSOCIATE EDITOR
Steven Marcus

EDITORIAL ASSOCIATE
Joan C. Schwartz

EDITORIAL ASSISTANTS
Rachel Hadas
Estelle Leontief
Rosanna Warren
Jane Uscilka

CONTRIBUTING EDITORS
Kathleen Agena
Daniel Bell
Peter Brooks
Morris Dickstein
Daphne Merkin
Leon Wieseltier
Dennis Wrong

CONSULTANTS
John Ashbery
Frank Kermode
Barbara Rose
Susan Sontag
Stephen Spender

PUBLICATIONS AND ADVISORY BOARD
Joanna S. Rose, Chairman
Lillian Braude
Carter Burden
Cynthia G. Colin
Joan Ganz Cooney
H. William Fitelson
Gerald J. Gross
Marjorie Iseman
Shirley Johnson Lans
Vera List
Robert H. Montgomery, Jr.
Lynn Nesbit
David B. Pearce, M.D.
Ethel Person, M.D.
Al Silverman
Anne W. Simon
Roger L. Stevens
Robert Wechsler

CORRESPONDING EDITORS
Leslie Epstein, Eugene Goodheart, Donald Marshall, Roger Shattuck, Mark Shechner

PARTISAN REVIEW

The 50th Anniversary Edition

Edited by

WILLIAM PHILLIPS

STEIN AND DAY/*Publishers*/New York

Library of Congress Cataloging in Publication Data

Main entry under title:

Partisan review.
   Published also as v. 51, no. 4 and v. 52, no. 1 of
the Partisan review.

   1. Phillips, William, 1907 Nov. 14-   .   II. Partisan
review (New York, N.Y.: 1934)   III. Partisan review &
anvil.   IV. Partisan review (New York, N.Y.: 1936)
AC5.P36   1985   081   85-40325
ISBN 0-8125-3061-X
ISBN 0-8128-6244-9 (pbk.)

CONTENTS

COMMENTS

PARTISAN REVIEW

The 50th Anniversary Edition

Edited by

WILLIAM PHILLIPS

PARTISAN REVIEW THEN AND NOW. Just to reread the editorial in the first issue of the new *Partisan Review* is to be reminded how much the world has changed and how much we have changed. Yet there is a clear line of continuity in the magazine. Although some of our thinking has responded to changes in the intellectual and political atmosphere, our intellectual principles and our literary values have been fairly constant.

In 1937, when we had just broken with the communists, and we reappeared as an independent, Left literary and cultural review, we still avowed an allegiance to a radical movement and to the basic direction of Marxist thinking. At the same time, we were committed to the free play of ideas, and we were open to all literary tendencies. We were aware that the Soviet Union had become a totalitarian state and that the Communist Party was a corrupt instrument of Soviet policy. But it still was not clear, at least not to us, how much of what has gone by the name of radical or Marxist thinking had been perverted by Soviet — and Communist — nationalist purposes and machinations — how much of it was becoming "Left" cant.

As the early editorial indicated, we were trying to merge the modernism, the estheticism, and the avant garde impulses of the earliest years of the century with the new historical sense that the best part of the radical movement had introduced. But while we recognized that the esthetic of modernism was undergoing many changes, we could not foresee later cooptation by the media and by more popular trends in the culture.

We think, however, as we look back, that we were able to respond to the shift of the political and literary mind and to the changes in the world situation, while at the same time we managed to maintain our political and literary sanity. We think we succeeded, at least most of the time, in keeping a balance between traditional standards and values and an adventurous spirit in evaluating new ideas and forms.

Where are we now, as we are nearing the end of a violent and traumatic century? This is a difficult question to answer. Perhaps the most characteristic aspect of this period is that everything seems to be in doubt, everything in flux, everything problematic. Our literature, our culture, our politics are full of contradictions and reversals and polarizations. Under the banner of pluralism, everything is moving in all directions, and confusion has become a normal condition. This is not to say there is any lack of talent or critical thinking.

A time that can produce a Mailer, Bellow, Malamud, Ozick, Kundera, Solzhenitsyn, Lessing, Naipal, to name only a few outstanding novelists, is surely a creative epoch. And there are too many accomplished figures to list in the academic disciplines. Yet the prevailing atmosphere is one of specialization, academicism, and uncertainty. In literary criticism, for example, there are still a few critics who are neither journalists nor academics, such as Irving Howe, Alfred Kazin, Mary McCarthy, Stephen Spender, Robert Penn Warren. But academic criticism is dominated by a highly abstract, self-perpetuating literary theorizing, most of it under the influence of an Americanized version of French deconstructionism, some of it under the spell of a jargonized and outdated Marxism. And the popular media, with their zest for novelty, create the feeling that we are living in a permanent intellectual carnival.

Beyond the intellectual questions are the larger ones of war and peace and the survival of Western democracy. We are living in a state of apocalyptic fear and fatality about the possibility of a nuclear holocaust — partly real, partly induced by a new wave of radical pacifism that has the effect of paralyzing the will of the West to defend itself against the growing power of the Soviet Union and its terrorist allies. And none of the solutions — or even the old categories — appear to furnish the answers to our problems.

It is often said that the terms "left" and "right" no longer have meaning. This is not true. They do have a meaning, but the meaning is not what it used to be. For much of the Left is not the old Marxist, revolutionary Left. Nor is it simply pro-Russian or pro-communist. The new Left is a complex of outworn Marxist notions, vaguely progressive ideas, trendy causes like environmentalism and various liberation movements, sympathy for something called the Third World, pacifism, anti-Americanism, an obsessive fear of nuclear power. All this is combined with a sometimes genuine, sometimes spurious concern for justice and human welfare. Unfortunately, the concern is often expressed in terms of blind government spending and in political pieties. This is not to say there is not a serious socialist Left, mostly in France and to a lesser extent in this country, but it is often overwhelmed by the more popular radical tide. On the other hand, in an inversion of their usual roles, conservatives are often more concerned over the preservation of liberal and democratic values than are the liberals on the Left, though a good deal of this concern is more rhetorical than real. Nevertheless, in matters of foreign policy, for example, conservatives tend to be more realistic and more reliable than the liberals and the Left. Liberals, as a rule, are caught in the crossfire between conservatives and radicals; many of them have been swept up in the tide of worldwide pacifist and anti-nuclear agitation. But, of course, a number of liberals have resisted the seductive and self-justifying assumption of the Left that to be on the side of progress and decency, one has to be "gauchist" — that to be "gauchist" is itself a positive value and ideal. These liberals now know that Left or Right stances are, as they say, part of the problem not the solution, and that each issue must be examined on its own.

Such is the policy that *Partisan Review* seeks to follow. It is, we think, an extension to our hopes and dilemmas today of the principles we stated in our early editorial. We are still opposed to political reflexes, cultural cant, and literary obfuscation. Our history, we feel, has demonstrated that we are committed to publishing those works that best represent the creative and critical intelligence of our time.

W. P.

*   *   *   *

Of the original contributors, some have died, but several writers who appeared in early numbers of *Partisan Review* are represented in this Anniversary Issue. Sidney Hook and Lionel Trilling, who had much to do with the political and literary direction of the magazine at the start, have characteristic contributions (Trilling posthumously). We regret that Philip Rahv, who had a major role as an editor, and Fred Dupee, who was also a leading figure in the early life of the magazine, could not be in this issue. Other writers associated at the beginning were Lionel Abel, Eleanor Clark, Clement Greenberg, Mary McCarthy, Dwight Macdonald, and Diana Trilling. The second generation represented here includes Daniel Bell, Nathan Glazer, Irving Howe, Alfred Kazin, Norman Mailer, Bernard Malamud, Robert Motherwell, Norman Podhoretz, Philip Roth, and Arthur Schlesinger, Jr. The other figures have joined us more recently.

Those invited to contribute to the Anniversary Issue were asked to submit a poem, story, essay, part of something they were working on, or a brief statement about how their views have changed over the years. All contributors were asked to make their pieces short, because we wanted to include as many writers as possible within the obvious space limitations.

Fifty years is a long time, and we hope the contributors to this volume give some sense of what made our longevity possible.

Immediately following is the original editorial statement from the first issue of the new *Partisan Review*.

EDITORIAL STATEMENT*

As our readers know, the tradition of aestheticism has given way to a literature which, for its origin and final justification, looks beyond itself and deep into the historic process. But the forms of literary editorship, at once exacting and adventurous, which characterized the magazines of the aesthetic revolt, were of definite cultural value; and these forms *Partisan Review* will wish to adapt to the literature of the new period.

Any magazine, we believe, that aspires to a place in the vanguard of literature today, will be revolutionary in tendency; but we are also convinced that any such magazine will be unequivocally independent. *Partisan Review* is aware of its responsibility to the revolutionary movement in general, but we disclaim obligation to any of its organized political expressions. Indeed we think that the cause of revolutionary literature is best served by a policy of no commitments to any political party. Thus our underscoring of the factor of independence is based, not primarily on our differences with any one group, but on the conviction that literature in our period should be free of all factional dependence.

There is already a tendency in America for the more conscious social writers to identify themselves with a single organization, the Communist Party; with the result that they grow automatic in their political responses but increasingly less responsible in an artistic sense. And the Party literary critics, equipped with the zeal of vigilantes, begin to consolidate into aggressive political-literary amalgams as many tendencies as possible and to outlaw all dissenting opinion. This projection on the cultural field of factionalism in politics makes for literary cleavages which, in most instances, have little to do with literary issues, and which are more and more provocative of a ruinous bitterness among writers. Formerly associated with the Communist Party, *Partisan Review* strove from the first against its drive to equate the interests of literature with those of factional politics. Our reappearance on an independent basis signifies our conviction that the totalitarian trend is inherent in that movement and that it can no longer be combatted from within.

But many other tendencies exist in American letters, and these, we think, are turning from the senseless disciplines of the official Left

---

*Original *Partisan Review* Editorial Statement.

to shape a new movement. The old movement will continue and, to judge by present indications, it will be reënforced more and more by academicians from the universities, by yesterday's celebrities and today's philistines. Armed to the teeth with slogans of revolutionary prudence, its official critics will revive the petty-bourgeois tradition of gentility, and with each new tragedy on the historic level they will call the louder for a literature of good cheer. Weak in genuine literary authority but equipped with all the economic and publicity powers of an authentic cultural bureaucracy, the old regime will seek to isolate the new by performing upon it the easy surgery of political falsification. Because the writers of the new grouping aspire to independence in politics as well as in art, they will be identified with fascism, sometimes directly, sometimes through the convenient medium of "Trotskyism." Every effort, in short, will be made to *excommunicate* the new generation, so that their writing and their politics may be regarded as making up a kind of diabolic totality; which would render unnecessary any sort of rational discussion of the merits of either.

Do we exaggerate? On the contrary, our prediction as to the line the old regime will take is based on the first maneuvers of a campaign which has already begun. *Already*, before it has appeared, *Partisan Review* has been subjected to a series of attacks in the Communist Party press; already, with no regard for fact — without, indeed, any relevant facts to go by — they have attributed gratuitous political designs to *Partisan Review* in an effort to confuse the primarily literary issue between us.

But *Partisan Review* aspires to represent a new and dissident generation in American letters; it will not be dislodged from its independent position by any political campaign against it. And without ignoring the importance of the official movement as a sign of the times we shall know how to estimate its authority in literature. But we shall also distinguish, wherever possible, between the tendencies of this faction itself and the work of writers associated with it. For our editorial accent falls chiefly on culture and its broader social determinants. Conformity to a given social ideology or to a prescribed attitude or technique, will not be asked of our writers. On the contrary, our pages will be open to any tendency which is relevant to literature in our time. Marxism in culture, we think, is first of all an instrument of analysis and evaluation; and if, in the last instance, it prevails over other disciplines, it does so through the medium of democratic controversy. Such is the medium that *Partisan Review* will want to provide in its pages.

FROM THE NOTEBOOKS OF
LIONEL TRILLING *

(1927)

It has gone to only 1000 words, a very rough sketch of the beginning of the 1st chapter. (There is no particular reason why it should not be done in chapters: they are no more arbitrary than the whole notion of a novel.) So far three persons have been introduced, and as yet, Headland, the young man, is so different — or different only in that he already is not so sloppy — from the usual "young man." The trick is to be kept "tight," sensible, and unhysterical — in short, if he is to be puzzled, he is also to be intelligent. He is to have humor but no wit. Unfortunately (because, I suppose, it will be a "self-portrait") he cannot be very interesting: that is, he will have no real physical or emotional abnormality. Perhaps it might be well to give him one soon, but I fear he will always be the least dramatic person in the book, no matter what he does, because the most intellectual — i.e. he will be seeing most. Probably he will have the dull truth of David Copperfield rather than the active, real truth of Micawber. Perhaps not.

Advice: Do not be afraid of strangeness and "improbability."

Advice: Do not be afraid of action. You can manage it. The destiny of this y[oung] m[an] by p. 300 is to win freedom, of some sort, for the book is to be a comedy.

(1928)

To become a friend to yourself! Emerson addressed himself as "dear" in his Journals!

(1928)

Being a Jew is like walking in the wind or swimming: you are touched at all points and conscious everywhere.

(1928)

I have spoken twice (to women) that educating a son I should allow him no fairy tales and only a very few novels. This is to prevent him from having 1. the sense of romantic solitude (if he is worth anything he will develop a proper and useful solitude) which identification with the *hero* gives. 2. cant ideas of right and wrong, absurd

---

* Lionel Trilling (1905–75) contributed regularly to *Partisan Review* in the period covered by these excerpts. His notebooks were not a conventional diary. They contain comments on books, people and happenings in his life, records of certain important events, suggestions for stories and novels. These entries were selected by Christopher Zinn, a graduate student of English at New York University.

systems of honor and morality which never never will he be able completely to get rid of, 3. the attainment of "ideals," of *a priori* desires, of
a priori emotions. He should amuse himself with fact only: he will
then not learn that if the weak younger son do or do not the magical
honorable thing he will win the princess with hair like flax. It is objected that he will not ever learn of beauty and he will never desire:
but he will and if he do not that is his choice. If he read a true account of a polar expedition he will find both misery and glamor & he
may balance his account. He will learn the so-necessary thing that
every lovely thing may — must? — have a sordid disagreeable foundation. He will come out for the world without preconceptions, without
self-deceptions which it will take him years to set right. — Poetry he
might read because of the element which Wordsworth notes of formal unreality. The great books taught me, they never made me dream.
The bad books made me dream and hurt me. I was right when 4 years
ago I said that the best rule-of-thumb for judgment of a good novel
or play was — Do you want to be the hero? If you do, the work is bad.

(1931–32?)

Humor seems almost never to be revolutionary — as the common
opinion makes it out to be: see the *Nation's* praise of Peter Arno[1] &
Cohen's[2] anger that Arno really exalts and defends the class he
seems to attack. But Aristophanes was a Tory & hated Socrates' seriousness with the usual Tory's hate of it. The fabliaux were not
discouraged by the Church (see the Churl in Heaven). Cervantes
was far from revolutionary. Rabelais defended an aristocratic ideal.
Dickens . . .[3] Carlyle says that a sense of humor is a kind of inverted
sense of sublimity: it raises what is generally lowly into our affections. By affording a comic katharsis, Falstaff and Charlie Chaplin
draw off our resentment of what is above us. Probably it is impossible for humor to be ever a revolutionary weapon. Candide can do little more than generate irony.

(1931–32?)

Reading Mill's Autobiography for the about 3rd time. Remembering how I used to find it dull and gray and now enormously rich and
exciting, I understand how very changed I have become. Especially
the parts relating to his difficulties with the problems of government
are exciting. . . .

---

[1]Cartoonist for *The New Yorker*.
[2]Elliot E. Cohen, editor of *The Menorah Journal*.
[3]Trilling's ellipsis.

Dec 19 (1933)

Saw a letter which Hemingway wrote to Kip[4] — a crazy letter, written when he was drunk — self-revealing, arrogant, scared, trivial, absurd: yet felt from reading it how right such a man is compared to the "good minds" of my university life — how he will produce and mean something to the world . . . how his life which he could expose without dignity and which is anarchic and "childish" is a better life than anyone I know could live, and right for his job. And how far-far-far- I am going from being a writer — how less and less I have the material and the mind and the will. A few — very few — more years and the last chance will be gone.

Tues April 20 (1936)

Jacques B[5] called to report content of his dinner with Steeves[6] as follows. That I am considered the most brilliant of the younger instructors, that I am most devoted to teaching of all of them & most conscientious. That I have done brilliantly in the colloquium & am irreplaceable in that course: that my two yrs of work in the 19th century were splendid. With freshmen I am not so utterly successful: a little too much for them (not true, I think). The reason for dismissal is that as a Jew, a Marxist, a Freudian I am uneasy. This hampers my work and makes me unhappy. E.E. Neff[7] (a Columbia professor!) concurs in this opinion! (And Mark?[8])

Tues May 5 (1936)

Interview with Steeves. 1½ hours. Me cool and positive. Him friendly and "realistic."

Explains it as decision of college profs. (i.e. Neff, Weaver,[9] Van D., Everett,[10] Dick[11]). Two reasons adduced: 1. That it is better for me to get out, I being superior to all the other men in the Dept who because of their inferiority or mediocrity . . . will easily get jobs at any time. Believe me unhappy here. Act motivated by concern for my welfare. I replied that if this is so I might well have been con-

---

[4]Clifton Fadiman.

[5]Jacques Barzun.

[6]Harrison Ross Steeves, Chairman of the Columbia College English Department.

[7]Emery E. Neff.

[8]Mark Van Doren.

[9]Raymond Weaver.

[10]Charles Everett.

[11]Harry K. Dick.

sulted, that I agreed that it might be well for me to move on, that, however, I had plans which involved a few more years of teaching at C in order to get started on my work of writing. (2) That I had been failing as a teacher. That I irritated many freshman students by talking about literature as sociology and psychology. I asked how his run of the mill teachers taught Babbitt and Point Counterpoint [*sic*] as anything else. Said that E.E.N. considered that my 1st year of work in 65–6 was excellent but felt I had fallen off in 2nd year. Replied that this constituted disingenuousness on N.'s part, for he had assured me that my work had been good, that my removal had been for administrative reasons, that he was trying to get the course for me again. Said at a later time N. dissatisfied with my grad. work. Replied that I considered this equally disingenuous in view of his praise. Said Neff was an excellent friend. Replied Neff knew less about me than almost anyone.

I said that nothing could convince me that I was not a good teacher, & that 90% of my students thought me so. I said I could say this because I had not the slightest intention of trying to convince *him.* Said I thought I was particularly adapted to Columbia as I thought he wanted it to be. He said that he was sure that I was a very good teacher as teaching should be done but that they needed routine men, that the whole dept was to be cleaned out, the most routine men (Eng A & C) to be kept the longest. — Said that my work in Colloq. could not be done better. I said that I was not unhappy at Colum though I might be unhappy, & that my emotions had nothing to do with my teaching. I said he was making an awful indictment of his department if what he said was true. He inclined to agree and include the whole college system. — I asked him how he knew of my condition & its effects on my work. Said it was generally felt. I forced him to say it was a mere intuition. At the end he said would I want to stay another year if the other men agreed. I said I was not asking for it, nor had I the slightest thought of doing so but that I had no desire to be quixotic and that a year would be useful. He said he would see how things *went* (meaning my teaching) and he would delay positive action. I said since I felt that his altruistic motive had to be rejected, and since I preferred to consider that I was being dropped because I was a bad (or too good) teacher, I felt that I could not accept this implication that I was rebuked and would try to improve. He said I was not being rebuked and he would talk to the other men. I said only if he understood and would make clear that I had not asked for an extension of time. He said he understood this.

Tues May 5 (1936) Interview with Mark 5:30–6:15 P.M.
Told him account of interview with Steeves. Listened and approved. Started to say he had no part in the meeting. I warned him that Steeves had said he had concurred. He said that when the attack on me had taken place he had not said anything. Why? Doesn't know. Could only say he admired me, that I was a nice fellow; weight of numbers was against him; had no evidence such as teaching a course with me. Did I not understand that? Might I not act in the same way? Yes I might but I should not feel very proud of it. He felt ashamed, said he.

Weaver had of course spoken against me but W. is usually discounted. Dick had been silent. Everett had said that he had certain reports from students: didn't set much store by them. Steeves rather silent.

(Says Weaver dislikes me because thinks I like to be stepped on too much: too meek. Said W. will be impressed by my standing up to Steeves!). . .

Telephone conversation with Irwin[12] *May 5 (1936)* 8: P.M.
Told him of interviews. . . . He told me of having lunch with Edgar Johnson. Neff sits down. Conversation turns to Schappes at C.C.N.Y. Edgar asks what doing about tenure at Columbia? Neff begins to make speech. Some people being fired for incompetence, some for their own good, some because they didn't fit. Irwin asked what about L.T., into what category does he fit? He is not . . . nor . . . — E.E.N. says that is very complicated. "I have followed L's career for a long time with the greatest interest. But . . . His great gift is his literary sense.["] Irwin: Seems good thing in a teacher of literature. E.E.N. But he has involved himself with Ideas. . . . He is too sensitive . . . Doesn't fit because he is a Jew. At any rate, he was appointed against the will of the dept!!

Called E.E.N. and made date to annihilate him on Thursday.

6 May (1936) Interview with H.K. Dick 20 minutes
Stated case as put by Steeves. He replied that he knew nothing of my teaching, saw no way he could know. Knew nothing of effect of "happiness" on my teaching: Said that he had heard some complaints about my emphasis on "Sociology." Said he did not teach

---

[12]Irwin Edman.

"Lovers" "Intermezzo" or "PCP"[13] any more partly because of feeling
that it might shock boys & that they did not understand the matters
in works [sic]; also there was consideration of parents' raised eye-
brows. Said that the cause of the movement to drop me was the general policy of the department to "rotate." Insisted he knew nothing of
my teaching.

May 6 (1936)

J.B. reminds me of E. Neff's old sociological complex. In Eng
5M-6 he could think of nothing in a poem save what it reflected —
democracy, the factory system, religious conflict etc. Caring nothing
for the music or mood. Of course he used to preach sociology and
econ. in literature to all of us. But my last conversation with him
about poetry brought out the opinion that ideas do not matter in
poetry — the music was everything. Interpretation obvious: in 1924 it
was OK to write about Carlyle Mill & the factory conditions. But
now it is getting near and real and he is running for cover into
"music."

May 7 (1936) Interview with Everett 11–11:15

Said I wanted to ask him about what he testified in the
meeting. He said I must be sure that I do not believe there was un-
friendliness to me at the meeting. I said cooly I was neither doubtful
nor interested in the matter of friendship. He told me his part: it was
as Mark had described it. I told him so. He said he could not do
otherwise by his conscience than to tell the truth. I said of course but
I said that I could do no otherwise by my pedagogical conscience
than to raise hell to say that the way I taught was the right way. I
asked him how he taught the books we used. He said he had great
difficulty teaching PCP. He said I should not lose my head; that he
had been fired once and that the situation had suddenly broken. I
said I wasn't much interested.

Interview with Neff *May 7 (1936)* 12:15–1:30

He very friendly, I cold but amicable. Found it impossible to
be furious with him personally but was inflexible in my positions. I
gave a very clear and well-put summary of my interviews with Steeves
& Van Doren. Told him what I had been told of his declaration about
my 1) 65 work & 2) about my thesis.

---

[13]Probably *Sons and Lovers,* by D.H. Lawrence; "Intermezzo," by Arthur Schnitzler;
Point Counter Point, by Aldous Huxley.

He said about 1) that Steeves must be mistaken in the attribution. Had only the highest admiration of my work there as he had said to me. Told him to tell this to Steeves, said he wld. About 2) he said he had not wanted to tell me about his reservations about my thesis, because it was still inchoate (when else? I asked) & that he had mentioned them because he felt that my sociological tendencies had hidden my literary gifts in the thesis as in the classroom. But that his reservations were not fundamental.

He said that he did not want me to stay because my position was bad and likely to get worse. In what way bad? He explained my question about my Jewish-sensitivity: had not meant that: had meant that I was too sensitive to Weaver's "brutality." I said I ignored it. He admitted that there was no fault to find with my teaching that could not be corrected by a word of suggestion to me. What it really got down to was that Weaver pressed hard & my contemporaries had disliked my teaching (and me presumably) & that this had counted. I blew up & asked him if he really meant to say that this minority, part of it unrepresented, had swung a majority. He said things always happened so. I used no uncertain terms.

He told me that the trouble had started with my appointment. Said it had been forced by Thorndike[14] & put through without the democratic consent of the dept. Said he understood I had told Thorndike I was in trouble at Hunter, would get no job & was in desperate financial straits. I denied that I had ever spoken to Thorndike in this way. (Henry Ladd perhaps did.) (This accounts for Weaver's feeling I like to be stepped on?)

Finally I asked him if I might tell Steeves that in his (Neff's) opinion my dismissal had nothing to do with my teaching at all but only with the dislike of Weaver and a few of my contemporaries. He said, heartily, that I might quote him so and even gave me a formulation of that opinion to use.

I said that apparently I was being fired for all the qualities I admired in myself & that I considered the whole matter a triumph for me. He said (defending his success) that it was not a triumph but luck. — I did not admit at any point the decency of his getting me fired for my own good, though his absurd mind is sincere about it, I believe. He said the whole matter was not to have been as peremptory as it was with a short time set and hinted vaguely that it might

---

[14]Ashley Thorndike.

be adjusted as to time. The whole business he had thought would be a warning not a dismissal: nonsense.

There remains to see Steeves and tell him what I now know and to insult Weaver, publicly if possible.

Note that Mark concurs with Steeves about Emery's position and intention!

June 13 (1936)

Going through change of life and acquiring a new dimension. Principally a sense that I do not have to prove anything finally and everlastingly. A sense of life — of the past and present. Am no longer certain that the future will be a certain — Marxian — way. No longer measure all things by linear Marxian yardstick. But this is symbolic. A new emotional response to all things. New response to people, a new tolerance, a new interest. A sense of invulnerability. The result of my successful explosion at Columbia? The feeling that I can now write with a new illumination, getting rid of that rigid linear method that has irritated me in my reviewing for so long. . . . — An easier understanding of poetry and painting — and of opinion. — Less responsibility put on people. — Sense of my own stature & less concern with it. — Effect visible in O'Neill essay.

(1936)

To tell students: In reading poetry do not assume that you are in an audience listening to music; assume rather that you are yourself the musical performer — the poem is your score and you have to make someone understand it — as we say, you have to *interpret* it.

(1936)

An essay on the "ambivalent moments" — those moments in our reading when we neither hate nor love what the author is saying but hate and love together: when our mind is poised over a recognition of a truth which attacks other truths, or when the author has brilliantly caught half the truth, and denies the other half. These are the most fertile moments. They are the moments of the critic:

Santayana, Arnold, Carlyle: Nietzsche, etc.

(1936)

Story of a teacher and his student: the boy has just graduated: transformation of the teacher's rather sentimental regard: the change from a false charming relationship to a real disagreeable one. The student's rivalry seen, etc.

Story of a university teacher who had never got to write, meeting the

woman he had known as a girl who had written and become very successful: with such "perceptive" stories, such revolutionary stories and
now is wealthy and Stalinist. To be a story of literary criticism: on
the nature of writing.

(1944)

The evening at the Rices[15] with John Matthews—how much I
laughed—realization how seldom we laugh, in that cathartic way, although we laugh almost continuously in a social group. How much
pleasure I got when he was doing imitations of vaudeville patter—my
pleasure in being able to cap his gag at the right moment—he stood
on a stepladder in order to bite himself on the head. How I loved the
memory of vaudeville, but how I used to hate vaudeville as a boy. I
was romantic and vaudeville gave only worried, harrassed people.
Joe Cook was the only exception and he was a delight. But even he
had a great deal of unhappy meaning; still, he could *do* so much. But
what I always looked forward to was the "sketch" with its drama.
Actually, vaudeville comedy represented *adult* life.

Being taken to Morrison's theater in Rockaway Park to see Belle
Baker by my Uncle T. —I disliked her and thought her vulgar—
the surprise at this at home and the great pleasure—the surprise was
insincere, the pleasure sincere: I was innately "refined"! —That
Morrison's theater (1912?) was out of one of Howells' Rockaway
sketches—The movies were for me much better than vaudeville—
the fantasy was what I liked—and even the medium gave me a sense
of safety. —Remembering myself then, at 7,8,9?, I have the impression of someone enormously mature, much more mature than my
uncle T., toward whom I must have felt some of the family's condescension—but I have the reminiscent sensation that I looked on
this scene with a remote and censorious eye, the sense that there
were better things!

(1944)

I began this notebook after reading Henry James's regret that he had
so long neglected to keep one. After the usual burst of dutifulness, I
gave up. But it is imp't in my situation to keep it, really to make a
habit of it so as to fix my mind always and continuously and as much
as possible on the job I still think must be done.

Reasons for not keeping a notebook: 1) the ambiguity of the

---

[15]Kitty and Philip Blair Rice.

reader—it is never quite oneself. 2) I usually hate the sight of my handwriting—it lives too much and I dislike its life—I mean by "lives," of course, betrays too much!

(1945)

At the Harvard Club—the sense from the faces and manners of the greater possibility of drama than one gets from the general run of middle class people. Money & snobbery—together—are the basis of the novel & one sees the signs of both here. And with money & snobbery, the "mustache" on which all good novels depend—eccentricities—meaningful ones—of manner: and here one gets them more than in most places.

(1945)

A theory of the middle class: that it is not to be determined by its financial situation but rather by its relation to government. That is, one could shade down from an actual ruling or governing class to a class hopelessly out of relation to government, thinking of gov't as beyond its control, of itself as wholly controlled by gov't. Somewhere in between and in gradations is the group that has the sense that gov't. exists for it, and shapes its consciousness accordingly. It does not have the sense of a perfectly real or immediate connection with gov't.: ideals, desires, emotions intervene. With this definition we can better understand the present trade union situation & mentality; also the Russian social situation.

(1945)

The Victorians have lost all charm for me—they make my *parent* literature, the reading with which I was most cosily at home—I could feel their warmth and seemed always to know my way among them —now they bore me utterly—I cannot read them—I cannot teach them with any conviction. . . . Dickens is the exception—possibly Newman—

(1945)

In three-four-decades, the liberal progressive has not produced a single writer that it itself respects and reads with interest. A list of the writers of our time shows that liberal-progressivism was a matter of contempt or indifference to every writer of large mind—Proust, Joyce, Lawrence, Eliot, Mann (early), Kafka, Yeats, Gide, Shaw— probably there is not a name to be associated with a love of liberal democracy or a hope for it. Thus the enormous breach between the journalism of liberalism—the "serious" writers—and the important

works of the imagination of our time. That is put badly. — Better:
that there does not exist a continuity of imagination and action. The
19th century had by and large such a continuity. — Importance of
this. — When a man does begin to court the liberal-democratic ideal,
it is either a sign or the beginning of spiritual collapse in his work. . . .

(1945)

A birthday — the 40th — incredible that it should have been the first
really happy one that I can remember! — inside and outside causes
— so much cleared away within — a charming party — the Browns,[16]
the Rahvs, Wm Phillips, Quentin Anderson, Philip Rice — everybody quiet and nice — imagine Phil Rahv singing Happy Birthday — (an American folk expression now, a real one: When Wm Ph.
came in late he said seriously when he heard the occasion: But we
have to sing Happy Birthday.) — To have a birthday with friends &
without family delightful — sad this should be — so happy I feared the
consequence of hubris!

(1945)

"Well," said my mother when I told her I wished to go to no
Thanksgiving dinner this year, "Well, I suppose that's all there is to
it — and I must accept. There are many things in my life that I don't
like that I must accept." And the unconscious meaning was so clearly
"In *my* life" that I said sharply "Exactly the same as in my life" —
       She seemed taken aback & agreed at once, "Yes, of course." Yet
I saw as never before the assumption in which I was reared — the assumption that life lay with my mother (and father), that something,
not life, better than life, was for me. That pain, disaster, frustration
might touch them, but not me . . .

(1946)

. . . I meant to write here a note that I had just got over a period of
abt. 6-8 weeks of insatiable desire for praise & notice — nothing satis-
fied and the more I got the more I wanted — grew by what it fed on —
I had to make conscious effort to check this & not allow it to be
publicly seen — I would *court* affirmation and flattery — also about
this time a period of terrible sleeping, in which consciousness seemed
increased in sleep & nightly problems were presented to me which
had to be solved — I could see-smell-feel the aura of philosophy — the
classroomy, textbooky aura of abstraction, terribly engaging, terri-

---

[16]Beatrice and Alan Brown.

bly repelling — life depended on solving the abstract problems presented to me — I wld wake with a hideous sense of desolation and loss
— absolutely hopeless — dominant in my thoughts the desire for children — one night near the end of this period a great sense of being on
the point of *connection* — the connection between 2 things never before
connected, which if reconciled would be of incalculable good — it all
depended on my mental effort — but I could not do it — desolate — at
the same time (end) a great sense that by not doing criticism, not
using my "mind" I was losing all force and poetry whatever — giving
myself only to the novel was making me go all soft and nothing — at
the same time the novel was beginning to open up, but almost to
seem too easy — this association of events came suddenly of itself & is
almost too pat! — that old dodge: too pat! — facing sexual scenes of
novel — sexual fantasy in connection with them.

(1946)

Kenyon Conference — Laski[17] and his charm attack on the little Rice
boy — "Do you know what his name is? His name is Oogly-Moogly.
Oogly-Moogly. And do you know what he did last night?" etc.
(climbed the moon). — But the boy responded to it, loved it. He was
a thing to be conquered. — Laski's aptitude to have a story for every
discussion — what Henry James said — beaten by Laughlin at tennis
— what Uncle Joe said — (what Uncle Joe said was that he was a flexible man but that Molotov was not and that Beria could work wonders by deferring to Molotov a little — he knew that Britain & U.S.
were without imperialist designs but he could never hope to convince
his Politbureau [*sic*] so long as our emissaries were acting as they
did.) His views on Russia were those of the man in the street with
PM[18] — it was astonishing — no cliché was too much for him — he had
deceived himself for so long that now he believed himself thoroughly — his Oxford Union manner on the platform — impossible to
suppose that such a man had anything to do with a nation's course.
— Yet he could charm — because he wished — because he had been
connected with events.

(1946)

At Kenyon: Frost's strange speech — apparently of a kind that he often gives — he makes himself the buffoon — goes into a trance of aged
childishness — he is the child who is rebelling against all the serious

---

[17]Harold Laski.

[18]A New York newspaper which began publication in 1940.

people who are trying to *organize* him — take away his will and individuality. It was, however, full of brilliantly shrewd things — impossible to remember them except referring to the pointless discussion of skepticism the evening before, he said: "'Skepticism,' is that
anything more than we used to mean when we said, 'Well, what
have we here?'" — But also the horror of the old man — fine looking
old man — having to dance and clown to escape (also for his supper)
— American, American in that deadly intimacy, that throwing away
of dignity — "Drop that dignity! Hands up" we say — in order to come
into anything like contact and to make anything like a point.

(1946)

Kafka: The Trial — what is the mystery here when we remember
that every neurosis is a primitive form of legal proceeding in which
the accused carries on the prosecution, imposes judgment and ex-
ecutes the sentence: *all to the end that someone else should not perform the
same process.* In writing about Kafka — whenever — it is important to
remember the function of this sui-trial. (See Ancient Mariner at very
opening of our era)

This is very important in making a judgment of the tendencies
of modern culture. The masochistic character of the estimate of
survival — to adopt a form of being that will differentiate oneself from
the dominant father-culture — to take strength-weakness from that —
to indict the Philistine-father by strength-weakness — the str.-w. of
the legal process of the neurosis.

(1946-47)

Spirit. The modern feeling that spirit should find its expression *immediately* in the world of necessity and that all that falls short of the
full expression of spirit is repulsive. I see this often in gifted students
of a particular kind who when they find that, say, a graduate school
is not up to their standard and expectation, cannot endure staying
and abandon their projects. They have, one might say, no irony —
for irony, perhaps, is the awareness with acceptance of the breach
between spirit and the world of necessity — institutions etc. They insist that spirit be wholly embodied in institutions. If what I have just
written were put to them, they would say, why of course, why not?
Yet the fact is that there is a weakness of spirit within that keeps them
from enduring — they do not believe that they really exist and can
exist if what they recognize as good within themselves is not matched
by external forms, received and established by something. This has,
of course, its social source — for once, no doubt, apart from institu-

tions, there was an agency that established spirit within a man, so that he could say that what he felt within himself was really right and true, no matter how little it was existent outside. This agency was religion itself but also a more extensive thing & view of which religion was a part. In a sense this explains the feelings of the *Politics* group. My students discussing Billy Budd, feel that there is really nothing to be said about the story. Vere is, to them, wholly culpable, Budd being good. Law does not express spirit — even kills it: they insist that this is the whole, and final truth in the matter. They think that Vere is a not-exactly-bad man, but a stuffy one, and in objective result bad. They do not understand the *tragic* choice. They want the reign of spirit immediately. What they do not understand is that: if spirit exists in its purity, so does evil in the form of Claggett and that Claggett makes Vere necessary as an intermediate force between him and Budd. . . .

(1947)

"Dostoevsky could not have had certain of his insights if he had not been psychotic" (Delmore Schwartz). But we value these insights because they are "correct" by the standards of normal reality.

(1947)

The attack on my novel that it is gray, bloodless, intellectual, without passion, is always made with great personal feeling, with anger. — How dared I presume?

Fitzgerald, Lalley, Warshow, Prescott.

(1948)

. . . At *PR* dinner we talked of the situ. of Am. intel. & I spoke of how he cld not be poor & how he bec. isolated from his group — Sid. Hook protested this last pt & I said that I felt that as I defined my position and character by my work I found that I felt more and more alone. He said in a very kind way: that is because you are growing independent and establishing yourself and young people begin to make their way & define themselves by attacking you. Later, speaking with W. Barrett on same subj., B. said "You have managed to estab. your life on an equilibrium, a precarious one, etc" — speaking, nicely, of my life as if it were an observable thing. (Scholarship without pedantry, university teaching without academicism — bec living in N.Y. — a N.Y. continuity etc.) Flattered on both occasions, I had a twinge of pain both times — and that night woke with indigestion and the sense of some awful doom impending by reason of this belief

of others that I was established. A scene in which I was the oldest
and therefore terribly isolated — out on a limb — woke in the morning
with the sense that at 42 I had no more time, no more time. . . .

(1948)

Nowadays, we are all Aristotelian in our aesthetics & we are certain
that the theory of art that Plato proposes in *The Republic* is false &
naive. Yet there is truth in the belief that we become assimilated to
the literal content of the arts we contemplate. And really Aristotle
did not do more in the correction of Plato than to enumerate the conditions under which this did not need to happen; he seems to have
had a very clear sense that it could happen. — It is possible that the
contemplation of cruelty will not make us humane but cruel; that the
reiteration of the badness of our spiritual condition will make us consent to it.

(1948)

We are at heart so profoundly anarchistic that the only form of state
we can imagine living in is Utopian; and so cynical that the only
Utopia we can believe in is authoritarian.

(1948)

Cowardice: let it be a lesson —
Attracted to the committee being formed to get in touch with Italian
radicals & intellectuals, I hesitated, feeling it was naive and sentimental etc. Asked Rahv what he was doing about it — he spoke with
contempt. — So also Barrett — So that I felt ashamed to join, although exactly the naivety of the committee was what drew me — I at
last said no — saying I had no reasons but simply wasn't "drawn" to
it. Mary McC tells me that the *PR* people are joining — *making a virtue of it:* I then decided that I properly stood alone, acting on my own
impulses!

(1948)

The dissatisfaction of the parents of my generation with their
children — the children show no signs of intellectual addiction & even
are hostile to the intellect — is this the cultural tendency (for children,
I am sure, make cultural breaks & smell out the cultural scents &
make large cultural decisions), or is it the contrast between two
generations of Jews? Or is it simply the response of the children to
the neurosis of their fathers? — the particular quality they give to
their intellectuality?

(1948)
Received this morning official announcement of my promotion. If anyone had told me even a year ago that I should be a "full" professor at Columbia at $9,000, I should have been pleased; two years ago I should have been delighted; if anyone had told me that I should be not only indifferent but annoyed because I do not receive $10,000, I should not have believed him. My only satisfaction is that I do not have to make any more bids for promotion & that I do not have to carry a modified title. For the rest indifference. And a sense of the absurdity of my having this rank at all—for no one could be more ignorant than I, without knowledge of any classical language, without any real command of any modern language, with no very wide reading and a great and growing laziness about reading and no wish for investigation. I have only a gift of dealing rather sensibly with literature, which surprises me for I always assume my intellectual feebleness. My being a professor and a much respected and even admired one is a great hoax. But sometimes I feel that I pay for the position not with learning but with my talent—that I draw off from my own work what should remain with it. Yet this is really only a conventional notion, picked up from my downtown friends, used to denigrate myself & my position, to placate the friends, to placate in my mind such people as Mark VD, who yearly seems to me to grow weaker & weaker, more academic, less a person. Suppose I were to dare to believe that one could be a professor and a man! and a writer! —what arrogance and defiance of convention. Yet deeply I dare to believe that—and must learn to believe it on the surface.

September, 1948
Read my paper on the novel[19] to the English Institute, the response seemed very warm, hearty and prolonged applause. Ernest Birnbaum, an elegant old gentleman with a little white beard, rose and delivered an eloquent eulogy of the speech; he spoke to me afterwards about my Wordsworth essay: when I was 20 or 21 and looking for a job he was chairman of the dept at Illinois & responded with extreme coldness to my application. A very young man arose and said that he agreed with me in everything except my phrases "overvaluation of love" & "overvaluation of art"—he gave the Aquinian sense of love and art—I thought "what an attractive, strange, earnest

---

[19] "Art and Fortune."

young man" & replied with polite condescension (I fear). He came
up to me afterwards — it was Philip Wheelwright — The effort of reading 7500 words in 50 minutes enormous — to keep up the rhythm and
intensity — I did it well, but ended hoarse and exhausted — wanted
desperately to be praised by Schorer[20] and Fiedler,[21] who said nothing — Schorer having vanished. The praise of the others profoundly
depressed me — utterly — sickened me with my profession — depressed
all evening, but not as it were personally — very unhappy about my
essay which I consider academic, simple-minded, philistine, regres-
sive — great sense of the superiority of the "others" — Warshow,[22]
Fiedler, Rosenberg[23] (who had written slurringly about me in *Commentary*) Bellow, Kaplan[24] (who had liked my book), not Schorer.
On Sunday both Jacques and Philip[25] called me & said the piece was
a great cultural statement, both using the same phrase. I had sent it
to Ph.R. to tell me whether it was suitable for *PR* & now he is wild
for it. — What am I after? . . .

(1948)

The man who served with me on the jury who questioned me about
the teaching of writing. He wanted to know why, if the teachers
knew so much, they didn't write themselves. I made the usual distinctions between the teaching & performing gifts & impulses &
made comparison with the teaching of music. I said the teacher of
writing didn't want to write. This he brushed aside impatiently:
"Who wouldn't write if he could?" I pressed him: "Do you mean
everybody wants to write?" "Everybody without exception" — He was
a man of youngish fifty, shabby, intense. He ran a full dress rental
establishment in the Bronx. His son, 25, a graduate of CCNY, was
in process of being a novelist.

(1949?)

Allen Ginsberg in to see me — he is a convalescent patient at the
Psych. Institute. He was very well dressed in a checked suit, yellow
pullover and a good tie. He is very well-treated — no distinction be-

[20]Mark Schorer.
[21]Leslie Fiedler.
[22]Robert Warshow.
[23]Harold Rosenberg.
[24]Probably H. J. Kaplan.
[25]Philip Rahv.

ing made at the Inst. between the patients who pay and those who
don't. He will soon have a private room to write in. He speaks of
himself as being "dulled" by the psychiatric therapy, not actually
helped. An analysis is planned for him. He thinks much in terms of
sanitoriums — the Hartford Retreat, one in the South, near Washington, preferring that because it is warm. My sense of fatigue and
indifference — the absence of some grain, some resistant element.
Like a different *kind* of humanity. This always there — and perhaps
all the sad history has been the search for that. — Strange that I never
took notes on all the process of law and psych. that I went through
after his arrest, and of his own account of what had been going on
with him. But perhaps just as well. The events will form of themselves.
— We spoke of Kerouac's book. I predicted that it would not be good
& insisted. But later I saw with what bitterness I had made the prediction — not wanting K's book to be good because if the book of an
accessory to a murder is good, how can one of mine be? — The continuing sense that wickedness — or is it my notion of courage — is
essential for creation.

(1951?)

If one defends the bourgeois, philistine virtues, one does not defend
them merely from the demonism or bohemianism of the artist but
from the present bourgeoisie itself, which is exactly no longer a bourgeoisie itself, — not *burgerlich,* having no sense of "business" and "affairs," no feeling for "hard practicality," but rather a highly politi-
cized group, extravagantly sensitive to trends, tendencies, demands,
ideals — which it does not have the mental equipment to deal with. I
speak here from experience of the university — the administrators
have no bottom, no sense of fact, far less than the intellectuals on the
faculty. They are bewildered and confused, they are excessively concerned with their own status, not in a simple obvious way but in the
sense of wanting to be in accord with a certain "spirit," a certain
rightness which they cannot define. They have no tradition, no sense
of themselves as achieved personalities — they look to the future to
realize themselves. — The old 19th century hard-headed type has
been destroyed. In politics we have mainly the demagogue (ideals
again) and the conscious idealist. — After meeting Del Paine and
being impressed by his quality of mind I said to Diana that it was
strange that a person whose mind was so humanistically flexible, so
literarily comprehensive, should have gone into journalism and administration to become managing editor of *Fortune,* rather than into

some actual intellectual and literary profession—and then caught myself and understood that a culture in which men of mind inevitably went into the intellectual professions was doomed.

(1951)

Harry Levin sends me a paper on The Tradition of Tradition with the inscription "forgive the gibe"—he refers to a "sly" association of the phrase "the liberal imagination" with conservatism or reaction: he is ever forward. And with this paper I know that I could never go to Harvard—for there they would take me *seriously,* with that seriousness of men who have no real sense of reality, but who believe they should have. Here at Columbia I am of my own kind—if there is any hostility and dislike there is no slightest attempt to meet me on my own ground, at best a secret inner *flounce.* But at Harvard, nothing is beyond a Harvard professor. I should not be allowed to make my writing cancel their scholarship as here—they too are critics; and if not critics then serious men who would hold me *to account* for what I say. Here no one tries to understand except E.N. & I am left in peace.

(1951)

A catbird on the woodpile, grey on grey wood, its breast distended, the feathers ruffled and sick, a wing out of joint, the head thrown back and the eyes rolled back, white. Looked so sick I thought of killing it, when another bird appeared, looked at it, took a position behind it, and assumed virtually the same attitude, although not so extremely. To distract me? This it did once more, although with rather less conviction the second time, then flew away. Suddenly the first bird pulled itself together, flew to a tree above, sat there for a moment seeming to adjust its wing, or exercise it, then flew away.

(1951)

When I gave my last lecture on American literature in May—a poorish one on Henry Adams, in which I spoke chiefly in defense of Adams—my class applauded terrifically, keeping it up after I was out of the room, down the hall and up the first flight. They knew that I was giving up the subject, hence this extra response. I was naturally moved and gratified and even thought that perhaps I had done wrong to give up the subject if I could so please people with my handling of it—thought too that no subject I might ever treat wld ever involve people so much *a priori,* & that I cld never again win such easy victories. But one reason I gave it up was the ease of the victories. And then I hated dealing with contemporary figures or nearly contemporary, for several reasons: I did not like to speak personally, or close to personally, of men alive or recently dead; I hated dealing with the men of my youth as if they were long historical, and of talking of the twenties & the thirties as if they were the last century: I shld like to feel that I am myself a fact in American literature & that makes dealing with it awkward, or it denies my being part of it. The true judgments & explanations were too hard to make in public, almost impossible, and the judgments available for lectures repelled me. The subject really must be dealt with in a wholly serious, systematic way, and, I feel sure, as "history of culture" rather than as a study of individual authors, and this, aside from the subtlety & complexity, needs a total intellectual & emotional involvement that I shld never want to make, although I feel that the result might be very good. And then the students dismay me, the particular students who choose contemp. Am. lit to satisfy some strange unspoken need. But then all graduate students trouble & in a way repel me and I must put down here the sensation of liberation I experienced when I arranged for my withdrawal from the graduate school, from seminars and the direction of dissertations. That involvement, the result of vanity, lack of clearsightedness, a little cowardice . . . has cost me much. I was a free man when I taught in the college and ceased to be free when I taught in the Grad. school. For one thing I became a public character and always on view, having to live up to the demands made upon a public character, & finding that the role seemed to grow inward. The relation with the students who worked under me was unpleasant, although sometimes seductive — most of them were badly prepared, poorly endowed. One was led to "reject" them, and then because of their personal situations, to become terribly partisan with them. And the time one had to give, and the personal involvement, almost worse than the time! And the colleagues in the Gr. School, with whom it was almost impossible to converse . . . the childish naivety — together with, of course, the considerable knowledge which I did not have & which really abashed me. . . . The sense that I was part of an enterprise that I could in no way defend, and did not want to defend. . . . And the day I made the arrangement with Campbell[26] to withdraw I felt liberated, what a foolish mistake it had been, & how entirely discreditable to me. And here I should set down my ever-growing dislike of teaching & of the systematic study of literature — more and more it goes against the grain.

---

[26] Oscar Campbell.

FICTION, POETRY, AND DRAMA

John Ashbery

NOTHING TO STEAL

What's growing? Will it start
In the next few minutes, leaving us
Far from each other? I think he said
The sun is going down in Florida, but the proverb
Tells us there is no night in light,
No respite, no ticking in the separate seconds.
The prospect is such verbiage, a winter
Landscape, dense, tangled.

A loner spied it in his vocabulary
And, about to shy, made the rest
Into man instead. Dread is the pillow
Of those who flee, making more in the morning.
By midafternoon the machine
Has gasped its last. There are no things to be,
Only a detective. A light dusting of snow
Was all he was appalled to find. On the tree
A mile away some dim, swollen, waxen fruit. He couldn't
Go on
Enumerating. They came for the sale,
Students weighing protests, a light on
In the garage. Those in the superette
Shirked their idea more hazily. The sun
Had now returned to the kitchenette.

Bite harder, the old man tells them, the next time
The rabbit wars loom and you got all scratched
In the basin. Next time. And wear wool
Headgear 'cause the car's scrapped, the children
Came out to see what was wrong and we all turned
In that direction, only to have it disappear.
There are parking lights shining and who knows
How much of it they take in let alone
Understand though the stairs are nice

And the companions in the yards too who fall
In all directions. Standing's the comparison
For them as don't want to sleep yet after
All, after it was all over, one sees some
Disappointment in breaths sucked in, in
The decision to wait until the same time tomorrow
For the wolf to be on, whose hunger
Made him leave the woods, and the sea
Must be part of that too. The wire sea.

John Ashbery's latest book of poems is A Wave, *recently published by Viking Press.*

Harold Brodkey

EGYPT AND FLESHPOTS, JOHNNO AND WILEY

Noisy party. 1956.

You can hear the music—jazz in those days: a saxophone and drums—from the cobbled, ill-lit street. There's no sidewalk, only loading docks with marquees over them. Leather factories, meat processing plants, other somber industries—boneyards, ragshops— deserted at this hour except maybe for a guy with a German shepherd on a leash on one of the loading docks—a watchman. The elevated highway between us and black Hudson carries a fairly solid stream of cars, tusked with lights. Up shaky stairs past a sausage skin plant and its smells to a room with only a few lights on, people scattered here and there in the dim expanses, big windows open showing black windows in other buildings, black roofs. The neighborhood has few residents—derelicts, artists, prowlers—at this hour.

Near the door, a larger than life-sized canvas with a blurred portrait of Eisenhower in a toga on it smeared with brown paint that had on it in one corner the letters F E C E S.

"I see the honesty of it," I said.

And an portrait of the painter's current psychoanalyst, a woman: she stood naked by her desk—looking lost; she was blurred but her genitals were carefully drawn, and that portion of the picture was circled with red and inscribed H O M E H O M E O N T H E R A G E.

Johnno was thirty-two, thirty-three. I was twenty-six.

Johnno talked for a moment to a woman painter about Matisse and Picasso—*the idyllic and the enraged*—Johnno had announced in a series of pieces that *the topic of the year was clearly rage.*

The woman thinks I'm uptown money, a boy collector. She wants me to buy a picture: "I'm doing flowers saturated with time—"

"*Drenched* with time," Johnno corrected her.

He told her who I was. She said in a tough, challenging way, "Hey, those stories of yours must make a lot of money."

Editor's Note: This is the opening section of a work to be continued.

"Naw. I'm starving."

She made a face.

The painter whose loft it was — Bruno Ultto — (Johnno had helped name him; Bruno's real name was Shultz) — the year was in him: he wore an undershirt and paint-stained white workman's pants and he was playing bongo drums — that was very stylish then, advanced — primitive and advanced.

One of the things I'd told Johnno as we'd walked here was about the depth, the validity of a present moment, even if it's only named as a date, as 1956: "It is when whatever was real *was* — the date, the moment *then* — "

Johnno then patiently tried to tell me his theory, that a poem or a painting must have a real present tense in it — doing it has to be real and present — the artist's life has to be present in the moment of action, in the act, in the blind, sensory, *prior* rush of action — prior to meaning — and then the judgment: yes, no, let it stand, do it over . . .

This is the quality that is perceived as *art*, he said; whereas when there is no such drama, when the thing is rehearsed and known from the start, it is merely memoir, it is merely anecdotal then, it is without any real value as life and art at all.

The woman I live with is not allowed here. Johnno can't stand her. And Ultto gets upset at the way she acts. She had dinner with Johnno and me, part of a dinner, and then she went home: but she is not considered an artist, and I am.

WHY I AM AN ARTIST: my circumstances were these.

I was adopted when I was two, shortly after my real mother died. First, she was ill — she vanished when I was eighteen months old or so. I was taken from the care, or custody, of a drunken woman, who was my father's lover. He was a minor gangster off and on, a gambler, a brawler — it depends on the date what it is he was: a semi-pro boxer for a while known for the brutality of his attack. He was an immigrant —

But why go on.

I admire people who are not artists.

JOHNNO SAID, THERE IS NOTHING YOU CAN BE BUT AN ARTIST, SO RELAX AND BE IT.

I SAID, I DON'T TRUST MYSELF OR WHAT I KNOW.

AS A MATTER OF LICENSES: PERMISSIONS: HERE IS A PARTIAL PORTRAIT OF JOHNNO:

He was a very good, very interesting poet of the second rank if you consider only his own work, but if you add in his life and his concern for *art* and his ties to other artists, then he was a poet of major presence.

This thing of being a poet, he used all his time that way—which is not surprising—but I mean that he worked for a salary, ate, slept, telephoned—talked, looked—read, wrote as *a poet* and not so much as a man or human being—or as a faun or boy, either. He led a professional life, self-consciously embarked on, self-consciously announced, self-consciously carried out—it had its madness.

It was rooted in words—and brushstrokes—and friendships and a certain kind of information and influence—gestures of art—in nothing else. He had a compacted solidity of purpose, an ability to bear being hated (by rivals, by those he thought untalented, by those who refused to live by his discipline and wanted him to be a fool, or to appear to be so, so that they might seem smarter by comparison), he could bear all sorts of daily and hourly and yearlong strain, and this showed in his body, which, although thin—a little airy—yet had a dense, compacted quality after he'd been in New York for a while and had begun to be known—

Which means to be hated—and admired.

He wore sneakers, always clean ones; he was short-legged, phenomenally erect, the erectness was a gothic strut in his case—the determining grotesquery by which you recognized him even when he was seated (that and the extraordinary cleanness of his face: he was supremely well-scrubbed and laundered)—especially since his hands and head (and shoulders) opened like fans from thin piers of skinny bone and muscle that in their turn alternated tightly, elegantly—no: *neatly*. The speed, the velocity of his will was more apparent as a considerable fluster in his voice—and eyes and lips—than his movements which were self-conscious and sternly stylish—bordering on cute. His face maintained a deadpan that yet sparked and buzzed with signals like a terminal for a complex electrical system—which in a way it was—until his sensibility, increasingly famous downtown (and derided or ignored uptown and then paid attention to)—that is, his *fame*—his *position*—increasingly slowed and dulled the operations of his face and, in fact, he grew coarse and tough (in a way) and *clever*—that is to say, dishonest; and the quick, semi-anguished face of his youth—in its separate category of pained beauty—intelligent, luminous—vanished in the purposes and methods and necessities of his becoming famous—memorable—a star. Always a worthwhile star, however. But it became hard to *see* his face except as the methods he used for making it visible in this other, rarer framework of being an embattled and newsworthy poet — mostly in peripheral publications however — except as those methods presented it: the techniques of the art he admired tugged and shaped his face but obscured him, the person. The methods of presentation of the poet's face became Johnno's face. The movement of his thought in the backyard part of consciousness, the dimmer area, in which sacredness erupts, grew limited and then was hidden from view. His mind was pressed forward toward the world — in the manner of *the retort.*

Tonight, though, he is approximately in the chronological center of his most fecund period.

He is already citified — he is semi-famous — he is bony and treeless. The animal peculiarity of intelligence in him is a nervous commandingness and courage — the courage is as it was in school: to speak, to be bullied for it, to persist and *dare.*

Much of his style was taken from his reading and from — well, it was stolen — but thefts of things devised by others are relationships to others, so that his manner was a scrapbook of affections. That part of his intelligence once devoted to the sacred is an evolving self-conscious devotion to art now. Around him spreads the horizontal biography of his work, his managing to live and work as he does, his publicizing himself and others (painters, never writers) combined with his particular aspirations, sexual and social — to be notable at the party — to impress me.

Johnno moves on the floor of the loft to the table which is the bar, above the mocking skuhh and squeak of his sneakers on the poorly finished wooden floor. The hard-willed and densely armored and pained *elegance* his eyes have — their pursuit of sustenance suggest the natural state of the predator. Then the defenseless squeak of his sneakers suggests he is an ecological niche himself, alone.

I hear the words, "Macaw, Madam," — but it is Johnno's pronunciation of *macadam* in the noise of the party and the flutter of his lips — the faintly interpolated extra syllable, a pressure of the lips, helps in reading his poetry sometimes.

His preternatural posture causes his sweater to hang so *neatly* from his shoulders — it doesn't touch him until the ribbed waist circles the top of his pants — that it makes an extraordinary physical eloquence for that period — him and that linearity.

The schooleyness of that — the secular version of a sacerdotal alb quality — is parochial school papal; he consciously felt his youth as a formal moment — subject to being pillaged, violated, sinned against — because he was *beautiful and good:* therefore, to be demeaned. He is of a consequently conscious and sophisticated pillaging nature — but if I consider the ways in which he violated himself in order to write and to live, then his being ruthless, his kind of tireless mercilessness seems shadowed — heritable. . . .

His walk is American — he has an American gait: his is an American poetry. His perhaps ill-conceived elegance of person wasn't ill-conceived when you liked his poems — then he seemed authoritatively interesting. His physical proportions, fine-drawn in themselves but thickening every year, were now coarsened by fame — i.e., will, impatience, bad temper, perpetual self-defense, the hardening of the self, the sort of reality — citified, peculiarly symmetrical and outspread, and momentary — that is caused by turning a moment into art, an attempt at comparative eternity. And were dirtied by a kind of jaggedness, by being limited to the specific meaning of *this* flight toward art — but art as coarseness and strength and all sorts of other things — in his case, taut and nuanced — androgynous — daring.

Body and art were synchronized. In the light of being like *this,* he had *a kind* of erotic authority as a reality of strength and navigation — of accomplishment here — potent and nervous — not second-rate: he was more right about who and what was good than any other man or any woman alive at the same time he was. He had a captain's authority; he had explored the queer seas of taste and esthetics — and truth — and that is sort of sexual even if not quite sexual, *sexually* — if I can say it like that.

Here is another way to try to show it: his head was stonelike atop the enflamed pyramid of what he was and what he knew: his head deals with the room, the party: a woman who paints dull landscapes but who will be good in five years time, or thereabouts, is near us: she talks; Johnno extricates us; and a drunken Dutchman, large and thick, but with an uncommon — and unexpected if you went by a first glance — personal beauty, to a startling degree — it mixed power and loneliness and a workman's naivetè and rage with a very rare fineness, an artist's sad affection, unshared rage — and victimization by everything — but also by the shaky processes of esthetic performance — he had peculiarly knowledgeable-looking arms, I swear it — a physical intelligence that seemed connected to or even to be a form of, saintliness, weirdly —

The proud tin cut-out of Johnno was partly in the style of that man's sketches along with a sort of proud shock from dealing with varied creators' frequent revelations — all of them serious and far-

reaching—and a Harvardish resonating tin *brilliance* of his own devising—Johnno was not saintly but *was* martyred—and his head was
stonelike like a cathedral enclosing this stuff—the matter of spirit—it
was like a pyramid entombing something or other in the middle of a
desert. . . . He regards and scans and checks out the middle distance in a knowing way—with nervous irony—in experienced (and
aging) appetite: for complicated realities—he was the star at the
party as none of the women then in New York who tried to do this
sort of thing—to be entrepreneurs and mistresses and creators—
could have been. They were too tinged with the second-rate and
their being ashamed of admiring anything and their bitterness in
competition. Actually, Johnno was that way, too—but he was more
serious about art—and authority—which, in the end, is a matter
merely of persons—and he had it—authority—and they never did—
except as wielders of malice. They were all drinkers—those women
and Johnno and the artists of the time—and dark with prejudice and
malice when drunk. But Johnno was unmalicious until he was
drunk—he was helpful to anyone who cared about *art*—he would be
vengeful and enraged shortly, as he drank—he had a larger parish
and a smaller audience than any of the women would risk.

In a window near us is a view of lit stretches of as if rustling
cloud, shifting cloud, ravelling and moving fast, torn antimacassars
in migration past—phallic—water tanks. The set of Johnno's eye-
brows and their movements—his squinting wide-eyedness and the
cording of the neck and in the jut of the chin—he is toughly, staunchly
aware—and thoroughly drunk—he is on the cusp of malice—but the
period is still one of an evening's (civilized) affections—the broken
layers and stepped edges of his awareness are part of an as if moral
address for the occasion.

I helped father the non-abyss part of Johnno's esthetic and I
nagged it and advised him on it—the rest of him is him or is from
other sources.

In dreams he can be either a pyramid or a *layered* horse—a wild
horse alternating with the drawn and painted horses of pictorial
art—his look of *wit*—the racing (or stalled) commentary—of someone of publicly acknowledged *wit*—is like that. In a more personal
sense: his eyelids blink less than most people's—the gallows shadow
that the genital chance casts is on his face. Heat and forwardness
gust around his mouth. An unexpected aura of cleanliness—something like a shaved look on a shamed dog—lurks at the fork of his
legs.

His drunken mother comes and goes in him—he has a readiness for visits from phantoms—his body is slowed by air, by reality—as if by cottonlike batting in a chute—a long flinch of suffocation—but his head persists in its swiftness—its eyeliddedness. His fretful and combative love for things present in the moment is pitted by a civilized, drunken hatred for the same things.

His packed eyes shift—or hold—a topic less *educatedly* than when I last saw him and more personally, more maddenedly—drunkenly—he is an optical and ethical and careless device of fame and self-destruction at the same time—he is in a light he *knows* is local and brief—he is calculatedly boyish at moments still: "I will live forever."

"Forever in common usage means until one's death, don't you think?"

"I'm an *American* poet—I don't have to think."

He means to correct my style . . . to make his dominant. The pitch of his voice is set by the mannerisms for his style of The Retort. At dinner, I'd said I intended to live in this country and that meant one did not have to think in any even half-profound manner: what he says refers to that but that doesn't mean that you have to remember the earlier stuff but only that an explanation of sorts is in your head.

He and I compete—but we show off for one another, too . . . (I am much, much more famous uptown than he is.)

"You work by other methods."

He ignored what I said.

Sneakers and sweater, brown, straight hair, bare throat, 'intelligent' but eery look of youth, naked ankles, fingery, taut hands—and his drunken—maybe lecherous—mother in his eyes—

He doesn't mind it that the first person pronoun is boundless. His life is autobiography—I talked him into it—arguing that for anyone smart, the autobiographical is an ironic tone. Ideas set up earlier between us shape how we talk to each other now—

He wrote me when I was in college: *In my dreams it is often Cleveland—uncanny Lake Erie. I see myself: it is not what you say it is, it is NOT intellect pretending to be physical presence in some sort of model of the day—it is me, the cocksucker. Art has taught me how to see. You said you feel your face as a watery nothing. Well, tant pis if you want. That's up to you. I am the middle point of everything. I AM everything possible. This is very serious.*

He was younger then.

I won't quote from a poem but I'll say that for me the governing mode is the child-bliss in offering the captured creature, the poem; it's not like a cat's long-backed swagger. That stuff was sweet in him: he was drawn to sweetness in art although no one ever pointed it out. When seriousness was at too continuous a pitch, he pushed clear from it as a child might push his mother's hands from him — this is in his poems and in his tastes in art. Everyone knows he is crazy — and is getting worse — but no one does anything about it — and this is in his work, too. Ecstasy, the most extreme emotional presence, he knows only in art, if there. Daily pain and the recognition of death — that is what he is a master of.

Sexually, the search for extreme — and justified — presence ties him to vileness — by justified I mean within a frame of art's *private* meanings — and by presence, I mean suffocating his mind so that it matches his always suffocated body for a moment. I thought his sexual nature vile and wasted — maybe pathetic — but I respected it totally because it was *his* — he did those things and he was Johnno Finner — I am not a moral man, this means.

For him, sexually, as in poetry (and in painting) when the words were okay, it was felicity — for a while.

Harold Brodkey is at work on a new novel, sections of which have appeared in The New Yorker.

James Dickey

BLIND SNOW, WARM WATER

from the novel *Alnilam*

(Frank Cahill, a man in his fifties who has gone blind three months ago from diabetes, is in the small town of Peckover, North Carolina, where his son has been killed — or has disappeared — as the result of an accident in primary flight training. With his seeing-eye dog he is staying in a room over the local bus station. Takis Harbelis is an aviation cadet who has been a friend and follower of Cahill's son Joel. Cahill has just returned from walking with Harbelis in a heavy snowfall. The incident takes place in mid-winter of 1943.)

The door, the room opened inward, and he was prepared for the desolation. It was there, it was always there for the blind, no matter what they did, but he was continually ready for it: ready with routine, with slow meticulous activity, with finding and placing things, with control, with his body. He sat, now, untied his shoes and took them off, leaving his socks on temporarily, not wanting to put his bare feet on the cold linoleum. He footed into the bathroom, closed the door to hold the heat that would come, found the faucets, and sat on the side of the tub, his shirtsleeve turned up, adjusting the temperature of the water with one hand and testing it on the inside wrist of the other. He ran the water hard; the little room boomed and splashed; there was a slow urgency of filling, of water with heft, the weight of increase. In the deepening sound, the thresholding sound, he got up and methodically stripped off everything, the dark glasses last. He gripped the side of the washstand and felt the mirror before his face, passing his palm over it, imagining what it was giving back. He put a thumb- and forefinger-tip on his lids as if it were magic, withdrew his hand, opened his eyes and blinked into the new darkness, and smiled openly into the mirror thinking that anyone who saw him would be delighted at such an open, outgoing individual — so friendly, so easy to talk to you wouldn't believe it. Before getting into the tub he listened through the door to determine if Zack were moving around in the outer room, but the dog had evidently settled himself, perhaps gone to sleep from the cold, the snow, and the running. He put the whiskey on the floor and, holding on, stepped and felt into the tub, his eyes closed, sat on the end and slid by degrees down the smooth enamel, consumed by fiery water, his feet going for the far wall where the tap still ran thundering in on him, as in a cave. He leaned forward and quieted it and lay back with finality, almost floating, his muscles lengthening, his bones separating, breaking a facial sweat, waiting for nothing.

In unopposed arrival, responding as though called wordlessly by his whole body, like the opening of all his veins, the snow he had just left came to him, a directness, a seeking-out of piercing darts of flame which at the same time glanced off and disappeared, not being head-on when most head-on: small parts of a flock, of an enormous sheet, each meaning to be forthright but dying, as in a touch the essential fire that made it were leaving it. He had been wandering with Harbelis in a kind of wall, an unhinged black, a shadowed flocking, unballasted, hooded, hovering, unfurling, failing and oncoming. It was the right kind of scene for secrecy; the snow had something to do with a code of some kind. Also with an instrument; also with his son born Joel Hamilton Cahill twenty years ago in Atlanta, Georgia, and raised in Memphis, who had gone one year to a small college and had been, until recently, in this town.

He stirred the water, a turbulence in depth unguessed in the deepest seas of the world, reached over the side, picked up the bottle, hauled it in and tilted into his throat four strong swallows of the hot sick-tasting sweetness. He did not dissolve. He drank again and finished it all, the warmth around him in steam now and leaving the water. The presence of snow was also leaving: the ticks of flame in his face, the scatter as of hooded coins, the released and compulsive swirling about, the seething, the hiss from all sides, the in-ranging, the suggestion of hammers and anvils, paper-thin bells, forge-fires, the peltering of sparks, the bee-shower, the vague quick coals dying instantly, and the sense of disclosure there in all that hoodedness and numbness and unlikeliness — was that gone? What had Harbelis meant? Was he supposed to pick up on what it might have been? Guess it? Build a meaning that he could add to, when he went back to them tomorrow? He shuddered, now helpless, the whirling envelopment of the snow gone except as a memory of discomfort temporarily dispelled, but returning as the water cooled. The cold room outside the door waited also, with linoleum ready to frost the brain through the foot-soles before he could lump into bed, and beyond that the town purposelessly feathered and draped in whiteness, half-stunned, fro-

zen in mid-air and skidding underfoot, and beyond that the countryside, and the field with its silent aircraft, having nothing, not even
their engine-noise, to defend them. They are parked in rows, he remembered, preparing to get up from the tub-floor according to routine, as he did almost everything, envisioning aircraft in a long line
stretching away from him out of sight, and the top wings — Harbelis
had said they had two—formed, from his angle—which could have
been anywhere but was here—one single wing all the way to the horizon, a wing of snow, pure wing, ready for unimaginable flight when
the weather cleared, or ready now. He rose to both feet, steadied
and slow-hurdled out, tried to find a trash-basket for the bottle,
couldn't, backed it into a corner, left it, and toweled off. He felt
himself out into the other room, turned the bed down, stood over it
like a landmass, got in and went down.

James Dickey is the author of Puella, The Strength of Fields, *and*
Buckdancer's Choice *(recipient of the 1965 National Book Award), among
other collections of poems, and the novel* Deliverance.

Robert Fitzgerald

DEDECORA TEMPORUM

(Written in 1968)

Here is the armor, tons and tons,
Each by its own assembly line
Conveyed over old cobblestones
To make free gentlemen resign.
Lord, save us, or we drown.
This cry comes from a long way down.

Here is the horrorshow, record runs,
Here is a plausible genial swine
Teaching our longing daughters and sons
That Eros' lash is far from fine.
Lord, save us, or we drown.
This cry comes from a long way down.

Here is the addlepate, everyone's,
Here is the vanity, yours and mine,
Delivering gardenlands to guns
And vision to the low malign.
Lord, save us, or we drown.
This cry comes from a long way down.

Robert Fitzgerald, poet and translator, is Boylston Professor of Rhetoric, Emeritus, at Harvard University. He received the Bollingen Prize in 1961 for his translation of the Odyssey.

John Hollander

THE TWIN'S STORY

My twin brother and I had been placed in different families shortly after birth, and although I had known of his existence,
we never met until we were both in our early thirties. I grew up in the
city, he in the country, although the effects of this in our two natures
were not what you might think. For by that time our cities had
already become what they are today — had lost their cosmopolitan
character and had become massed villages, enclosures rather than
confluences. The country had lost its innocence, but of course had
never acquired the generous skepticism, the joy in the multiplicities
of life's versions, that the cities once engendered — wide as its exposure to nature was, the country afforded only a narrow window
onto human variety.

Well, then. My brother and I, different as our circumstances
were, finally met by some peculiar combination of chance and design. My parents — or rather, my foster parents, for my true mother
and father had been killed in a grisly and meaningless accident a few
months after my birth — had spoken of a twin brother who had been
taken away by distant relatives. But they had so casually managed to
dampen my natural curiosity, by means that I can now barely
manage to understand, that the details of the question never seemed
to matter. Perhaps I had been encouraged to feel that any attempt to
discover or encounter this brother would end in disaster, or that it
would be extraordinarily unseemly. In any event, I never felt much
interest in pursuing the problem. But this did not prevent me from
taking great comfort in the notion — even when I was very young —
that there existed somewhere in the world a strange kind of completion of my body and my consciousness. Although I was apparently
finished off — with no missing limbs, nor palpable deficiencies of
sense or metabolism or whatever that might need correction — I
alone knew and felt that, actual encounter or proximity aside, an
embodiment of the rest of me — rather than *more* of me — was part of
the available universe, and that he — who-and-wherever he was —
stood as some ultimately redemptive being for any missing element
or quality of which even I might be unaware. I grew so used to the
feeling of security to which this notion gave rise that I would leave it
undisturbed even by meditation.

It was not until I was old enough not only to have put away childish things, but to have returned to them, as it were, in the way that certain fortunate adults can manage to do, that I could consider this sense I had of the Other one, and what it all might mean. In those days, I traveled for a notions manufacturer, visiting both wholesalers and chain retailers that did a large business. Driving at night, or in buses or airplanes on short hops, I would often look out into the distant darkness, moving and motionless both, as if searching it not for someone else possibly hidden there, but for a truth or an answer in another kind of hiding: What did my unknown twin brother correct in me? What incompleteness did he add to? Would there be some reciprocating defect in his nature which was redeemed in mine? It was only in the year in which I finally realized my defective property — which was purely and simply my uniqueness itself — that I encountered my brother in a bar in a small New England town.

Outside it was dark — a late fall evening — and dark within, but I had an immediate sense, as I saw from a booth a figure with its back toward me standing at the bar, that this was someone I knew. When he turned around to leave, I saw who indeed it was and walked up to him immediately, leaving him no time in which to be startled. I set out at once to explain myself — and, in a way, himself — to him. I discovered that although he knew that his parents had been adoptive, he was unaware of my existence. But our identical resemblances, my story, and reasonable inference after his initial shock and disbelief, combined during the course of the evening to convince him.

We had walked to his home, a small house in an older part of town (like me at the time, he was unmarried), and we sat quietly there, drinking and talking, until very late. From that night on, we saw each other at long but regular intervals, either in the city on weekends, or in the town where he lived and worked in the management of a mill. All this is, actually, unremarkable enough. Both of us had lost our foster-parents and were without other relatives; we were both hardworking and solitary, both used to avoiding intimate friendships with the men of our acquaintance and to anything more than guarded, casual affairs with women. Neither of us was ready or willing to claim the other for a new-found and unsettling friendship, and our blood relationship — even this ultimate of those — could only be represented socially by improvisation.

For my part, my sense of completeness in another one remained undisturbed by the mere actuality of his presence. Given the banality of both our lives, an account of our subsequent relations might have remained banal as well. He never had the sense of completion that tinted even the darkest days of my life, and could barely understand what I meant on the one occasion at which I unwisely attempted to explain it. And, as I have said, his reality neither augmented nor diminished that feeling, nor would I allow it to alter my life in any other way. The fact of his existence was like that of a very important text, an explanation or commentary without which the text of my life would be unreadable; he himself was like a copy of the book, no less and no more.

Then one night he tried to kill me. Or rather, he came at me with what might have been murderous effects; the intent, if murderous itself, was not so much his as that of a drunken rage he had acquired and been unable to dispose of. We were both solitary but moderate drinkers; on our visits we would seldom go out, being unwilling to deal with the stares that adult twins seem to attract, and, even more, with the reflected sight of ourselves in store windows, or of the paired shadows whose sinister quality lay in their very innocence — they might have been shadows, for example, of any two men of roughly the same height. And so we would usually meet, eat, talk, and drink at his house or mine, and after a few years, this had become ritual. I would know exactly, during the evening, how it would end; I could anticipate the quality of the air on the street outside his door, or the strange light in the corridor outside my apartment, the words we always spoke after an interval of silence: "Well, then"; and he would answer, "I guess so."

But that night he drank much more than usual, and grew more and more silent between our brief exchanges. I felt uneasy, and since I had to leave very early the next morning for a long trip, I tried to bring the evening to an early close. The meeting was at my apartment, and I rose from my chair, walked to a table on which his trench coat lay folded, turned to where he was standing nearby and spoke:

"Well, then."

"No, not well at all, you bastard," he suddenly snarled and rushed at me with outstretched fists. I was so taken aback that defense against even this childish and ridiculously fragile assault was impossible for the moment. During that moment he reached me, battered me in the face, seized my neck, and started to choke me. Only after what was almost too long a time did outrage, terror, and

disgust combine to fuel my awareness and strength. I finally struggled free, kicked him several times in the groin and stomach, got him
to the floor, and pinned him there with my knees.

He groaned softly for a while and said nothing. He refused to
answer my question about the meaning of his attack, or about anything else. Suddenly taken by a painful thought, I wrestled his wallet
from his coat pocket, opened it up, and on an identification card I
found there, saw among other facts listed "in case of accident," his
blood type. It was not my own.

I shouted out something that started as a question and immediately dissolved into a cry of terror and dismay; then I ran from
my apartment, scarcely bothering to shut the door behind me, raced
down the stairs without waiting for the elevator, and rushed out into
the street. Mindlessly distraught, I walked through drizzling rain
without a coat, pushing through streets still busy with night traffic,
and still occupied by scurrying pedestrians. When I returned home
after an hour, he was gone, the door shut, and nothing disturbed
within. I never saw him again.

The problem, of course, was mine, not his; and even after
some months when I tried to check up on him, and found that he had
quit his job, moved, and left no forwarding address, it did not
change the situation. For there was no explanation he could have
given me that would have helped. Naive acquiescence, designing
guile, or whatever, motive seemed to me to have nothing to do with
the truth of what had happened.

Nature produces doubles as well as twins, but cannot be
blamed for the first of these any more than for the second. Twinship
is as much a learned as a given state, but one's relation to a double is
totally of one's own making. I had quested, without being fully
aware of how I was doing it, for a twin. But as in all significant
quests, the goal and the final task, as well as many of the later intermediate stages, are invented by the searcher. It is not only that
the nature and meaning of the task changes during the course of ex-
ecuting it. It is that the end gets reinvented during the later phases.

And so I had created my twin, but I had bungled somehow and
ended up with a mere double, another person whose otherness from
myself was so ordinary as to be trivial—someone with nothing to do
with me, someone as meaningless as a namesake. There had been no
significant change in my way of life while I still believed him to be
my twin brother, nor were our lives together of any consequence.
But the discovery of his existence, and the termination of his being

my twin, were profound and catastrophic. In the latter instance, it was as if I had made a stone image and then broke it; but whether the breaking was to bring good luck or bad I was not to know. The first of these events put an end to a strangely muted but obsessive kind of search. The second instigated a very different kind of one, a search for no guerdon, a mission toward no ultimate showdown, whether of real or figurative battle, a recircling journey toward no home. It was rather a search whose sea-voyages and treks inland, whose bookings and arrangements, whose map-readings and takings of stock, all occurred in the domain of questionings. Like some topological game requiring the player to move on a board through as many points as possible, this domain into which I had been thrust to live my moral life caused me to do so not by traversing the field, but to live among the questions and doubts that blossomed everywhere, wherever an answer fell.

But questions of the kind one would think might nag at me fell away long ago, questions about *him,* and what "actually" happened. The questions I live with are all about *me,* and about *it* (or everything else). And even what might appear to be a terminal or limiting question about all that (the years in which he was part of my life went by fifteen years ago) — What if he were not *your* double, but a double of some twin brother of yours, from whom you might have been separated, say, in infancy, a twin brother whom this person encountered once in the way he did you, a twin brother whom he either killed, or, more likely, caused to abandon him, and so forth? — even *that* question no longer looms up before me like a menacing indeterminacy along a forest road on a moonless night. It simply stands, like a funny rock formation at the far end of a field, more or less visible and more or less problematic in its possible figuration, depending upon the weather.

John Hollander is Professor of English and Director of Graduate English Studies at Yale University. His last book of poems, Powers of Thirteen, *was published in 1983 by Atheneum.*

Norman Mailer

AT THE CATHEDRAL OF ST. ISAAC
IN LENINGRAD

Great and ancient building
Dread reeks out of your damp
Huge fear stirs in your stone
You sit at the feast
    in gloom and splendor
You lie in copulation
    on our common air
Old histories have left a curse
    Your ghosts are the sons of failure
They swear to call again
We hear oaths from your dead
Great and ancient building
Odorous old beast
We revere you

Norman Mailer's most recent novel is Tough Guys Don't Dance, *published by Random House.*

Bernard Malamud

IN KEW GARDENS

Once as they walked in the gardens, Virginia felt her knickers come loose and slip down her ankles. She grabbed at her maidenhair as the garment eluded her frantic grasp and formed a puddle of cloth at her feet. Swooping up her underpants, with a cry of dismay she plunged into the bushes, shrilly singing "The Last Rose of Summer." As she stood up, the elastic knot she had tied, snapped, and the knickers again lay limp at her feet.

"Christ, Goddamn!"

Vanessa listened at the bushes.

"Don't be hysterical. No one will see through your dress."

"How can you be certain?"

"No one would want to."

She shrieked slowly.

"Forgive me, dear goat," Vanessa told her. "I meant no harm."

"Oh, never, no, never."

Insofar as I was ever in love I loved Vanessa.

George Duckworth, affectionate step-brother, carried his tormented amours from the parlor to the night nursery. He nuzzled, he fondled, he fiddled with his finger. To his sisters he was obscenity incarnate. He touched without looking.

"I meant no harm. I meant to comfort you."

Virginia lost her underpants and wondered where she had been.

Her erotic life rarely interested her. It seemed unimportant compared with what went on in the world.

I was born in 1882 with rosy cheeks and green eyes. Not enough was made of my coloring.

When her mother died she tore the pillow with her teeth. She spat bleeding feathers.

Her father cried and raged. He beat his chest and groaned aloud, "I am ruined."

The mother had said, "Everyone needed me but he needed me most."

"Unquenchable seems to me such presence": H. James.

The father moaned, "Why won't my whiskers grow?"

As Virginia lay mourning her mother, dreadful voices cried in the night. They whispered, they clucked, they howled. She suffered piercing occipital headaches.

King Edward cursed her foully in the azalea garden. He called her filthy names, reading aloud dreadful reviews of books she had yet to write.

The king sang of madness, rage, incest.

Years later she agreed to marry Mr. Leonard Woolf, who had offered to be her Jewish mother.

"I am mad," she confessed to him.

"I am marrying a penniless Jew," Virginia wrote Violet Dickinson. She wondered who had possessed her.

"He thinks my writing the best part of me."

"His Jewishness is qualified."

His mother disgusted her.

She grew darkly enraged.

In fact, I dislike the quality of masculinity. I always have.

Lytton said he had no use for it, whatever. "Semen?" he asked when he saw a stain on Vanessa's dress.

Vanessa loved a man who found it difficult to love a woman.

She loved Duncan Grant until he loved her.

She had loved Clive Bell, who loved Virginia, who would not love him. Virginia loved Leonard who loved her. She swore she loved him.

When Julia, the mother, died, the goat threw herself out of a first storey window and lay on the ground with Warren Septimus Smith. "He did not want to die till the very last minute." Neither had she.

The old king emerged from the wood, strumming a lyre. A silver bird flew over his head, screeching in Greek.

A dead woman stalked her.

Janet Case, her teacher of Greek, loved her. She loved her teacher of Greek.

She loved Violet Dickinson.

She loved Vita Nicolson.

Leonard and she had no children. They lay in bed and had no children. She would have liked a little girl.

"Possibly my great age makes it less a catastrophe but certainly I find the climax greatly exaggerated."

Vanessa wrote Clive, "Apparently she gets no pleasure from the act, which I think is curious. She and Leonard were anxious to know when I had had an orgasm. I couldn't remember, do you?"

"Yet I dare say we are the happiest couple in England. Aren't we Leonard?"

"My dear."

Leonard and Virginia set up the Hogarth Press but they would not print Mr. James Joyce's *Ulysses.* "He is impudent and coarse."

Mrs. Dalloway loved Warren Septimus Smith though she never met him.

"He had committed an appalling crime and had been condemned by human nature."

"The whole world was clamoring, kill yourself, kill yourself for our sakes."

(He sat on the window sill.)

He jumped. Virginia fell from the window.

As for *To the Lighthouse,* I have no idea what it means, if it has a meaning. That's no business of mine.

"(Lily Briscoe) could have wept. It was bad, it was bad, it was infinitely bad. She could have done it differently of course; the colour could have been bleached and faded; the shapes etherialized; that was how Mr. Paunceforth would have seen it. But then she did not see it like that. She saw the colour burning on a framework of steel; the light of a butterfly's wing lying in the arches of a cathedral. Of all that only a few random remarks scrawled upon the canvas remained. And it would never be seen, never be hung; and there was Mr. Tanslay whispering in her ear, 'Women can't paint, women can't write . . .'

"She looked at the steps; they were empty; she looked at her canvas; it was blurred. With a sudden intensity, as she saw it clear for a second, she drew a line there, in the centre. It was done; it was finished. Yes, she thought, laying down her brush in extreme fatigue, I have had my vision."

All I need is a room of my own.

"I hate to see so many women's lives wasted simply because they have not been trained well enough to take an independent interest in any study or to be able to work efficiently in any profession": Leslie Stephen to Julia Duckworth.

"There has fallen a splendid tear/From the passion flower at the gate." —Alfred, Lord Tennyson

"There was something so ludicrous in thinking of people singing such things under their breath that I burst out laughing."

The Waves.

The Years. The bloody years.

The acts among *Between the Acts.*

No one she knew inspired her to more than momentary erotic excitement throughout her life. She loved Shakespeare's sister.

Leonard gave up that ghost.

"They also serve."

She felt a daily numbness, nervous tension. "What a born melancholic I am."

They had called her the goat in the nursery, against which she tore at their faces with her tiny nails.

They had never found Thoby her dead brother's lost portrait. Vanessa had painted and forever lost it.

Her mother died.

My father is not my mother. Leonard is my mother. We shall never conceive a living child.

"I shall never grow my whiskers again."

She heard voices, or words to that effect.

"Maiden, there's turd in your blood," King Edward chanted in Ancient Greece.

Her scream blew the bird off its one legged perch and it flapped into the burning wood.

An old king strode among the orange azaleas.

For years she simply went mad.

She spoke in soft shrieks.

She wrote twenty-one books whose reviews frightened her.

"That was not my doing," said Leonard Woolf.

"Nor mine," sobbed her Greek tutor.

Perhaps it was mine, Vita Nicolson said, "She was so frail a creature. One had to be most careful not to shock her."

I loved Vita. She loved *Orlando.*

Virginia wrote a biography of Roger Fry. She did not want to write a biography of *Roger Fry.*

Leonard served her a single soft-boiled egg when she was ill. "Now Virginia, open your mouth and swallow your egg. Only if you eat will you regain the strength to write your novels and essays."

She sucked the tip of his spoon.

"Though you give much I give so little."

"The little you give is a king's domain."

At that time the writing went well and she artfully completed *Between the Acts,* yet felt no joy.

Virginia relapsed into depression and denied herself food.

"Virginia, you must eat to sustain yourself."

"My reviews are dreadful," Virginia said.

"I am afraid of this war," Virginia said.

"I hear clamorous noises in my head," Virginia said.

One morning, to escape the noises of war, she dragged herself to the river Ouse, there removed shoes, stockings, underpants, and waded slowly into the muddy water. The large rock she had forced into her coat pocket pulled her down till she could see the earth in her green eyes.

"I don't think two people could have been happier than we have been."

Bernard Malamud teaches at Bennington College. The Stories of Bernard Malamud *has recently been published by Farrar, Straus, and Giroux.*

Leonard Michaels

TOILER

"You can't say anything to her?"

"Certainly not in class."

"How about in your office?"

"I don't even know her name."

"Do you want my advice?"

"Yes."

"The minute she begins to do it, stop your lecture."

"Then what?"

"Then, in a strong voice, say 'Many of you in this room are picking your noses.'"

"You mean nose?"

"Many of you are picking your *nose?* Sounds like one nose is being passed around the room. Anyhow, the students will laugh and she'll stop doing it."

Bluma laughed.

At the next meeting, when the woman started doing it, I persisted in my lecture and tried to look elsewhere, but it was virtually impossible not to look at her. She tore at her nose and neck. I lectured in a trance of revulsion and thought I would go insane before the end of the hour. Finally, I dismissed the class and, amid the rush of students, stopped her in the hallway.

"I think you never signed the enrollment sheet."

She signed: Anna Toiler.

"Miss Toiler, have you noticed how students chew gum and writhe in their seats? This is an exceptionally nervous class."

"Do they do that?" She was inclined to smile, but chose not.

"There's a woman in the front row — she sits near you — who crosses her legs and swings the elevated foot all hour long. Her eyes glaze, the foot swings faster, faster."

"You must see everything."

"I do," I said, pressing her with my look; willing her to leap from the general to the particular. I stood close to her. Perhaps too close, which is how I felt.

She had fine hair, several shades below blonde. I'd noticed it before, yet it seemed like a sudden influx of reality. Strange, lovely hair. In me something gazed, desiring nothing, taking her in. Her eyes were blue, light as her hair, with flat dark pupils like spots. In her late twenties, older than most of my students. Her gray wool suit and black shoes were inappropriate to the hot, luminous, September morning. She wore a creamy silk blouse. A cameo sealed the collar high on her neck, obscuring some of the scratches she had inflicted on herself. She was overdressed; insulated by an idea of propriety; niceness. East Coast type, I supposed. Most of the students dressed somewhat like bums — dirty jeans, jungle boots, tee shirts with the names of rock bands printed on the chest. The hallway was nearly empty. It was time to speak to the point.

"You're not from California, are you?"

Thus, I changed the subject I never raised.

"My husband and I arrived this summer. He took a job with an engineering firm in Palo Alto."

We were in a coffee shop across the street from campus. The

dark centers of her eyes, afloat in silvery blue circles, seemed fallen
from other eyes. Among her Nordic ancestors, there had been an
Asian.

"Stanton is a geologist and an engineer, but he's mainly involved with management these days, which isn't what he studied in
college. He's just good at it and that's what the firm wants."

I imagined a tall Stanton, then thought no. He wouldn't be so
accomplished. Average height. Maybe a little guy with a lust for
power. She'd chosen him as she had the black shoes, for strength,
principles, authority. But I knew absolutely nothing. My mind
swung around the periphery of concern like my spoon in the coffee
cup.

"What about you?" I asked.

She gave me a quizzical frown. I didn't even know, I realized,
what I meant.

"Do you have children?"

"I go to school."

"Of course."

"I have horses." Smiling now with lips together, showing no
teeth, she looked prissy. The horses, then, were special; delicious.
Her secret pride.

Walking back to campus she talked about how she loved to ride
in the hills after dinner. Once, she'd seen a bobcat. I hardly listened,
but I imagined her riding alone at twilight. The conversation, a
failure for me, was interesting to her. She might have thought I
found her attractive. She was attractive, but, except for her eyes and
tic, not unforgettable. She didn't pick or tear at herself when we talked,
but pushed with her knuckles occasionally at her nose. Like a boxer.
No sense of distinct, strong personality came through. Only polite
reserve. A willingness to state facts, to confess her pleasure in
horses. She had spiritual hands. The skirt, tight-fitting, showed the
line of her thigh, good athletic legs. In the sunlight, her pupils
shrank into dense black dots.

"I should tell you that I'll be missing some classes. I'm sorry. I
have to go to doctor's appointments. They're doing tests."

"Nothing serious, I hope."

"That's what the tests should discover. They think I might have
a tropical parasite. Nigerian fluke or something. We lived in Africa
for a year while Stanton worked for an oil company." She smiled
again in the prissy way, as if she'd exceeded herself by talking this
personally, but went on. "It's probably an allergy. All the new

grasses and flowers. I've never lived in California. I'm told the Bay Area is a hotbed of allergies. Stanton loves it here. He doesn't blame me for ruining things, but I do feel guilty. In Africa, I had a persistent fever. Poor Stanton quit the job because of me. He loved Africa, too. He's so good. So healthy compared to me. He lifts weights. The only time he ever hit me was when I contradicted him. He was saying something. I can't remember what, but I contradicted him. He hit me so hard that I lost a contact lense." She grinned, then shrugged.

At the south gate of campus, we said goodbye, and I went to my office. The phone rang as I set down my books and papers. Bluma's voice said hello.

"The woman's name is Anna Toiler. Her husband, Stanton, is an engineer. They lived in Africa. He lifts weights."

"At least you talked to her."

"She likes to ride horses."

"If you don't mind my saying so, I think you have a character disorder."

"Why?"

"What's all this garbage about horses? You were supposed to tell her to stop picking her nose."

"She thinks she has an allergy. The Bay Area is a hotbed of allergies."

The door opened. Henry, whose office was down the hall, peeked in. "You busy? I'll come back later." I waved him inside, pointed to the chair beside my desk. He was carrying an unlit cigarette which meant he wanted to settle and talk.

"Bluma, I have to hang up."

"You can't face the truth about yourself. Talking to you is a futile activity." Her receiver knocked my ear.

As he sat, Henry lit his cigarette. The top of his spine pressed the back of the chair. His torso sloped to the front edge of the seat, catching it with his tail bone, arresting a slide to the floor. Neck down he was slung like a sack of broken sticks, but his head was fixed on his high, skinny neck, expression eagle-like, fierce and brainy.

"What's new exactly?"

"I have a student who tears at her neck and nose while I lecture. Ever have one like that?"

"Many times."

"What did you do?"

"Nothing."

"Drives me crazy."

"I never thought of you as squeamish."

"This is an extreme case."

"I could tell you about a hideously offensive student, but you won't believe it."

"Yes, I will." I was surprised at my readiness to believe.

"You'll never repeat a word of this?"

"I swear."

"If you repeat it, I'll deny I told it to you."

"Have I ever betrayed a confidence?"

"I don't care."

"I won't."

Henry straightened slowly, pressing his back against the back of the chair and staring at me as he put out his cigarette. "There's a gentleman in my class — a Mr. Woo — who has a mandarin fingernail."

"No shit."

"Do you know what a mandarin fingernail is?"

"Not really."

"On the little finger of his left hand, the nail is ten inches long. I mean this literally. Ask anyone."

"What does he do with it?"

"Nothing. It's a symbol of his leisurely life. His face is covered with puss pimples. He has an affected, mincing manner. Loves to talk about movies."

"Is the fingernail hideously offensive?"

"Why the hell should I care about his fingernail?"

"I don't know."

"Mr. Woo grins at me throughout the hour, as if everything I say is intended only for him. That's offensive." Henry sneered with disgust.

"Is he a little paranoical?"

"He's smug. It's the same thing."

"He would get to me, too."

"I want to throw a knife through his face."

"Do you feel hungry?"

"I'd have lunch with you, but I teach in fifteen minutes. What about Thursday? No; I have a conference with Mr. Woo. Friday. Three o'clock."

"That's very late."

"I really want to have lunch with you. I haven't had lunch, you know, in thirteen years." He lit another cigarette. His stare was grim. He wasn't joking.

"You're joking."

"No. Lunchtime is when I write."

"What are you writing?"

"A sentence."

"Can I read it?"

"You won't believe this — and you'd be perfectly right not to — but the other day I thought I'd actually written it."

"Can I read it?"

"Yes. I want your opinion. I'll show it to you in a month or so."

"After thirteen years, you lose perspective. It's probably finished."

"What were you saying before?"

"A woman tears herself to pieces while I lecture. It's not important."

"What's her name?" he asked, glancing at his watch.

"Toiler."

"Toilet is French. What an odd name. Do you call her Miss Toilet?"

"Toiler. Anna Toiler."

"Same word. Old French. It means battle, trap, trouble, one who labors, or one who engages in litigious disputes. It's also a kind of cloth. What else does she do?"

"Rides."

"Well, then, she's involved with drugs. Why else would she hide?"

"Rides. Rides horses."

"I've had many students who were in the circus."

"She isn't. She's a housewife from Palo Alto. Her husband is an engineer and a weight lifter. He beats her up. Anyway, once. That's what she said."

"There's a pilot in my class who is from Palo Alto. I've sworn never to tell his name."

"Why not?"

"He's a serious alcoholic. All pilots, surgeons, and judges are drunks. You do know this is true?"

"Everyone knows."

"That's correct."

Henry stood, turned to the door, then said, "Remember our lunch date. I must talk to you about something very important."

It occurred to me to ask what, but the door closed. I was alone.

After the next class, she waited for me outside the room, leaning against a wall. She pretended to be reading through her notes.

As I approached, she glanced up and smiled. Again, instinctively, I began to gaze; to study her.

She wore the same suit with a white shirt and thin black tie. She looked mannish, severe, and pretty.

"Would you like to have coffee? I'll buy it this time."

I couldn't remember saying yes or no, but I was in a coffee shop. As we talked, she didn't touch her face or neck. She'd been good in class, too, sitting very still throughout the hour. I'd forgotten she was there. I wondered if, somehow, I'd cured her of the tic by talking to her; seeming flirtatious. The sexual juices have healing powers. She said, "I won't be able to meet you after class next time. I go to my doctor."

The remark seemed a little strange. I hadn't asked her to meet me. I hadn't assumed these meetings had become an institution. But she missed the next class and the one after that. When she missed the third, I stopped thinking about her. It's easy to forget a student. First the name, then the face. Over the years whole classes go from memory, as if you'd been alone talking to yourself, hallucinating amid the flow of academic seasons. Thales, the first philosopher, said everything is water.

Then Bluma phoned and stopped the flow. "What happened to your student, Tiller?"

"Toiler."

"Toiler, Tiller. Same name. What happened with her?"

"She dropped the class, I think."

"I don't blame her. I wouldn't take your class in the first place."

"You wouldn't?"

"And I'd throw you out of mine."

"Because of my character disorder?"

"Because of everything. Listen, there's more important things to talk about. I heard a new joke."

"I heard one, too."

"Want to tell yours first?"

"You first."

"How can I tell it if you're thinking about your joke?"

"I won't think."

"Then you'll forget your joke and it'll be my fault."

"Tell me your joke. I need a laugh."

"In New York they have a number you can call for a joke."

"It's a desperate city."

"Do you want the number?"

"Tell me your joke, for God's sake."

She told it. I laughed, then told mine. There was silence.

"You didn't like it?"

"Theoretically, I liked it."

"Can you like a joke theoretically?"

"You told it wrong is what I mean."

"How should I tell it?"

As Bluma told me my joke, I looked out the office window at the Berkeley hills where black-green ragged trees stood against the glaring blue of a cloudless sky. In the north a hawk circled, looking for a kill. It seemed to me there were no jokes and nothing funny in nature.

The term was half over when, late one afternoon, I found Anna Toiler waiting for me outside my office. "I must talk about dropping the class," she said. I hurriedly opened the door, ushering her inside, gesturing toward the chair Henry had sat in. The window was behind her, a tall rectangle of light. She wore a new suit, summery cotton, lavender with a dull sheen. It had incipient vitality and suggested a compromise with California. Her blouse had the dark green solemnity of a rain forest and was open at the neck, as if negligently, revealing a bra strap. The scratches on her neck were like spears of thin red grass slanted this way and that by an uncertain wind. She wasn't cured, apparently, only restrained in my company. She didn't touch herself. I wondered what that cost her.

"You've missed a lot of work. Good idea, I suppose, to drop the course."

"It isn't that I don't like your course."

"You needn't explain."

"It's these doctor's appointments. They can't seem to tell me anything. All they do is give me different drugs."

"I see."

"What I'd like to know is whether I can take your course independently. I'll do the reading on my own and write a paper."

The window was slightly open and a breeze pressed the back of her neck. A soft breeze, but steady. She began shivering. She'd set her purse on the edge of the desk. Small, square, green purse with a brass clasp that looked efficient. Her hands lay side by side in her lap, more tense than composed. They braced her against the shivering.

"Aren't you uncomfortable? Move away from the window."

"I'm fine," she said, but the shivering continued.

"To do an independent study, you'd have to have conferences with me. It's late in the term. They might be hard to arrange. Then there's all the driving back and forth. You should consider that. Even with little traffic, it means hours on the highway for you."

Her response was a shrug. She was resigned to suffer the highway just as she was resigned to sit there shivering. The spasms became stronger as I talked, as if I were biting her with icy phrases, but she merely sat there, self-denying, proud. She belonged in the East, I thought, living a tight exquisite life like Emily Dickinson.

Attractive; handsome clothes; horse owner; but she wanted tedious hours on the highway, wanted to sit there shivering. The lavender suit set off her silvery eyes, dark centers like mysterious planets, and the ghostly hair descending to her shoulders. She'd said her husband, the weight lifter, hit her. Maybe her soul required tribulation. Her disease wasn't a mere allergy. I had her number, but felt annoyed at myself for having it. Not my business.

"This is ridiculous. You're freezing."

I rose abruptly and went to the window. Enough of this martyrdom. I'd shut the damn window. It was built in an old, luxurious style, plenty of oak and glass. As I strained to pull it down, I felt better about myself, doing this good thing for her, but the window moved only a little. Measured the truth in my heart? Then it stuck, fused in its runners.

"I'll move to the other side of the desk," she said.

I ignored her and tried for a better grip, determined to shut the window. She was looking up at me, her face close to my right hip, her expression dismayed and apologetic, with a kind of pre-Raphaelite pathos, sweet, other-worldly, faintly morbid. Her husband didn't blame her for ruining things, she said. I could see why. I could understand everything in my violent determination to shut the window; even why he hit her. Dreamy hair, eyes of a snow leopard, lacerated neck. I felt pity more than blame; anger more than pity. The window wouldn't move. I was beginning to sweat. My neck and shoulders burned with strain. Then fingers slid beneath the sash. Why? To help me. Pull from the bottom. But I had no time to think this. Delicate, ethereal fingers vanished beneath the sash as sixty pounds of wood and glass rushed down, smashing them. I screamed, lunging at the window, shoving it back up instantly; the bitterly adamant resistance gone; a strength of gorillas in my arms. "Oh God," I said, stepping toward her, leaning down to look, then immediately backing away in dread of making her pain worse. This close to her, me, the one who did the smashing, the feel of it still in my hands, wood crushing flesh. She whispered, "My fault, my fault," her eyes big, wild with silvery exhilaration, claiming all guilt, pleading with me for forgiveness. "I'm so sorry," she said. "I did it. It was my own fault."

I retreated slowly, fearfully, as if from a forbidden being, the awesome other, taboo. Her hands lay palms-up in her lap, fingers greenish-blue, pads shrivelled, looking waterlogged, squashed. They seemed like a memory of hands. In a photograph, I'd have guessed they were dead; so empty and still, they were in terrible pain. Without a word, I settled into my chair and waited for it to end. There was nothing to do, nothing to say. An immense passion, a weight of incoherent turgid feeling, enclosed us like the walls of a cave. At the bottom corner of the desk, she crossed her ankles, rubbing them together, soothing and hugging herself down there, out of sight, quietly, so that I might not notice. I noticed. In a slow, dull voice, I said, "Drop the course. Take it independently. Do it any way you like."

Though still big with pain, her eyes took on new urgency. "Don't you care what I do?"

I regretted having spoken, tried to change the effect, but managed only a feeble question. "What do you mean?" I put it very gently, each word a tender baby of concern.

"You know." This was sullen.

"I do?"

"Damn right. You started this."

"This?"

"Yes, this."

"But you sit there shivering in front of me. I go to the window. You stick your hand under it . . ."

"Oh please. Please don't go on like that. If you say one more word, you'll inflict irredeemable stupidity on both of us. There isn't enough time for little games. Don't pretend nothing has happened between us."

"What's happened? The window . . ."

She leaned forward, grit her teeth, and kicked me hard in the shin. Then neither of us moved or seemed to breathe. We sat facing each other across the desk, her purse between us, window light filling her hair with a cloudy glow. My heart beat in me like a bludgeon. Any word, any move, would be wrong. The green and lavender of her clothing now seemed intensely sensational, the open collar more dissolute than negligent. The torn neck fierce. Her posture and expression stiff, impassive, with no sign of resignation but rigid with effort to contain herself, the idea she had of something between us. Finally, she stirred, reaching to her purse, snapping it open. She removed a long pearly comb and drew it through her hair in a swift, automatic motion, then stopped, glanced at me, startled, as if remembering suddenly where she was.

"May I?" she said, her tone confused. "I don't usually comb my hair in public. I must have imagined nobody could see me." She was then crying; long gleaming tears; flowing in the way of children. "You are there, aren't you?"

"Let me do it."

She stared for a moment, then seemed almost to relax, to come down through miles of feeling as she handed me the comb and bowed her head. I combed her hair, trailing layers of dumb solicitude.

When she left I put my elbows on the desk, my face in my hands. I let time pass and tried to think but discovered no issue, only a picture of her inserting the comb into her purse, clicking it shut, standing, walking to the door in three brisk steps as if she had somewhere definite to go. The books and papers on my desk seemed unreal, meaningless clutter, but, gradually, as the office darkened, they gained substance and sense. I began gathering them together, putting them in order, as if with love.

About two weeks later, I received a note on heavy beige paper. It was written in a fine, small hand with no ego-distorting pressures. She said that she'd dropped all classes. Apologized for wasting my time. Thanked me for being patient. Under her name, squeezed into the corner, was her phone number. I read the note again, looking for more than it said, but the smooth clear script, with its even pressure throughout, expressed nothing inadvertently. I folded it, put it into my pocket, reached for the phone and dialed, surprised that I had memorized the number without trying. There was no answer. I listened to the ringing, monotonous ringing, day after day, until it became a sound of emptiness and futility in myself. I had only to dial her number to begin feeling I'd misspent my life making idle gestures, repeating them for no reason, though I always felt less anxious afterwards. I phoned from my office, from gas stations, drugstores, movie houses. . . .

One afternoon, on the way out for lunch with Henry, I said, "A student of mine lived in Africa and came back with a parasite. She calls it Nigerian fluke."

"Are you sure?"

"That's what she calls it."

"Nigerian fluke?"

"She thought it might be only an allergy."

"Nigerian fluke is fatal in every case. Ask her to be specific. I'm curious. I've had many students who were diseased. . . ."

"She dropped out."

"See?" Henry stopped, held my elbow, and grinned. He seemed pleased to think he'd been right, yet also horrified. "She's dead?"

"Dropped out. That's all I know."

"Were you smitten by her?"

I shrugged, instantly reminding myself of how she shrugged after telling me that her husband hit her. Henry waited for my answer, but, as we left the building, the daylight was so pure there seemed nothing to talk about. We entered it like creatures sliding into a lake without disturbing the surface.

"Oh," he said.

Leonard Michaels, author of The Men's Club *and other works of fiction, is Professor of English at the University of California at Berkeley.*

Vladimir Nabokov

THE GRAND-DAD

Drama in One Act

Introductory Note: The Grand-dad (Dédushka) was completed on June 30, 1923, at the Domaine de Beaulieu. It was published in *Rul'* in Berlin on October 14 of the same year. The English translation is based on a collation of the published text and two almost identical handwritten versions recorded by Nabokov's mother in her albums. What few discrepancies and lapses there were generally had resulted from oversights in copying.

CAST OF CHARACTERS
Wife
Husband
Passerby (de Mérival)
Juliette
Grand-dad

The action takes place in 1816 in France, in the house of a well-off peasant family. A spacious room, with windows giving on a garden. Slanting rain. Enter the owners and a stranger — a passerby.

Wife

. . . Come in. Our living room is over here. . . .

Husband

. . . One moment — we'll have wine for you. *(to his daughter)*

Juliette, run to the cellar, quickly!

Passerby
(looking around)
How cozy it is here. . . .

Husband
>   . . . Be seated, please —

here. . . .

Passerby
>   Bright. . . . And neat. . . . A carved chest in the corner,

a clock up on the wall, its dial adorned
with cornflowers. . . .

Wife
>   Aren't you soaked?

Passerby
>   Oh, not at all —

I ducked under a roof in time. A real
downpour! You're certain it's no trouble? May I
wait till it stops? As soon as it is over . . .

Husband
Oh, it's our pleasure. . . .

Wife
>   Are you from nearby?

Passerby
A traveler. . . . I've recently returned from
abroad. I'm staying at my brother's castle —
de Mérival. . . . Just a short way from here . . .

Husband
Yes, yes, we know it. . . .
(to his daughter, who has come in with the wine)
>   Put it here, Juliette.

There. Drink, good sir. It's sunshine in a glass. . . .

Passerby
(clinking glasses)
Your health. . . . Ah, what a fine bouquet! And what
a comely daughter you have too. . . . Juliette,
my sweet, where is your Romeo?

Wife
(laughing)
>   What is

a "Romeo"?

Passerby
            Oh . . . Never mind—one day
she'll learn herself. . . .

Juliette
                Have you seen Grand-dad yet, sir?

Passerby
Not yet.

Juliette
            He's nice. . . .

Husband
(to Wife)
                    Say, by the way, where is he?

Wife
Asleep inside his room, smacking his lips
just like a little child. . . .

Passerby
                    And your grand-dad—
he's very old?

Husband
                Near seventy, I reckon . . .
we do not know. . . .

Wife
                He's not our kin, you see:
it was our own idea to call him that.

Juliette
He's gentle. . . .

Passerby
            But who is he?

Husband
                        That's exactly
the point—we haven't the least idea. . . . One day
last spring an oldster turned up in the village,
and it was clear he came from a great distance.
He had no recollection of his name,
and smiled a timid smile at all our questions.

It was Juliette who brought him to the house.
We gave the old man food, we gave him drink;
he cooed with pleasure, licked his chops, eyes narrowed,
squeezed at my hand, with an enraptured smile,
but made no sense at all; must be his mind
was growing bald. . . . We kept him here with us —
it was Juliette who talked us into it. . . .
He must be coddled, though . . . his tooth is sweet,
and he's been costing us a pretty penny.

Wife
Oh, stop it, dear . . . the sweet old man. . . .

Husband
                                                I meant
no harm. . . . It was just idle chatter. . . . Drink, sir!

Passerby
I'm drinking, thanks. . . . Although it's almost time
for me to go. . . . What rain! It will breathe life
into your land.

Husband
                        Thank heavens. Only this
is just a joke, not rain. There, look — the sun's
beginning to peek through already. . . . No. . . .

Passerby
Look at that lovely golden smoke!

Husband
                                        See — you, sir,
can marvel at it, but what about us?
We *are* the land. . . . And our thoughts are the land's
own thoughts. . . . We do not need to look, but sense
the swelling of the seed within the furrow,
the fruit becoming plump. . . . When, from the heat,
the earth begins to parch and crack, so, too,
the skin upon our palms starts cracking, sir.
And, if it rains, we listen with alarm,
and inwardly we pray: "Noise, blessed noise,
be not transformed to hammering of hail!" . . .
And if that ricocheting clatter should
begin resounding on our windowsills,

it's then—then that we plug our ears, and bury
our faces in our pillows, just like cowards
who hear a distant fusillade! Our worries
are many. . . . As when, lately, in the pear tree,
a worm appeared—a monstrous, warty worm,
a green-hued devil! Or when aphids, like
a clammy rash, will coat a youthful vine. . . .
And so it goes.

Passerby

Yet what a sense of pride
for you, what joy it must be to receive
the ruddy, aromatic thank-you's that
your trees give to you!

Wife

Grand-dad, too, awaits
assiduously some kind of revelation,
pressing his ear first to the bark, then to
a petal. . . . He believes, it seems to me,
that dead men's souls live on in lilies, or
in cherry trees.

Passerby

I wouldn't mind a chat
with him—I'm fond of gentle simpletons
like that. . . .

Wife

I look and look at you but I
just cannot figure out your age. You don't seem
too young, and yet there's something. . . . I don't know. . . .

Passerby
Dear lady, I'm in my sixth decade.

Husband

Then
you've lived a life of peace—there's not a wrinkle
upon your brow. . . .

Passerby

Of peace, you say! *(laughs)* If I
wrote it all down. . . . Sometimes I, even, cannot

believe my past! My head spins from it as . . .
as it does from your wine. I've drained the cup
of life in such enormous draughts, such draughts. . . .
And then there were times, too, when death would nudge
my elbow. . . . Well, perhaps you'd like to hear
the tale of how, the summer of the year
seventeen ninety-two, in Lyon, Monsieur
de Mérival—aristocrat, and traitor,
so on, so forth—was saved right from the scaffold
of the guillotine?

Wife
                    We're listening, tell

us. . . .

Passerby
                    I was twenty that tempestuous year.
And the tribunal's thunder had condemned me
to death—perhaps it was my powdered hair,
or else, perhaps, the noble particle
before my name—who knows: the merest trifle
meant execution then. . . . That very night I
was to appear, by torchlight, at the scaffold.
The executioner was nimble, by
the way, and diligent: an artist, not
an axman. He was always emulating
his Paris cousin, the renowned Sanson:
he had procured the same kind of small tumbrel
and, when he'd lopped a head off, he would hold
it by the hair and swing it the same way. . . .
And so he carts me off. Darkness had fallen,
along black streets the windows came alight,
and street lamps too. I sat, back to the wind,
inside the shaky cart, clutching the side rails
with hands numb from the cold—and I was thinking . . .
of what?—of various trivial details mostly:
that I had left without a handkerchief,
or that my executioner companion
looked like a dignified physician. . . . Soon we
arrived. A final turning, and before us
there opened up the square's expanse. . . . Its center
was ominously lit. . . . And it was then,

as, with a kind of guilty courtesy,
the executioner helped me descend,
and I realized the journey's end had come —
that was the moment terror seized my throat. . . .
Lugubrious hallooing midst the crowd —
derisive, maybe, too (I couldn't hear) —
the horses' moving croups, the lances, wind,
the smell of burning torches — all of this
passed like a dream, and I saw but one thing,
just one: there, there, up in the murky sky,
like a steel wing, the heavy oblique blade
between two uprights hung, ready to fall. . . .
Its edge, catching a transient gleam, appeared
to be already glistening with blood!
To rumblings from the distant crowd, I started
to ascend the scaffold, and each step
would make a different creak. In silence they
removed my camisole, and slashed my shirt
down to my scapulae. . . . The board seemed a
raised drawbridge: to it I'd be lashed, I knew,
the bridge would drop, I'd swing face down, and then,
between the posts the wooden collar would
slam tight on me, and then — yes, only then —
death, with an instant crash, would plummet down.
It grew impossible for me to swallow,
my nape was racked by a presentient pain,
my temples thundered and my chest was bursting,
tensed with the palpitation and the pounding —
but, I believe, I outwardly seemed calm. . . .

Wife
Oh, I'd be screaming, lunging — my entreaties
for mercy would be heard, and I'd . . . But then —
then how did *you* escape?

Passerby
                                        A miracle. . . .
So — I was standing on the scaffold. They
had not yet bound my hands. My shoulders felt
the frigid wind. The executioner was
unraveling some kind of rope. Just then —
a cry of "fire!" and instantly flames shot

up from behind the rail; I and the headsman
were swaying, struggling on the platform's edge. . . .
A crackling—and the heat breathed on my face,
the hand that had been clutching me relaxed,
I fell somewhere, knocked someone down, I dove,
I slid, amid torrents of smoke, into
a storm of rearing steeds and running people—
"Fire! Fire!" the cry vibrated over and over,
choking with sobs of joy, with boundless bliss!
But I was far away by then! Just once
I looked back, on the run, and saw the crimson
smoke billowing into a vault of black,
the uprights bursting into flames themselves,
the blade come crashing down, set free by fire!

Wife
How dreadful! . . .

Husband
                         Yes, when you've seen death you don't
forget. . . . One time some thieves got in the garden.
The night, the darkness, fright. . . . I got my gun off
its hook—

Passerby
(interrupting, lost in thought)
                         —Thus I escaped, and suddenly
it seemed my eyes were opened: I'd been awkward,
unfeeling, absent-minded, had not fully
appreciated life, the colored specks of
our precious life—but, having seen so close
that pair of upright posts, that narrow gate
to nonexistence, and those gleams, that gloom. . . .
Amid the whistle of sea winds I fled
from France, and kept avoiding France so long
as over her the icy Robespierre
loomed like a greenish incubus, so long
as dusty armies marched into the gunfire
spurred by the Corsican's gray gaze and forelock.
But life was hard for me in foreign countries.
In dank and melancholy London I
gave lessons in the science of duelling. I

sojourned in Russia, playing the fiddle at
an opulent barbarian's abode. . . .
In Turkey and in Greece I wandered then,
and in enchanting Italy I starved.
The sights I saw were many; I became
a deckhand, then a chef, a barber, a tailor,
then just a simple tramp. Yet, to this day
I thank the Lord with every passing hour
for all the hardships that I came to know—
and for the rustle of the roadside corn,
the rustle and the warming breath of all
the human souls that have passed close to me.

Husband
Of all, sir, all of them? But you forget
the soul belonging to that flashy craftsman
whom you encountered that day on the scaffold.

Passerby
Oh, no—through him the world revealed itself
to me. He was, unwittingly, the key.

Husband
No, I don't get it. . . . *(rising)* Before supper, I
have chores to do. . . . Our meal is unpretentious . . .
but maybe you'll—

Passerby
                                    Why not, why not. . . .

Husband
                                            Agreed, then! *(going out)*

Passerby
Forgive my talkativeness. . . . I'm afraid
my tale was boring. . . .

Wife
                                    Goodness, not at all. . . .

Passerby
Is that a baby's bonnet you are sewing?

Wife
(laughs)
That's right. I think I'll need it around Christmas. . . .

Passerby
How wonderful. . . .

Wife
                 And that's another baby,
there, in the garden. . . .

Passerby
(looks out the window)
             Oh — your "grand-dad." Splendid
old man. . . . The sun gives him a silvery sheen.
Splendid . . . and there's a certain dreamy air
about his movements, as his fingers slide
along a lily stem, and he is bent
over the flower bed, not picking, just
caressing, all aglow with such a tender
and timid smile. . . .

Wife
             That's true, he loves the lilies —
he fondles them, has conversations with them.
He even has invented names for them —
all names of duchesses, of marquesses. . . .

Passerby
How nice for him. . . . Now *he* is one, I'm certain,
who's lived his life in peace — yes, in some village,
away from civil and from other tumults. . . .

Wife
He's good at doctoring. . . . Knows all about
medicinal herbs. Once, for our daughter —
(Juliette bursts in, laughing boisterously.)

Juliette
                Mother!
Oh, Mother! You'll die laughing!

Wife
              What's the matter?

Juliette
Grand-dad . . . out there . . . the basket. . . . Oh! *(laughs)*

Wife
               Come on,
let's hear it properly. . . .

Juliette
                              You'll die. . . . See, Mother,
I was just going—I was going through
the garden to pick cherries. . . . Grand-dad sees me,
gets in a crouch, then snatches at my basket—
the new one, the one with the oilcloth lining,
already stained with juice—he snatches it,
and heaves it all the way into the stream. . . .
By now the current's carried it away.

Passerby
How very odd. God only knows in what
directions, in his brain, the thoughts make bridges. . . .
Could be that . . . no. *(laughs)* Sometimes I tend myself
to strange associations. . . . Like that basket,
its oilcloth lining with the cherries' juice
incarnadined—it brings to mind. . . . Good God,
what chilling nonsense! You'll permit me not
to finish. . . .

Wife
(not listening)
                              What's got into him? Your father
will be angry. Twenty sous, that basket. *(leaves with her daughter)*

Passerby
(looking out the window)
They're bringing him. . . . It's funny how he sulks,
the old man. . . . Just like an offended child. . . .

Wife
(They return with Grand-dad.)
Here, Grand-dad, we've a guest. . . . Just look at him. . . .

Grand-dad
I do not want that basket here. There must
not be such baskets. . . .

Wife
                              It's all right, my dear. . . .
It isn't there. It's gone. It's gone for good.
Come on, calm down. . . . Good sir, perhaps you could
distract him for a while. . . . I have to go
and start preparing supper. . . .

Grand-dad

                                      Who is this?

No, I don't want . . .

Wife
(in the doorway)

                        But that's our guest. He's kind.
Sit down, sit down. What stories he has told us!
About the executioner in Lyon,
the guillotine, the fire! It's fascinating.
Tell it again, sir. *(leaves with her daughter)*

Grand-dad

                         What? What was that she
just said? That's strange. . . . The executioner,
the fire . . .

Passerby
(aside)

                    There, now he's frightened. Silly woman —
why did she ever have to tell him that?
(full voice)
It was a joke, Grand-dad. . . . Tell me instead,
what do you chat about out there with flowers,
with trees? . . . Why do you look at me like that?

Grand-dad
(staring at him intently)
Where are you from?

Passerby

                  Oh . . . simply passing by . . .

Grand-dad

                                            Wait,
just wait, don't go away, I'll be right back. *(goes out)*

Passerby
(pacing the room)
Odd character! Either he's had a fright
or he's remembered something. . . . I've an eerie,
a troubled feeling — I don't understand. . . .
The wine they have here must be strong. Tra-ram,
tra-ra. . . . *(sings)* What's wrong with me? I seem to feel
some kind of vague oppression. . . . Ugh! How stupid. . . .

Grand-dad
(enters)
And here I am. . . . I'm back. . . .

Passerby

Hello, hello. . . .

(aside)
Look how he's grown all nice and cheery now.

Grand-dad
(shifting from foot to foot, hands behind his back)
Here's where I live. Right in this house. I like
it here. For instance, over there, look at
that wardrobe. . . .

Passerby

Beautiful. . . .

Grand-dad

You know, that's an
enchanted wardrobe. . . . Oh, the things, the things that
go on inside! You see that chink, that keyhole?
Peek through it . . . Eh?

Passerby

Enchanted? I believe you. . . .
It's beautiful. . . . You didn't tell me, though,
about the lilies, and your talks with them.

Grand-dad
Peek through the chink. . . .

Passerby

I can see fine from here. . . .

Grand-dad
No, take a closer look.

Passerby

I can't — that table
is in the way. . . .

Grand-dad

Lie on the table — lie
on it, face down. . . .

Passerby

                Oh, come, it isn't worth it.

Grand-dad
Don't want to do it?

Passerby

               . . . Look, look at that sunshine!
And your whole garden sparkling. . . .

Grand-dad

                 You don't want to?
A shame. . . . A real shame. It would be much
more comfortable.

Passerby

          More comfortable? For what?

Grand-dad
For what? *(swings with the axe he has been holding behind his back)*

Passerby
       Hold on there! Stop!
(They struggle.)

Grand-dad

            No. . . . Wait. . . . You must
not interfere. . . . It is decreed. . . . My duty. . . .

Passerby
(knocks him down)
Enough!
      There — there, that's it — that madness. . . . God! . . .
I didn't expect it. . . . He was mumbling, purring —
then suddenly . . .
           What *is* this? I think it
already happened once. . . . Or did I dream it?
The same way, just the same, I struggled. . . . Up!
Enough, get up! Reply! . . . Look how he stares,
and stares. . . . Look at those fingers, naked, blunt. . . .
I've seen them once before, I know! You'll answer,
you will! . . . That stare. . . . *(bends over the prostrate figure)*
          No, he will tell me nothing.

Juliette
(in the doorway)
What have you done to Grand-dad? . . .

Passerby
                                                        Juliette . . .
You'd . . . better go.

Juliette
                        What have you done. . . .

Vladimir Nabokov's posthumous publications include *Lectures on Literature,* published in 1980 by Harcourt Brace Jovanovich, and *Lectures on Russian Literature* (1981) from the same publisher.

Joyce Carol Oates

MASTER RACE

    Why would you want to hurt me — ?
Why hurt another person — ?
Though the incident happens abruptly, and the worst of it, in a manner of speaking, is finished within sixty seconds, Cecilia is to remember it in slow motion: the arm pinioning her deftly beneath the chin, the clumsy staggering struggle on the sidewalk, her assailant dragging her into a narrow alleyway, pummelling and punching and tearing angrily at her clothes . . . and the rest of it. No warning, no one to blame (she thinks instantly) except herself, for hadn't Philip and the Americans at the Consulate cautioned her against. . . . She makes an effort, confused and feeble, to protect herself, pulling at the man's arm, using her elbows, squirming, turning from side to side. Stop, please, no, you don't want to do this, *please*—so Cecilia

would say in her reasonable soft-toned voice except for the fact that she can't breathe and her attacker is warning her to keep her mouth shut or he'll rip off her head. Yes the accent is American, low and throaty, South Carolina, perhaps, Georgia—yes she catches a glimpse of dark skin, long fingers, and blunt square trimmed fingernails, the palm of the hand lighter, almost pale.

Afterward Cecilia will recall the footsteps hurrying close behind her and her body's shrewd instinct to steel itself against attack, while a more mature—detached—rational—"intelligent"—part of her dismissed the reaction as unnecessary. She is not the sort of woman to succumb to fear, or even to take herself, as a woman, very seriously—not Cecilia Heath.

Nor is she the sort of woman—she has always supposed—who need fear sexual attack: her vision of herself is hazy and unreliable, but she has always assumed that men find her no more attractive than she finds herself.

Now she has been dragged somewhere, her smart linen jacket has been ripped partway off, her skirt lifted—she is being slapped, shaken, cursed, warned—her assailant appears to be both frightened of her and very angry, wildly angry. She doesn't see his face. She doesn't want to see his face. Her body goes limp with terror, she will discover that her clothes are soaked in perspiration, though still, *still,* that amazed stubborn voice of hers, that relentlessly civil voice, is trying to plead, to reason—*Please,* you don't really want to do this, there must be some mistake—

The man holds her from behind, panting and grunting; awkwardly, and angrily, he jams himself against her buttocks, once, twice, three times; then releases her as if in disgust, thrusts her away, gives her a hard blow to the side of her head; and it's over. Cecilia is sprawled gracelessly on the ground, her nose dripping blood, her breath coming in shudders.

Her assailant is gone as abruptly, and very nearly as invisibly, as he appeared. She hears his footsteps, or feels their vibration, but she can't move to look around. "Oh but *why.* . . ?" Cecilia whispers. "Why at this time in my. . . ."

Fortunately, she thinks, she hasn't been badly injured; perhaps she hasn't been injured at all. Fortunately she is not far from the Hotel Zur Birke, three blocks away in fact; and Philip will probably not be waiting for her; and no one has witnessed her humiliation; and no one need know. (Though, surely, humiliation is too extreme a word, too melodramatic?—Cecilia Heath does not consider herself a melodramatic woman. Her instinct is simply to withdraw from trouble and attention. In any case she has not been humiliated, she has been ill-used — the result of bad judgment on her side.)

She gets to her feet shakily, carefully. She dreads someone approaching, a belated witness to the encounter, someone who will discover her in this vulnerable exposed state: an American woman, an American woman who speaks very little German, not a tourist precisely, well, yes, perhaps she would be considered a tourist, with some professional connections, her case would be reported not only to the Mainz police but to the United States Consulate and to the United States Army since her assailant (she knows, she cannot *not* know) was an American serviceman. . . . One of the hundreds, or are there thousands, of American servicemen stationed nearby. . . .

"Oh why did you do it, *why*," Cecilia says half-sobbing, "I meant only to be friendly. . . ."

Her right ear is ringing, blood seems to be dripping down the front of her English silk blouse, she's dazed, her heart racing, of course she isn't seriously injured; the assault would not be designated rape; the man hadn't even torn off her underwear, hadn't troubled.

Nor had he taken her purse, Cecilia sees, relieved. It is lying where she dropped it, papers and guidebook spilling out, her wallet safe inside, her passport safe . . . so there is no need to report the embarrassing incident at all.

At this time — early summer of 1983 — Cecilia Heath is traveling in Europe with a senior colleague from the Peekskill Foundation for Independent Research in the Arts, Sciences, and the Humanities, a specialist in European history named Philip Schoen. Philip is fifty-three, almost twenty years older than Cecilia; he claims to be in love with her though he doesn't (in Cecilia's opinion) know her very well. He is also married — has been married, as he says, "most of his life — not unhappily." Why does he imagine himself in love with Cecilia Heath? — she can't quite bring herself to inquire.

In the past fifteen years, since the publication of his enormous book *The Invention of Chaos: Europe at War in the Twentieth Century*, Philip Schoen has acquired a fairly controversial, but generally high, reputation in his field. Cecilia has been present when fellow historians and academicians have been introduced to Philip, she has noted their mode of address, a commingling of gravity and caution, deferential courtesy, some belligerence. She has noted how Philip shakes their hands — colleagues', strangers' — as if the ceremony were something to be gotten over with as quickly as possible. Do men squeeze one another's fingers as they do ours, Cecilia has often wondered. Do they dare. . . ?

Though Philip Schoen avidly sought fame of a sort, as a young scholar, by his own confession "fame" now depresses him. Perhaps it is the mere sound of his name, *Schoen* having taken on qualities of an impersonal nature in recent years, since he was awarded a Pulitzer Prize, a Rockefeller grant, a position as Distinguished Senior Fellow at the Peekskill Foundation. . . . He jokes nervously that his rewards are "too much, too soon," while his wife would have it that they are "too little, too late."

A tall, spare, self-conscious man who carries himself with an almost military bearing, Philip Schoen is given to jokes of a brittle nervous sort which Cecilia cannot always interpret. (Her own humor tends to be warm, slanted, teasing — not the sort to make people laugh loudly. She has always remembered her mother and grandmother murmuring together, in some semi-public place like the lobby of a theater, about a fast-talking young woman close by who was making a small gathering of men laugh uproariously at her wit: *vulgar,* to have that effect upon others.) Philip is impressed by what he calls Cecilia's anachronistic qualities, her sweetness and patience and intelligent good sense; he really fell in love with her (or so he claims — it makes a charming anecdote) when she wrote a formal thank you note after a large dinner party given by the Schoens: the first note of its kind they had ever received in Peekskill, he said. ("Do you mean that nobody else here writes thank you notes?" Cecilia asked, embarrassed. "Not even the *women*. . . ?") Half-reproachfully Philip told her she was the most defined person of his acquaintance. She made everyone else seem, by contrast, improvised.

Cecilia has known Philip Schoen only since the previous September but she has been a witness, in that brief period of time, to a mysterious alteration in his personality and appearance. His manner is melancholy, edgy, obsessive; his skin exudes an air of clamminess; the whites of his eyes are faintly discolored, like old ivory, but the irises are dark, damply bright, with a hint of mirthful despair. By degrees he has acquired a subtle ravaged look that rather suits him; his sense of humor has become unexpected, abrasive, inspired. If asked by his colleagues what he is working on at the present time he sometimes says, "You don't *really* want to know": meaning that doing professional work in the history of Europe, or, by extension, in history of any sort, is a taxing enterprise. Also, he has confided in Cecilia that it's an unsettling predicament to find oneself

posthumous while still alive—to know that one's scholarly reputation, like one's personality, is set; that the future can be no more
than an arduous and joyless fulfillment of past expectations. Failure
is a distinct possibility, of course, but not success: he *is* a success.

"But why call yourself 'posthumous'?—I don't understand,"
Cecilia said.

"Perhaps one day you will," he said.

In late March he dropped by unexpectedly at Cecilia's rented
duplex and asked her rather awkwardly if she would like to accompany him on a three-week trip to Europe. He was being sent by the
Foundation to interview prospective Fellows for one of the chairs in
history—men in France, Belgium, Sweden, Finland, and Germany;
and he had the privilege of bringing along an assistant of sorts, a
junior colleague. Was she free? Would she come? Not as an assistant
of course but as a colleague?—a friend? "It would mean so much to
me," he said, his voice faltering.

They looked at each other in mutual dismay. For weeks Philip
had been seeking her out, telephoning her, encountering her by accident in town, for weeks he had been watching her with an unmistakable air of suppressed elation, but Cecilia had chosen not to see;
after all he was a married man, the father of two college-age children. . . . Now he had made himself supremely vulnerable: his
damp dark eyes snatched at her in a sort of drowning panic. "Of
course I can't accompany you," Cecilia heard her soft cool voice explain, but, aloud, she could bring herself to say only: "Yes, thank
you, it's very kind of you to ask, yes I suppose I would like to go . . .
but as an assistant after all, if you don't mind."

He seized her hands in his and kissed her, breathless and
trembling as any young suitor. Did it matter that he was nineteen
years older than she, that his rank at the Foundation was so much
superior to hers, that his breath smelled sweetly of alcohol. . . ? Or
that he was married, and might very well break Cecilia's heart. . . ?

On the flight to Frankfurt Philip tells her about his family background in a low, tense, neutral voice, as if he were confessing
something shameful.

His paternal grandparents emigrated from the Rhine Valley
near Wiesbaden in the early 1900s, settling first in Pennsylvania,
and then in northern Wisconsin: they were dairy farmers, prosper-
ous, Lutheran, clannish, supremely German. Until approximately
the late thirties. Until such time as it was no longer politic in the
United States, or even safe, to proclaim the natural superiority of

the Homeland and the inevitable inferiority of other nations, races, religions.

"The Germans really are a master race," Philip says, "—even when they—or do I mean we?—pretend humility."

Though he has visited Germany many times for professional purposes he has never, oddly, sought out his distant relatives. Perhaps in fact he has none; that part of Germany suffered terrible devastation in the final year of the war. Yes he had relatives in the German army, yes he had an uncle, a much-honored bomber pilot who flew hundreds of successful missions before being shot down over Cologne. . . . "As late as the fifties I had to contend with a good deal of family legend, stealthy German boasting," Philip says. "Of course if hard pressed my father and uncles *would* admit that Hitler was a madman, the Reich was doomed, the entire mythopoetics of German-ness was untenable. . . ."

He believes he knows the German soul perfectly, he says, but by way of his scholarly investigations and interviews primarily: not (or so he hopes) by way of blood. Historical record is all that one can finally trust, not intuition, not promptings of the spirit; a people is its actions, not its ideals; we are (to paraphrase William James) what we cause others to experience.

He breaks off suddenly as if the subject has become distasteful. He tells Cecilia, laughing, that there is nothing more disagreeable than a self-loathing German.

"But do you loathe yourself?" Cecilia asks doubtfully. "And why do you think of yourself as German rather than American. . . ?"

Philip takes her hand, strokes the long slender fingers. His gesture is sudden, surreptitious, though no one is seated in the third airliner seat and in any case no one knows them. He says lightly: "My wife would tell you that the secret of my being is self-loathing— by which she means my German-ness."

A symposium on contemporary philosophical trends was held that spring at the Peekskill Foundation. No aesthetician participated; no specialists in metaphysics or ethics. There were linguists, logicians, mathematicians, a topologist, a semiotician, and others— all men—who resisted classification. The chairman of the conference began by stating, evidently without irony, that since all viable philosophical positions were represented it was not unreasonable to expect that certain key problems might finally be solved. "Only in the presence of my colleagues would I confess to such optimism," the gentleman said, drawing forth appreciative laughter.

The sessions Cecilia attended, however, were consumed in disjointed attempts to define the "problems" at hand. Equations were
scrawled on the blackboard, linguistic analyses were presented, the
philosophers spoke ingeniously, aggressively, sometimes incompre-
hensibly, but so far as Cecilia could judge the primary terms were
never agreed upon; each speaker wanted to wipe the slate clean and
begin again. One particularly belligerent philosopher made the
point that the habit of "bifurcated" thinking, the "hominine polarity
of ego vis-à-vis non-ego," was responsible for the muddled communication. Which is to say, the custom of thinking in antitheses;
the acquired (and civilization-determined) custom of perceiving the
world in terms of opposites; the curse, as he phrased it, of being
"egoed." Hence civilized man is doomed to make distinctions between himself and others: mind and body: up and down: hot and
cold: good and evil: mine/ours and yours/theirs: male and female. . . . The list went on for some time, including such problematic opposites as vocalic and consonantal, reticular and homo-
genous, violable and inviolable, but Cecilia drifted into a dream
thinking of "male" and "female" as acquired habits of thinking. *Acquired habits of thinking. . . ?*

But why, Cecilia wonders, holding a handkerchief to her bleeding nose — why hurt another person?

Cecilia and Philip, in Mainz, in Germany, are no longer quite
so companionable. In fact they are beginning to have small mis-
understandings, not quite disagreements, like any traveling couple,
like lovers married or unmarried.
Cecilia speaks very little German, which gives her a kind of
school-girl innocence, a perpetual tourist's air of surprise and interest and appreciation. Philip's German is fluent and aggressive, as
if he half expects to be misunderstood; he responds with annoyance
if asked where he is from. Though he had enjoyed himself previously—especially in Paris and Stockholm—he now seems distracted, edgy, quick to be offended. The clerk at the Hotel Zur Birke,
for instance, was brusque with him and Cecilia before he realized
who they were and who had made their reservations, whereupon he
turned apologetic, smiling, fawning, begging their apologies. ("The
very essence of the German personality," Philip muttered to Cecilia,
"—either at your throat or at your feet.") His eye for local detail
seems to be focussed upon the blatantly vulgar—American pop
music blaring from a radio in the hotel's breakfast room, "medieval"

souvenirs of stamped tin, graffiti in lurid orange spray-paint on walls, doors, construction fences (much of it in English: KILL, FUCK, NUKE, PRAY) which Philip photographs with a tireless grim pleasure. The enormous tenth-century Romanesque cathedral which Cecilia finds fascinating, if rather damp and oppressive, Philip dismisses as old Teutonic *kitsch,* preserved solely for German and American tourists; the Mainz Hilton he finds a monument to imperialist vulgarity, a happy confluence of German and American ideals of fantasy, efficiency, sheer bulk; even old St. Stephen's Church, partly restored after having been bombed, offends him with its stylish Chagall stained glass windows . . . the blue so very pretty, so achingly pretty, like a Disney-heaven.

Cecilia is surprised at his tone, and begins to challenge him. Why say such things when he doesn't really mean them, or when they can't be all he means? — why such hostility? "I have the caricaturist's eye, I suppose," Philip admits, "— of looking for truths where no one else cares to look."

But Philip is beginning to find fault with Cecilia as well. His objections are ambiguous, likely to be expressed half-seriously, chidingly. . . . Frankly, he says, she puzzles him when she isn't exacting enough by ordinary American standards; when she's overly tolerant; quick to excuse and forgive. In the hotel's newspaper and tobacco shop, for instance, Cecilia returned a few German coins to a clerk who had, in ringing up her purchase, accidentally undercharged her by about sixty cents; and the man — heavy, bald, bulbous-nosed — became inexplicably angry with Cecilia and spoke harshly to her in German, in front of several other customers. Whatever he said hadn't included the word *Danke,* certainly. "And you think the incident is amusing?" Philip says irritably. "How can you take such an attitude?"

"I'm in a foreign country, after all," Cecilia says. "I expect things to seem foreign."

Walking in Mainz on their first evening, trying to relax after the strain of the Frankfurt airport, Cecilia and Philip find themselves in a slightly derelict section of town, across from the railroad station, by the Hammer Hotel, where a number of black American soldiers are milling about in various stages of sobriety. They are touchingly young, Cecilia thinks — nineteen, twenty years old, hardly more than boys. And self-consciously rowdy, defiant, loutish, *black,* as if challenging respectable German pedestrians to take note of them.

One of them, laughing loudly, tries to grab hold of a Binding Bier sign affixed to the hotel's veranda roof, but falls heavily to the street. A driver in a Volkswagen van sounds his horn angrily as he passes and for a minute or two there is a good deal of shouting and fist-waving among the soldiers.

"Strange to see them here," Cecilia says, staring.

"Yes. Unfortunate too," Philip says.

They are stationed at a nearby army base, Philip explains, probably employed in guarding one of the United States military installations. It might even be a nuclear weapons site, he isn't certain.

Cecilia has been reading about recent anti-war and anti-United States demonstrations in Germany, in the *Herald Tribune*. The Green Party is planning an ambitious fall offensive — the hostility to the American military is increasing all the time. She feels sorry for these soldiers, she says, so far from home, so young. . . . They must feel totally confused and demoralized, like soldiers in Vietnam. And so many of them are black.

"Yes. It's unfortunate," Philip says, urging her along. "But the situation isn't at all analogous to Vietnam."

A heavy-set black soldier is staggering about in the street, clowning for his buddies and two very blond girls, German teenagers perhaps, who are whistling and applauding him. Cecilia slows, watching them. She feels an odd prick of guilt — or is it a confused sort of compatriotism, complicity? The soldiers are here, stationed in West Germany, thousands of miles from home, only because they are in the service of their country; protecting, in a manner of speaking, private citizens like Cecilia Heath and Philip Schoen. It is a sobering reflection to think that, if necessary, the men would die in that service. . . .

When they are some distance away, headed back toward the Neue Mainzerstr. and a more congenial part of town, Philip says: "We're only about one hundred miles from the East German border, don't forget. It's easy to forget, in a place like Mainz."

"What do you mean?"

"I mean that our soldiers are political hostages of a sort, under the protection of the United States military. Their presence isn't very agreeable to anyone but it is necessary."

"'Hostages'. . . ?"

"The fact that there are thousands of American soldiers in West Germany makes it less likely that the Soviets will attack: it's as simple as that."

Cecilia draws away slightly to look at her companion. She cannot determine whether Philip is speaking ironically, or with a certain measure of passion. Since coming to Germany he hasn't seemed quite himself . . . not quite the man she believes she knows. The edge of antagonism in his voice has the curious effect of provoking her to an uncharacteristic naivete. "But is a Soviet invasion a real possibility?" she asks. "Isn't it all exaggerated, as the anti-arms people say?"

"For Christ's sake, Cecilia, nothing is exaggerated *here,*" Philip says. "Don't you know where you are?"

But still the matter does not rest. Their odd disjointed conversation, their discussion-on-the-edge-of-quarreling, continues even at dinner. Cecilia supposes it is pointless of her to question Philip Schoen on such issues, her knowledge is haphazard and blurred, much of it, in truth, garnered from the *Herald Tribune* of recent days; but she cannot forget the black soldiers, their foolish conspicuous behavior, their air of . . . wanting to be seen, noted. If Cecilia Heath does not take note of them, who will? Yes, she says, the situation resembles Vietnam in certain ways: an army consisting of many impoverished blacks, very young ill-educated men, men who probably know little about why they are where they are, or even, precisely, where they are. In a way it's a tragic situation.

Philip laughs irritably. He says that, in his opinion, the "tragedy" is Germany's. He feels sorrier for the Mainz citizens than for the United States soldiers. In recent years the soldiers have caused a good deal of trouble in Germany: drunk and disorderly behavior, drug-dealing to young Germans (even school children), assaults, vandalism, even rape and robbery. Maybe even murder, for all he knew. Such things were hushed up. As for the blacks. . . . "The Germans ignore them completely," Philip says. "They aren't sentimental about certain things, as we are. They don't assume virtues when they don't have them."

Seeing her startled expression Philip says that he isn't a racist — she shouldn't think *that* — but he likes to challenge liberal pieties; he wouldn't respect himself as a scholar and an historian otherwise. It is his role as a professional to challenge, for instance, the media's image of such countries as Poland, Czechoslovakia, Hungary. How innocent are they, historically — objectively? What are their records concerning the treatment of Jews and other minorities, and neighboring countries — ("provided the neighboring countries are weaker")? Fed by a sentimentalist public media, how many Americans know anything at all about Poland's terrifying history of anti-Semitism — or of Hungary's belligerence against Rumania—or of the cruelty of the Czechs toward any number of defenseless minorities? One might in fact argue that Poland provoked Germany into the invasion of 1939, for instance, by way of her intransigence in the early 1920s— insisting upon mythical rights against the Germans, and invading German territory by force; invading Lithuania as well, and the Ukraine, and even Russia—in a grotesque attempt to consolidate a little empire. Did anyone in America know? Did anyone want to know? Truth isn't very popular these days.

If the Germans became outlaws, Philip says, who could prove that, following the catastrophic Treaty of Versailles, they were not forced into an outlaw mentality: which is to say—outside, beyond, *beneath* the law? Perhaps Hitler was no more than the Scourge of God.

Cecilia protests faintly, scarcely knowing what to say. Her field of training is art history, particularly nineteenth-century American art; it is probably insulting to Philip for her to attempt to argue with him. Quoting statistics, referring to treaties, invasions, acts of parliament, acts of duplicity and vengeance of which Cecilia, frankly, has never heard ("to understand Hitler's Reich, and by extension present-day Germany, you have to understand Bismarck's 'siege mentality' of the 1880s"), Philip makes Cecilia appear to be something of a fool. What has triggered this episode? Merely the sight of those eight or ten black soldiers by the Hammer Hotel? Cecilia is so upset she drinks several glasses of wine quickly, fighting the impulse to tell Philip that she doesn't care for his facts, his precious History, if they contradict what she wants to believe.

Finally she makes the point that not all Germans are racially prejudiced, as he'd said ("Now Cecilia of course I didn't say *that*") —what of the two young German girls who were with the soldiers by the hotel? They all appeared to be getting on very well together.

Philip shifts uneasily in his seat—they are sitting now in a dim, smoke-hazy cocktail lounge in the Mainzer Hof, as a way of post-poning the awkwardness of returning to their own hotel and their separate rooms—and makes an effort to smile at Cecilia, as if to soften his words: "Those 'girls,' Cecilia, were obviously prostitutes. No other German women would go anywhere near those men, I assure you."

It throws you back upon yourself, the starveling little core of yourself—so a friend of Cecilia's once told her, lying in a hospital bed, having been nearly killed in an automobile accident. He meant the suddenness of violence; its eerie physicality; the fact that, as creatures with spiritual pretensions, we do after all inhabit bodies.

It throws you back upon yourself, the starveling little core of yourself. The aloneness.

Cecilia thinks of her assailant, who was not quite visible to her, but irrevocably real. Oh yes real enough — convincing in *his* physicality. She will never know his name, his age, his background; whether he is married; has children; is in fact considered a "nice guy" when not aroused to sexual rage. (He had been drinking too, Cecilia recalls the odor of beer, his hot panting breath, the smell of him.) She will never know whether he felt any legitimate pleasure in performing his furtive act upon her, or any remorse afterward. Whether in fact he even remembered what he'd done, afterward. Did men remember such things?

The German prostitutes were so young, no more than seventeen or eighteen, surely. And so blond, so pretty. Cecilia sees them vividly in her mind's eye, she notes their blue jeans, their absurd high heels, their tight-fitting jersey blouses, their unzipped satin jackets — one crimson, the other lemon yellow. She notes their glowing faces, their red mouths, the drunken teetering in the street, the clapping of hands (had the black soldier's antics genuinely amused them, or was their response merely part of the transaction?), the streaming blond hair. *The starveling little core of yourself*, Cecilia thinks. *The aloneness.*

The evidence Cecilia Heath will not provide, either to Philip Schoen or to the authorities: while Philip spent the afternoon at the Johannes Gutenberg University, speaking with graduate students in the American Studies Department, Cecilia, grateful to be alone, spent the time in the Mainz Museum (paintings by Nolde, Otto Dix, Otto Moll which she admired enormously), in the Gutenberg Museum (a sombre, rather penitential sort of shrine, but extremely interesting), and in a noisy pub on the Kaiserstr. where, believing herself friendly and well-intentioned, she struck up a conversation of sorts with six or seven black soldiers.

It's true that such cheery gregarious behavior is foreign to Cecilia Heath. She is usually shy with strangers; even with acquaintances; she spends an insomniac night before giving a public lecture, or meeting with her university classes for the first time; someone once advised her — not meaning to be unkind — that she might see a psychotherapist to help her with her "phobia." Yet for some reason, here in Mainz, liberated for a long sunny afternoon from Philip, she must have thought it would be . . . charitable, magnanimous . . . the sort of thing one of her maiden aunts might do in such circumstances: *How are you, where are you from, how long have you been stationed in Mainz, when will you be going back home, do the peace demonstrations worry you, is it difficult being in Germany or do you find it . . . challenging? The German people are basically friendly to Americans, aren't they?*

(Cecilia takes on, not quite consciously, the voice and manner of her Aunt Edie, of St. Joachim, Pennsylvania: the woman's air of feckless Christian generosity, her frank smiling solicitude. In the early fifties this remarkable woman had helped to organize a Planned Parenthood clinic in St. Joachim, had endured a good deal of abuse, even threats against her life; but she'd remained faithful to her task. Even after the clinic was burned down she hadn't given up.)

So it happens that Cecilia Heath talks with the soldiers for perhaps fifteen, twenty minutes. Cecilia in her dove-gray linen blazer, her white silk English blouse, her gabardine skirt, her smart Italian sandals. Cecilia carrying a leather bag over her shoulder, a little breathless, shyly aggressive, damp-eyed, her hair windblown, a fading red streaked with silver. (She wonders afterward how old she seemed to them, how odd, how "attractive." They were so taken by surprise they hadn't even time to glance at one another, to exchange appraising looks.) She introduces herself, she shakes their hands, she makes her cheery inquiries, she can well imagine Philip Schoen's disapproval; but of course Philip need not know of the episode.

Harold is the most courteous, calling her Ma'am repeatedly, smiling broadly, giving her childlike answers as if reciting for a school teacher (he's from New York City yeh he likes the Army okay yeh he likes Germany okay there's lots of places worse yeh he's going home for Christmas furlough yeh ma'am it sure is a long way off), Bo is the youngest, short and spunky, ebony-skinned, brash (No ma'am them Germans demonstratin an shootin off their mouths don't worry *him* — howcome she's askin, do they worry *her*), Cash, or "Kesh," asks excitedly if she is a newspaper reporter and would she maybe be taking their pictures. . . ? They talk at the same time, interrupting one another, showing off for Cecilia and for anyone in the pub who happens to be listening; they make loud comments about Mainz, about the Germans, about the food, the beer (they insist upon buying Cecilia a tankard of beer though it was her intention to treat them to a round); but two others whose names she hasn't quite caught — Arnie, Ernie? — Shelton? — regard her with sullen expressions. Their faces are black fists, clenched. Their lives appear clenched as well, not to be pried open by a white woman whose only claim to them is that she and they share American citizenship . . . in a manner of speaking.

Cash half-teases her that she must be a reporter, else why would she be bothering with *them,* and Cecilia, flushed, laughingly denies it. "Do I look like a reporter?" she says. And afterward wonders why she made that particular remark.

For an art historian she doesn't always *see* clearly enough; she isn't exacting; in fact she can be "perplexingly blind" — so Philip has said, critically, kindly; so Philip has been saying since their arrival in Germany. For a critic of some reputation she isn't sufficiently . . . critical. After all, to be sentimental about foreign places and people simply because they are foreign is a sign of either condescension or ignorance. It can even be (so Philip hinted delicately) a sign of inverted bigotry.

Again and again Cecilia will tell herself that she wasn't condescending to the soldiers, she isn't that sort of person, in fact she feels a confused warm empathy with nearly everyone she meets . . . but of course her intentions might be misunderstood. Her empathy itself might be angrily rejected.

Yet is there any reason, any incontrovertible reason, to believe that her invisible assailant was actually one of the men in the pub. . . ? There is no proof, no evidence. The soft gravelly Southern accent might have belonged to any number of Americans stationed in Germany. And of course she didn't see the face. Hearing the running footsteps — feeling the acceleration of her heart — she had not wished to turn her head.

It takes her approximately ten painful minutes — walking stiffly, her arms close against her sides — to get to the Hotel Zur Birke. Only on the busier street do people glance at her, frowning, disapproving, wondering at her disheveled hair and clothes; but Cecilia looks straight ahead, inviting no one's solicitude.

(Yet it is a nightmare occasion — Cecilia Heath alone and exposed, making her way across a public square, along a public street, being observed, judged, pitied. A dream of childhood and early girlhood, poor Cecilia the object of strangers' stares, in a city she does not know, perhaps even a foreign city. . . . How ironic for it to be coming true when she is an adult woman of thirty-four and her life is so fully her own. . . .)

Fortunately there is an inconspicuous side entrance to the

hotel, and a back stairway, so that Cecilia is spared the indignity of the central foyer and the single slow-moving elevator. On the stairway landing she sees her reflection in an ornamental coppery shield: sickly-pale angular face, pinched eyes, linen jacket torn and soiled, signs of a recent nosebleed. The sight unnerves her though it should not be surprising.

She will deal with the situation efficiently enough: she will soak herself in a hot bath, prepare to forget. There is a dinner that evening at eight hosted by a German literary group and Cecilia doesn't intend to miss it.

Her hotel room is on the third floor, near the rear of the building; Philip's is close by. While she is fitting her key in the lock, however, Philip suddenly appears — he must have been waiting for her. He says at once in a frightened astonished voice: "What has happened to you? Good God —"

Cecilia refuses to face him. She tells him that nothing has happened: she had an accident: she fell down a flight of stairs, five or six steps maybe, nothing serious: nothing for him to be alarmed about.

"But Cecilia, your face, your clothes — is that *blood?* What happened?"

He touches her and she shrinks away, still not looking at him.

Now follows an odd disjointed scene in the corridor outside Cecilia's room, which she is to recall, afterward, only in fragments.

Philip seems to know that something fairly serious has happened to her but he cannot quite think what to do, what to say. He keeps asking her excitedly what *exactly* happened, where did she fall, was it out on the street, were there witnesses, did anyone help her, how badly is she hurt, should he call the downstairs desk and get a doctor, should he call the Consulate and cancel their plans for the evening. . . . Cecilia, turned away, half-sobbing, ashamed, insists that she hasn't been injured, it was only a foolish accident, a misstep, a fall, she banged her head and one knee, tore her jacket, her nose started bleeding, she has only herself to blame . . . won't he please believe her?

Philip takes hold of Cecilia's shoulders but she wrenches sharply away, ducking her head. He doesn't repeat the gesture and she thinks, *He's afraid of me.* For some seconds they stand close together, not touching. Each is breathing audibly.

He *should* call a doctor, Philip says hesitantly. She might have a sprain, a concussion. . . .

No, Cecilia insists. She *hasn't* been injured, she *isn't* upset, won't he please let her go inside her room?

But he should cancel their plans for the evening, at least, Philip says. He had better call the Consulate. . . .

No, says Cecilia, that isn't necessary. If she doesn't feel up to going out by eight o'clock he must go alone, certainly there's no need to cancel his evening, the dinner after all is primarily in his honor and not hers.

But he couldn't do that, he couldn't leave her. . . .

Yes, please, oh yes, Cecilia says, trying to calm herself, she isn't at all injured, she's only a little shaken, if she can be alone for a while . . . if she can relax in a hot bath. . . . Please won't he believe her? Won't he leave her alone?

Cecilia has managed to unlock her door. Philip, reprimanded, rebuffed, doesn't try to follow her inside the darkened room. He stands in the doorway, staring, so visibly distraught that Cecilia can't bear to look at him. *He knows,* she thinks. *That's why he's so afraid.*

As Cecilia is about to close the door he says, again, in a faltering voice, that he'll be happy to cancel their plans for the evening if she wants him to. He doesn't want to go to the dinner alone, he'd only be thinking of her, *is* she all right . . . really?

"Yes," Cecilia says, her face now streaked with tears. "Yes. Of course. *Yes.* Thank you for asking."

As she is undressing the telephone rings. It is Philip, agitated, rather more aggressive. Where exactly did she fall? — did someone push her? — was her wallet taken? — why did she stay out so long, alone? — *it was one of those soldiers, wasn't it* —

Cecilia quietly hangs up. The phone doesn't ring again.

In her bath she lies with her head flung back and her eyes shut tight, tight. It is her head that aches, that buzzes, the other parts of her body are numbed and distant. Her buttocks are not sore — they have no sensation at all.

She imagines her mother, her mother's sisters, even her father, her family's neighbors, gathered to sit in judgment on her. Whispering among themselves that Cecilia Heath should not be traveling with a man not her husband . . . a man who is another woman's husband . . . even if they are not lovers. Especially if they are not lovers.

It isn't like Cecilia. It *isn't* Cecilia.

She recalls her first gynecological examination at the age of

eighteen, the sudden piercing pain, the surprise of it, the uncon-
trolled hysterical laughter that had turned to sobs . . . and hadn't
she done something absurd, dislodging one of her feet from the
metal spur, kicking out wildly at the doctor? . . . angering him so
that he'd said something mean and out of character: *You had better
grow up, fast.*

And so she did.

But perhaps she did not. . . ?

In the other room the telephone is ringing. But the sound is
faint and distant and not at all threatening.

A long time ago, a decade ago, Cecilia Heath was in love and
more or less engaged, but nothing had come of it; nothing comes of
so many things, if you have patience.

She keeps her eyes shut tight so that she needn't see the soldiers'
expressions, the grinning flash of teeth, the faint oily sheen of dark,
dark skin; she wills herself not to hear again that command, *Shut up,
keep your mouth shut,* low and throaty, she had supposed it a Southern
accent but in truth it might be any Negro accent at all, New York
City, Baltimore, Washington, South Carolina, Georgia, hadn't Bo
said he was from Atlanta, and what of Arnie, or Shelton, who had
stared at her with such hatred, *Keep your mouth shut or I'll rip off your
head.*

She sees no face, no features; she can identify no one; she has
nothing to report. Philip is quite mistaken—her wallet wasn't
touched. Her passport wasn't touched. Consequently it would be
pointless to report the incident to the authorities, pointless and embarrassing to all concerned, the Mainz police, the United States
Consulate, the United States Military Police, pointless and embarrassing, a matter of deep shame to both her and Philip. She has
Philip Schoen to think of as well as herself. *Keep your mouth shut or. . . .*

She has scrubbed away all evidence of her attacker. Semen,
sperm. Perspiration. She has discarded her stained underwear, she
will never again wear the linen skirt and jacket, the expensive silk
blouse is ruined past recovery, far simpler to fold everything up
carefully and throw it away. (She recalls as if from a distance of years
her girlish vanity, her excitement, when she bought these clothes for
the trip; for her honeymoon fling with Philip Schoen *who claimed to be
in love with her.*) No evidence, nothing remains. A few bruises. That
ringing in her head, in her right ear. Impossible to press criminal
charges against a person whose face you have not seen and whose

voice you did not clearly hear, impossible to press charges against such impersonal anger, such sexual rage.

Your feelings are wounded, aren't they. Not your flesh.
You liked the soldiers and wanted to think . . . yes, badly wanted to think . . . they liked you.

*   *   *

Though doomed, the evening begins successfully.
There are nine of them around the table — Cecilia, and Philip, and an information officer from the Consulate named Margot (a German-born American woman, Cecilia's age), and six Germans (five men, one woman) who are writers, and/or are involved in American studies at the University. To disguise her sickly pallor and the discoloration on the right side of her face Cecilia applied pancake make-up hurriedly purchased in the hotel's drugstore — Cecilia, who never wears make-up, who has always thought the practice barbaric — and the result is surprisingly good, judging from the others' responses. (Philip has said very little. Philip is going to say very little to her throughout the evening.)
Yes, the German gentlemen behave gallantly to Cecilia, even rather flirtatiously. Perhaps they sense her new, raw vulnerability — perhaps there is something appealing about her porcelain face, her moist red lips. August who is a philologist and lover of poetry, Hans who teaches English, Heinrich who has translated Melville, Whitman, Emily Dickinson . . . and fiery young Rudolph who will shortly publish his first novel . . . and even the most distinguished member of the German contingent, the white-haired professor of American history Dr. Fritz Eisenach . . . all appear to be quite taken with Miss Heath of the Peekskill Foundation. Dr. Eisenach addresses her so that all the table can hear, querying her on nineteenth-century American art, in which he claims an interest of many years — for such "supreme" figures as George Fuller and John La Farge. As it happens Cecilia is the author of a monograph on Fuller, published when she was still in graduate school in New Haven; and her main project at Peekskill is to do a study of La Farge whom she has long considered an important painter . . . indeed, it is Cecilia Heath's professional goal to raise La Farge from his respectable obscurity and establish him as a major American artist. So her replies

delight Dr. Eisenach, and for some heady minutes Cecilia finds herself the center of attention.

Philip smiles in her direction, sucking at his pipe, saying nothing. When asked about La Farge he professes innocence: he intends to wait, he says, for Cecilia's book.

They talk variously of American art, German art, the journals of nineteenth-century German travelers in North America, the history of Wagner's *Ring* in America, the mingled histories of American and German transcendentalism in its many permutations and disguises . . . they spend a good deal of time on the menu . . . the Germans' intention being to treat their guests to a fully German dinner, a representative German dinner, yet not the sort too readily available back in the States. (Cecilia is to sample, with varying degrees of appetite, such delicacies as Räucheraal — smoked eel; Gänseleber-Pastete — goose liver paté; Ochsenschwanzuppe — oxtail soup; Rheinsalm — Rhine salmon; Schweineleber and Schweinhirn — pork liver, pork brains; Hasen — hare; and any number of wines and desserts.) The food is hearty and tasty, the Germans speak English fluently, the conversation rarely flags, Cecilia feels herself borne along by the very current of her hosts' sociability, hearing her own frequent laughter, glimpsing her reflection in a bay window opposite. (The dinner is being held in a private dining room in a restaurant on the Bahnhofplatz, candlelit, charmingly decorated with oaken beams, paintings of the Rhine Valley, a massive stone fireplace piled high with white birch logs. The atmosphere is warm, gracious, convivial, a little loud. Cecilia wonders how she and the others appear to passers-by who happen to glance inside: very like old friends, probably, even relatives, men and women who are extremely close. She wonders too how Philip and she appear to their hosts. They are lovers, surely? But lovers who have traveled together for years, lovers who know each other's secrets, who have forgiven much, whose courtesy toward each other has become second nature. . . . Called Frau Schoen by the German woman, at the beginning of the evening, Cecilia felt obliged to correct her; and wondered if Philip overheard. Frau Schoen, she might have added, is back home in Peekskill, New York.)

The talk shifts to politics, the films of the late Fassbinder, an organization in Frankfurt for refugees from the East, pacific and ecological and vegetarian movements among the young. . . . Philip and Cecilia will be flying from Frankfurt to West Berlin on the following afternoon, they are leaving the Federal Republic of Germany, consequently tonight's celebration has an additional symbolic value. Yes they have enjoyed their brief stay in Mainz very much. Yes they hope to return again someday soon. And next time — so August Bürger insists — they must stay longer, two weeks at least.

Cecilia and Philip glance at each other, smiling, compliant, pretending to be flattered. Cecilia is reminded of the way Philip and his wife Virginia glanced at each other from time to time in their home — how effortless it is, to put on a mutual front, to deceive observers. There is even a kind of pleasure in it.

By degrees the dining room becomes over-warm, the conversation too intense. Cecilia would like to return to her hotel room but cannot bring herself to move. Her head aches again, her breasts are sore. Had her assailant pummelled them? . . . she can't recall. Philip and Professor Eisenach and the shrill-voiced Rudolph are discussing the Green Party, and the international peace movement, and the hoax of the Hitler diary ("a disgraceful episode," the Professor says, shaking his jowls, "brilliantly hilarious," says young Rudolph), and Aryan mythology, and the manufacture of Nazi memorabilia in the German Democratic Republic, for export to the West. (This too is disgraceful, and cynical, says the Professor; but Rudolph insists that it is justified — if idiots in the F. R. G. want to buy such trash, and kindred idiots in the United States, why not sell it to them? "Such arrangements are only good business," Rudolph says.) They discuss the ironies of the new dream of German unity ("a dream acknowledged only in the West," says Hans), and the hunger of all people for national heroes . . . for something truly *transcendent* in which to believe. . . .

("So long as the 'transcendent' is also good business," Rudolph cannot help quipping, a bad little boy at his elders' table.)

Cecilia drifts off into a dream and finds herself thinking of her mother, but her mother is dead . . . and of her father . . . but, dear God, her father is dead also: they died within eighteen months of each other, during the confused time of Cecilia's "engagement." When she rouses herself to attention the atmosphere has quickened considerably. Hans is speaking passionately, his forehead oily with perspiration; August is speaking, laying a hand, hard, on Rudolph's arm, to keep him from interrupting; Professor Eisenach warns sternly of the "Fascistoid" left; the German woman Frau Lütz reminds them, should they require reminding, that the students of the 1920s were far more anti-Semitic than their teachers and parents — as, she believes, Dr. Schoen himself discussed in his excellent book.

Philip graciously accepts the woman's praise. He surprises his listeners, Cecilia included, by rather contemptuously dismissing the peace movement: after all, he lived through the sixties in the United States, he'd been teaching at Harvard at the time, he'd had quite enough of "youthful idealism."

Rudolph begins to speak loudly, excitedly, waving a forefinger. It isn't clear to Cecilia — part of his speech is in German — if he is attacking Philip or siding with him. Perhaps he is attacking the red-faced Eisenach? Rudolph's sympathy with socialism, he says, is such that he has come to the conclusion that the "forced de-Nazification" of Germany by the United States was an act of imperialist aggression; so too, the "forced democratization" of Germany. He believes in a Left that is pitiless and unforgiving of its enemies — especially its German enemies. He believes in a Left that proudly embraces German destiny. As for History, he says with majestic scorn, spittle on his lips and his eyes wickedly bright — History has no memory, no existence. If he had his way he would ban all books written before 1949 . . . which is to say, six years before his own birth.

Philip laughs and regards him with a look of affectionate contempt. "No German born in 1955 can be taken seriously," he says.

Everyone at the table bursts into laughter except Cecilia and Rudolph, who sit silent.

Belatedly, Margot from the Consulate tries to change the subject. Did Philip and Cecilia visit St. Stephen's Church, did they see the famous Chagall window? — but Philip ignores her. He and Rudolph are staring at each other, clearly attracted by each other's insolence. So very German, thinks Cecilia, feeling a wave of faintness. It is an old story that has nothing to do with her.

It is late, nearing midnight. Coffee and brandy are served. Chocolates wrapped in tinfoil. Too many people are smoking, why has no one opened a window. . . ? Frau Lütz who teaches English and American literature at the University asks the Americans their opinions of "Black Marxist street poetry"; the smiling gat-toothed Heinrich asks about "revisionist gay" readings of Whitman and Hart Crane. Again the subject of Fassbinder is raised, arousing much controversy; and does Werner Herzog ("the far greater artist," says August) have a following in the States; and is there sympathy for Heinrich Böll, his attitude toward disarmament, his involvement in the blockade of the American military base at Mutlangen. . . ? In the midst of the discussion Rudolph says languidly that he himself would not wish the enemies of Germany destroyed; for as the aphorism has it, our enemy is by tradition our savior, in preventing us from superficiality. At this August bursts into angry laughter and tells the Americans to pay no attention to Rudolph, who is drunk, knows nothing of what he says, and has never visited the East in any case.

"How dare you speak of my private business! — you know nothing of my private business!" Rudolph says in a fierce whisper.

It is no longer clear to Cecilia what the men are arguing about, if indeed they are arguing. It seems that Rudolph is only courting Philip, in his brash childish manner. . . . In the flickering candlelight he looks disconcertingly young; his face is long and lean and feral, his eyes hooded, his lips fleshy. Stylized wings of hair frame his bony forehead, stiff as if lacquered. The *enfant terrible* of the Mainz circle, petted, over-praised, spoiled, he has nonetheless a charming air of self-mockery. (Unfortunate, Cecilia thinks, that he isn't qualified to be a Fellow at the Peekskill Foundation — he and Philip would certainly liven things up there. But it is Dr. August Bürger, the philologist-poet with the impressive credentials, whom Philip has been interviewing in Mainz.) Now Rudolph and Philip are speaking animatedly together, for the benefit of the entire table, of the folly of German submersion in "European civilization" — that phantasm which had no existence, could never have had any existence, since Europe is by nature many Europes, nation-groups, language- and dialect-groups, clamoring for autonomy but, for the most part, fated to be slave states. Slave states! — Does Cecilia hear correctly? Or is she simply exhausted, depressed! The expression arouses a good deal of comment on all sides, but Philip and young Rudolph pay no heed.

Hans, sighing, draws a large white handkerchief out of his coat pocket and wipes his gleaming face and says in an aside to Cecilia: "I am teaching four courses each term, Fraülein Heath, elementary and intermediate and advanced English, and am not given to idle speculation, but what of the new Pershing II rockets, Fraülein, which your country is so generous as to wish to store with us? Germany has become a land-mine, Fraülein, in payment for its sins. Do you agree? Are you informed? The Soviets boast that they will destroy us how many times, and the Americans are to retaliate by destroying them how many times. . . ? Forty, sixty, one hundred, five hundred? Yes, Fraülein," he says, showing his teeth in a broad damp smile, "it is only a joke, no offense is meant, we have here not the privilege of offense after all. For Rudolph and his comrades the destruction of Germany is perhaps no loss, as for your President Reagan also, just payment for our sins. Please, Fraülein, on the eve of your departure from Mainz, do not take offense — I am but making jokes printed in the newspapers every day, a commonplace."

Cecilia, flushed, slightly light-headed, would say that she favors peace and disarmament, she doesn't favor war, or even the stockpiling of weapons; but so banal a statement might provoke mocking laughter. Even now Rudolph is laughing with a hearty brutality at something Philip has said, a reference perhaps to the Schoen who flew a bomber for the German Air Force, or is there another Schoen, a Nazi major, about whom Cecilia has yet to hear. . . . Professor Eisenach makes a passionate drunken speech, his eyes damp and his voice trembling, in Wilhelmian Germany and yet again in the 1930s the Church freely acquiesced to the State, and did the *intelligentsia* protest? Not at all. Never. A disgraceful history of abnegation, a disgraceful history of. . . . There must be worship, and gods, and devils, and sacrifice; when there are untroubled times it is the peace of apathy and impotence, young men and women indistinguishable from one another in hair style, costume, behavior . . . it is all *a waiting for the end.* The others listen to the Professor's rambling speech with barely concealed impatience. Then August brings up the subject of the East, addressing the Americans (but Philip especially): Does their country feel sorry for the East Germans? — is their special sympathy for the East Germans? If so they are fools and must be better informed, for the East Germans went from Hitler to Stalin with ease — "*It is all the same to them! The same!*" At this Rudolph stammers in protest; and August accuses him of being a traitor and a fool; and Philip, sucking on his pipe, expelling a thin gray cloud of aromatic smoke, assures the table that he himself feels no sympathy for the East Germans, his sympathy is solely for the West Germans, amnesiac for so many years, and made to be on perpetual trial in the world's eyes . . . made to feel shame for being German. Indeed, words like "shame" and "guilt" strike the ear, Philip says, as distinctly hypocritical. Is German "shame" indigenous, for instance, or a matter of import? And "guilt". . . ?

Several of the Germans propose a toast to Philip, in German, but Professor Eisenach demands to know if Dr. Schoen is mocking them? What can such sympathy mean?

"But Professor, we are foolish to question sympathy, from any quarter!" Frau Lütz says chidingly.

"You carried it off quite well," Philip tells Cecilia quietly on their way back to the Hotel Zur Birke. His voice is just perceptibly slurred; there is a slight drag to his heels. But clearly he is in high spirits — a good deal of his soul has been restored.

Cecilia doesn't ask what he means. She says, "And so did you."

But Philip, keyed up, nervous, isn't ready to end the day, the long festive celebratory evening. He finds his hotel room depressing, as he has said several times, would Cecilia care to have a final drink, a nightcap, at that Rathskeller up the street. . . ? Philip is pale, smiling, aging around the eyes, a wifeless husband, a lover without a beloved, clearly deserving of female sympathy. But Cecilia is suffused with a sense of irony as if her very flesh might laugh; Cecilia draws unobtrusively away. They have not touched since that awkward meeting in the hotel corridor—they have hardly dared look at each other all evening. Cecilia understands that it falls to her to assuage this man's guilt for thinking her despoiled by denying the very premise for such thinking, she understands that he is eager as a small child to be assuaged, eager to believe whatever she tells him; but she does not intend to tell him anything.

They are standing in front of the Hotel Zur Birke, a solitary tourist couple, apparently indecisive about what to do next. It is late, past midnight, the wind has picked up, clearly Mainz is not Frankfurt or Berlin in terms of its nightlife, why not give up, why not simply go to bed? But Philip doesn't want to go to bed alone. Philip seems to be frightened of being alone. He detains Cecilia, asking what she thought of the Germans at dinner. Wasn't it all supremely revealing? The casual remarks as well as the political—? That quintessential German-ness he'd find amusing if it weren't so terrifying—the secret gloating pride in their blood, in their race—in sin, guilt, history, whatever they choose to call it—

Cecilia surprises him by laughing, laughing almost heartily, as she slips past him and enters the hotel.

There, in her room on the third floor, she falls asleep almost at once, as soon as she turns out the light and finds a comfortable position in her bed. She will not be accompanying Philip to West Berlin the next day—she will make her own arrangements at the Frankfurt Airport to fly back home. It should not be very difficult, she thinks; even informing Philip about her decision should not be very difficult. She supposes he will understand.

He will never have to touch me again, she thinks.

Released, profoundly relieved, she sinks through diaphanous layers of sleep, aware of herself sinking, drifting downward, her physical weight dissolved. She sees a creek out of her childhood— the St. Joachim—she smells the wet, newly mowed grass in the

cemetery where both her parents are buried—she hears her Aunt
Edie's voice raised in welcome: Cecilia, a child of eight or nine, shyly
poking her head into her aunt's kitchen, standing on the rear porch,
holding the screen door open. It is summer but quite windy. Rain-
drops the size of golf balls are pelting the roof. A river has overflowed its banks, a lake has overflowed, the very light is strange, pale
and glowering, a sunken city is rising slowly to the surface, a city of
spires, towers, old battlements, partly in ruins, blackened by
fire . . . and now a cathedral of massive dimensions, its highest
tower partly crumbled, its edifice stark and grim . . . and now a
cobblestone street, puddled with bright water that strikes the eye like
flame . . . Cecilia, alone, is half-running along the empty street, she
is both relieved that it is empty and on the brink of terror, for what if
she is lost?—Yet she cannot be lost since she seems to know where
she is headed, hurrying forward as if in full possession of her senses,
looking neither to the left nor the right. She is barefoot, only partly
dressed. She is breathless with fear. No matter, she seems to know
where she is going, behind her footsteps suddenly sound, close
behind her, overtaking her, but she does not intend to turn her head.

Joyce Carol Oates's latest book is *Mysteries of Winterthurn*,
recently published by E. P. Dutton.

Amos Oz

ONE SUMMER'S MORNING, IN THE VILLAGE

All night long mist rises from the green swamp, spreading
a smell of decay among our huts. Objects made of iron rust here
overnight, the wooden walls are disintegrating in the clutches of the
sickly vegetation, straw and hay turn black like scorched fields, mos-
quitoes swarm in the dank air, our rooms are full of flying insects

---

Editor's Note: Translated from the Hebrew by Nicholas de Lange.

and reptiles, and the very soil seems to bubble. Our children suffer from boils and rashes all through the summer, the old folk die from degeneration of the respiratory tract, and even the living exude a stench of death. I, who have been sent here by the Bureau for the Assistance of Underdeveloped Regions, still go out every day, towards evening, to spray the swamp water with disinfectants and to dispense carbolic acid, ointments, essential hints on hygiene, DDT, and chlorinated water to the settlers. I am still holding the fort until a replacement arrives. And in the meantime, I am pharmacist, teacher, notary, go-between, and peacemaker. Before I arrived, a few years ago, perhaps four years, though the old people stubbornly insist it was six, the District Commissioner came on a tour of inspection with his staff, and gave orders for the river to be diverted immediately so as to put an end to the malignant swamp. The Commissioner was accompanied by officers and clerks, surveyors and men of God, a legal expert, a singer, an official historian, and representatives of the various branches of the secret service. They spent a whole day here, and the Commissioner recorded his findings: dig, divert, dry out, purify, and turn over a fresh page.

Since then nothing has happened.

The old folk and the babies continue to die and the youngsters are growing older. The population, according to my cautious calculations, is declining. By the end of the century, so says the table I have drawn up, there will not be a single living soul remaining here — apart from the insects and reptiles. Large numbers of babies are born, but most of them die in infancy and their death hardly seems to stir a ripple of grief any more. The young men run away, the girls farm potatoes and wither before my eyes at the age of fifteen or twenty. Sometimes desire bursts out and inflames the whole village to nocturnal orgies by the light of bonfires of damp wood, and they all run riot, old folk and children, girls and cripples; I cannot record the details, because on nights like these I lock myself into the dispensary and put a loaded pistol under my pillow, in case they get some mad idea. But such nights are infrequent. The days are blazing hot. The work in the potato fields is apparently crushing. Some time ago, two of the gravedigger's sons joined a gang of smugglers. The two widows with their children moved in with the youngest brother, a mere lad, not yet fourteen. As for the gravedigger himself, a stubborn, silent, broad-boned man, he determined not to pass over the matter in silence. But the years are slipping past in silence. The gravedigger himself moved into the hut of his surviving son, more and more babies were born there, and no one could say which were the offspring of the runaways and which were the youngest brother's, or which were sired by the father. In any case, most of the babies died almost as soon as they were born. Other men came and went, and also dim-witted, big-bodied girls in search of a roof, a man, a child, or food.

The Commissioner has not replied to three successive memoranda, each more strongly-worded than the last, sent to sound the alarm against the seriousness of the moral situation. I was the outraged sender of these memoranda. The years are slipping past in silence. Nothing happens here. Apart from the strange occurrence which I witnessed this morning, and which I shall report without comment.

In the morning the rising sun had transformed the mist from the swamp into a kind of incandescent, unclean rain. The villagers had left their huts and were preparing to set out for the potato fields. Suddenly a stranger appeared at the top of the small hill which stood between us and the rising sun and began waving his arms, describing curves and circles in the air, kicking or bowing, hopping and jumping on the spot.

"Who is he," the men asked, "and what does he want here?"

"It's not one of us and it's not one of the smugglers," said the old men.

And the women said, "We've got to be careful."

While they were discussing what to do, the early morning air was suddenly full of different sounds, screeching birds, barking dogs, talking, lowing, humming of insects as large as your fist. The frogs also began to croak, the chickens tried to outdo them, and harnesses jangled. And the sounds were all distinct.

"That man," said the gravedigger's youngest son, "has been sent to break up the village and we must kill him."

"That man," said the innkeeper, "is trying to seduce the girls."

The girls shrieked, "Look he's dancing, look he's naked, look he's white like a corpse!"

And the old gravedigger said, "What is there to chatter about? The sun is up, and the white man has vanished behind the hill. Words won't help; a hot day is starting and we must go to work. Whoever can work, let him endure in silence. And whoever cannot bear it any longer, let him die. That's that."

PASSPORT PHOTOGRAPH

A veteran member of the kibbutz appears in a sepia photograph taken in Lodz some fifty years ago.

It shows a pudgy youth of seventeen, with his shirt buttoned up to the neck but without a tie. (Perhaps a compromise between respectability and pioneering ideals.) An open, slightly ingenuous face, a spoiled mouth, and a frank, direct look in the eyes. An expression which seems to be saying, "I have no complaints, and I am sure that no one has any complaints about me. I'm perfectly all right. Everything's perfectly all right. It'll be OK."

The hair is brushed straight back, apart from a single unruly lock, suggesting a schoolboy-but-definitely-not-a-child: "You all think that I'm a simple, straightforward, likeable sort of lad, and you're not mistaken. I certainly am one of those decent chaps you can rely on, but you should know that if we're talking about, say, girls, I'm perfectly capable of getting up to a spot of mischief, and in fact I've already managed one or two japes, I'll leave it to you to guess what."

It is still possible to compare the old photograph with the man's face as it is now — wrinkled, tired, sunburnt, and windlashed, and yet, not healthy. Now, almost at the very end, all that is left of that cultured-but-pioneering smile is a disillusioned grin: "All right. That's the way it is. So be it." The hair has receded and the furrowed brow extends almost to the top of the skull. The ears, large and pendulous, have finally found their rightful place. The chin is more pointed now, and underneath it there are pockets or bags, as though this were an elderly philanderer instead of a veteran Zionist socialist and an exemplary working man.

And the concerns now: "It's all over. It's all happened. Not that it was bad or disappointing, or — heaven forbid — a bad bargain, but it's simply all over." What a terrible thing. All over. Girls. Wars. Discussions. Children. Work. Rifts and reconciliations. Grandchildren. Assignments. Victories. All over. Now the ideals have faded and the desires have grown cold, and of all the old longings, only a handful are left. A little honor. A little peace and quiet. A little affection. And, no muckraking. A little politeness please. Remember who you're talking to. Mind your manners. I haven't spoken my last word yet, and I can still cause a fair amount of unpleasantness if I decide to speak up. So, if you don't mind . . . And the astonishment: ("What?! So that's it? All over? How on earth?") And the fear, together with a tremor of despair: ("That's it. That's all. Finished. That's the way it is.")

What does this old veteran have to say to me when we are sitting over supper in the dining hall on one of those autumn evenings? First, politics: "Why do I jump around so? Carter, Shimon Peres, *Gush Emunim,* Kissinger, *Hashomer Hatsair,* perhaps I'll be good enough to listen for a moment before I give vent to hasty opinions? After all, we've been through it all before, one way or another, and it's always turned out all right in the end. It's wrong to worry so, and to spread panic. Don't get so worked up, Amos, we've been through much more problematic times in the past, and you see, we've survived, thank God. This mood will also blow over. Do you have a cigarette by any chance? No? Have you really managed to give up? Hand on your heart—have you really stopped? Truly? (A hint of Polish in the accent still.) So perhaps you'll share the secret, and tell me how it's done? These cigarettes are killing me. Literally killing me. Hey, how'd you do it? *Nu?* How? Wait, don't say anything, I'll tell you exactly how it's done. Wait a minute, let me finish a sentence, I'll tell you exactly and don't you interrupt."

Amos Oz, the Israeli novelist, has recently published In the Land of Israel, *from Harcourt Brace Jovanovich.*

Philip Roth

THE PHENOMENON OF ALIENATION
IS NOT APPROVED OF FROM ABOVE

Bolotka occupies a dank room at the top of a bleak stair-well on a street of tenements near the outskirts of Prague. He re-assures me, when he observes me looking sadly around, that I shouldn't feel too bad about his standard of living — this was his hide-away from his wife long before his theater was disbanded and he was forbidden to produce his "decadent" revues. "It excites young girls to be fucked in squalor." He is intrigued by my herringbone tweed suit and asks to try it on to see how it feels to be a rich American writer. He is a stoop-shouldered man, large and shambling, with a wide Mongol face, badly pitted skin, and razor blade eyes, eyes like rifts in the bone of his skull, gray slitted eyes whose manifesto is, "You will jam nothing bogus into this brain." He has a wife somewhere still, even children; only recently her arm was broken when she tried to prevent the police from entering their apartment to impound her absentee husband's library of several thousand books.

"Why does she care so much about you?"

"She doesn't — she hates me. But she hates them more. All the old married couples in Prague have something to hate now even more than each other."

Just a month earlier the police came to the door of Bolotka's hole at the top of the stairwell to inform him that the country's lead-ing trouble-makers were being given papers to leave. His was the name at the head of the list. They would allow him forty-eight hours to get out.

"I said to them, 'Why don't *you* leave? That would amount to the same thing, you know. I give *you* forty-eight hours.'"

But would he not be better off in Paris, or across the border in Vienna, where he has a reputation as a theatrical innovator and could resume his career?

"I have sixteen girlfriends in Prague," he replies. "How can I leave?"

I am handed his robe to keep myself warm while he undresses

Editor's Note: This is excerpted from a work in progress.

and gets into my suit. "You look even more like a gorilla," I say, when he stands to model himself in my clothes.

"And even in my terrible dressing gown," he says, "you look like a happy, healthy, carefree impostor."

Bolotka's story.

"I was nineteen years old, I was a student at the university. I wanted like my father to be a lawyer. But after one year I decide I must quit and enroll at the School of Fine Arts. Of course I have first to go for an interview. This is 1950. Probably I would have to go to fifty interviews, but I only got to number one. I went in and they took out my 'record.' It was a foot thick. I said to them, 'How can it be a foot thick, I haven't lived yet. I have had no life — how can you have all this information?' But they don't explain. I sat there and they look it over and they say I cannot quit. The workers' money is being spent on my education. The workers have invested a year in my future as a lawyer. The workers have not made this investment so I can change my mind and decide to become a fine artist. They tell me that I cannot matriculate at the School of Fine Arts, or any-where ever again, and so I said okay and went home. I didn't care that much. It wasn't so bad. I didn't have to become a lawyer, I had some girlfriends, I had my prick, I had books, and to talk to and to keep me company, I had my childhood friend Blecha. Only they had him to talk with too. Blecha was planning then to be a famous poet and a famous novelist and a famous playwright. One night he got drunk and he admitted to me that he was spying on me. They knew he was an old friend and they knew that he wrote, and they knew he came to see me, so they hired him to spy on me and to write a report once a week. But he was a terrible writer. He is still a terrible writer. They told him that when they read his reports they could make no sense of them. They told him everything he wrote about me is un-believable. So I said, 'Blecha, don't be depressed, let me see the reports — probably they are not as bad as they say. What do they know?' But they *were* terrible. He missed the point of everything I said, he got everything backwards about when I went where, and the writing was a disgrace. Blecha was afraid they were going to fire him — he was afraid they might even suspect him of playing some kind of trick, out of loyalty to me. And if that went into *his* record, he would be damaged for the rest of his life. Besides, all the time he should be spending on his poems and his stories and his plays, he was spending listening to me. He was getting nothing accomplished for himself. He was full of sadness for himself over this. He had

thought he could just betray a few hours a day and otherwise get on
with being National Artist, Artist of Merit, and winner of the State
Award for Outstanding Work. Well, it is obvious what to do. I said,
'Blecha, I will follow myself for you. I know what I do all day better
than you, and I have nothing else to keep me busy. I will spy on myself and I will write it up, and you can submit it to them as your
own. They will wonder how your disgraceful writing has improved
so overnight, but you just tell them you were sick. This way you
won't have anything damaging on your record, and I can be rid of
your company, you shitface.' Blecha was thrilled. He gave me half of
what they paid him and everything was fine — until they decided that
he was such a good spy and such a good writer, they promoted him.
He was terrified. He came to me and said I had gotten him into this
and so I had to help him. They were putting him now to spy on big-
ger troublemakers than me. They were even using his reports in the
Ministry of Interior to teach new recruits. He said, 'You have the
knack of it, Rudolf, with you it's just a technique. I am too imaginative for this work. But if I say no to them now, it will go in my record
and I will be damaged by it later on. I could be seriously damaged
now, if they knew you had written the reports on yourself.' So this is
how I made a bit of a living when I was young. I taught our
celebrated Artist of Merit and winner of the State Award for Outstanding Work how to write in plain Czech and describe a little what
life is like. It was not easy. The man could not describe a shoelace.
He did not know the word for anything. And he saw nothing. I
would say, 'But Blecha, was the friend sad or happy, clumsy or
graceful, did he smoke, did he listen mostly or did he talk? Blecha,' I
would ask, 'how will you ever become a great writer if you are such a
bad spy?' This made him angry with me. He did not like my insults.
He said spying was sickening to him and caused him to have writer's
block. He said he could not use his creative talent while his spirit was
being compromised like this. For me it was different. Yes, he had to
tell me — it was different for me because I did not have high artistic
ideals. I did not have any ideals. If I did I would not agree to spy on
myself. I certainly would not take money for it. He had come to lose
his respect for me. This is a sad irony to him too, because when I left
university, it was my integrity that meant so much to him and our
friendship. Blecha told me this again only recently. He was having
lunch with Mr. Knap, another of our celebrated Artists of Merit and
winners of the State Award for Outstanding Work, and secretary
now of their Writers' Union. Blecha was quite drunk and always

when he is quite drunk Blecha gets overemotional and must tell you the truth. He came up to the table where I was having my lunch and he asked if everything is all right. He said he wished he could help an old friend in trouble, and then he whispered, 'Perhaps in a few month's time . . . but they do not like that you are so alienated, Rudolf. The phenomenon of alienation is not approved of from above. Still, I will do what I can . . .' But then he sat suddenly at the table and he said, 'But you must not go around Prague telling lies about me, Rudolf. Nobody believes you anyway. My books are everywhere: schoolchildren read my poems, tens of thousands of people read my novels, on TV they perform my dramas. You only make yourself look irresponsible and bitter by telling that story. And, if I may say so, a little crazy.' So I said to him, 'But Blecha, I don't tell it. I have never told it to a soul.' And he said, 'Come now, my dear old friend—how then does everybody know?" And so I said, 'Because their children read your poems, they themselves have read your novels, and when they turn on TV, they see your dramas.'"

Philip Roth's latest novel is The Anatomy Lesson, *published by Farrar, Straus, and Giroux in 1983.*

Roger Shattuck

INCOMPATIBLE COMPONENTS

This stereo must be alive.
When you turn it off
it dies
the way I'm prepared to die —
no cut to black, rather
sound and image holding after the click,
all those warm circuits still glowing
in slow fade.

Psychic scientists and old wives concur:
on the way to outer darkness we screen
a monogrammed freeze-frame feature
undercranked and overexposed
all scenes shot
with all scores settled.
"Snatched from the jaws of death,"
the headline says,
"Sea captain saved from drowning
tells of passing over and coming back
reborn into his own life."
Dr. Clay squirts mind-bubbling drugs
into college prisoners and death-row students,
claims he can simulate death
all but the sting.
His emissaries stagger back
bearing tales of comic geometry
and paleolithic memory traces
too stark to be fake.

Case histories stir up the old refrains —
Humani nihil a me alienum . . .
Ontogeny recapitulates . . .
Something like that.
I shudder to think
the distance traversed may be equal
coming in and going out.
O death
where is thy click?

For all its transformational grammar
of recorded sounds and satellite signals
I'm not so sure
I want this radium-eyed
immortal daily-dying zombie
in the house.

Roger Shattuck's new book The Innocent Eye: On Literature and
Art, *is forthcoming this fall from Farrar, Straus, and Giroux. He is Commonwealth Professor of French at the University of Virginia.*

Isaac Bashevis Singer

STRONG AS DEATH IS LOVE

My aunt Yentl and her cronies were talking about love, and Aunt Yentl was saying, "There is such a thing as love. There is. It even existed in former times. People think that it's new. It is not true. Love is even mentioned in the Bible. Laban gave his daughter Leah to Jacob, but Jacob loved Rachel. Imagine, a saint like this. Still he was flesh and blood. One glance at a person and you see his or her charm. The only difference is that in olden times once you liked someone you got married. Nowadays, couples get engaged but still look for others.

"Not far from Turbin there was a squire and they called him the crazy squire. Actually, all the nobles were somewhat pixilated. They lived in so much luxury that they didn't know whether they were coming or going. This squire, Jan Chwalski, was completely befuddled. He didn't speak, he screamed. He kept warning his serfs that he would whip them to death but he never laid a finger on anybody. When a peasant became sick, he sent in a doctor or at least a healer to cure him. He had a court-Jew named Betzalel whom he often threatened to hang and shoot. Still, on Purim he sent him a Purim gift. When Betzalel married off his daughter, the squire sent her a wedding present. He came to the wedding and danced a Kossack dance with the Jews and made himself so ridiculous that the people almost choked from laughter. Chwalski never married because he was in love with a noble woman who had a husband. Her name was Aliza and she was not really such a beauty as he imagined. Not bad, gentle and slender. Gentiles, as a rule, are blonde but she was a brunette with black eyes and with a most charming smile. Her husband, Count Lipski, was the biggest drunkard in the whole of Poland. No one had ever seen him sober. He drank away his entire fortune. He knew that Chwalski was in love with his wife, but these things did not bother him. It was said that he used to wake up in the middle of the night and drink vodka from a pitcher through a straw. If this Aliza would have been a loose woman she could have committed the worst sins. But she was a dignified lady. She used to plead with Chwalski not to chase after her since she was married, but Chwalski loved her too much to comply. He wrote daily love letters to her and sent them by messenger. Maybe once a year he received a reply. It always said the same thing, 'I have a husband.' On Sunday Chwalski used to go to church just to be able to gaze at her. When both of them were invited to the same ball, Aliza only accepted one dance with him. It seemed she liked him too, but she did not want to betray her husband. The priest often beseeched Chwalski to leave Aliza in peace. But Chwalski said, 'From all the women in the whole world there is only one Aliza. All week long I live with one hope, to see her on Sunday.'

"Count Lipski, her husband, was a tall fat man with a perpetually red face and broken veins covering his nose. He drank until he burnt out his lungs. The doctors forbade him to drink but he drank to the last day. A doctor in our town said, 'If a man drank as much water as Count Lipski drank spirits, he would become mortally sick.' Chwalski on the other hand, never got drunk. He was drunk from Aliza.

"Count Lipski had the eyes of a madman. He never knew what was going on with his estate. Everything was handled by a manager who stole as much as he could and the rest was lost through bad management. As to Aliza, she kept to herself and did not interfere with business matters. She liked to read books and to take long walks through the orchards. She never had any children. Who knows? Count Lipski might have been even too drunk for anything. In his last months, he could no longer walk. The liquor had gone to his legs. He had also developed diabetes since vodka contains a lot of sugar. One way or another he died without last rites, without confession, without a will. I was told that after his death his body blew up and became like a barrel. Almost no one from the gentry came to the funeral because he had insulted all his neighbors and blasphemed God and all the Christian saints. The hearse passed by our windows. I was still a young girl and I watched the procession. It is the custom among the Gentiles that two men lead the widow. Aliza had a brother somewhere whom I saw then for the first time, and the other man was Jan Chwalski. Just as Count Lipski was tall and broad, so was Jan Chwalski small and lean with a long yellowish mustache which reached to his chin. Aliza was dressed in black. Chwalski held onto her arm as if in fear that she might run away. Love is a kind of madness.

"Lipski died, he was buried. Everyone thought that the widow would immediately marry Chwalski, but she insisted that he wait a year for the period of mourning. When Chwalski found out that he would have to wait he raised Heaven and Earth. Hadn't he waited long enough? But Aliza contended that she would never marry him before a year passed. Lipski did not leave a will, and a gang of would-be heirs emerged. They came, God knows from where, and they took everything away from Aliza. On the other hand there was not much to take. Whoever could, grabbed a piece. This is how people are. They imagine that they themselves will live forever. When Chwalski heard what was going on, he took a gun and came running ready to kill all of them. But Aliza said to him, 'You don't interfere.' And her word was holy to him. There are such people who will silently allow others to rob them. Perhaps it was gentleness or perhaps foolishness. It was known that she came from very high nobility and with some of them money has no meaning. Their main passion is their honor. One way or another she remained with nothing. All they left her was the empty walls. Lipski had had a court-Jew by the name of Yankel. But how can a Jew fight off Gentiles? He came to her and said, 'Your Excellency, they take away everything from you.' And she answered, 'They cannot take more than I possess.' She had suffered all these years with Count Lipski but no one ever heard her complain. Some people are wolves, others are sheep. But ultimately no one takes anything with them. They brought her a document and she signed it without blinking an eye.

"Not a month had passed and a marshal of the court came with some officials and they told Aliza to move out. Neither the house nor the furniture belonged to her anymore. Again Chwalski came running ready to defend her: a little man and yet hot-blooded. If Aliza would have asked him to jump into a fire for her sake he wouldn't have hesitated for a moment. But Aliza told him to leave matters alone. He wanted to bring her to his estate but she refused to go with him as long as they were not married. To make it short, she found some wealthy peasant—a village elder. He had a little hut beside his house where he kept flax and other objects and he cleared them away for her to live in. Her husband's relatives had left her a single bed and her books. That's all she needed. She had managed to hide some of her personal jewelry which Yankel had later sold for her and on this she supported herself for the year. On Sabbath afternoon the tailors' and shoemakers' apprentices and the seamstresses took a walk to the village to peer into her window and see what the haughty Countess was doing. She didn't even leave herself a maid. On Sunday the elder took her in his britska to church. Chwalski again and again tried to persuade her to move to his estate but she did not let herself be persuaded. A pure soul, you should forgive the comparison, almost a rebbitzin.

"A year passed and she became a Squiress again. All the nobil-

PARTISAN REVIEW

ity of the neighborhood came to the wedding. It is not the custom
that a bride, even if she is a widow, should be dressed in mourning
when she remarries. But Aliza insisted that she dress in black for the
wedding. They showered her with flowers and gifts. The priest gave
a sermon. One has never heard of peasants attending a noble wedding on their own volition. But peasants came from many villages.
Since she lived in a peasant's hut, they considered her one of their
own. She came to the wedding in the elder's britsk. But from the
church to Chwalski's estate she rode in a carriage drawn by eight
horses and peasants dressed like dragoons rode in front. They had
erected a gate hung with plants and flowers at the entrance of
Chwalski's estate. A Jewish and Gentile band played a 'good night'
melody for the couple. Chwalski was not especially rich, but he
guarded his possessions and nobody could steal from him. It seemed
that Aliza's bad luck had begun to shine. But wait a minute, I need
a drink."

I brought Aunt Yentl a pitcher of water, and she murmured a
blessing and drank. "Don't laugh at me," she said, "I feel like crying."
And she blew her nose into her batiste handkerchief. Then she continued:

"Shortly after the wedding, Jan Chwalski threw the type of ball
which was considered rare even for a king. It was a few weeks after
Passover and the weather was balmy. Aliza was against it. She was
quiet, proud, and no longer young. But Chwalski wanted to an-
nounce his joy to the world. He invited hundreds of nobles who even
came then from far away cities. Carriages rolled in early in the
morning and it lasted all day. The stores in Turbin profited. There
was a band from Zamosc and another from Lublin. For years people
spoke about that ball: the food, the wine, the dances, the music. Reb
Betzalel revealed later that Chwalski was forced to sell a portion of
his forest for less than nothing to pay for all this. Of course Jews and
peasants were not invited. But many young people stood outside
and listened in, even dancing. The servants treated them to wine
and food. The next day the nobles went hunting and killed, God
knows, how many animals. When they left, the estate was in sham-
bles. Aliza had pleaded with Chwalski not to squander his fortune.
But he was insane from happiness.

"My dear people, all this good fortune lasted not longer than a
year. Suddenly one heard that Aliza was sick. What the illness was I
don't know until today. But Aliza slowly began to waste away.
Chwalski again sold a part of his estate and sent for the biggest doc-

tors, but no one could help her. Our own healer, Lippe, was called in, and he heard one of the doctors say that her blood turned to water. God forbid, when the time comes, the Angel of Death will find a way. The sickness lingered for months, and although everyone had given up on her, Chwalski kept on bringing new doctors, professors, various quacks. He even went to the rabbi and offered him money for charity to light candles for Aliza's sake in the synagogue. Nothing availed. Aliza was dying. The priest came and she made her confession. He poured holy water on her and soon Aliza was no more. Reb Betzalel told us that she passed away like a saint. Who knows? There are good souls even among them. It is written in a holy book that good Gentiles go to Paradise.

"The way Chwalski cried and moaned and howled cannot be described. But dead is dead. They took her to the church and there her body stayed until the funeral. Chwalski had bought plots for her and for himself. He grew pale and emaciated as if he had consumption. His clothes hung on him. His mustache became white. He walked and spoke to himself like a madman.

"But if one has years, one lives. He tried to poison himself but someone forced two fingers into his mouth so that he should vomit. Whatever was left from his fortune was lost, although Reb Betzalel tried to save as much as possible. A year or two passed and Chwalski still lived. He had a portrait of Aliza and he stared at it day and night. He spent more time at the cemetery than at home. Every day he laid flowers on her grave. He ordered a headstone for her with the figure of an angel carved to resemble her. He kissed the stone and spoke to it. He no longer concerned himself with business matters. Reb Betzalel had practically taken over. A number of years passed. There is a saying that what the earth covers must be forgotten. But Chwalski could not forget. The priest reproached him saying that it is forbidden to mourn too long. Chwalski was visited by other squires and relatives who tried to cheer him up, but he could not be comforted. He also took to drink. There was no lack of beautiful women in the neighborhood but he wouldn't even look at another female.

"Now, listen to this. After Aliza was buried Chwalski locked the bedroom and no one was allowed to enter, even the chamber maid. He also kept her boudoir locked. Every stitch of clothing—even things she simply touched—became sacred to him. He himself slept in her nanny's bedroom. The cook prepared food for him but he barely touched a thing. He became even smaller than he had been and his mustache appeared even longer. In time he dismissed all his servants. And only the nanny remained, an old woman, deaf and half blind.

"That winter was one of the coldest. The seeds in the fields froze. So much snow fell that many houses became snowed-under and the people had to dig themselves out. In the midst of this cold spell, Chwalski did not miss a day at the cemetery. One day Chwalski took a spade to the cemetery, most probably to shovel the snow away from the grave and the headstone. It was strange to see a squire carrying a spade over his shoulder, but people had become accustomed to his idiosyncrasies. He often spent all day at the cemetery and sometimes late into the night. Gradually, it became warmer and the snow melted. The water flowed over the village like a river.

"One time after Passover the cemetery watchman came to the police and reported that the earth around Aliza's grave had been tampered with. There were thieves at that time who stole corpses from graves and sold them to doctors who used the bodies to perform autopsies. But those vandals only stole fresh corpses. Who would perform an autopsy on a corpse which is already decayed? In Turbin people said that Aliza rose up from the grave and roamed the city at night. When such talk begins, witnesses immediately emerge: this one saw her, that one heard her. She was standing on the bridge, she was washing linen by the river, she was knocking at someone's shutter. The rumors reached Chwalski and he only shouted: 'Idiots, I refuse to listen to such superstition.'

"Nu, but when an entire town talks it is not baseless. The Russian authorities ordered a few soldiers to dig under the headstone and to open the coffin.

"When Chwalski heard this he became wild with anger, but he seemed to have forgotten that Poland was no longer independent. The Russian soldiers pushed him back, dragged out the coffin, unscrewed the lid, and the casket was found to be empty. Half the town came running together to look at the black wonder. Somebody had stolen Aliza out from the grave. You could never imagine the things that went on every day in Turbin. They ran to tell Chwalski the news, but he hollered like a madman. Reb Betzalel was still alive, but he was no longer a court-Jew. For a few days the whole town was boiling like a kettle. Jews were afraid that false accusations would be brought against them. There were already those who barked that the Jews used her blood for matzohs.

"In the middle of all this a new commotion broke out in the

town. It happened like this. The old woman who served the squire
was cooking grits for him and lit a fire. Her hands were shaky and a
piece of burning kindle-wood fell. It soon became a blaze. The old
woman began to scream and peasants came to see what was going
on. The firemen came running with their half-empty water barrels.
Someone burst open Aliza's locked bedroom door. It gives me the
creeps to talk about this. The squire lay in bed snoring — it seemed
he was drunk — and next to him lay a skeleton. Yes, Chwalski
himself had stolen Aliza from the grave. He yearned for her so, that
one winter night he dug her up, pried open the coffin, took out her
remains and carried them home. The night was a dark one and nobody saw. He admitted to everything when the police officials took
him in for a hearing. She was already decayed he said and he peeled
off the flesh leaving only the bones. The Russians did not believe
their own ears. 'How is it possible that a person can do such a wild
thing?' they asked. And he answered: 'I just could not bear the longing. Better bones than nothing. If you want to hang me, hang me,
but bury me near her.'

"Nobody among the Russians knew what sort of punishment to
give for such a crime. They wrote a report out to the gubernoton in
Lublin. In Lublin they didn't know what to do either and inquired in
Warsaw and from there to Petersburg. Meanwhile they allowed
Chwalski to remain free. The skeleton they buried again. Chwalski
lived only one year more. He had become like a skeleton himself.
They buried him with all the honors right near his Aliza.

"What I mean to say is: a person gets some idea in his head and
it begins to grow and take over the brain. It becomes an obsession.
You can even call it a dybbuk. Both he and she were people with
souls. If there is a paradise for Gentiles I am sure they will rest there
together forever. How is it written in the Holy Book, 'strong as death
is love, cruel as the grave is jealousy.' Well, the Sabbath is over. I see
three stars in the sky. A good new week to all of us."

"Strong as Death Is Love" is included in the volume The Image and
Other Stories, *published by Farrar, Straus & Giroux, Inc. Reprinted
with permission. Isaac Bashevis Singer's new work,* Love and Exile, *will
published by Doubleday this fall.*

Stephen Spender

FROM MY DIARY

'She was,' my father said (in an aside),
'A great beauty, forty years ago.'
Out of my crude childhood, I stared at
Our tottering hostess, tremulous
In her armchair, pouring tea from silver —
Her gray silk dress, her violet gaze.
I only saw her being seventy,
I could not see the girl my father saw.

Now that I'm older than my father then was
I go with life-long friends to the same parties
Which we have gone to always.
We seem the same age always
Although the parties sometimes change to funerals
That sometimes used to change to christenings.

Faces we've once loved
Fit into their seven ages as Russian dolls
Into one another. My memory
Penetrates through successive layers
Back to the face which I first saw. So when the last
Exterior image is laid under its lid,
Your face first-seen will shine through all.

A GIRL WHO HAS DROWNED HERSELF SPEAKS

If only they hadn't shown that cruel mercy
Of dredging my drowned body from the river
That locked me in its peace, up to their surface
Of autopsy, and burial, and forms —
This, which was my last wish, might have come true —
That when the waves had finally washed away
The remnants of my flesh, the skull would stay —
But change to crystal. Things outside
Which it had looked at once, would swim into
Eye-sockets that looked at them: through
The scooped-out caverns of the skull, would dart
Solid phosphorescent fish, where there had been
Their simulacra only in the mind.

A CHORUS OF OEDIPUS

O human generations, I consider
Life but a shadow. Where is the man
Ever attained more than the semblance
Of happiness, but it quickly vanished?
Oedipus. I count your life the example
Proving we can call no human blessed.

With skill incomparable he threw the spear;
He gained the prize of an unchallenged fame:
He killed the crooked-taloned maiden
Whose singing made the midday darken:
He was our tower that rose up against death
And from that day we called him king of Thebes.

But now whose history is more grievous
Plagued with the loss of all that greatness his?
Whose fortunes ever met with such reverse?
I pity Oedipus for whom that soft flesh couch
That bore him, also proved his nuptial couch.
Oh how can soil in which your father sowed
Have secretly endured your seed so long?

Time, all-revealing, finally tracked you down,
Condemned the monstrous marriage which begot
Children upon her, your own begetter.
O son of Laius, would my eyes had never seen you.
I weep like one with lips formed for lament.
Until today it was you who gave me light.
Today your darkness covers up my eyes.

CHORUS FROM OEDIPUS AT COLONOS

Stranger, this is shining Colonos,
Famed for horses, loveliest place.
Nightingales pour forth their song
From wine-dark depths of ivy where they dwell
Close to the god's inviolate bowers.
Heavy with fruit and never visited
By scorching sun or tearing wind.
Here Dionysos revelling runs
The nymphs that nursed him, his companions.

Each dawn, narcissus clusters, washed
In the sky dew, upraise their crowns,
Those worn of old by the great goddesses,
And crocuses like shafts of sunlight show.
Fed by eternal streams, the fountains
Of Cephysus fan through the plains
Bringing their swelling breasts increase.
Nor are the Muses absent from this place.

And here a miracle, a thing unknown
In Asia, flourishes perpetually—
The self-renewing vast-trunked olive tree,
Bastion for us against our enemies
And for Athenian children, nurturer.
Nor youth nor age can cause it damage
For Zeus smiles on it, and grey-eyed
Athena holds it in her keeping gaze.

And most of all, I have to praise the horse
Poseidon's gift to this land, glorious,
Running beside white horses of the waves.
And Colonos is where Poseidon taught
Man bit and bridle for the horse the horse
To tame the wild colt and to curb his speed:
And taught him carve the wood for prows and oars
Chasing the Nereids through the waves.

Stephen Spender's most recent book, with David Hockney, is China Diary, *published in 1983 by Harry N. Abrams, Inc.*

Robert Penn Warren

UPWARDNESS

It is hard to know the logic of mere recollection.
Is Time the nexus? No, for Time does not

Define sequence of recollection, only
Of event, and of event as the death-black humus

In which pale hair-like roots of recollection
Probe in ghostly aim, or aimlessness.

Look! Coming down the street of the little town,
Book-satchel on shoulder, what idle wonderment

In head, the small boy passes homeward, not
Yet knowing where love lived, or what it was.

He gives you a totally blank stare which denies
Your very existence — as you, in the mirror, are often

Inclined to do. There have been mountains. Deserts. Seas.
In moonlit deck-swell there has been head laid to your shoulder,

Hair sweet, name unknown. A lamp has gleamed all night
As print, enchanted, squirmed, live, across the page.

Down Sierra curves, in the old open Buick back,
The standing young man is hurled sidewise, seatward, the gin bottle

Overside. The driver is screaming in ecstacy.
What was happiness? There must have been such a thing.

* * *

Yes, silently, out of nothing, again it comes true:
Side by side, on night grass lying, one palm to one palm,

And silently, silently, four eyes fixed upward as though
Straining beyond the infinite starwardness.

Robert Penn Warren is a recipient of the MacArthur Award. His New and Selected Poems *will be published by Random House in the spring of 1985.*

Rosanna Warren

HISTORY AS DECORATION

Float over us, Florence, your banners
of assassination, your most expensive
reds: Brazil, Majorca lichen, cochineal.
Let the Neoplatonic Arno flow
crocus yellow. Let palazzo walls
flaunt quattrocento dyes: "little
monk" and "lion skin." We pay for beauty: beautiful
are gorgeous crimes we cannot feel,

they shone so long ago. And those philosophies
too pretty in spirit ever to be real.
City of fashion. Leonardo chose
the hanged Pazzi conspirator for a theme:
"Tawny cap; black satin vest," he wrote,
"Black sleeveless coat, lined; turquoise
jacket lined with fox; Bernardo di
Bandino Baroncigli; black hose."

So dangled the elegant corpse, *bella figura*
though its tongue stuck out. The keen, gossipy
faces still peer from Ghirlandaio's walls
and from the streets we elbow through today.
History flashes in banknotes. Gold, jade, corals
twinkle from hand to hand, while the spectral glare
of Savonarola's sunset bonfire licks the square
and his cries ascend and blend with Vespers bells.

Rosanna Warren teaches in the University Professors Program at Boston University. A collection of her poetry, Each Leaf Shines Separate, *will be published this fall by W. W. Norton.*

ESSAYS

Jacques Barzun

SHAW VERSUS STENDHAL

Comparative literature is a fruitful branch of learning, but comparisons between two authors are usually sterile. "The Good Society in Carlyle and in Ruskin," "The Incidence of Crime in Dostoevsky and Edgar Allan Poe" are topics that appeal to graduate students, but they yield only parallel enumerations: "Carlyle thinks this, and Ruskin says that." How much better for everybody to read Carlyle, then Ruskin, and store the opinions of each side by side in the memory.

Yet it sometimes happens that a comparison closely pursued leads the mind to an instructive difference, a single and striking divergence among similarities, which helps to mark a change of direction in culture, an epoch in history or human psychology. This possibility, I think, justifies the attempt to bring into one view what Stendhal and Shaw wrote as critics of music. The outcome is by no means limited to the realm of art.

What is required to make such a comparison productive is that there be a large common ground between the two minds or two bodies of work — not merely a large *subject,* but a position within the subject showing many points of congruence up to the sought-for point of disparity.

Now in bringing together Stendhal and Shaw, the common *subject* is: What should be said about music? And the common ground or position is what I am about to describe. The musical scene no doubt changed between 1810 and 1890, but the repertoires of the two periods overlapped to a very large extent. The two critics are moreover alike in being primarily writers of fiction, each with a unique place in the first rank. Both men began to write music criticism early in life, simultaneously with other kinds of criticism (including that of painting) and before they produced any of their great fictions. (Plays, we should recall, *are* fiction. The illogical habits of modern librarians should not obscure that ancient fact.)

But these fundamental similarities are far from exhausting the list, even of externals. Stendhal and Shaw acquired their passion for music largely through self-education, by listening and reading widely, though each had a start in early music lessons. Shaw emerged as the better trained of the two, because his mother and quasi father were both professionals; but Stendhal also had some training—enough to make him resent his family's failure to provide him with better teachers —and the notion that he was a musical illiterate is now entirely discarded.

The body of music criticism that each of our men has left us is abundant. Though some of Stendhal's is scattered in diaries and travel books, it may be estimated as not far from equal in bulk to Shaw's six volumes of collected reviews, speeches, and letters to the press—all about music. What is amazing after we take in that fact is that neither writer went on to make a musician a principal figure in any of his fiction.

It could be argued that this generality is partly blurred by the character of Owen Jack in the third of Shaw's five and a half novels, *Love Among the Artists* (1881). But the chief trait of Owen Jack is his rude arrogance, arising from the consciousness that he is a genius among philistines—so much of a genius that he decides against marriage as an impediment to art. His role in the novel is to upset the fuddy-duddies who run the Antient Orpheus Society and are petrified by his new music; the novel makes no attempt to describe the inner workings of a composer's mind. Its purpose, Shaw later explained, was to show the difference between people who enjoy the fine arts as dabblers and those in whom it is a passion. Whatever one concludes about this figure in Shaw's prentice work, it remains noteworthy that in none of his fifty-three plays is there a leading character who is a musician. Indeed, there are only two artists: Marchbanks, the fledgling poet in *Candida,* and Dubedat, the immoral painter in *The Doctor's Dilemma.*

In Stendhal the absence of musicians is likewise complete. Nor is much use made of music as part of life in the imaginative work of either writer. In Stendhal the one conspicuous incident involving music is the effect of hearing Cimarosa's *Matrimonio segreto* on Mathilde in *The Red and the Black*: she detests music, but the opera releases her pent-up passion of love, and she bursts into a torrent of tears. In the rest of his fictions, Stendhal is content simply to name concerts or operas as a means of suggesting contemporary reality. In a few places he refers to music for comic effect, and so does Shaw— for instance in the fourth act of *Caesar and Cleopatra,* where the queen's professor of music, after teaching her the harp for two weeks, is to receive a flogging for every wrong note that she plays. In *The Music Cure,* subtitled "a piece of utter nonsense," pieces by Chopin, played by a beautiful girl, rescue a young diplomat from hallucinations. The playlet is insignificant. In another farce, a chorus of angels sings "Bill Bailey"; in *The Simpleton of the Unexpected Isles,* a matter-of-fact trumpet ushers in the Last Judgment; and in *Methuselah* we hear three trombone calls reminiscent of the Masonic symbol in Mozart's *Magic Flute.* Half a dozen other "musical in-terventions" in the plays could be listed — all trifling and purely at-mospheric, as in Shakespeare. Their fewness is in fact remarkable, for the theater of Shaw's time made much use of incidental music. The unions had not yet made the practice prohibitively expensive.

The only serious role given to music in Shaw's work occurs in *Man and Superman,* whose plot is derived from Mozart's *Don Giovanni* and where the famous scene in Hell is heralded by three musical quotations from the opera. The introductory chords resound three times more during the scene. But as we shall see, none of this pre-pares us for what the play winds up saying about music. The value Shaw assigns to it in relation to himself and to society is complex and unexpected, and as it forms the "difference" here looked for, it must be kept back until the end.

As to the esthetic influence of music on Shaw and on Stendhal, a curious remark has been made by the students of each — indepen-dently, since, so far as I know, nobody has coupled the two disparate geniuses before now. The remark is that their greatest works "fol-low musical form." I myself was caught in that trap, when thirty years ago I was asked to write a commentary on the "Scene in Hell" for a recording of it by a quartet of famous actors. Most recently, in 1979, a doctoral dissertation at the Sorbonne pointed out musical patterns in Stendhal's two great novels. After reflection, I have come to think that these discoveries are false criticism. They are based on such things as the recurrence of themes and the verbal tagging of characters and situations, which presumably correspond to effects of timbre and tonal choices. All these suppositions about musical form through words, I think, exemplify only our modern love of meta-phorical nonsense. It is shown to be nonsense by two plain facts: every art is distinct in its means and methods; and all the arts employ repetition and recurrence, harmony and contrast between parts, because the human mind, in order to think at all, demands order and iteration in anything and everything it touches.

One more point of resemblance between Stendhal and Shaw:

neither was a sedentary listener; both pursued music wherever it could be heard. Stendhal's travels in Austria, and the Germanies, and in Italy as far as Naples greatly added to what he heard in Paris. Shaw covered the British Isles and visited Bayreuth and Paris. We should also remember that their main musical fare was opera. In the nineteenth century it was the leading genre, with religious music second. For the public, those forms were the test by which a composer was judged; and for our purpose, we note that opera, oratorios, passions, and requiems are all dramas in music.

We are now ready for what our two men did and thought as critics. They intended from the outset to write for the general reader and to proselytize for certain ideas. Shaw repeatedly made fun of so-called technical criticism, showing by parody that he was fully able to write the gibberish of program notes and saying why they were useless. Stendhal could not have done the same, but then the public he was aiming at — the opera-going high society — would not have stood it, or understood it, if he had. His indications without technical terms are precise and sufficient to make his points, just like Shaw's.

Their propaganda runs in parallel. Stendhal was bent on rescuing from neglect Mozart and the former repertory (Cimarosa, Pergolese, and other composers of the late eighteenth century), and at the same time he was trying to preach the modern, which for him was Rossini. Shaw was bent on rescuing from neglect Mozart and the former repertory (Berlioz, Verdi, Schubert, and other early nineteenth-century composers), and at the same time he was battling for the modern, which for him was Wagner.

It would be too much to say that after his crusade Shaw was not fully committed to Wagner, but it is evident that for him "the master of masters" was Mozart. More markedly, Stendhal had reservations about Rossini, and for him the greatest of masters was Mozart.

Though propagandists for a cause, our pair were first and always critics, which means granting virtues to what they disliked and seeing faults in what they admired. In doing this kind of justice, their estimates of Meyerbeer and Rossini are strikingly alike. Moreover, as conscious critics of themselves they were oddly self-depreciatory. Stendhal declared himself "mistalented" for music; and Shaw, asking rhetorically, "Who am I to criticize. . . ?" answered (at least, he did so once): "Simply nobody but a man of letters of no musical authority at all."

A common element in our critics' writing is their historical sense. They drew analogies over a wide range in all the arts. They illustrated by reference to the well known, and in music they defined schools and innovations, both in composition and performance. They were teaching music history at the same time as appreciation. And in doing so, they never hesitated to express shocking opinions or to satirize the mind and the behavior of contemporary audiences. Stendhal, as his friend Mérimée noted, was courageous in the salon no less than in anonymous print; and Shaw earned his reputation as a rude iconoclast first of all as a reviewer of music. What enabled them to survive protests and resentment was the compelling attraction of prose styles such as had never been seen before.

Stendhal and Shaw obviously shared the dramatic temperament; the latter wrote plays, the former long tried to — he even took courses in dramatic elocution from a professional. In each of them the temperament went deeper than love of the stage and its smell of grease paint. They conceived of life itself as drama. Stendhal loved Italy and castigated France, because the Italians alone lived dramatically. The violence of their passions had not shrunk into the petty hostilities of a polished society. Shaw's revolutionary ardor sprang from an Early-Christian belief that the individual must save his soul by fighting for righteousness. He thought the greatest passage in English literature was the scene of bloodshedding in *Pilgrim's Progress*. True, the librettos of opera usually trivialize moral conflict, but the music does not, if the opera is great. And in religious music, the same life-and-death issues inform the oratorios and other works based on sacred history and prophecy.

The mark of the dramatic temperament is that it abhors sentimentality and is at ease with strong effects in art, sentimentality being the refusal to act out one's emotions in life, and strong effects in art being but the expression of strong passions in life. Accordingly, Stendhal and Shaw had nothing but scorn for people boasting of artistic sensibility who thought that art should always be delicate and gentle, music particularly. When respectable Londoners objected to the "shocking noise" made by the Salvation Army bands, Shaw went to hear their music and pronounced it excellent. "Imagine a band with forty-three trombones!" Like Berlioz, our two wanted music to "make their nerves vibrate." Stendhal, indeed, has been misunderstood precisely because he laid stress on the physicial force of music. He did not know that one day Shaw would write about the Rakóczy March in the *Damnation of Faust* that if it had gone on one minute longer, he would have rushed out and taken Trafalgar Square by storm.

In a word, music was an expression of life passionately felt. Music does not depict scenes or describe objects or tell stories, but it mysteriously embodies the continuous motion and emotion that we experience at the sight of objects and scenes and events. On this point, Shaw and Stendhal (and Berlioz, who was a great critic too) are absolutely at one. Their unanimity explains why after a lifetime of critical writing all three ended up as worshippers of Mozart.

So far, then, musical intelligence in Stendhal and Shaw runs along the same straight track, from sensation and sensibility to expressiveness and the energy of live ideas. But within this realm of ideas their paths diverge, for an excellent reason in each case.

Stendhal concluded, after much meditation on his conscious and unconscious life, that music was the expression of love in a special sense. In listening to perfect music, he felt the perfect bliss that he felt in the presence of the beloved. That bliss was a unique concentration of all the faculties, which made him aware of his true self. This awareness, in turn, must find further expression, that is, it is impelled to the creation of art. Music, love, and art formed a circle and an equation. Along the circle and between the terms of the equation was the deep self of the man and artist, which everybody agrees differs from his public personality, and in some cases from his verbalized beliefs.

The introspective Stendhal not only sensed that deeper self directly, he also had theories about it, derived from the writings of Destutt, Cabanis, and others who, under the name of *Idéologues,* were the first to study abnormal psychology as a key to the normal mind.

And for Stendhal this — so to speak — musical knowledge of the self, this account of the genesis of art, had an importance beyond the satisfaction of understanding. Like his fellow romanticists, he believed in the power of art to regenerate society. Men in society were stunted by convention, which he saw as collective cowardice — everybody afraid to *be* himself, because afraid of others and afraid of his deep self. The artist-genius comes upon the scene and acts as liberator. By exhibiting a true self, he shocks. By saying what he really thinks, he prompts others to give up repeating lies. And possibly by the ideality of the work of art and the perfection of its form, he offers a model for life and society to follow.

Another way of putting the same romanticist creed is to say that art reveals reality and new art breaks up the cake of custom. The fortunes of that creed are suggestive but too complex for any summary. We can only make a leap of three-quarters of a century and rejoin Shaw for his views — his divergent views — on the same subject. The year is 1903, and Shaw has just finished *Man and Superman,* including its preface and its appendix, *The Revolutionist's Handbook,* which winds up with some 180 "Maxims for Revolutionists."

Inside the play is the scene in hell, and there Don Juan, who is temporarily the shade of the play's hero as well as the spokesman for Shaw, launches into a tirade against art. He acknowledges that, thanks to art, he has cultivated his senses and derived "great delight for many years." But the artist "with his love songs and his paintings and his poems . . . led me at last into the worship of Woman. . . ." And this "beauty worshipping and happiness hunting and woman idealizing was not worth a dump as a philosophy of life."

In case this indictment should not be strong enough, Shaw gives his hero three splendid aphorisms. First, a true philosophy of life "reduced art to the mere schooling of my faculties." Second, "Music is the brandy of the damned." And third (one of the maxims for revolutionists), "The nineteenth century was the Age of Faith in the Fine Arts: The results are before us."

That maxim is the clue to the previous onslaught and to Shaw's difference from Stendhal. Stendhal's philosophy had succeeded in the nineteenth century *as a belief*—the romanticist belief in regeneration through art as the expression of true individual selves. But at the dawn of the next century, his alter ego Bernard Shaw, an artist brought up in the same creed, sees that man and society are still unregenerate, and he looks for another remedy. The remedy is twofold: the economic remaking of society through socialism and life enhanced by the further evolution of man's intelligence.

This one ultimate difference between the two music critics, or rather, the artistic and historical perspective that it affords, was the point of my taking the risk of a comparison.

I should logically stop with this *quod erat demonstrandum*. But as in *Don Giovanni* and *Saint Joan,* there is need for a brief epilogue. Shaw continued after *Man and Superman* to be a passionate devotee of music and the other arts. He kept writing criticism and thinking like a nineteenth-century man. That forgivable inconsistency reduces his divergence from Stendhal in one material way, for, of course, Stendhal never repudiated art. And the attentive reader will surely have noticed another reconciliation: these two artists acknowledged alike that there was something above and greater than art, which is life itself. Hence the absence of musician- or artist-heroes from both the novels and the plays.

Jacques Barzun formerly was provost and is Emeritus Professor of History at Columbia University. His latest book is Critical Questions: On Music and Letters, Culture and Biography 1940–80, *recently published by the University of Chicago Press.*

Daniel Bell

OUR COUNTRY—1984

The title of the original *Partisan Review* symposium of 1952 was "Our Country and Our Culture," and the question was whether the situation of the intellectual and the artist had changed in American society, whether the alleged hostility of the country to art — which had sent the nineteenth-century writers packing to London, and the twentieth-century writers to Paris — was now different. And this was the issue to which almost all of the original participants, twenty-four in number, responded.

I do not wish to speak about "Our Culture," for two reasons. One is that in the last thirty or so years, I have not heard much that is new about traditional culture, popular culture, folk culture, mass-cult, mid-cult, lowbrow, highbrow, class culture, elite culture, adversary culture, counter-culture, modernism, postmodernism, avant-garde and kitsch, or *pompier* and *spettacolo*; and I, at least, have nothing to add.

The other reason is that the original *Partisan Review* statement had a more pregnant theme, one which was almost submerged and which was put in just one sentence: "Politically, there is recognition that the kind of democracy which exists in America has an intrinsic and positive value: it is not merely a capitalist myth but a reality which must be defended against Russian totalitarianism."

If the symposium thus represented a turning point in the attitude of the writers and intellectuals, it was not in the "celebration" of America culturally, but in the retreat from a moral relativism that had dominated left-wing thinking for so long. This was the idea, going back to Marx's analysis of liberalism in *The German Ideology* (where he dubbed Kant "the white-washing spokesman of the German bourgeoisie"), that political democracy was "bourgeois democracy," and that "bourgeois freedom" was a sham. It was the basis of the doctrinaire belief that the ruling class only "tolerated" democracy and would jettison it when threatened, and that "proletarian democracy" (in the Leninist version, as interpreted by the Party) was of

Editor's Note: This is a revised version of remarks at the Y.M.H.A. colloquium on January 12, 1984, on the original *Partisan Review* theme.

a higher moral order and possessed the only true claim to universalism and freedom. Politically, this belief was the justification of the Communist effort to undermine the Weimar Republic, to attack the Socialists as "social-fascists," to insist that fascism was "the last stage of monopoly capitalism," and even, as Georg Lukács stated in that startling last testament (published in 1971), that "I have always thought that the worst form of socialism was better to live in than the best form of capitalism." *

The larger framework of the *PR* sentence was the Cold War. This was 1952. There had been the takeover of Czechoslovakia and the defenestration of Jan Masaryk. A whole new series of purge trials had unrolled in Europe. In Prague, Rudolf Slansky, the general secretary of the Party, and the other defendants "confessed" to being "Zionist agents" in league with R. H. Crossman and Koni Zilliacus, the left-wing leaders of the British Labour Party, in a plot against the Soviet Union. In Hungary, it was Rajk; in Bulgaria, Petkov. Zhdanovism had been reinstated in Russian culture and Akhmatova denounced as a whore. The Jewish writers and artists, Bergelson, Feffer, Michoels, had disappeared (and been murdered). The city of Berlin had become divided.

In Europe the intellectual lines were sharply drawn. Merleau-Ponty, the French philosopher and an editor of *Les Temps Modernes*, had written a book, *Humanisme et Terreur*, restating the justification of terror as a necessary defense of the Revolution. Sartre declared that one should not discuss the Soviet concentration camps, lest that give aid to its enemies and help the United States. Brecht had gone back to East Berlin. Ernst Bloch, the philosopher, had returned from New York to Leipzig. Lukács had resumed his apologias in Budapest. In Paris, Louis Aragon, dominating the French literary establishment, led an onslaught against the critics of Stalinism. On the other side were the voices of Koestler, Silone, Aron, Sperber, Milosz and Orwell—but they were in a minority and were looked on as "renegades," with the revulsion that some individuals felt (at that time) for defrocked priests.

---

*See, *Georg Lukács: Record of a Life,* edited by Istvan Eörsi (London: Verso Editions, 1983), p. 181. See also the editor's introduction, pp. 16–20, for the psychological basis of Lukács's fear of being "excommunicated" from the Party. "In his eyes, Stalin's death camps were now a world-historical necessity, now surface pimples on the blooming face of the totality," writes Mr. Eörsi.

What is surprising, and in its way quite extraordinary, is how little of this is reflected in the pages of the *Partisan Review* symposium. Lionel Trilling does make reference to "the commanding position of Stalinism in French cultural life." And Philip Rahv suggests the end of ideology, which he calls the end of utopian illusions. But much of the debate centered upon the themes of mass culture, the alienation of the intellectuals, and the justification of nonconformity, issues that were posed most sharply and aggressively by three of the dissenting voices in the symposium. C. Wright Mills, in the habitually truculent posture of the outrider, wrote: "Imagine 'the old *PR*' running the title 'Our Country.' . . . You would have cringed." Norman Mailer found the symposium "shocking" and "wonder[ed] if there has been a time in the last fifty years when the American artist has felt more alienated." For Irving Howe, "America has entered the stage of kitsch, the mass culture of the middlebrows." Capitalism as a world-system is exhausted, American vitality is maintained by a war economy. Yet "the power of Stalinism does not permit one to settle on an isle of rectitude equidistant from both sides. . . . Veering and tacking as history compels him, the socialist intellectual must try to defend democracy with some realism while maintaining his independence from and opposition to the status quo."

Since the position of the dissenters did represent the earlier *Partisan Review* attitudes, most of the contributors in one way or another wrestled with those themes, the ghosts of that past, rather than the existing actualities abroad.

Sidney Hook, with his characteristic lucidity, declared: "There are all kinds of alienation in the world and one can get startling effects by confusing them." And he proceeded in his shrewd manner to disentangle three meanings. On the matter of non-conformity, Hook remarked: "I see no specific virtue in the attitude of conformity or non-conformity. . . . [They] are relational terms. Before evaluating them I should like to know *to* and *with what* a person is conforming or not conforming, and *how*." A sensible statement, but sociologically the postures of submission (as in the instance of Lukács) or of rebellion (as that of Sartre) are rooted in the character of these individuals who, in their ability to exemplify these attitudes, embody an historical *sensibilité* of segments of the intelligentsia. That is the source of their appeal.

Ever the "realist," James Burnham chided those who believed that America had become the land where the citrons of culture bloomed: "This is the generation . . . of the triumph of the Book Clubs, columnists and radio, the relative decrease in the number of book titles published, the Hollywoodization of a continuous series of writers . . . a dull local tradition in painting [*pace* Hilton Kramer] combined with an offshoot of European non-representation which ran its second-hand course in a decade and a half, a philosophic waste. . . . Culturally we remain what we have been: a 'semi-barbarian superstate of the periphery' . . . with Rome and not Athens the potential form of the future."

Burnham, still the Machiavellian, declared: "Let us not build a case out of counterfeit. The objective justification for the intellectuals' 'reaffirmation and rediscovery of America' is in the first and sufficient instance political and military." Soviet totalitarianism "is the worst possible secular evil," and "American power is thus the lesser evil." Therefore, "if it comes to full war," the case for America is "just and right, and rightly to be preferred."

*   *   *

Thirty years later. Thirty years wiser? I wish to discuss three themes: what one means by our *country;* who is the *our* we are talking about; and the change in the nature of partisan intellectual divisions in the last two decades.

Marx had said that the workers had no country and that one's loyalty was to the international working class. Today, not only is there no real international working-class movement, but there is less internationalism among the workers than at any time in the twentieth century when, at the Basle congress of the Second International in 1912, Jean Jaures threatened a European-wide general strike to halt the threat of war. If not the working class, the leftist intellectuals still cling to the lingering idea that *they* have no country. The idea of alienation, which was resurrected only forty or so years ago (see, for example, the failure to include an article on "alienation" in the standard *Encyclopedia of the Social Sciences* published in the late 1930s), has represented the "true consciousness" of these intellectuals, the sociological distancing of themselves from the society.

But what is the "society," and how does one establish one's attitude towards it? To assess the character of a country, one has to go back to a distinction made by Burke between a *society* and a *regime*. A society embodies the underlying values and beliefs, the cultural traditions, the commitment to the continuity of that character of a country. A regime or administration is, by its nature, transitory.

In the Soviet Union, the regime identifies itself with the society, but it is not *accountable* to the society and, based on a privileged class,

rules over the society. In Poland, a regime, the Army, seeks to crush
and subdue the society — which is the working class, the Church, and
the peasantry. In Chile, a society and social structure which long
was democratic is now ruled by a narrow-based Army regime which
seeks to create capitalist and market forces by decree!

In the United States, the regime has always been subordinate
to the society. The values of the society are economic freedoms, civil
liberties, and individual rights; a limitation of state power through
checks and balances; a Constitutional system with emphasis on due
process and guarded by judicial review. These may, and sometimes
have been, twisted by regimes (particularly as the administrative
state and public bureaucracies compete with the corporate bureaucracies), but the values remain and the regimes are accountable to the
society.

Equally, in the United Kingdom and in the United States, the
protection of liberties and the rule of law antedate the capitalist
economy and are maintained by a strong institutional tradition, a
cumbersome yet basically protective legal system, and the play of
civil as against ideological politics. Any destruction of democracy
derives more from the polarization of a society into irreconcilable
factions than from the dominant economic class becoming fearful of
the "masses."

To identify the administration with the society, or the culture
of the country, coarse as it may be in many ways, with the character
of its underlying values, is not only quite wrong but leads to gross
and misleading equations. Thus, in *The New Yorker,* that imposter of
Parnassus, George Steiner, wrote of George Orwell that he was
"resistant to both the Stalinism and the detergent inhumanity of a
technocracy and mass-media hypnosis of the kind toward which the
United States seems to Orwell to be moving."

To the extent that Orwell was a "little Englander," as many
British writers are, he would seek a different way from the mass
society of the United States and the closed, repressive society of the
Soviet Union. But on the overriding issue of the defense of freedom
and decency, his choice was unambiguous.

So, to the extent that we live in a society whose values are
rooted in traditions of freedom and pluralism, and are embodied in
continuing institutions in which accountability and consent remain
the foundations of the political order, we can say, without apology,
that this is "our country."

*   *   *

A more difficult question: the word "our." Who is the "we"? The *we* are not just those born here, schooled here, who have voted, taken part in political controversies, pay taxes, and think of ourselves as Americans; the *we* now think of ourselves also as Jews. Most of the intellectuals in the reprise of the *PR* symposium are Jewish.* In the original symposium, eleven of the twenty-four participants were Jewish; two others had Jewish parents but do not consider themselves Jews. What is quite striking is that in the original symposium — I am not being invidious, because I probably would have done the same — no one spoke of the problem of a double tie. Even though almost all the Jewish respondents were children of immigrants, the discussion of culture was a claim to the inheritance of American culture, with no mention of the particular role of the Jewish experience. Yet today almost all, I would say, are highly conscious of being Jewish; many are involved with the Jewish community; and the relation to and the survival of Israel loom large in our lives.

Yet we are American Jews. We do not think of ourselves as Jewish-Americans, in the way that one still writes of Italian-Americans, or Irish-Americans, or Polish-Americans. What is the nature of this tie? Is it a double identity, or is there something unique in the relation of Jews to American life?

It was difficult for intellectual Jews in Western Europe, not only in Germany but also in France and Italy, to think of themselves as Jews in addition to their identification with their country. They were Germans or Frenchmen or Italians who had been or were also Jewish, but often only if they retained an affiliation with some *Gemeinde* or had religious ties. The Dreyfus case may have made many persons aware of anti-Semitism (and we forget that individuals such as Cézanne and Degas were anti-Dreyfusards), but the case was complicated by the fault lines of clericalism and anticlericalism, the secularists and the antisecularists, the partisans of the Revolution or the Restoration, all of which derived from the deep historic divisions of the society. Léon Blum on the left and Georges Mandel on the right may have suffered the indignity of being called *les sales Juifs*

---

*I refer here to the four sessions of the Y.M.H.A. meetings. The two non-Jews were William Barrett and Christopher Lasch. The other participants were Hilton Kramer, Leslie Fiedler, Irving Howe, Leon Wieseltier, William Phillips, and myself.

when they headed or served in French cabinets in the Third Republic, but they thought of themselves primarily as Frenchmen. (Yet both, of course, were taken to concentration camps, and it was in Vichy France that the latent anti-Semitism in the country became more manifest.)

But the United States has been different: in part because we were a "created" nation and lacked the long threads of history and culture that gave other nations a distinctive cast; in part because of the idea, *au fond,* that we are all foreign-born. There have been distinctive stamps. New England Puritanism and transcendentalism shaped a large part of American culture. The South has been a region with a common culture, rooted in a way of life which fused family, land, and *apartheid,* and decried the levelling of industrial life. And there has been a long history of WASP supremacy, largely in the social and economic spheres, and a great deal of anti-Semitism. Yet none of these were large enough or strong enough to contain the restlessness and dynamism of the technologically-driven economy and the large admixture of foreign-born groups who, in their own regional and urban concentrations, created a diversity of striated hues.

Thus, as Jews, it has been easier for us to think of ourselves as Americans and as Jews in a way different from other subordinate Jewish communities in the world—whether in Argentina, Mexico, South Africa, or the Soviet Union. In those countries, Jews still have a special status, or lose their identity. In the United States we are, as American Jews, a natural designation.

This has been particularly true since World War II, which has seen the rapid onrush of Jews into the centers of academic, cultural, and public life. *Partisan Review* itself has been a platform for the American Jewish writers: Saul Bellow, Bernard Malamud, Isaac Rosenfeld were first published in these pages. Jews are prominent in the major universities. At Harvard, where before World War II there were few Jewish professors (and these largely in the professional schools), one finds major Jewish figures in almost every department of the university. The rise into the professions and upper-middle-class status of the children of the East European immigration is one of the remarkable feats of social mobility in modern times. American culture, elite and mass, has been indelibly etched with Jewish influences—in the rhythms of inflection and language; in the number of Nobel laureates in literature, economics, physics, and medicine; in the wisecracking wit of Broadway and Hollywood, the music of Tin Pan Alley; and in the literary criticism of the New York

Jewish intellectuals. In all ways, the Jews have the greatest stake in the continuing strength of pluralist institutions in the United States.

But now there is also a whole new set of problems. Fifty years ago, few persons would have predicted the upsurge of ethnicity not only in the United States but in almost every country in the world. The focus on the economic conflicts between capitalist and worker, as shaped by Marx, predisposed most sociologists to regard class as the most salient division in contemporary society. Ethnicity was thought to be an anachronism which would be submerged under the single national identification of a country, or dissolved into the class identifications within a society. Yet this has not been the case. Almost every country in the world (with the exception of Japan, and to some extent the Scandinavian countries) is a plural society, with large admixtures of self-conscious minorities. And today almost every society is being challenged or torn apart by rancorous ethnic divisions.

The United States is not immune to these strains. There are the regional conflicts over resources (such as energy and water). There are the political and cultural conflicts, prompted by the rapid growth of Hispanic minorities with their concentrations in the southern tier of states: California, New Mexico, Texas, and Florida; and the black concentrations in the major urban centers, Chicago, Philadelphia, Newark, Washington, D.C., Atlanta, Detroit, and Los Angeles, all of which have black mayors. The cultural strain is aggravated because the arena in which the ethnic groups are making their demands is the political one, and conflicts in the political arena, as against the market, are focused and visible, and the outcomes tend to be zero-sum situations.

The Jews are in an especially difficult position. Though particularistic as a group, Jews have always insisted on universalistic and meritocratic criteria in the competition for place, position, and privilege in society. But precisely those criteria are under attack by the disadvantaged minorities who seek quotas and representation and similar particularistic rules as the means for increasing their position and status in society. Under conditions of adversity, such conflicts are bound to multiply.

There is, also, for the Jews, the precarious position of Israel. Before 1967, most American Jewish intellectuals were uninterested in Israel. As liberals or socialists, they focused on the radical reform of American society. But Israel today is a crucial symbol and reality of Jewish survival. In the Middle East today, who would say that class, not nation, is the salient division among peoples?

All of this was sketched in a remarkably prescient way by the forgotten member of the Marxian triad, Moses Hess. (Since Marxism always emphasized the dialectic, there had to be a third man.) Moses Hess was the first communist in Germany. He converted Engels, and together they edited a communist newspaper in the Rhineland, and he was an editor with Marx and Ruge of the *Deutsch-Französische Jahrbücher*. Hess split with Marx after 1848, and thereafter was subject to the vituperation that Marx reserved for his party opponents.

In his extraordinary book *Rome and Jerusalem,* written in 1862, Hess recalls some of his reflections of 1840 (written "in the midst of my endeavors in behalf of the European proletariat") following the Damascus affair:

> The proper understanding of this persecution of Jews must evoke a return to Judaism. . . . [Those] who for the sake of emancipation would like to persuade themselves and others that modern Jews no longer feel any trace of nationalism, do not understand how it is possible that in Europe in the nineteenth century men can give credence for a moment to so gross a medieval lie as the 'Mamser Bilbul'. . . . the Germans after their War of liberation not only repudiated the Jews who fought with them against France but moreover even persecuted them with the cry of 'Hep-Hep.'

For Hess, nationalism was still the most powerful current of belief. "In spite of all enlightenment and emancipation, the Jew of the Diaspora who denies his nationalism will still not win the respect of the nations." And in concluding his foreword, Hess ends with a peroration which stands in sharp contrast to the views of Marx:

> All of past history was concerned with the struggle of races and classes. Race struggle is primary; class struggle is secondary. When racial antagonisms cease, class struggle also ceases. Equality of all special classes follows on the heels of equality of races and finally remains merely a question of sociology.

Merely! The worldwide storms of race are still before us. And with them come precarious times for the Jewish community, and for the United States.

*   *   *

In 1952, the idea that a number of New York intellectuals might extol the virtues of America occasioned, as I have noted, astonishment, incredulity, and even outrage. In 1984, we see a different phenomenon on the cultural scene: a set of highly vocal conservative intellectuals for whom the affirmation of America and capitalism has become the ground of their existence, and for whom criticism of America is an affront. These intellectuals have positions in the government, a number of vigorous and influential magazines (*The Public Interest, Commentary, The New Criterion, This World*, blanketing the areas of domestic public policy, foreign policy, the arts, and religion); more specialized magazines such as *Public Opinion, Regulation*, the *Policy Review;* a half-dozen student magazines. And, as the guardian of public virtue, the Committee for a Free World.

In the normal course of events, all of this would be welcome. Conservatism, while having a distinguished lineage in English and European history, has never been central to American thought and debate. Henry Adams was a soured, embittered man who detested the plutocracy for its coarseness and the government for its corruption and rawness. H. L. Mencken mocked the "booboisie." The Southern Agrarians (John Crowe Ransom, Allen Tate, Robert Penn Warren) spoke eloquently of a rooted tradition, but their gossamer politics was one of nostalgia. Walter Lippmann, the only intellectual who invoked natural law (in his *The Public Philosophy*), was feared by the Midwestern Republicans for his anglophilia and admired by the liberals for his style and sentiments, but never read seriously by either. The striking thing, in fact, is that the conservative current in late-nineteenth and early twentieth-century America was deeply anticapitalist, and decried the grossness of uninhibited money-making and the destruction of "traditional" American values by the rising industrialism.

The appearance of a group of sophisticated individuals who themselves had emerged out of the detritus of Marxism and the pieties of radicalism gave rise to a genuine set of intellectual debates on the crucial issues of political philosophy—the character of distributive justice; the nature of rights and obligations; the limits, if any, on individualism; the virtues, and what they might be, of capitalism; the possibilities of community; the role of morality in foreign policy.

Unfortunately, those intellectual debates of the 1970s have shrivelled in the 1980s. And one also sees, in odd instances, the rapprochement of neoconservatives with the New Right, against the traditional conservatives, on questions such as supply-side economics, or a hard line on foreign policy.*

Perhaps such simplifications and cross-overs become inevitable when tender-minded discussions of philosophy and principles give way to the tough-hearted play of politics and polemics. Yet much of this becomes disturbing when it begins to affect the tone and temper of political discourse. Four illustrations:

One, although now growing in influence, the neoconservatives sound and talk often like a hunted band of men and women huddled together against the "cultural hegemony" of the liberals and the Left. It is true that the cultural mood of the intellectual community has been primarily "liberal" — a heritage of the rejection of small-town provincialism and the embrace of modernity; a politics influenced by the New Deal and progressivism; a sociology concerned with class and inequality; a disposition to romanticize the Third World combined with a fear of American military power. But to assume that this is a unified force when much of it is in disarray (with the neoliberals questioning government social programs and championing the rebuilding of American military strength) indicates a parochialism which has stopped time and is skewed by partisan politics.**

Two, there is the dyspeptic unwillingness of some conservatives to make relevant distinctions between social democracy and com-

---

*The ironic fact is that eight or so years ago, not only did the New Right question the commitment of the neoconservatives but, given its conspiratorial bent, feared that this was a move, abetted by the Eastern establishment-oriented national news media, to sabotage or take over the conservative movement and to abort the growing right-wing populism movement, out of the fear that such populism might become the basis of a new anti-Semitism. And on the issue of foreign policy, Pat Buchanan, a former Nixon speech writer and syndicated columnist, declared: "This *Commentary* crowd . . . didn't come around to our way of thinking until the Soviet threat to Israel became apparent." (See Jonathan Martin Kokey, *The New Right,* University Press of America, 1983, pp. 338–339.) The further irony, of course, is that today vocal anti-Semitism has emerged not out of the rednecks of the South, but from some black leaders in the ghetto. It is not only that politics makes for rumpled bedfellows, but that a drive for power and the use of demagogy override principles.

**Who would have thought, in 1972, that the main domestic political issue in 1984 would be whether Mr. Reagan or Mr. Mondale could more quickly balance the budget and reduce the deficit? Or that the Democratic candidates would embrace "family values" in such a wholehearted way? Or that Gary Hart would be repudiated

munism. Thus, writing in *Survey* (London) in a special issue on capitalism, Edward Shils remarked that socialists and communists are from the same family and that the fierce enmity which later developed between them derives from the original fraternal, and then fratricidal nature of the movements. Now, to a Mohammedan it may be that all Christians are alike, since he makes no distinction between footwashing Baptists and High Church Anglicans. But it is false, theoretically, to take a single axis and categorize all distinctions entirely along that line. If one felt that these issues were being raised to clarify the complex facets of beliefs, viewed from different perspectives or vantage points, all this would be legitimate. But one senses that this is not a debate but a desire to discredit. And that is where it becomes invidious.

Three, there is the fact that the formulations of many conservative intellectuals are increasingly couched in ideological terms. Ideology is reification, a frozen mimicry of reality, a hypostatization of terms which gives false life to categories. One reads, increasingly, (in capitalized letters), of The Media, The Liberals, The Universities, and then such assertions as "The Media are favorable to the Soviet Union" or "The Liberals are unpatriotic." In some ways this reification is the most disturbing of all. Not only is it a debasement of language, but it is the formulation of issues in combat terms. (Lenin once described all politics as *Kto-Kvo,* or "who-whom.") And there is no middle ground. At the extreme, this leads to the reduction of beliefs to motives, and the denial of legitimacy to one's opponents.

Four, underneath much of this fanfaronade is often an attitude of self-righteousness and rectitude. This shriving attitude has become characteristic of *Contentions,* the monthly newsletter of the Committee for a Free World. If one reads the newsletter to find out who are the enemies of the free world, it is astonishing to read attacks on Michael Walzer for proposing some rules for equality, or on Irving Howe for his memoirs. Walzer's and Howe's views may deserve criticism; but as enemies of the free world? Sometimes it is hard to distinguish the Committee for a Free World from the Watch

---

by George McGovern and championed by *The New Republic.* What many neoconservatives do not wish to admit (or even understand) is that they have largely carried the battle of ideas of the 1970s. But to admit that is to "lose" an enemy; and in *ideological* politics, one never loses an enemy but reincarnates him in different guises in order to maintain one's original momentum.

and Ward Society, since both seem to have the same zealot's conceptions of morality and vice.

The strength of neoconservatism had been its critique of the simplicities of liberalism and of utopian illusions. But if one seeks today for some consistent presentation of a conservative anchorage or standpoint, one finds incoherence. On the one hand, William Barrett and Hilton Kramer defend modernity and modernism. At the deutero-symposium of *Our Country and Our Culture*, held by the Committee for the Free World in February 1983, William Barrett declared: "What the artist is against is the spirit of modernity as such. . . . And what the artist secretly, or otherwise, hankers after is the society before 1789 . . ." (A strange statement, considering the infatuation of the Bauhaus [Gropius, Moholy-Nagy and Mies Van der Rohe] with technology, or the geometric rationality of de Stijl, Mondrian, the constructivism of Gabo and Pevsner, or the modernity exemplified by Malevich, Tatlin, and El Lissitsky which they identified with the Russian Revolution. And I thought it was de Maistre and his hangman who hankered after "religion, myth and tradition" and the *douceur de vivre* before 1789.) For Kramer, modernism is the great expression of the features of high capitalism. And the advent of postmodernism, the Tom Wolfe-like celebration of the features of representation, or Philip Johnson's architectural eclecticism, and other artifacts of bourgeois taste, is cultural rubbish.

Whatever the historical veracity of these views, (for Trilling and myself, modernism has been part of the adversary culture), the salient fact is that both men are unabashedly defending the serious view of high culture and an elite view of the arts. But against whom? The curious fact is that those who unabashedly proclaim the contrary *populist* view of art and politics are their fellow-conservatives. There is Edward Banfield's egregious defense of the market principle in culture (which Kramer rightly denounced), and the generalized adoption of a populist stance by Irving Kristol as a logical extension of the "common sense" of the people against the elite and the professionals, and of the notion that the market should be the arbiter of taste and preference.

Perhaps the most startling paradox of contemporary politics is the unvarnished victory of "populism" as a political doctrine, embraced by both Left and Right. In the progressive tradition, populism was the hallmark of agrarian radicalism, the embattled defense

of the little man against Wall Street, the bankers and the railroads, a
view that prevailed until demolished in large part by the work of
Richard Hofstadter, who demonstrated the soured rancor, the conspiratorial paranoid view, the anti-Semitism, the anti-intellectualism,
and the antimodernity in the spirit of populism. A dozen or so years
ago, Jack Newfield of the *Village Voice* wrote a book seeking to reclaim populism for the "Left." At the same time, George Wallace was
proclaiming a new populism for the Right. Today populism has become the code word for anti-establishment, anti-elite attitudes.
Richard Viguerie, the most vigorous spokesman and fund-raiser for
the New Right, writes a book called *The Establishment vs. The People.*
And Ronald Reagan's regional base, as Kevin Phillips has pointed
out—the Sun Belt, Farm Belt, and West—"coincides with the traditional populist and anti-elite component of U.S. political geography."

The philosophical conservatives ("the old conservative-core
movement of Burkean scholars, Austrian emigres, Catholic tradi-
tionalists and converts and recusant Communists," in Phillips' description) scorned the populists as political boors, radical extremists,
and demagogic disrupters of tradition, but as right-wing populism
gained ground, the original "spokesman" for that conservative
mélange, the *National Review,* slowly turned and endorsed the con-
servative-populist alliance, even though Chilton Williamson, Jr.,
the literary editor of the *National Review,* wrote an essay, entitled
"Country and Western Marxism," which stated that as populism
gained influence "the last gossamer threads that connect conservative politics to the conservative mind" were being snapped. The
curlicues of youth culture being what they are, we have today a new
generation of country western *and* rock-and-roll music that is politically conservative though sexually hanging loose!

What is striking today is that almost nobody defends elitism or
the establishment, or even the idea of having an establishment,
though in the traditional Bagehot view the establishment, the dignified part of society, was the guardian of morality. The populist view
is a distrust of authority and a rough-and-ready egalitarianism
which, in practice, often becomes a levelling spirit.

Kristol, a man profoundly aware of all these contradictions—we have argued them often enough—creates a strange hybrid
of "bourgeois populism," a mixed metaphor of Aristotelean measure
within the burgher's suit of clothes, which by prudence, reflection,

and moderation would dissolve the fevers and black humors of political choler. The difficulty is that the description is more fitting of
Lord Monboddo, the leader of the Common Sense School, than of
Ronald Reagan; of the Scottish Enlightenment than of American
politics.

If one accepts the theorem that the market should be the arbiter
of preferences, the inevitable question arises: how far? Here the
boundaries become blurred. Does one admit the rampant sale of
pornography because this is what sells best in the market? Kristol
would say no, because the extension of individual choice to such
matters, and to abortion, would transgress common morality. And
what of sexual acts between "consenting adults"? Again, freedom
becomes a problem. So, subtly, one passes over into moral tutelage
on virtue, while upholding populism on "economic" matters, a realm
where virtue has lost its loveliness.

The difficulties of establishing a "conservative" doctrine are
notorious. One current of conservative thought, being empiricist,
rejects the notion of a doctrine altogether, while another fixes its
gaze firmly on the *telos* of classical thought. Some are completely
libertarian, seeking to live only with a minimal state; others believe
in hierarchy and order and the instilling of family values in the
populace. But this is no different than the equally notorious difficulty of establishing a coherent doctrine of liberalism. The more
troubling problems arise when one crosses the divide from philosophy to politics.

Here I have to declare my interest. I was, with Irving Kristol,
the co-founder in 1965 of *The Public Interest*. The hope was to tran-
scend ideology through reasoned public debate and the inquiry into
knowledge. "Knowing what one is talking about,'" the opening
statement declared, "is a deceptively simple phrase that is pregnant
with larger implications. . . .we must admit—or, if you wish, assert—that such an emphasis is not easily reconcilable with a prior
commitment to an ideology, whether it be liberal, conservative or
radical."

For Kristol, today, all politics is ideological, and the issue as to
"who owns the future" is which ideology we will be governed by.* As
he wrote in the 1983 preface to his *Reflections*, "Neo-conservatism has
the kind of ideological self-consciousness and self-assurance—most
of its original spokesmen, after all, had migrated from the Left—and
even ideological boldness which has hitherto been regarded as the
legitimate (indeed exclusive) property of the Left." For Kristol,

understandably, politics maintains a primacy over economics. But what happens when ideology becomes the battering ram of politics? And what happens to a society when one begins to acquiesce in a *Weltanschauung* of "who-whom"?

I have not dealt with foreign policy, even though this is a highly charged issue within the intellectual world today. As Kristol wrote in 1967: ". . . it is the peculiarity of foreign policy that it is the area of public life in which ideology flounders most dramatically. Thus while it is possible — if not necessarily fruitful — to organize the political writings of the past three hundred years along a spectrum ranging from the ideological Left to the ideological Right, no such arrangement is conceivable for writings on foreign policy. There is no great radical text on the conduct of foreign policy — and no great conservative text either. What texts there are . . . are used indifferently by all parties as circumstance allows."

The liberal doctrine — using liberal in the historically-rooted sense of the term — believed in the "non-intervention" of the state because of its desire to reduce the role of *politics* in all areas of life, from free enterprise within to free trade without. Yet Hobbes, also a liberal, in his reduction of society to the individual as the relevant social unit, felt that the political role of sovereignty had to be paramount, lest the civil society be a war of each against all and all against each, the logic of which would lead, in an era of international interdependence, to a world state. But when in the political world, the idea of national interest becomes paramount and legitimate (even with Kant), the assessment of an enemy becomes primarily not an ideological, but an empirical matter. (Is Communist China today an "evil empire" or "totalitarian"?) Perhaps the most thoroughgoing realist theorist of international affairs, Hans Morgenthau, opposed the United States role in the Vietnam War because of the

---

*Since I believe that friendship is more important than ideology, I resigned as co-editor of *The Public Interest* in 1973, and from the publications committee in 1982. As Kristol wrote about our early years at the City College of New York forty-five years ago: "Daniel Bell . . . was that rarity of the 1930s: an honest-to-goodness social-democratic intellectual who believed in 'mixed economy,' a two-party system based on the British model, and other liberal heresies. . . . Over the years, his political views have probably changed less than the rest of us, with the result that, whereas his former classmates used to criticize him from the Left, they now criticize him from all points of the compass."

disproportionate use of means to the ends. Norman Podhoretz, in his retroactive endorsement of the American role, does so because he is a moralist. Yet does moralism lead inevitably to a "hard policy"? After all, Woodrow Wilson was a moralist. Yet I suppose it does if one is a "hard moralist." Irving Kristol, as a neoconservative, has retreated from the idea of "prudential politics," in an ideological world. Yet (not so surprisingly perhaps, because he is, by temperament, a sober man), in foreign affairs he has espoused a "realist" policy of prudence, going so far, even, as to call for the renunciation of the use of nuclear arms in a first strike.

I would not wish to repeat, in this catalogue of intellectual misprision, the error I have accused some of the neoconservatives of making, of seeing them as one unitary movement organized in combat posture. There are large differences among them in tone, from the urbanity of *The Public Interest* to the relentless combativeness of *Commentary*, as well as in point of view. My complaint, addressed as much in the past to liberal and Left intellectuals, is (philosophical differences apart) about conduct, the decline of civility (which conservatives presumably would embody) and the violations of what years ago Sidney Hook called "the ethics of controversy." These are matters not just of temper and tone, of manners and *moeurs;* in a fragile society, they are central to the nature of political discourse.

*   *   *

The reprise of the *Partisan Review* symposium has shown that not only have the old political categories atrophied, but the old partisan distinctions have gone askew. The serious or academic literary culture in the country, now that it has exhausted the theme of alienation, repeats in its dismembered new novels the jagged *nouveau romans* of French yesteryears or the arid deconstruction of the infinite regress of meanings. The polity is fragmenting, with few persons who stridently promote the claims of rights (in legal theory as well as social practice) accepting or even discussing the equal claims of obligations, and an administration which tells a people not to trust government.

The death of socialism, as I wrote previously in these pages, is the most tragic political fact of the twentieth century, and those who still mouth phrases about strategies for revolutionary change rarely, if ever, match that utopian ideal with the brutal consequences that have followed everywhere in its wake. The free world, without quotation marks and apologies, is a meaningful term if we accept, as the criterion of freedom, the simple idea stated (but never observed) in the preamble to the United Nations Declaration of Human Rights: that a person has the right to leave a country he or she does not like.

We need a new public philosophy, rooted in liberalism, a liberalism which has the "negative capability" of not reaching for closure on all issues. The "single" vision of liberalism is its distinction of realms, the separation of the public from the private, and the effort to set forth relevant rules of law and morality, merit and allocative principles of resources, appropriate to each. What undergirds such a pluralism is not any unbounded individualism, with its denial of community, or a rhetorical egalitarianism which ends in the division of society by group attributes, but the idea of "republican virtue," the hope of Montesquieu and Tocqueville (out of a strange Machiavellian lineage) that a society could be maintained by constitutionalism, comity, and civil discourse. (For Montesquieu, republican virtue was love of one's country; in a democratic society, one needed to emphasize frugality and equality. For Tocqueville, "In America . . . it is not that disinterestedness is great, but that interest is well understood. . . .") The exact balance of these principles is where the philosophical liberal-conservative debate would have to join issue.

In the end is our beginning, and I close with two propositions: this *is* our country and our culture; and one can be a critic of one's country without being an enemy of its promises.

Daniel Bell is Henry Ford II Professor of Social Science at Harvard University. A new edition of his book The End of Ideology *will be published by Harvard University Press.*

Peter Berger

ROBERT MUSIL AND THE SALVAGE
OF THE SELF

To have a self is an essential human quality across all the differences of history and cultures. Yet each age and each society modifies this anthropologically constant figure, to give birth to "Hellenic man," or to the "Chinese mind," or to *homo hierarchicus,* and so on. In each of these cases, a prime analytic problem is the delineation between that underlying self, which all human beings have always possessed, and the historically specific self that is the construction of an age and a society.

A good case can be made that literature, and especially the specifically modern form of literature that is the novel, may well offer the best guide to the delineation of modern Western individuality. This, obviously, is not the place to make that case. But one example from the argument can be explored — an example important and persuasive enough to make one optimistic about the outcome of a more comprehensive demonstration. The example is that of Robert Musil (1880–1942), the Austrian novelist whose work is slowly winning recognition. Indeed, Musil's major novel, *Der Mann ohne Eigenschaften (The Man without Qualities)*, on which he worked for some twenty years and left unfinished at his death, has as one of its explicit central themes the question of the modern self, a question to which Musil brought not only his great gifts as a writer but also his background (probably unique in modern Western literature) as a professional philosopher.

Like Ulrich, the protagonist of *The Man without Qualities*, Musil in his youth was a man of shifting careers. Brought up in a military school (immortalized in his first novel, *Young Toerless*), Musil became an officer in the Austro-Hungarian army, strongly disliked this way of life (at least for himself — he always retained a lingering respect for it), and resigned his commission. He went to study engineering at the technical university in Bruenn (today's Brno, in Czechoslovakia), where his father was a professor. But engineering did not suit him

Editor's Note: This essay was first presented at a conference at the East-West Center in Honolulu, Hawaii, August 1984.

either. And so, again after successful graduation, Musil went to Berlin to study philosophy, mathematics, and experimental psychology. He obtained his doctorate, with a dissertation on the Austrian philosopher Ernst Mach (often viewed as one of the fathers of the Vienna School and of neopositivism generally — curiously, Mach inspired Lenin to write his only philosophical treatise). Only then did Musil decide to devote himself entirely to writing. Until the end of his life, he wrote under mostly penurious circumstances as a refugee from Nazism in Geneva, the town (as he was very conscious of) that brought forth Jean-Jacques Rousseau, father of modern subjectivism, and that in the 1930s and 1940s was marked already, by the abstract internationalism that characterizes it today — a place of hotels full of strangers with indeterminate nationalities.

During his years in Berlin, and in order to be helpful to a friend who experimented in optical perception, Musil invented a laboratory gadget that he patented under the name "*Variationskreisel*," or "variation wheel" (it was apparently designed to experiment with the perception of colors, and Musil hoped, wrongly, that he would make money on it). The name would fit perfectly the structure of Musil's major novel, which contains an ever-shifting kaleidoscope of social worlds, roles and personalities, ideas and world views; indeed, a good argument has been made by Goetz Mueller to the effect that Musil intended the novel to be a comprehensive critique of existing ideologies. The subject of Musil's doctoral dissertation is equally relevant to the novel. One of Mach's most influential propositions was that the classical (especially the Cartesian) notion of the self can no longer be maintained — the proposition of the "non-salvagable self" (*das unrettbare Ich*). *The Man without Qualities* is one extended effort at salvage.

The action of the novel occurs within the space of one year, from August 1913 to August 1914, ending with the outbreak of World War I. Ulrich, the protagonist, is a man in his early thirties, a mathematician who interrupts a successful career abroad to return to Austria for a year. He intends to take a year's "vacation from life," as he calls it, in order to get to the bottom of a vague feeling of dissatisfaction with his life and to discover how he can best apply his considerable talents. More or less by accident he becomes involved with a patriotic project (called the *Parallelaktion,* because it is initiated in response to a similar undertaking in Germany) designed to prepare the celebration, in 1918, of the seventieth anniversary of the coronation of the Emperor Franz-Joseph. On this occasion the true meaning of the Austro-Hungarian state is to be proclaimed to the world, and the work of the project is to figure out just what that meaning is. The reader, of course, is aware of the ironic fact that the year 1918 was to see not the proclamation of the true meaning of Austria-Hungary but its cataclysmic destruction. Later in the year Ulrich's father (a professor of law in a provincial university) dies, and on that occasion Ulrich is reunited with his estranged sister Agathe. The two siblings decide to live together in Vienna in order to pursue the mystical quest for "the other condition" to which both have become committed. The posthumous materials of the novel allow no certain conclusion as to whether Musil intended this quest to succeed or fail.

Ulrich (like Musil) is convinced that one cannot acquire the perspective of modern science and go on looking at the world as one previously had. What is more, no solution to the problems of human life (political, moral, even religious) that ignores the scientific perspective is tenable. The opening paragraph of the novel gives the precise weather report for Europe, with all the antiseptic language of meteorology, ironically ending with the summation that it was a beautiful August day of the year 1913. The tension between scientific exactitude and the wealth of subjective emotional meanings implied in the last sentence could not be more graphically expressed. In the text, the last sentence is half-apologetically introduced with the statement that it is "somewhat old-fashioned." Yet virtually everything in human life that has subjective value can be so described; indeed the self, or rather the idea we have of it, is "somewhat old-fashioned." One might put the question, without violating Musil's intention, whether a good meteorologist can actually have a self or not.

The definition of the scientific method (Ulrich, incidentally, endlessly explains all this to Agathe and to various other interlocutors) is that reality is taken apart into component parts which are then perceived as interacting in causal chains. In other words, what was once perceived as a whole now comes to be perceived as a system of variables. This same process of disintegration applies to the self. Put differently, it becomes more and more difficult to see the self as the center of the individual's actions. Instead, these actions come to be perceived as events that happen to the individual, separate from himself, explainable in terms of both external (social) and internal (organic and psychic) causes. The Cartesian self, which was capable of pronouncing *"cogito ergo sum,"* is dissolved in a Machian flux of objectivities. Modern subjectivity, as it were, eviscerates itself.

This perception is sharply developed with two characters in the novel, one insane to begin with, the other in the process of going insane. The first character is Moosbrugger, a demented simpleton who is on trial for the apparently senseless murder of a prostitute and in whose fate Ulrich develops a passing interest. (It may be remarked that Musil's lengthy descriptions of Moosbrugger's perceptions of himself and of the world are masterpieces of clinical imagination. Moosbrugger is a simple, friendly man, liked by everyone (including his jailers), who suddenly erupts into homicidal frenzy. Who is the true Moosbrugger and what motivates him? The lawyers at his trial, the consulting psychiatrists, and Ulrich must all ask this question. At his trial the court tries hard to understand him as an acting person. The court has no other option, since it must determine whether, under the law, Moosbrugger can be held accountable for his actions (it so happens that Ulrich's father wrote his *magnum opus* on the concept of accountability in the legal thought of Pufendorf). But these efforts at understanding Moosbrugger as an acting person are in total contrast with Moosbrugger's self-experience, in which everything, including his own actions, just happens to him and in which he remains "eternally innocent." The main reason why Ulrich is interested in this case is his strong suspicion that allegedly normal people are really not very different from Moosbrugger in this self-experience. Perhaps there is no "true" Moosbrugger — and no "true" Ulrich either.

The other character is Clarisse, wife of an old friend of Ulrich's, a brilliantly gifted musician, who is also strongly drawn to Moosbrugger (she wants to liberate him from prison because she senses that he is musical) and who eventually descends into madness herself. On one occasion Clarisse visits a mental hospital in which Moosbrugger is being examined. The narrator observes that many people are afraid of madness because it would mean losing themselves — madness, that is, reminds even normal people of the precariousness of what they cherish as their self. One of the patients salutes Clarisse as the seventh son of the Emperor and stubbornly refuses to accept her denial. In rising panic she discovers that she is quite prepared to believe him, and she and her companions leave the hospital without having seen Moosbrugger. The question here is a variation of the earlier one: Who is the true Clarisse and why is she going mad?

In this perspective, madness is a liberating simplification, because the madman is paradoxically much more certain of who he is than the allegedly sane individual. The quest for the true nature of things is replicated throughout the earlier part of the novel by the patriotic project. The question here, of course, is: What is the true Austria? The chairman of the project, Count Leinsdorf, a deeply pious and at the same time deeply skeptical aristocrat, is convinced that everything and everyone has a true nature; he is also convinced that, intuitively, he knows what these true entities are. Resting in this (certainly very "old-fashioned") certitude, he can afford to preside over a committee of quarrelling intellectuals, each of whom has a different view of reality. He does not expect any interesting insights from this ideological pandemonium; his approach to the enterprise is purely tactical and political. Even if his certitude is finally based on illusion, Musil conveys the impression that Leinsdorf is a lucky man. (So, incidentally, is the representative of the war ministry, General Stumm von Bordwehr, a character drawn by Musil with very great sympathy.) But the order of the state is about to disintegrate as the order of the self has disintegrated in Moosbrugger and Clarisse, and the coming war will be a collective madness — infinitely more murderous than Moosbrugger's and yet, at least initially, experienced as a great liberation (one of the plans for the novel was to end it with a description of the enormous enthusiasm with which the outbreak of war was greeted in Austria as in the other belligerent countries on both sides).

The idea that the self is some sort of central entity, and that every individual therefore has a "true" self, is an illusion. Perhaps an individual may, through great effort, acquire such a center; but it does not exist as a given of human nature. Rather, the self is a "hole" which must somehow be "filled," both by oneself and by others. This reciprocal enterprise of endowing individuals with definable identities is described especially in the relationship between Ulrich and Agathe (again with great psychological precision, which is strongly reminiscent of George Herbert Mead's description of the social genesis of the self). In practice, for most people, the best way to "fill" this "hole" is by means of action (in Meadian terms, the individual performs his socially assigned roles, and the aggregate of these roles constitutes what he "is"). For those people who fancy themselves to have a "soul" (intellectuals, poets, those with a sense for the "finer things"), there is another method. In the words of a chapter heading, "ideals and morality are the best means to fill the big hole that one calls soul." The implication, of course, is that it matters little *which* ideas or *which* morality are employed to this end.

Early on in his participation in the patriotic project, Ulrich suggests that there ought to be "a general secretariat for exactitude and soul," to provide guidance for people in the quandary of combining these two ideas. One surmises that this suggestion for a sort of ministry of general psychotherapy is only half-facetious. The intellectuals associated with the project discuss the Marxist and psychoanalytical theories about the true foundation of human action, that substructure *(Unterbau)* which, if one only knew what it was, would explain everything. But, of course, they all disagree, leading Leinsdorf to complain about the unreliability of the people in the superstructure—a statement wonderfully summarizing his disdain for the intellectuals, his misunderstanding of the theories at issue, and his unshakable confidence in the reliability of the old order. Clearly, it would not be easy to carry out Ulrich's suggestion.

The novel is full of ruminations about the problem of order—or, more accurately, the problem of ordering. The patriotic project is to legitimate the order of the state. Moosbrugger understands his acts of violence as desperate attempts to restore order to his world (at one point he himself is described as "an escaped parable of order"). The only order that Clarisse knows is that of music, and Ulrich finds solace in the cool order of mathematics. In one conversation Ulrich, only half-ironically, explains to General Stumm that the military is the most spiritual of all institutions, because spirit is order, and who can deny that the military is the most orderly institution, down to the exact spaces between the buttons on an officer's tunic? In the same way, there are various ways of trying to order the self, to somehow fixate it in a way that makes sense. The law (to which Ulrich's father has devoted his life) is the most important "official" agency for this ordering of the self. In one episode Ulrich is caught in a political altercation on the street and is briefly arrested. During his interrogation at a police station, where he is asked about his age, profession, and the like, with no regard for all the allegedly "finer" aspects of his existence, Ulrich experiences a "statistical disenchantment" of his person—and, strangely (or, in Musil's perspective, not so strangely), finds a certain satisfaction in this experience. Psychiatry, using categories different from, even contradictory to, those of the law, also seeks to impose some sort of order on the self. All these efforts, though, are ultimately illusionary. They are, in Musil's term, "utopian"—literally nowhere. The self is and remains an unfillable "hole." Yet there also remains the profound urge, and perhaps the possibility, of finding a self that will be (precisely) "reliable." The quest for "the other condition," whatever its religious or metaphysical components, is also the quest for a coherent, ontologically real self. Musil may have been unsure to the end whether that quest was not "utopian" too, but evidently he was unwilling to conclude that it was. In any case, if such a "true" self was possible, it would not be a given, a *datum,* but rather something to be attained, achieved as the result of an enormously difficult effort.

Possibly the self always has been a "hole," but in earlier times people were less aware of this; or perhaps this species of what could be called *Lochmensch (homo lacuna?)* is an anthropological innovation of the modern age. Be this as it may, the title of the novel deliberately and self-consciously points to what Musil understood to be a central feature of modern man. Ulrich is first characterized as "a man without qualities" by Walter, Clarisse's husband, who is very critical of this aspect of his old friend. Walter feels that this is a new type of human being created by our age; this type can now be seen in millions of cases. Walter goes on to say that people today (with the exception of Catholic clergy) no longer look like what they are. Ulrich is supposed to be a mathematician. But what does a mathematician look like? At best, he looks generally intelligent, but this does not express any particular content. Ulrich seems to have many qualities, but really he has none. "Nothing is firm for him," everything may be changed again, and he has no idea what he is as a whole. (To which description Clarisse replies, to Walter's intense irritation, that this is precisely what she likes about Ulrich.) It follows from this that, in Musil's words, the man without qualities is *ipso facto* the man of *possibilities.* In other words, the modern self is characterized by its open-endedness, its being-in-process — or, one might venture, by its high degree of freedom. That freedom (if that is what it should be called) is not necessarily pleasing in actual experience; on the contrary, it can be felt as a burden — as it is felt by Ulrich.

In a later passage, the man without qualities is described as a man whose qualities have somehow become independent of him. Indeed, it seems as if these qualities have more relations with each other than with him. Events just follow each other, as *B* follows *A,* surprising the alleged actor as much or even more than those watching him. This was not always so. In the past, a person was much more certain of himself. To be sure, external dangers may have been

greater — natural disasters, disease and war — but the individual belonged to himself in a much clearer way. These observations could
all be subsumed under the proposition of Arnold Gehlen that ancient
man had "character," while modern man has "personality." The difference is that, paradoxically, the sociological theorist Gehlen
deplored this change, while Musil, the philosopher-turned-*Dichter,*
welcomed it, despite all the difficulties it created, as an advance in
human self-consciousness.

If Ulrich is a man without qualities, Austria-Hungary (or
Kakania, as Musil calls it) may be called a nation without qualities.
The linguistic confusion underlying Austro-Hungarian institutions
reflects the uncertainty regarding the true nature of the monarchy.
In a long satirical excursus, a chapter aptly entitled "A State Which
Perished Because of a Speech Defect," Musil elaborates this point.
The Hungarian half of the monarchy had a clear national identity,
even if this had to be imposed coercively by the Magyars on their
various Slavic subject populations (that imposition too, of course,
failed in the end). But the Austrian half did not even have a name for
itself. Its official name was the "Kingdoms and Lands Represented
in the Imperial Parliament." How could anyone identify himself
with such a designation? Yet, as Leinsdorf and General Stumm
knew very well, there was such a thing as Austrian patriotism — a
curious mixture of the archaic (this empire, after all, had been in existence for nearly a millennium) and the ultramodern (a nation-state
without a nation, faithfully reflecting the "hole" character of modern
man). The patriotic project is designed to remedy the "speech defect"
by producing the "true Austrian idea." Leinsdorf is quite suspicious
of such a project, though he wants to make use of it politically. He
suspects that too much reflection on the nature of the state cannot
help but subvert its taken-for-granted order. He is right, of course;
political loyalty based upon reflection on an idea is, by definition,
fragile and fugitive (Edmund Burke would certainly have sympa-
thized with Leinsdorf). Like all real conservatives, Leinsdorf relies
on intuitive certainties rather than intellectual conclusions. His
tragedy (and that of Austria-Hungary) is that modern man does not
come easily to intuitive certainties; more precisely, he dismantles, by
way of reflection, those certainties with which he had to begin.
Helmut Schelsky has called this modern propensity "permanent re-
flectiveness" *(Dauerreflektion);* it is as subversive of the political order
("critical consciousness-raising") as, in the mode of modern psychology, it is subversive of the order of the self. Thus the patriotic

project is a *Parallelaktion* in an additional sense; its ideological self-evisceration is parallel to Ulrich's mathematical-scientific disaggregation of the Cartesian self. In Meadian social psychology it is evident that an individual is more real to others than he is to himself — at least, real in the sense of being perceived as a coherent, comprehensible entity. Ironically, it is a foreigner, the Prussian business tycoon and would-be great thinker Arnheim, who seems to have a better grasp of "the Austrian idea" than the native intellectuals.

The political problem of the modern world is that all systems of order are put in question. The geometrically parallel problem of modern personality is that all its systems of order become equally questionable. There is one grand solution to these twin problems, which is the solution of collectivism. In the novel it is represented mainly by the figure of Hans Sepp, a sort of proto-Nazi (who, ironically, is the boyfriend of the Jewish girl Gerda, with whom Ulrich also has a brief and unsatisfactory affair). Sepp and his group of young German nationalists despise Austria-Hungary (later, they try to disrupt the patriotic project which they view as a Slavic plot); they are anti-Semitic because of the alleged intellectualism of the Jews; and Sepp particularly dislikes Ulrich because of his skeptical questioning of every "wholesome" idea. Sepp and his friends find a seemingly reliable collective identity in what they call "national feeling," which Musil contemptuously describes as "that merging of their perpetually quarreling selves in a dreamed unity." But they are not the only ones to find illusionary solace in a "dreamed unity" *(ertraeumte Einigkeit)* of collective solidarity. In Musil's posthumous materials a minor role is played by a militant socialist, Schmeisser (the German word denotes a machine-pistol), whom Musil describes with equal contempt. Ulrich and Agathe converse in pejorative terms about the false collective identity bestowed by institutional religion as well. And, most important of all, the entire novel moves toward that sublime eruption of "dreamed unity," the ultimate collective madness, which greets the outbreak of war.

The disaggregated modern self is a plural self. The qualities of the person detach themselves from him and become mere appendages of his variable social roles. Early in the novel it is stated that today every individual, not just Ulrich, has at least nine characters — linked consecutively to his vocation, nation, state, class, geographical context, sexuality, consciousness, unconscious mind, and, perhaps, his private life (whatever that means as an additional category) — and, somehow, he must juggle all these characters from day to day. Thus, an individual may be a professor, a Czech, a subject of Austria-Hungary, a person of petty-bourgeois antecedents, a lecher, a moralist with an immoralist libido, and on top of that, perhaps, someone with a profound appreciation of art. It is not always easy to keep in motion this menagerie of discrete selves. But then there is also a tenth character, which Musil describes as "the passive fantasy of unfilled spaces" ("die passive Phantasie unausgefuellter Raeume"). This is the human capacity for "utopian" dreams; all of these dreams, whatever their ideational or normative content, are finally dreams of a self restored to unity, to "wholeness."

One wonders how Musil would have thought of these matters if, instead of being reared on Mach, he had been familiar with Meadian social psychology and its ramifications in the sociology of knowledge. Be this as it may, Musil is aware, though the point is not elaborated much, that the plural self corresponds to a plural social world. Such a world means that an individual must choose. Put differently, the world presents itself to the individual, not as taken-for-granted destiny (the prototypical case through most of history), but rather as specific sets of options. This begins with the most mundane areas of everyday life. When Ulrich acquires a house in Vienna (which later becomes the locale of his mystical experimentation with Agathe), he faces the problem of how to decorate it. He cannot decide on a style. So he decides to leave the choice to his furniture suppliers, as a result of which the house becomes a random and incongruous collection of styles. Here too, in trivial consumer options, the individual hovers between a near-infinity of possibilities.

Yet, upon closer inspection, these mundane options are really not trivial at all. We owe to Ernst Bloch the philosophical concept of "accommodating oneself in the world" (sich in der Welt einrichten) — in ordinary German, the word "accommodating" refers to the acquisition of furniture. The individual furnishes his life as he furnishes his house, and very often the latter furniture symbolizes the former. In Ulrich's case, clearly, the disorder of his lodgings is a visible sign of the invisible disorder of his mind. There are, of course, individuals who acquire a "style." They now pretend to superior good taste, to always knowing the right object for the right place, the right gesture for the right occasion. However, these patterns of "wholeness" are social or ideological artifacts. They are, in principle, arbitrary and therefore subject to revision; in the terminology of Alfred Schutz, what we have here are styles "until further notice." By the same token, such styles are "utopian."

The intellectuals in the patriotic project in Musil's novel ac-

quire ideas as Ulrich acquired furniture. Here too there is a be-
wildering array of choices. Nothing is certain any longer, to be taken
for granted. In one of the most hilarious passages in the novel, General Stumm recounts how he tried to put some order into this
ideological chaos. Good staff officer that he is, he employs a small
platoon of subordinates to draw up a battle plan of ideas. Dominant
ideas are shown as advancing armies, there are strategic hillocks of
concepts, skirmishes are fought between categorial regiments.
Despite these efforts, entered on the map with multicolored pencils
(as Stumm learned to do in staff college), an order fails to material-
ize. The lines between the ideational armies keep shifting, the intellectual generals keep stealing weapons from their opponents and
use them to attack their own rear, important categories suddenly
disappear, and so on. The general has a deep respect for the life of
the mind, but he cannot suppress the mounting suspicion that
perhaps the entire battlefield is a sham. He is not so much bothered
by the fact that everyone in Diotima's *salon* tells him something different. But, as he explains to Ulrich (who used to be an officer and
must therefore have some sense of order), he is troubled by the feeling that the longer he listens to these intellectuals the more they all
sound alike. It follows that, in the end, the choice of ideas and
moralities is as random as the choice of decorating styles.

The social world allows the individual to choose different careers. Thus Ulrich is, in succession, an officer, a mathematician,
and a religio-psychological experimenter. With each possible career
go specific roles — and, of course, specific ideas and moralities. Needless to say, this Musilian insight could be vastly elaborated with the
use of categories derived from social psychology and the sociology of
knowledge. A perfect case of such an analysis of plural roles, with all
the appropriate ideational and moral attachments, would be the case
of Bonadea, with whom Ulrich has an affair early in the novel.
Bonadea is both *une brave bourgeoise,* proper wife and mother, and a
wildly roaming nymphomaniac. Somehow she manages to keep both
of these discrete social worlds going and segregated from each other.
She does feel some unease about this (manifested in very boring self-
accusations after each time she has gone to bed with Ulrich), and she
has the "utopian" fantasy that somehow, someday, she will integrate
the discrepant sides of her being into some sort of "whole." She
believes (mistakenly, it turns out) that Diotima commands this
"mystery of wholeness," and, in quest of salvation from herself, she
insinuates herself into the patriotic project. But then, to her great

shock, she discovers that Diotima is having an affair with Arnheim. The high cult of "wholeness" and soul is disclosed to be not very different from the little furtive games of adultery that Bonadea knows all too well. Another "utopia" collapses.

Musil's *The Man without Qualities* is an extraordinarily rich source of insight into the modern self. The insights are not comforting. The self, as traditionally defined in Western civilization (minimally since Descartes) and as still taken for granted in everyday life as well as in the solemn fictions of the law, is disclosed to be an illusion. At its core is a sort of emptiness (strikingly reminiscent of the classical Buddhist conception of *shunyata*). This is what scientific analysis suggests, but the disturbing news is penetrating beyond the small world of scientists. More and more people are uncertain as to who they are, what their motives are or should be, and they are also uncertain as to the true identities and motives of even their most intimate associates. Consequently, there is the pervasive "utopia of the motivated life," as Musil calls it — that is, the dream of a restored unity of self, action, and reality. But all projects to bring this about, individually or collectively, are equally uncertain; to repeat Count Leinsdorf's biting comment, all these people in the superstructure are unreliable — be they philosophers, psychologists, political ideologists (of whatever stripe), or poets. There are still some people walking around in modern society who represent an older mode of being, a traditional "wholeness." Perhaps they are lucky and to be envied. But for those who have drunk of the fountain of modern relativism there does not appear to be a way back. Reactionary restorations are illusionary. So are innovative, "progressive" constructions of "wholeness"; the ultranationalist Sepp and the socialist Schmeisser are mirror images of each other. And the constructions of "wholeness" based on individual eccentricity, in the mode of Clarisse, are likely to end in madness or crime.

Yet Musil is clearly not prepared to give up this utopia of self-realization. Within the logic of the novel, two avenues are left open. One is the skeptical, scientifically reflective, but nevertheless passionate endorsement of modern freedom. The other is the religious quest for the true self revealed in transcendence. There is a secular and a mystical Ulrich, and Musil leaves us in suspense as to which one will prevail at the end of the novel.

The posthumous chapters can be arranged differently. Adolf Frise, the editor of the standard edition, arranged them in such a way that Ulrich's experiment with "the other condition" fails (after a dramatic journey to Italy, during which he commits incest with Agathe); after this failure Ulrich returns, much sobered but unbroken, to the partial and insecure self-realization of ordinary life. The English translators of the novel have criticized this arrangement of the *Nachlass,* believing that Musil intended the novel to end with the so-called "holy conversations" between brother and sister, thus implying that the religio-mystical experiment had succeeded. A nonspecialist examining the Musil archives will incline to the view that Musil himself did not know which outcome to choose. He was clear about one point: There is no secular solution to the "mystery of wholeness." If there is a true self, it can only be revealed as true in a transcendent frame of reference. Alternatively, to paraphrase Dostoevsky, if God does not exist, any self is possible. The dilemma of modern man, but also his challenging opportunity, is that this alternative has become very sharply defined.

Peter Berger is a University Professor at Boston University. His latest book, with Brigitte Berger, is The War Over the Family, *published by Doubleday in 1983.*

Robert Brustein

THE THEATER OF METAPHOR

About twenty years ago, I wrote: "If politics is the art of the possible, art is the politics of the impossible." I was at the time too enraptured by the Latinate balance of the epigram to feel any

---

Editor's Note: A longer version of this essay was commissioned by the Tocqueville Forum of Wake Forest University for their recent series on "Politics and the Arts." It will be included in their book to be published this fall by University Press of America.

responsibility for explaining it. This essay is my tardy effort to face that task.

The relationship between politics and the arts in the theater has been a matter of contention ever since Thespis first broke ranks with the Chorus. The first to start these fevers roaring was Plato, who refused to admit the illusion-making dramatist, or any artist for that matter, through the portals of his ideal republic. Plato believed in a reality beyond the tangible or material, where an idea is more real than the physical object itself. Since a painting of a chair is an imitation of an already unreal object, it is even more distant from the truth; and an actor impersonating a character in the theater virtually obliterates reality altogether. For Plato, the dramatic artist is a fabricator and, hence, a menace to a republic which puts a premium on the faculty of truth-telling. (In less obdurate moments, Plato is willing to tolerate an art which holds up ethical models of behavior for humankind to imitate — what he called *ethos*. But nevertheless, he maintains that the artist is a serious threat to a utopian politics.)

Aristotle's *Poetics,* written not too long after Plato rejected the artist, may very well have been an effort to refute this argument. Rather than considering the dramatist a liar, Aristotle held that works of art, particularly tragedies, were among the highest forms of human activity; far from masking reality, they had the capacity to bring us even closer to the truth than politics or philosophy. It is significant that, in listing the elements of tragic writing, Aristotle found *mythos* — variously translated as plot or fable or action — to be preeminent, while *ethos,* or character, he placed second in order of importance. Behind these was *dianoia* — what a character says about the course to be pursued, what a person believes, his social morality — which is sometimes translated as "politics" or "thought."

In short, Aristotle considered the imagination to be not a source of fantasy or illusion, but rather the supreme human faculty, and imitation, which Plato scorned, to be an important mode of understanding. He didn't exclude politics from the drama but he believed that one's morality was of interest less for being right or wrong, than for the way it illuminated action and character. In this regard, Aristotle's concept of *hamartia* assumes a crucial importance in his tragic theory. Although sometimes translated as tragic flaw — medieval Christians appropriated the word to mean sin, suggesting a severe judgment on human morals and behavior — *hamartia* more accurately means tragic error, which is to say a mistake that brings on tragedy. We suffer tragedy not because of our character or beliefs but because we have broken some inexorable law of the universe—like sticking a wet finger in a live electrical socket.

The disagreement between Plato and Aristotle was whether the theater has importance as an instrument of moral and political action, or whether it is an imaginative experience for the purgation and exaltation *(katharsis)* of its audiences. Platonic theater is political theater, in the sense that it is intended to influence behavior, because it offers to resolve moral, social, even religious issues through ethical improvement and persuasion, and it embodies a precept which continues after the play is concluded. Theoretically, Platonic theater carries the seeds of its own extinction, since it will have no function once the Utopian state has arrived (a prospect that appalled such latter-day Aristoteleans as Nietszche who believed that imaginative experience is a compelling human need, that we have art so as not to perish from the truth).

Still, this "anti-theatrical prejudice," as Jonas Barish calls it in a book of that title, is the motif underlying the Platonic political view of the theater, and it dies hard. It can be detected even among some practicing dramatists in the modern age, where the conflict between the Aristotelean and Platonic, or aesthetic and utilitarian, views of the stage continues unabated. In Ibsen, the conflict is internalized, becoming the basis for his continuing quarrels with himself, not to mention persistent disagreements among his interpreters. For example, is *A Doll's House* Platonic or Aristotelean? What about *Ghosts*? Or *An Enemy of the People?*

Clearly, as the theater grows in intellectual sophistication, let alone moral authority, it assumes a greater burden of responsibility for solving the pressing questions of the day. Ibsen is deceptive because on the surface he seems to be embracing this responsibility. He has been claimed by both liberals and conservatives—as an advocate of the women's movement, a proponent of euthanasia, a supporter of companionate marriages, a firm believer in social responsibility. Doubtless, Ibsen was interested in these issues, but he continued to insist that his interest was artistic rather than political. Addressing the Norwegian League for Women's Rights, he decisively repudiated any conscious ideological intent: "I am not a member of the Women's Rights League," he said. "Whatever I have written has been written without any conscious thought of making propaganda. I have been more the poet and less the social philosopher than people seem generally inclined to believe. . . . True enough, it is desirable to solve the woman problem, along with all the others; but that has not been the whole purpose. My task has been the *description of humanity*."

This is the answer Ibsen gave to every group that tried to appropriate him for its cause and explains why he always appeared so inconsistent to his progressive followers. "I shall never agree," he wrote to one of them, "to making liberty synonymous with political liberty. What you call liberty, I call liberties; and what I call the struggle for liberty is nothing but the steady, vital growth and pursuit of the very conception of liberty. . . . The state must be abolished! In that revolution I will take part. Undermine the idea of the state; make willingness and spiritual kinship the only essentials for union—and you have the beginning of a liberty that is of some value. Changing one form of government for another is merely a matter of toying with various degrees of the same thing. Yes, my friend, the great thing is not to allow oneself to be frightened by the venerableness of institutions. The state has its roots in time; it will reach its height in time."

This is not a Platonist talking, but an anarchist who would blow up even the ideal republic in order to create breathing space and room for life. It is true that Ibsen occasionally becomes tendentious, even propagandistic, on behalf of his individualist philosophy—particularly in *An Enemy of the People*—but it is not long before he is announcing a contrary point of view lest he settle into a single fixed position. The only permanent structure that Ibsen can long tolerate is the structure of his own art, because only there can he accommodate the contradictions and antitheses that for him constitute the fabric of truth.

Anton Chekhov is even less of a Platonist than Ibsen because in his plays he seems to have virtually no formal beliefs of his own, and displays scant respect for the beliefs of his characters as well. Ibsen wrote indignantly after *Ghosts:* "They endeavor to make me responsible for the opinions which certain of my characters express," but compared to Chekhov, this impersonal dramatist almost seems like a ventriloquist: No one labored harder than Chekhov to keep the theater free from political imperatives and utilitarian demands. "To hell with the philosophy of the great of this world," he writes in an uncharacteristically rancorous mood. And even more pointedly: "I am not a liberal and not a conservative, not an evolutionist, nor a monk, nor indifferent to the world. I would like to be a free artist, and that is all."

"In my discussions with other writers," Chekhov writes in a letter of 1888, "I always insist that it is not the artist's business to answer narrowly specialized issues. . . . For specialized issues we have the specialist; it's their business to pass judgment about the peasant communes, the fate of capitalism, the damage of heavy drinking, boots, or women's ailments. As for the artist, he must pass judgment only about matters he can grasp. . . . Anyone who insists the artist's domain covers all the answers . . . has never written or has had no experience with images. . . . You are right in requiring from the artist a conscious attitude towards his work, but you confuse two aspects: *the answer to a problem and the correct presentation of a problem.* Only the second is an obligation for the artist."

Chekhov was said by his contemporaries to have had an ambiguous attitude towards what one of them called "the *burning questions* of the day," and he was proud that his characters were not created out of preconceived ideas or intellectual assumptions. This does not mean that he excluded social/political questions from his plays. The debates over the future that permeate *Three Sisters* were undoubtedly overheard by Chekhov in Moscow drawing rooms, and the original speeches of the revolutionary student Trofimov in *The Cherry Orchard* were said to be so inflammatory that the play was threatened with suppression until he agreed to modify them. On the other hand, these opinions are never the property of the playwright; they belong to the people who express them and exist, in Aristotelean fashion, to reveal character. In short, Chekhov introduced political, social, and philosophical discussions into his work, because this was the reality he was eager to present. But he was careful never to take sides or hint at solutions. As he put it in his favorite courtroom metaphor, "It is the duty of the judge to put the questions to the jury accurately, and it is for members of the jury to make up their minds, each according to his own taste."

Just as he tried to protect his characters from conventional moralistic interpretations of their behavior, so he tried to preserve their integrity as complicated human beings against narrow ideological interpretations of them as figures in a political chess game. Chekhov provided his characters with class roles, political convictions, and philosophic attitudes, but he never entirely defined them by these elements, even when they wished thus to define themselves. For Chekhov, the political animal and the suffering human often seem mutually incompatible.

It was because of their desire to protect the privacy of the individual from public impositions that both Ibsen and Chekhov adopted, in their art, a stance aloof from civic responsibilities. The concept of the "free artist," immune to political imperatives, ignoring any claims to become a mouthpiece for a movement or even a citizen of a state, was something they held in balance with a deep, abiding feeling for the human potential, a hatred of injustice, and a love of truth. Living in pre-revolutionary times, Chekhov and Ibsen were perhaps the last dramatists able to maintain a precious individualism and yet also deal with social reality.

The concept of the "free artist," however, was soon to find a more disembodied and fantastic expression, in the work of those poets, painters, novelists, and playwrights who sought to divorce themselves from the coarse reality of the modern industrial state. The idea animated the aesthetic movement of the late nineteenth century, perhaps the most extreme example we have of the separation of art from politics, if not from life. Villier de l'Isle Adam, the aesthete, announced: "As for living, our servants can do that for us"; Dada was devoted to an art of randomness and chance; and the symbolist playwrights (especially Maeterlinck) took refuge from life in a world of supernal unreality.

The advent of aestheticism was bound to stimulate an adversary reaction from playwrights with a strong political conscience. And, sure enough, the drama of the twentieth century became dominated by two figures—Bernard Shaw and Bertolt Brecht—who not only held a more or less Platonic view of the stage, but often scourged the Aristotelean tendencies of past and present writers.

Consider Shaw's attitude towards Shakespeare, a dramatist whose "romantic" theater of lies and dreams, as he called it, he wanted to replace with a theater of preachment and propaganda—"Plays for Puritans" was his significant subtitle. Calling himself an "artist-philosopher" rather than an artist, Shaw wished to expel all art which relied on "mere" feeling instead of thought and, through the agency of artist characters like Marchbanks and Dubedat, he ridiculed the aesthetic tendencies of those who used poetry or painting for "mere" self-expression, or who ignored the good of humanity while seeking the perfection of artistic forms. Platonist though he was, however, Shaw continually tried to find ways to include the artist in his ideal republic, if only by proving that the artist had utilitarian value. For at the same time that Shaw is a Platonic thinker, he is also an Aristotelean maker whose ideas are only one element, and not always the most important one, in the body of his dramatic work. William Archer first came upon Shaw in the British

Museum reading *Das Kapital* side by side with Wagner's *Ring,* and
though Shaw tried to justify Wagner's aestheticism by interpreting
The Ring as an allegory of the Industrial Revolution, the split in his
own nature between the ethical and aesthetic ideals of art was never
fully resolved.

Bertolt Brecht couldn't heal that split either, but not for want of
trying. Nobody in modern history worked harder to annihilate the
Aristotelean theater of feeling and replace it with a theater of didactic thought devoted to promoting political change. Brecht's struggle
against Nazism and his embrace of communism are the central
themes of his work from the early thirties until his death in the fifties,
and it is not inaccurate to say that he is the first dramatist to define
himself entirely in relation to modern totalitarianism. Having
chosen one tyranny over another, he spent his later years trying to
justify this decision to himself and others; but once having put his
poetic genius in thrall to an ideology, he rarely flinched from the
brutal consequences of his choice. In plays such as *The Measures
Taken,* for example, which demonstrate the necessity to sacrifice the
life of the individual to the demands of the Party, he managed to em-
barrass the Party with the inexorable logic of that dialectic; his
ideological writings are sometimes interpreted as among the most
virulent, if unwitting, indictments of the whole communist system
because of that logic.

Brecht's instinct for survival, coupled with his pride about being more practical and committed than the most cynical Party hacks,
sometimes makes his plays look like raw demonstrations of how the
end justifies the means. But even in his crudest ideological works,
there is a subtle and ironic dialectician quarrelling with the would-be
propagandist, a yogi arguing with the commissar. *The Good Woman of
Setzuan,* for example, is designed to show how a person can be virtuous in a capitalist society only by becoming schizophrenic, split-
ting off one's charitable impulses from the venal, ruthless necessity
to pursue wealth. But even in that work, Brecht manages to thwart
his own thrust, concluding the action not with a call to revolution
but with a characteristic note of irresolution. The three deaf gods,
who have come to earth to reinforce their conviction that the current
moral and social codes are perfectly compatible with the prevailing
economic system, witness ample evidence that justice and survival
are at odds, yet they ascend to heaven still firmly believing in the
status quo. "Should the world be changed?" they ask. "How? By
whom? The world should *not* be changed!" To which the battered,
anguished heroine can only murmur, "Help."

In short, while Shaw was able to imagine utopias, Brecht was
too honest to do more than suggest why they were necessary. As a
secret Aristotelean, a suppressed tragic writer, he was compelled to
examine the cruel exigencies of contemporary life, but his Platonic
impulses were not strong enough to let him indulge in fantasies of
the future. If Brecht was among the first to put his poetry at the service of the mass state, he was perhaps the last to find a channel —
using a strategy of simultaneous engagement and detachment — between the Scylla and Charybdis of art and politics. After Brecht, we
find the theater more openly divided between the utilitarians and the
aesthetes, between those who find an exclusively social-political
function for the theater, and those who largely deny all interest in
the public dimension.

Thus, in totalitarian countries, theater is used primarily as a
form of political consolidation, reinforcing the existing regime, or as
a covert form of subversion and resistance, while the theater of the
capitalist countries, despite occasional eruptions of political consciousness, grows increasingly private, limited largely to escapist,
domestic, psychological, even narcissistic subjects.

It is a generalization, of course, that admits of many exceptions
in the Western countries. I am happy to acknowledge them, though
few are particularly distinguished works. America in the thirties, for
example, produced a highly engaged political theater (Clifford Odets,
John Howard Lawson, the Federal Theatre, Theatre Union, etc.),
vestiges of which would appear during the postwar years, especially
in the drama of Arthur Miller, while the anarchic Living Theatre,
typifying the radical sixties in its Platonic scorn of imitation, tried to
break down barriers between stage and audience altogether. The
theater in Great Britain, from the time of the "angry young men" in
the late fifties until today, has featured a strong strain of radical consciousness, partly in reaction to the mainstream tradition of West
End drawing room comedies and seaside resort dramas, from the
plays of John Arden and John Osborne twenty years ago to the current work of David Hare, David Edgar, Howard Brenton, and Caryll
Churchill. And there is probably no more committed political writer
in the contemporary theater than the Marxist Italian farceur, Dario
Fo. Still, I believe that the Platonic and the Aristotelean approaches
to the stage have each grown more extreme, in response to the pressures and exigencies of the mass industrial state. Political theater has
tended to become either official propaganda, on behalf of the socialist present, or polemical preachment in support of a fancied Utopian
future, while the mainstream aesthetic theater has settled for those

specious and mindless products of what Brecht called "the bourgeois narcotics factory."

At present, then, we seem to be caught between a theater of ideology and a theater of quietism, the one devoted to exhortation and outrage, the other to bright if mindless entertainment. Is there no way for drama to assume a public dimension without developing a didactic form, or falling into that "grey exacting realism" which Camus identified as the official aesthetic of totalitarianism? How can the stage address such critical contemporary questions as injustice, inequality, inhumanity, war, and the threat of nuclear annihilation, not to mention the dwindling possibilities for freedom in the mass industrial state, while maintaining an individual style free of self-righteous melodrama? What is the dramatist's relationship to the political problems of his society, and how can his social responsibilities be combined with his own creative imperatives?

I believe there is a way for contemporary theater to preserve both poetry and political responsibility, to synthesize its Aristotelean and Platonic functions, and that is through the medium of metaphor. Dramatists are not equipped to solve problems — if they were, they would no longer be artists — but through imaginative metaphors they are certainly in a position to present them correctly. The advantage of metaphors is that they are suggestive rather than exact, reverberant rather than precise; they represent a poetic avenue to the truth. That metaphors describe rather than proscribe, preserves the autonomous nature of theater art; that they can permit a wider reality than domestic crises and marital woes, allows the theater artist to maintain his public function.

All great modern drama has been metaphorical, from Ibsen's metaphor of ghosts as a symbol of a rotting bourgeois social inheritance, to Chekhov's metaphor of the cherry orchard as a symbol of an aristocracy dying because it has lost its purpose, to Shaw's metaphor of a house shaped like a rudderless ship as a symbol of Europe drifting aimlessly towards extinction, to Brecht's metaphor of Mother Courage's canteen wagon, collapsing under war's venality and carnage, through Beckett's metaphor of two tramps lost in a void decorated with a single tree. It is this metaphorical art that seems to me missing from minor contemporary drama, whether political or domestic; the common run of plays tends to be discursive, prosaic, simplistic, lacking the complications of a poetic structure. Still, the secret has not been wholly lost. The best of our theater writers are continuing to mine a metaphorical vein, and it is these writers that I would like to discuss for confirmation and illustration.

Most of them, interestingly, are American. Aside from Edward Bond, and occasionally Harold Pinter, British playwrights are usually too enamored of verbal gymnastics and witty discourse to enter the realm of metaphorical suggestion; contemporary English drama is more akin to rhetoric than poetry. But the best American drama, perhaps because it is usually lacking in eloquence, sometimes manages to formulate images that penetrate and illumine.

Consider, for example, Jean Claude van Itallie's *America Hurrah*, particularly the final play in that trilogy, *Motel*. *Motel* is a monologue spoken by a female motel keeper, an enormous aproned doll wearing a huge carnival mask, complete with hair rollers and granny glasses. Her speech drones on about rooms ("rooms of marble and rooms of cork, all letting forth an avalanche"), rooms throughout history, and specifically this motel room with its antimaccasars, hooked rugs, plastic Japanese flowers, television sets, automatically-flushing toilets. As the motel keeper catalogues the room's possessions, the door opens with a blinding flash of headlights and a young couple enters — two more mannequins on raised shoes, their huge heads obscenely bobbing, their bodies moving with the jerky menace of animated monsters. Slowly, they undress for the night, coming together in a grotesque papier-mâché embrace, rubbing their cardboard bodies together, then turn on the television and, to the accompaniment of raucous rock-and-roll, cheerfully proceed to demolish the room: ripping off the toilet seat, breaking the bedsprings, pulling down doors and windows, scrawling pornographic graffiti on the walls with lipstick, and, finally, tearing the motel keeper apart, head and all. Nabokov, in *Lolita*, used motel culture as an image of our squalor and rootlessness; van Itallie uses it as a metaphor of our violence, our lunacy, our need to defile.

Or consider Sam Shepard's *Buried Child*, set somewhere in the heartland of America, where a family tries desperately to inter its past crimes and sins, including the murder of a little child, only to have the very earth erupt and expose the transgressions. Throughout the play, Tilden, a hulking idiot son, is covering his sleeping father with produce that has grown up overnight — husks of corn, carrots, wheat — even though the fields are barren and no crops have ripened for thirty-five years. At the end of the play, Tilden has appeared with the remains of a dead child in his arms, a bunch of bones wrapped in a muddy brown cloth, and starts up the stairs to his parents' room, as his mother babbles on about the effect of good hard rain on the roots of growing things. The corpse of the child that has broken through the crust of the earth, nourished by the rain, is not simply the rotten inheritance of this American family, but perhaps the buried promise of America itself—the possibilities of our country, once so pure and exceptional, whose abandoned innocence keeps surfacing to plague us.

Or consider another American example, a work by Arthur Kopit called *End of the World (With Symposium to Follow)*. This black comedy is written in the style of a film noir, and concerns a playwright approached by a mysterious stranger who wants to commission a play about doom. The playwright responds to this curious commission like a private eye hired to find a murderer, and in the course of the action investigates a number of witnesses with knowledge of our nuclear strategy.

What the playwright discovers is that our nuclear policy is crazy, and what is more, *everybody knows it, including its architects*. The policy is a "closed loop system": assured destruction and flexible response both lead to the same result; there's no way out unless you break the system itself. It is an Escher box—an illusion of reality. Though it looks feasible, it won't work, but because it looks workable, people can't stop working on it. The playwright concludes that writing such a play is impossible and abandons the project, along with all hope.

His final speech is the metaphor, and I would like to quote it at length. "My son had just been born," he says. "We'd brought him home. He was what, five days old I guess." (pause) "And then one day my wife went out . . . And I was alone with him. And I picked up this living thing, and started walking around our living room. We lived on a high floor. We overlooked the river, the Hudson. And I . . . looked down at this creature, this tiny thing, and I realized . . . I realized I had never had anyone completely in my power before." (pause) "And I realized he was completely innocent. And he looked up at me. And whatever he could see, he could see only in innocence. And he was in my power. And I'd never known what that meant, never had felt anything remotely like that before. And I saw I was standing near a window. And it was open. It was but a few feet away. And I thought I could drop him out. How easy to drop him out. And I went towards that window, because I couldn't believe this thought had come into my head, where it had come from, not one part of me felt anything for this boy but love, not one part, my wife and I had planned, we were both in love, there was no resentment, no anger, nothing dark in me toward him at all, no one could ever have been more in love with his child than I . . . and I was thinking,

I can throw him out of here, and then he will be falling the ten, twelve, fifteen, twenty stories down and as he's falling I will be unable to get him back, and I will feel a remorse . . . of infinite extent . . . and nothing will ever be able to redeem me from this, I will be forever outside the powers of redemption, if there is a God then with this act I am forever damned. And I felt a thrill, I FELT A THRILL, IT WAS THERE! I FELT A THRILL AT THE THOUGHT OF DOING SOME ACT WHICH HAD NO REASON WHATSOEVER AND WOULD LEAVE ME FOREVER DAMNED! God will notice me with this, I said. And of course I resisted this. And moved away from the window. It wasn't hard to do. Resisting wasn't hard at all. BUT I DIDN'T STAY BY THAT WINDOW. AND I CLOSED IT! I resisted it by moving away, back into the room. I sat down with him." (pause) "I don't think there's a chance I would have done it, not a chance." (pause) "But I couldn't take that chance; it was . . . very, very seductive. . . . If doom comes . . . it will come that way."

I am reluctant to comment further on this passage, because it is itself so much more powerful than comment, which is precisely the point I am trying to make about dramatic metaphor. Without evading his responsibilities as a citizen under nuclear threat, indeed by frontally facing these responsibilities, Kopit has managed to understand our terrors and turn them into art.

Let me conclude with one more example, a work that embodies better than any I know the tensions between the Platonic and Aristotelean visions of reality: Jean Genet's *The Balcony*. Genet imagines bourgeois society through the metaphor of the brothel, in which the status quo is preserved by means of erotic fantasies. The agencies of power — government, the law, the army, the police, and the Church — prosper by being impersonated in the brothel by ordinary citizens. The threat to this system comes not from whorehouse imposture but from a rebellion which is raging in the streets of the city, dedicated to destroying all the masquerades through which the system perseveres. This is the purpose, at least, of the rebel leader, the proleterian Roger, who wants the rebellion to adhere to a chaste Puritan ideal and put an end to role-playing. Roger knows that if the rebellion does not begin by "despising make believe," it will soon come to resemble the other side. Everything must be aimed at utility. Skirmishes must be fought without gestures, elegance, or charm. Reason must prevail. And when the great figures of the regime are captured, their costumes must be ripped off.

But Roger is a dreamer, for the rebels cannot give up their hunger for emblems, heroes, banners, and a legendary figure to worship. Chantal, the *la passionaria* of this revolution, has learned "the art of shamming and acting in the brothel"; now she applies it to the revolution, becoming its female emblem. This dooms the rebellion, modelled by Genet on the French revolution, which also began by despising artifice before developing its own ceremonies. The Puritan Roger, with his devotion to reason and virtue, is obviously modelled on Cromwell or Robespierre, whose Platonic idealism could not survive the people's love of sensation. The need for change is undermined by the need to play a role; rebels adjust themselves to already defined characters; even the revolutionary leaders become play actors, their chaste and simple dress serving as another kind of costume. Thus, Robespierre introduces a terror much more bloody than the atrocities of the *ancien regime*; Stalin creates a bureaucracy far more murderous than the feudal hierarchy of the Romanoffs. All progress is a dream, because reality is unattainable. For if real time moves forward, illusory time moves in circles, and humankind is doomed to repetition by its love of masquerade.

In Genet's vision, then, theater and politics live uneasily side by side, and the concept of imitation, which Aristotle made the focal point of his *Poetics*, becomes a method of enshrining the status quo. Yet, if Genet believes that the reality desired by Platonic revolutionaries is neither desirable nor achievable, he manages nevertheless to make a profound revolutionary statement of his own by means of theatrical metaphor. And, ultimately, that is the most one can ask of dramatic art in regard to politics — not that it solve our problems, but rather that it increase our understanding, not that it accommodate the possible, but rather that it preserve our belief in the impossible. As I once wrote in another context: "Art encompasses politics but refuses to affirm it. The artist lives in compromised reality, but he lives in another world as well, the world of the imagination, and there his vision is pure and absolute. . . . Politics demands resolution; dramatic art is content to leave us in ambiguity. . . ." To that extent, and perhaps that alone, metaphor creates a bridge where politics and theater meet, and it is there, at that imaginary junction, that Plato and Aristotle settle their ancient argument and join their venerable hands.

Robert Brustein, Professor of English at Harvard University, is Artistic Director of the American Repertory Theatre and theater critic of The New Republic.

Eleanor Clark

A SAHARA SILHOUETTE

If neither French nor Roman Catholic nor a Sahara buff, a traveler to the vast lower quarter of Algeria, the part of the Sahara called the Hoggar, may never have heard of the Atakor range of mountains or of a certain candidate for sainthood associated with one of them. His image clings to the whole region around the town of Tamanrasset and to its nomad people, the Tuareg, for whose language early in this century he wrote the first dictionary, grammar, and translations of a great store of oral poetry. Later it came to seem very peculiar indeed not to have known about this odd priest, subject of innumerable books. At least to the tourist trade, and in the perception of any in the outside world who have chanced or cared to look into it, his name looms over the Hoggar like Lenin's over Red Square, and greater difference than between those two gentlemen the human race can rarely have conjured up. His name was Charles de Foucauld, and he was murdered in Tamanrasset, called Tam thereabouts, in 1916. The mountaintop linked to him, because he built a little hermitage there (although he actually didn't spend very much time there), is the Assekrem.

A legend already in his lifetime, now still not officially declared a saint, Foucauld was first proposed for sainthood at the Vatican in 1927. At the time of his death, he was fifty-eight years old and probably would have died soon anyway, as a result of extreme self-inflicted deprivations throughout the second half of his life. The fact of his death can doubtless be taken as an answer to his prayers over many years; the manner of it stands in a causal relation to the most dire days of World War I for France. They were bound to be days of strain and sorrow for this fanatic and aristocrat whose patriotism was almost on a par with his Christian zeal.

After the first presentation of his cause in Rome, in 1927, more than a half-century would pass before the formal petition for beatification and canonization, apparently still in abeyance, was made in 1979. The time in the celestial waiting room isn't always so long, as witness the last-stage elevation a while ago of the Polish priest-martyr of World War II. Obviously, as with all international awards, recognition of sainthood can entail political expediences and general horsetrading. Conceivably, if all or any big majority of Père de Foucauld's compatriots were begging for his canonization and being offended by the hierarchy's delay, the matter would have taken a different turn before now. But he can never have been the darling of the French left wing in general, and to a number of others who know little more than his name, his several roles in turn-of-the-century North Africa are likely to be viewed on a scale from passé to pernicious.

Meanwhile, the books about him have gone on pouring forth; how many fewer there would be without this era's travel craze and consequent boosting of the holy father's hut on the Assekrem is anybody's guess. The writings are, of course, mostly laudatory, of pious intent and often no political or historic sense whatever. Two in English by devout women journalists are likely to raise more hackles than paeans of praise. For one thing, it is beyond question that the same virtues in a person born in poverty and social obscurity would have occasioned no such great notice then or later, but then a lot of the drama could never have occurred, since wealth and social position along with high army connections were key factors, in adventure as in renunciation. More surprising than the character's appeal as not just a viscount but a rich one, is the prevailing lack of psychoanalytic insight in writings about him, in a period and for a personality that would seem to make these tools impossible to avoid. Granted, we are all so sick of psycho-nonsense in every branch of history and biography, it might be thought refreshing to find one character of stature and life of high drama treated with comic-strip innocence. But the pause that refreshes can soon become the refreshment that palls; and where there is no guideline but dogma, no thought, for instance, even of effects on such a child of a mother's early death, together with other violent losses, clearly no cause is being well served, either of faith or of veracity.

Pettier flaws, in this orthodox-inclined literature, can add up to almost equal offense, as in ignorance of the rule for the aristocratic *de* before a French proper name, to wit: unless preceded by the title or first name or some other antecedent as for military rank, the surname drops the *de* except for names of one syllable, the most familiar violation in this country being de Tocqueville. We also get an *s* added to Tuareg for the plural, which is not altogether at odds with French orthography but nearly so. The name is itself plural; singular *targui* male, *targuia* female.

A more general ignorance together with almost rabid dislike of the Tuareg comes in too, keeping strange company with the story of

a life so much given to them, in so much love. They are called in-
variably filthy, busy with their "disgusting courts of love," commit-
ting infanticide as a matter of course. Of Foucauld's assassins, one
such biographer writes that all the Tuaregs (sic) in the group were
black, none were white, whatever that may mean when the blacks in
the region were not Tuareg at all, and no targui comes under any
usual meaning of white.

With such admirers, to borrow the old gag, who needs detrac-
tors. But of course not all who have found a good deal to praise and
even to be awed by in the life of Foucauld, the burning, God-bitten
bachelor of the Sahara, are either sloppy or bigoted. Even quite profound appreciation can stop short of idolatry. Of downright denigra-
tion there seems to have been less than one could expect in print,
given the holy man's role in sustaining and fostering the French colonial grip on the area. A power in that respect he certainly was, in a
way and to a degree far beyond the common period picture of the
priest with cross and holy water giving supposedly divine sanction to
the troop movements of some advanced nation or other, against the
benighted heathens of a less sophisticated or, anyway, less technocratic one. For that role he had extraordinary qualifications; he was
a superstar and, proportionately, more guilty than an ordinary cleric
by the anti-colonialist lights of later generations and of many in his
own time, no doubt, insofar as they had ever heard of him. After all,
he was killed just two months before the start of the Russian Revolution. Plenty of able thinkers and organizers had been railing for
decades against just such stooges of imperialist occupations, not to
mention religion itself as the opium of the people. Between that
minority and the hermit of the Hoggar, ignorance was probably mutual, not that Foucauld was a stupid or ignorant man. He showed
himself a fine student and scholar when his interests required. But
except for his ground-breaking work in *tifinar,* the written form of the
Tuareg language, after his conversion at the age of twenty-eight, the
incipient Trappist, subsequently ex-Trappist and priest, seems, outside of his own enormous correspondence, to have read little if anything except the gospels, and breviary, and military reports—not
that he showed himself all that dedicated to the army during his
regular youthful military service.

There was still a good deal of the spoiled brat about him at that
stage. The early deaths of both parents, the father's of what sounds
like some kind of cerebral corrosion, left the little boy and his sister

to be raised by a grandfather and must have figured then, as in his
later and far more dramatic quests. The Franco-Prussian war that
drove what was left of the family from their native Strasbourg, in
1870, must surely have helped, too, to set up a lifelong pattern of
dislocation. Poverty, obvious hardship might perhaps have been better, in at least driving a person to some steady occupation, than the
range of temptations lying around this unmoored young aristocrat
with no particular calling and too much pocket money.

A remark attributed to him around the time of his only higher
education at a normal age, at the military academy of St. Cyr, was
that he didn't need to choose a life work or work at all, since he was
rich. He was quite fat and in photographs of the time looks overin-
dulgent in general. His studies for the priesthood came much later,
when he was almost forty. His earlier reputation for laziness and
sloppiness must have had some basis in fact, since according to one
of his French biographers, he was rated number 333 in his class of
386 at St. Cyr, and in cavalry training at Saumur afterwards he was
eighty-seventh out of eighty-seven. He became known for his wild,
expensive parties, at which, as he would tell it in later years, a grim
moodiness was apt to seize him before the end of the evening. He
took a mistress named Mimi to Algiers and set her up in an apartment there, in the guise of his wife, to lighten his military service,
from which he was shortly discharged because of objections to that
arrangement. He was still in the reserve, however, and before long,
having ditched Mimi after some boring months with her in a hotel in
Switzerland, he was back for another hitch in uniform. He resigned
that time, in order to prepare for a project both daring and in itself
worthy enough, but this too was only for a pampered darling of society. A young man of small or no income could not have considered it.

He was about to undertake a geographical exploration of
Morocco, disguised as a Jew, since no Christian was then allowed
across the border. As guide he hired an elderly rabbi who knew the
country well. The journey would end up taking eleven months, after
at least as many of preparation. The budding explorer had first to
learn Hebrew, perfect his Arabic, take a crash course in surveying
and map-making, acquire the necessary costly instruments and de-
vise ways of hiding them about his person, bone up on all possible
aspects of that then quite forbidding segment of the Maghrib. At
least as much as the courting of danger in the enterprise, the fierce
intellectual labor entailed might seem at odds with the pudgy and
licentious spendthrift of the same period, who had already squan-

dered so much of his inheritance that it had been taken out of his control and given to a cousin to manage for him. But this other character had also been there long before, not necessarily in any great tug-of-war within the psyche. In a letter written in his quite early teens, the future pioneer scholar and translator of *tamahaq,* language of the Tuareg and their own name for themselves, described a most impressive program of study and translation from the Greek and Latin classics, by way of fun in summer vacation. "Un lettré fêtard," the rollicking bookworm or Goodtime Charlie with his nose in a book, he was called by his devoted army friend Laperrine.

The volume that resulted from the Moroccan journey, Foucauld's only writing published in his lifetime, was honored with the gold medal of the National Geographic Society and is said to have been the work officially used by the French army in Morocco many years later. The country was then so badly and unjustly run, many are said to have been hoping for French conquest, which was not to be for another thirty years. One of the great disappointments of the former explorer's life was that when that conquest did occur in 1912, his old friend and army comrade, General Louis Lyautey, future Marshall of France, did not send for him to accompany the troops. Before then he had gone with Lyautey on at least one long expedition in Algerian parts of the desert, and he yearned to be summoned to Morocco. Still the leading French authority on the geography of the country, he seems to have been a good horseman in his salad days, in spite of his record at Saumur, and he could still hang on creditably for long treks, in spite of a body by then half-wasted away.

This was far indeed from the figure of the young man of twenty-four who in 1882, one year after a notorious massacre by other tribesmen in another part of that desert, made his way in Jewish garb from the Mediterranean to the Atlas mountains, as often in danger from robbers as from the authorities, such as those were away from the few towns. For years now he had eaten mainly barley and water, plus a few ground dates once in a while. He slept on floors, preferably in a space too small for him to stretch full length ("Could Jesus stretch out on the cross?"); roused himself at three or four a.m. for holy offices in his outlandish, lonely little habitations; and wore a costume as outlandish, designed by himself, of threadbare sandals, a probably often filthy white gandoura with a big red heart of Jesus clumsily sewn on the front, and an oversized rosary serving as a belt.

T. S. Eliot, who had given some thought to saints in deserts, has been quoted as disapproving of the extreme physical deprivations Foucauld went in for and praising him for having finally let up in that regard. There I believe Eliot was misinformed. The regime remained pretty close to what most people would consider slow torture, with a very rare glass of wine or nibble of meat taken just in the cause of sociability. With Lyautey, for one, he might have had to give in that far on occasion, the general being quite a bon vivant who traveled desert or no with his own chef and a collection of bawdy phonograph records for entertainment in the evening. He may have found this haggard, skinny, burning-eyed old comrade, judging by pictures possibly verging on toothlessness too, rather too much of a good thing for a whole campaign. However, he later gave a moving account of a mass said by Father de Foucauld in his rickety little chapel at Béni-Abbès. That was his first place of residence as priest in Algeria — a small town fairly close to the Moroccan border, far north and to the west of Tamanrasset. There, along with constant unofficial charity among the local population, he served as chaplain to the French garrison. Later on he would divide his time between there and Tam, scarcely commuting as we understand it; this was several hundred trackless desert miles, not for anything with wheels, and he is said to have often preferred to walk behind the camels rather than ride, just as an act of humility.

After describing the miserable poverty of the tiny chapel with its sand floor, Lyautey wrote, "I have never heard Mass celebrated as it was by Father de Foucauld that Sunday morning. I could imagine myself in the bare desert with the early Christian hermits. It was one of the lasting impressions of my life."

With a much closer old army comrade, his "incomparable friend" Colonel Laperrine, Foucauld went on several military treks including a long one across the still uncharted and scarcely pacified Hoggar, to Timbuktu. There the troop was stopped not by any band of natives but by a rival and very jealous French officer prepared to fight his own countrymen rather than cede an inch of colonial prerogative. Laperrine judiciously withdrew from that uncertain border, but remained the leading military authority in the Sahara, and it was with him that Foucauld was mainly communicating on matters of regional armament and defense in the World War I years.

In that role, aside from contriving his own death, he can rather easily be accused of putting country before God and army even before country. He drew up the plans and supervised the construction of the fort at Tam, decided the amount and type of arsenal as well as manpower needed there, provided the French command posts with almost daily bulletins on threats from this quarter or that. Whatever the valor and glamor of the Zouaves and other French North African troops far across the sea in Picardy, down in the lower reaches of the Sahara it was an ideal time for rebellion, and there cannot have been much manpower to spare for colonial police work. The Tuareg had come around to formal acceptance of French dominion in 1904, and their current *amenukal,* or top chief, reputedly a man of impressive quality, was in some sense a friend of both Foucauld and Laperrine. After the assassination he wrote a letter of what has been taken to be genuine sorrow and condolence to the priest's sister in France. But anti-Christian fervor was rife, and whatever the actual part played by members of the Senoussi sect, they had converts and influence there as elsewhere in the Moslem world.

The ins and outs and accusations and suspicions about that December night in 1916 have been hashed over in various quarters ever since. The victim's term for himself from way back, "universal brother," sounds pompous enough out of context but as translated into his daily life seems to have been nothing of the sort. While refraining from any effort at conversion, except what might germinate from his example and that turned out to be nil, he was indefatigable in acts of kindness to the local Tuareg, who were at his door for help and handouts all the time, and his cheerful lack of censure of their foibles, individual or generic, would put at least one of his English-language biographers to shame. He did report that they seldom washed and were averse to any new kind of work; this goes with such impartial observations as that they didn't weave or shear sheep, so their clothing was mostly from hides. In general, his relations with them must have been based on a high degree of mutual respect and sympathy.

So who was in the group of assassins? Would he have opened the door that night if he hadn't heard a trusted voice? Were there some who knew of the plot and could have warned him but chose to be away just then instead? Tamanrasset at the time was a small village, not the kind where such a plan would stay secret long. Where, that night, was the young tauregui named Uksem, whom Père de Foucauld had taken to France with him three years before, in 1913, for three and a half months? The trip was evidently meant to impress the youth with the glories of French civilization, which he would see at its most glamorous among the holy viscount's family connections. Departure was first postponed several weeks so the candidate for the honor could get married, amid the usual tribal motion and commotion. Then wrenched from his bride and from everything familiar to him, he was dragged in his desert garb through the glittering salons where he is reported, rather understandably, to have been lonely and homesick; probably the food disagreed with him too. The strange pair also did a swing through Switzerland and the French Alps, with what results either religious or cultural or political in the protégé's outlook is not clear. Nor is it clear how he can have been ignorant of the plot against his benefactor, or on what grounds he failed to warn him if he knew of it. But then the subsequent French anti-Foucauld camp, either leftist Catholic or anti-clerical altogether, would not all be above picturing the principal as well warned and opening his door to the bullets on purpose, in order to be a martyr.

Whether pro or con, it is refreshing, not to say humbling, to find an antidote to such zeal in a little book by a Moslem writer, who, while not veiling any imperialist unpleasantness of the period insists on showing it in context. That includes as fair a picture as has been drawn of Foucauld's true intentions, not to proselytize but to exemplify the teachings of Christ. There was no limit to his generosity. He gave and gave and gave — food, clothes, lodging, money; his tough debate with himself, over a life of service versus contemplation, became solved half and half without his decision, by the flock of needy at his door, in both Béni-Abbès and Tam. Slavery in Algeria was not only among the Tuareg; he bought slaves whenever possible in order to buy their freedom, often with little thanks for his pains except perhaps from on high. In recalling that long social service and his grueling work in *tamahaq* vocabulary, grammar, and literature, this unassuming Islamic commentator, Ali Merad, justly presents him as the antithesis of the not too untypical French profiteer and exploiter of the same territory, or their counterparts in any other colonizing nation. The French have often been praised, in contrast to some of those other powers, for their policy of infusing French education and culture into the peoples under their dominion, instead of looking on them solely for grab value; which is not without some truth but left plenty of grabbers.

As context for the priest's so widely shared assumption that ultimate good for humankind could come from Christianity alone, the same Moslem study presents quite a battery of big guns of the time, in a ruling power that happened to be also a bastion of intellectual supremacy, and makes a very cogent plea for the case to be judged accordingly. There was Ernest Renan calling Mohammedanism the enemy of scientific inquiry and source of intellectual stagnation, and Cardinal Lavigerie, one-time Archbishop of Algiers, saying the mission of France was to save North Africa from barbarism. It could be added too that the contents of the Bibliotèque Nationale and the Louvre as well were apt to be pulled down on the heads of any so benighted as to disagree; also that the far from unenlightened St. Simoniens, those pre-socialists drawn in many cases from the prestigious intellectual ranks of the Hautes Écoles, while often differing from their country's officials on motives and tactics, were all for its spreading the blessings of its superior culture wherever possible.

On the purely religious side of the picture an odd note, probably not unique to this case, is that Foucauld stood in some degree of debt to the heathens, those "barbarians," in his own Christian conversion. Most likely the actual text of the Koran had little if any part in the matter. What did deeply affect the young Charles de Foucauld, as army officer first and then probably far more in his year as explorer in Morocco, under more frequent solitudes and silences, was the quiet religiosity of the desert-dwellers he was seeing, whatever their characters and occupations otherwise. He returned from that often perilous sojourn, in the kind of landscape once dear to Christian saints, in a state not yet of readiness to believe but of some kind of awakened sensibility leading that way.

Actually it led first to his getting engaged to be married — an unfortunate and it would seem rather cruel little episode lasting a couple of weeks in the immediate sense and a lifetime for the lady in another sense. She did eventually marry, but long after Foucauld's death, in response to inquiries in connection with the opening moves for his beatification, would speak of him as the abiding adoration of her life. He has been charged with throwing her over under pressure from his family, because although she was from a respectable French family in Algiers, she was not of the nobility and lacked a *de* to her name, which hardly holds water, as various Foucauld relatives had married outside the aristocracy. In speaking of the engagement as a stupid mistake, which had cost him some pain to get out of, he sounds self-centered not to say self-enclosed, perhaps not too uncommon a prelude to the most extreme monastic discipline. From that much self it must indeed be a relief to be divorced.

He also had to deal with what cries out to be taken as nearly ruinous frustration in his love for a married and ultra-pious cousin a few years older than he, Marie de Bondy. It was through her that he came to know the remarkable abbé who would be his guide and mentor for the rest of his life; and it was on an outing with the Bondy family, the beloved Marie and her husband and children, that the doting skeptic first visited the Trappist monastery where he would soon choose to be immured.

He did not stay for very long in that particular house. His seven years as a Trappist, except for the first few months, would be spent at Akbès in Syria, followed by three years of more drastic but self-appointed abjection in Palestine, mixed finally with studies for the priesthood. Cousin Marie, his constant correspondent through all this and for the rest of his life, in what could make a feast for Freud-flies, had turned into "Dearest Mother," heading of all the hundreds of letters. The little orphan has found a mother at last, has turned this unavailable love of his life into his mother in Christ. But there is one letter, the first of his Trappist immurement, written on the evening of his arrival at the monastery, that stands apart from all the rest and from any ordinary class of writing; hasty, tragic, a compound of eloquence, commitment, and probity that forbids the most crucial outpourings of a breaking heart, it is a document ranking high in the love literature of the world. They had spent the last precious hours in Paris together, earlier that day, and he is reliving every minute of those hours in the anguish of permanent and total loss. He has entered a house of God, said goodbye forever to the usual human condition, but is not yet ready, that night, with her presence so fresh in his eyes and nostrils (although this he may not say), to suppress the almost explicit cry of his longing. It is, only in part between the lines, not from the beautiful peaks of faith that he writes, such as his name would come to be associated with on the Assekrem, but from the all too human and intolerable, except that it must be tolerated, abyss.

Soon, in his different immolations in the Near East, we find him not only humble as can be but in love with humiliation. After being out in the street one day, he came back radiant with joy because some children had jeered and thrown rocks at him. This was a step forward in the imitation of Christ. He was extremely upset when a new rule allowed a little oil and butter in the food, the "dear diet" loved for its frugality; when he left the order at last, with all due approval, it was because for him the regime was neither solitary nor penitential enough. In Nazareth he was given a hut in a nunnery garden and, wanting only the most menial work, was happy to serve as gardener, evidently thinking the Lord would guide his shovel and hoe, since having grown up with plenty of hirelings around for that sort of thing, he didn't know one tool or plant from another. He was so sweet and kind, the nuns watching from their windows must have smiled behind their hands and either given him a few lessons or found him some other drudgery.

Next we hear of him sending home to family financial guardians in Paris for a rather huge sum with which to buy a certain mountain of holy connotation outside Jerusalem, at the request of an appropriate institution wanting to be established there. Such was the viscount's anonymity in his rags and tatters, one would have to marvel at his unworldliness if he ever honestly thought he would be just Brother Alberic or later Brother Charles of Jesus, with letters arriving for him all the time on the most elegant crested and monogrammed stationery.

In pursuing his belated studies for the priesthood he was more or less ordered to Rome but got away in a couple of months. Nothing pleased him there, which may or may not figure in Rome's delay in furthering his cause now. He can't have failed to notice that the city's more conspicuous brands of Christian reverence were not at all up his alley, and besides, the French have usually not liked Rome much unless they were conquering it. Furthermore, it is far truer of Rome than of most places that to appreciate it you really need to appreciate life, and Brother Charles was at his nadir for that. Life was a trial that must be undergone in order to merit the light everlasting, but he yearned for the end of the trial. After pulling through what was taken to be incipient tuberculosis, at the monastery at Akbès, he wrote that he had not had the good luck to succumb; after a cholera epidemic, being spared meant for him being unworthy, as also in connection with a nearby massacre of Christians, mostly Armenians, by the Turks. He was still alive; alas, it had not yet been his turn; he had not been chosen.

A subsequent wonder, to minds unversed in such matters, may be that the Trappists seem never to have resented his leaving the order, and his is reported to be a name of worldwide veneration among Trappists now. As for his own motives in becoming a priest instead of a monk, and a priest in spots of his own choosing, it is hard to avoid a passing thought of the silver spoon that that mouth was born to. It would be replaced by the most wretched utensils, serving the poorest, most tasteless, and inadequate food. What would not be relinquished was that the person in question would somehow go on call-

ing the shots and doing at nearly every move what he pleased — until
the silence from Lyautey about Morocco that must have been rather
a kick in the teeth, and with the continuing exception in the so different sphere of his hope to found his own order.

Both in Béni-Abbès and later in Tam he kept sending out appeals for like-minded believers — or fellow-nuts, some would say (and
some in French ecclesiastical circles did say) — to share his regime of
utmost privation, in one of the least luxuriant spots on earth. His
friends the White Fathers finally turned up a young novice crazy
enough to accept the challenge, but whether because he was literally
crazy or for some other reason, the arrangement soon blew up. Father de Foucauld would die absolutely alone, in his courage, in his
folly, and in his faith, leaving traces that refused to disappear and
would finally blow into the semblance of an order after all.

Eleanor Clark's most recent work, Tamrart: Thirteen Days in the
Desert, *is forthcoming.*

Nathan Glazer

JEWISH INTELLECTUALS

One of the ways of participating in the celebration of the
fiftieth anniversary of *Partisan Review* suggested by the editor was to
submit something from one's current work. When the time came to
respond to this invitation I was working on an essay on the relationship between anti-Semitism and anti-Zionism, another on the question of the nature of American Jewish political influence on American policy-making.

Neither of them seemed suitable for *Partisan Review.* And it occurred to me that this raised an interesting question: what was there in the relationship between the *Partisan Review* world and Jewishness that might make sections of papers on anti-Zionism and Jewish political influence unsuitable? Perhaps they were only unsuitable in my mind. There was of course no dearth of Jewish contributors to *PR*. On occasion, there were references to the fate of the Jews, perhaps even a translation of the work of a Hebrew or Yiddish writer. One felt, however, that Jewish topics entered only if they passed a test of universal significance. The Hebrew Bible, if it were discussed, was in terms of literary considerations; Hebrew and Yiddish writers would have to enter through the gates kept by a universal literary sensibility; political issues of concern to Jews (and *PR* of course on occasion dealt with political issues) would have to demonstrate a universal significance. Jewishness as such, in a word, was parochial. No great surprise there: Italianness, or blackness, or Irishness, or any sort of other ethnic affiliation, if insisted on too exclusively, would have been equally out of place in *PR*, and thus the question may simply already be answered, and the reasons for my reluctance to consider my current work suitable involves no further examination.

But I would argue Jewishness might well have had more of a claim on *PR* than it did; as against all other forms of parochialism, it applied to a good part of its editors and writers, as other ethnic affiliations (aside from American) did not. If American issues had a claim on them, as an American journal of literature, culture, and (on occasion) political thought, so, too, might Jewish concerns. Yet another reason for a larger claim was that the Jews and Jewishness were involved intimately in all those issues of modernity and radicalism that were the basic concern of *PR*. Whatever the potential claim, there was almost nothing on Jews and Jewish issues in *PR*. Editorial judgment alone, as I suggest, might simply have considered them too parochial. Assuming for the sake of further consideration that doesn't explain everything, what else might explain it?

I don't think I have an answer, only uncertain speculations, but one must clear out of the way answers that clearly are wrong. One wrong answer would be to say that there was any effort to *deny* Jewishness on the part of the intellectuals who were involved in the creation and sustaining of *PR*, and who were also Jewish, by birth, if not by any current religious practice or social or political allegiance. By the 1930s, certainly the later 1930s, Jewish intellectuals, at least those stemming from the East European Jewish world, did not display signs of Jewish self-hatred, of denial of Jewish identity, of the

conscious assimilatory strategies that were common among Jewish
intellectuals in central Europe. Perhaps this very acceptance of Jewish identity explains the absence of any strong Jewish concerns: they
were not seen as problematic. In Germany, in contrast, the idea of a
return to Judaism or to Jewishness, such as that inspired by the work
of Martin Buber and Franz Rosenzweig in the 1920s, had substantial appeal to German Jewish intellectuals just because it was a response to a prevalent and undignified self-denial and self-hatred.
Such a return would have had less meaning in the world of the immigrant generation of Jewish intellectuals of New York in the 1930s
because there was no similar effort to deny, or turn away from, Jewishness in any formal and decisive way. None of those involved in
the founding and subsequent history of *PR* ever would have dreamed
of converting: and it was to this final threat to Jewishness that Buber
and Rosenzweig responded.

For Jewish intellectuals in Germany (or at least some of them)
the great attraction was Christianity, as a central element of the culture of the Western world, and one therefore which demanded an
explicit denial of Jewishness. Obviously there were also social components in the attraction of conversion: opening the way to better
jobs, social interaction with Christian elites, better opportunities for
one's children. But there was also the attraction, it seems clear, of a
religion and culture of (it then seemed) universal claims and universal appeal, something very different from what Judaism, or the
Jewish social world, offered. If then one rejected this central attraction, one was immediately thrown back on Judaism and one had to
take a more serious attitude to it than any of the Jewish intellectuals
of the *PR* world ever did.

I make such an interpretation with some hesitation: perhaps I
am too influenced by a current reading of Gershom Scwolem's memoirs, *From Berlin to Jerusalem: Memories of My Youth,* and *Walter Benjamin: The Story of Friendship.* Conversion was a strong attraction, not
only for social but for intellectual reasons. Because, too, German
Jewish intellectuals were steeped in German philosophy, a philosophy which defined itself in large part by a relationship to Christianity (not so, after all, the philosophy of William James and John
Dewey), Judaism was by that fact alone given a greater significance
in the sphere of thought, a significance it could not have for contemporary American Jewish intellectuals.

Alongside Christianity and conversion and their social attractions was the strong appeal of Marxism and its variants, communism and socialism, and forms of utopian reform, such as the youth

movement and anarchism. These attractions of course existed in the
United States, too, in Jewish and (formally) non-Jewish versions.
Here there was a strong parallel between the situation of German
Jewish and American Jewish intellectuals. But once again one senses
that Judaism or Jewishness — specifically, Zionism — formed a more
significant challenge to the universalistic Marxist and reform movements in central Europe than in the United States. After the fact, of
course, one can say why: it was there a matter of life or death, as it
never was in the United States. But was this understood in the 1920s
and even 1930s by Jewish intellectuals? Not by most of them, who
died or escaped to the West or Palestine as a matter of survival that
had little effect on their ideas. But I would argue the reality that it
did turn out — certainly from 1933 — that the debate between a universalistic Marxism and reform and a particularistic Jewish choice
might be a matter of life and death, and gave the Jewish alternatives
a seriousness that they could not have in the United States.

For the contemporary American Jewish intellectuals of the
1930s, too, one great alternative attraction to Jewishness then was
socialism and its heirs, possibly communism. That was the major
form in which universalism combatted their particularistic Jewish
tendencies. But rejecting these in the United States implied nothing
it seemed about any Jewish alternative, led to no necessary involvement in any Jewish issue, even though inevitably one detected a
modest rise in Jewish interest as commitment to Marxism, communism, or socialism declined, a rise sometimes leading to (as in the
case of Will Herberg) full involvement. But there was an infinite
regress of other alternatives in the United States: if one rejected
Stalinism, one could go back to Leninism; if one rejected Leninism,
there was socialism; if socialism, democratic socialism. If any or all
of the above were found unsatisfactory, there was in the United
States Americanism (for which the *PR* intellectuals were roundly
abused).

Once again, the contrast with central Europe is fascinating:
there was no Germanism (or add any other central European or
Eastern European national culture) to fall back on for Jews, except
for some eccentrics: Jews were totally rejected. The situation was
different, as well as the psychological dynamics. In rejecting Christianity and Marxism, some German Jewish intellectuals of great
stature infused Jewish thought with an intellectual energy that as yet
a much larger and in one sense more "Jewish" American Jewish community has not yet matched.

There was then no obvious, formal, direct denial of Judaism

and Jewishness among the American Jewish intellectuals of the 1930s
and 1940s. Few hid their Jewish social origins; few were tempted to
conversion; few were desperately eager to enter a social world that
denied Jews, for that reason alone. There was, among the radicals,
the adoption of "party names," uniformly non-Jewish. But the fact of
being Jewish was not hidden. One can perhaps detect a denial of
Jewishness in the adoption of socialism and communism. No American intellectuals were interested in the variants developed in central
and Eastern Europe to accommodate national differences and ethnic
diversity: It was not the Jewish Bund, or socialist Zionism, or the
thought of Karl Renner and Otto Bauer that attracted them. It was
socialism and communism as universal movements, denying the
significance of religion, ethnicity, race as against the overarching
divisions of class, that attracted them.

One may push the argument to encompass modernism in literature and art, a much more substantial and steady concern of *PR*.
This, too, was a way of embracing universalism against particu-
larism. There was a paradox here, in that some of the creators of
modernism (Kafka, Proust, by descent) were Jewish, and others,
non-Jews (Joyce), were incredibly particularistic, and yet it was
modernism as providing a universal model, freed from ethnic and
religious allegiances despite its dependence on ethnicity and religion
for materials, that *PR* advocated. There were many articles on Kafka:
hardly any made anything of the fact that he was a Jew, in a uniquely
Jewish environment, and intensely so. (Perhaps the member of the
PR circle most cautious about Marxism and modernism was Lionel
Trilling. And yet he, for a half-dozen years in the late 1920s, was
connected with the Jewish magazine *The Menorah Journal*, whose
young managing editor, Elliot Cohen, was to become the first editor of *Commentary* in 1945. See the very interesting paper by Elinor
Grumet, "The Apprenticeship of Lionel Trilling," in *Prooftexts*, Volume 4, 1984.)

Was there an undue avoidance? Should *PR* have paid more attention to Jewish issues? Should the Holocaust, the creation of the
state of Israel, Jewish writers, the rise of the American Jewish community to a position of great influence in intellectual, cultural, and
academic life, have provided subjects for *PR*? (All these topics entered into *PR* — I speak of weight, proportion.) The fact is there were
other journals, some sharing many of the same writers, that were doing these things (*Commentary, Dissent*). And yet, looking over the
decades of *PR*, recognizing the remarkable achievement of its editors
and writers, one detects, or I do, in retrospect, a surprising absence.

And now? Now matters are somewhat different. Marxism and all its variants are in ruins, if one views them in serious intellectual terms. That there are (and more than ever) Marxist sociologists and historians and literary critics in American and other universities must be viewed as mere intellectual curiosity from the point of view of a serious criticism of ideas, even if it is of great significance as a weapon in political struggles. As for modernism: What is that any more when experiments in form, in writing and art, are simply old hat, and traditional elements of storytelling, even if affected by the history of modern experiment with form, and modern thought, return — and are even to be found in *PR*? On a purely intellectual level, the literature of Zionism, for example, might make as great a claim to attention today, when universalism weakens everywhere before the steady and strong attachment to national group, as Marxism. And when Christianity is in crisis, and yet religion seems to be more legitimate intellectually than it has been for a hundred years, one might even ask, why not Judaism?

But I make no predictions and no prescriptions. My interest is only in asking why a magazine that was in such large measure created by Jewish editors and writers had so little to say about Jews, Jewishness, or Judaism. The Jewish component it seemed could enter only when a universal and non-Jewish source of authority or point of reference gave it an appropriate cachet. One suspects that won't be the case in the future.

Nathan Glazer is Professor of Education and Social Structure at Harvard University and co-editor of The Public Interest.

Juan Goytisolo

TWENTY-SIX RUE DE BIÈVRE

Recently, in Paris, I dined with several friends at a small Moroccan restaurant at twenty-six rue de Bièvre. Over dinner I thought back to that time in the early seventies when a group of writer friends — most of whom were associated with the Latin American "Boom" — and myself opened an office for *Libre*, our new magazine, at this same address. We thought, then, that this journal of the Hispanic literary world would further unite us as a group. Instead, the personal relationships which had united us soured, and the original cordiality and comradeship of the old days corroded into an atmosphere of hostile mistrust. The event that was to tear us apart was the famous Padilla affair.

It all began in the spring of 1970, when I met Albina du Boisrouvray, who wanted to finance a cultural and political journal geared to the Spanish-speaking world. Albina was very young, extraordinarily beautiful, and passionately interested in literature, film, and social justice for Latin America. (She also happened to be the granddaughter of Nicanor Patiño, the Bolivian tin magnate.) She agreed to advance one hundred thousand francs to start the magazine, and, at the same time, to allow us complete editorial independence. I gave Albina a rough sketch of my ideas for the journal, and then I contacted those writers I had suggested to Albina: Julio Cortázar, Carlos Fuentes, García Márquez, Jorge Semprún, Mario Vargas Llosa, and Severo Sarduy. When Sarduy heard about our angel he exclaimed, "Young, beautiful, cultivated, millionaire, and, on top of that, leftist. Wow! It can't be true. Or, if it is, she must have cancer."

At that time Julio Cortázar had a summer place near Avignon, and, as Carlos Fuentes had a play which was part of the Avignon Summer Theater Festival, his friends had a good reason to gather at Cortázar's house to discuss our plans for the new magazine. Julio was already separated from his wife, Aurora, and his new companion, Ugné Karvelis, was serving as hostess. He had just returned

Editor's Note: Translated from the Spanish by Barbara Probst Solomon with René Campos.

from Cuba and brought me personal regards from the Cuban poet, Heberto Padilla, who, although already a controversial figure there, had not yet been arrested.

During our discussion about the journal, I stressed that our main purpose should be what Sartre, several years before at the Leningrad Writer's Conference, had called "the demilitarization of culture." We were as concerned by the grave social and political problems mounting in Latin America as by the hardening of the Cuban Revolution which had created a cold war climate in the world of Hispanic letters. But we still believed that an independent publication such as *Libre,* which would continue to give *critical* support to Cuba, thus preventing its cultural isolation, would, at the same time, stabilize the position of those independent intellectuals such as Padilla who remained in Cuba. Heberto had already gotten himself in hot water there by his outspoken support for Guillermo Cabrera Infante. (The author of *Three Sad Tigers* and former Cuban diplomat was one of the first Cuban writers to blow the whistle on the revolution and had gone into self-exile in London.) Indeed, it was almost inevitable that the informal conversation in Cortázar's garden should be over whether or not to include Cabrera Infante in the editorial board. Julio firmly announced it would be he *or* Cabrera Infante. I don't remember what the others said — except that the Chilean novelist, José Donoso, was as surprised and irritated by Cortázar's vehemence as I had been. With the advantage of hindsight, I realize that we immediately should have stopped our plan to publish *Libre.* But, at that time, the strength of Cortázar's political arguments mistakenly made me accede. What had convinced me then was the idea — although a bit risky — that a dialogue between Cuba and the non-Communist Left in Latin America and Europe would be worthwhile.

I felt that in maintaining a link with the Cuban Revolution we would be able to help those intellectuals in Cuba who were living in increasingly bad conditions, and this overcame my repugnance at the conditions being exacted. Thus, from its very birth *Libre* was the fruit of intrigues and compromises. Castro's hardline pro-Soviet position during the Czechoslovakian coup had produced increasing disillusionment and alarm among writers. Even by then, roughly speaking, our group seemed to split into two directions. There were those writers (later associated with *Libre*) like myself, Octavio Paz, Carlos Fuentes, García Márquez, José Donoso, and Severo Sarduy who continued to publish in another "Boom" literary magazine, *Mundo Nuevo,* despite the fact that it and its editor — Emir Rodíguez Monegal—had been falsely accused by ardent Castristas of being a CIA operation. But another faction, including Cortázar and the group involved with the Cuban magazine put out by Casa de las Américas, kept their distance.

Casa de las Américas, a unique cultural center which had existed in Cuba long before Castro's time, had its own magazine and gave coveted literary prizes. Important—intellectually and literarily—within the world of Hispanic letters, we still hoped that "Casa" could serve as our link to those writers. As Cortázar and Vargas Llosa had permanent ties to it, they seemed to us, then, to be ideal intermediaries. During our Avignon meeting, they both promised to defend the idea of *Libre* at the next editorial meeting of Casa de las Américas. Later that evening, we innocently drank a toast to the future success of our shared venture.

"Avignon" took place in 1970. But it had been my own last brief visit to Cuba in 1967 which had convinced me of the disintegration of the Revolution. Along with fifty or so other writers and intellectuals I had been invited by Carlos Franqui—one of Castro's closest comrades during the early days of their struggle—to join Cubans to celebrate the anniversary of the Revolution. Most of the guests, especially those Europeans who didn't speak Spanish, considered their Cuban junket a great success. Marguerite Duras, Nadeau, Guyotat, and the surrealists Leiris and Schuster were delighted with the marvelous atmosphere of freedom; alongside of which their own ordinary Parisian freedom suddenly seemed insignificant. The Cuban honeymoon of European intellectuals had reached its high point. According to Castro, they were "the only real friends of Cuba" and he still showed himself willing to accept their criticisms.

In spite of our cordial reception, I was quick to sense unpleasant undercurrents. One of the journalists who had interviewed me warned me against publicly mentioning Cabrera Infante's name. But the next day, on the radio, I said that the two best modern Cuban novels were *Three Sad Tigers* and Laezama Lima's *Paradiso*. The following morning Laezama Lima telephoned me at my room at the Hotel Nacional. He thanked me and asked whether I realized that this was the first time someone had dared mention his novel on Cuban television.

In my talks with Carlos Franqui, Heberto Padilla, and others, I was told about the omnipresent police force and the havoc being created by censorship. The writer Virgilio Piñera, anguished and fearful, came to see me. He immediately insisted that we go for a walk in the hotel garden where we could talk without being overheard. While we strolled, he explained in detail the harassment of homosexuals in Cuba. Because of his homosexuality, Piñera had become a target for blackmail and lived in constant fear of being reported to the police and being shipped off to the UMAP enforced labor camps. Despite the thick garden foliage he spoke in whispers. His suffering, in solitude and moral misery, was unbearable.

During my 1967 visit my vision of the revolution creating a free society had been replaced by what I had already become familiar with during trips to countries in the Soviet orbit, where there is, as Rudi Dutschke has so aptly put it, "real socialism — where everything is real except the socialism." The following year Carlos Franqui joined the ranks of Cubans in exile. And Cuba had ceased being my political model. As I had come of age in Franco's Spain, until this period I had assumed that a free society was to be found in what was the antithesis to Franco. But now reason led me to abandon "lyrical effusion" for a more sober, prosaic view of the Cuban reality. My time of political innocence was over.

The next shock came on November 8, 1968, when *Le Monde* reported that the official newspaper of the Cuban Army, *Verde Olivo,* had denounced Heberto Padilla for counterrevolutionary actions. The paper accused Padilla as the ringleader of a group of Cuban writers who, brainwashed by foreign decadence, were purported to have published "soft literary pieces which were a blend of pornography and antirevolutionary ideas." And he was said to have misused public funds during his time as manager of Cubatimpex.

Clearly Padilla's consistently unpopular literary and political stands had gotten him into hot water. When in 1967 Padilla had defended the literary merits of Cabrera Infante's *Three Sad Tigers* over a mediocre novel written by a high-ranking Cuban cultural commissar, he had exacerbated his suspect position. His strong stand against official literary mediocrity had caused the Cuban writing world to split into two camps: those who saw in his stand a necessary protection of literary values and those who wished to solidify their position with the literary *caciques* of the Cuban Revolution. Padilla seemed almost oblivious of the risks he was taking by engaging in a fight against a closed authoritarian regime.

In addition to arousing the anger of the Cuban Army magazine, Padilla's sarcastic attacks concerning the docility and conformity of Cuban writers provoked a series of rebuttals from a group of the "young revolutionary writers" of *El Caimán Barbudo,* the magazine associated with Casa de Las Américas. And, before that polemic had a chance to die down, Guillermo Cabrera Infante's public rupture with the Cuban Revolution (he was already in exile) worsened Padilla's position because of his previous support of Guillermo. Finding himself in a tight jam, Padilla reacted to the situation with his characteristic ambiguity. On one hand, he immediately disengaged himself from Cabrera Infante; on the other hand, he continued his provocations — within an official perspective — against the Cuban establishment. His position was extremely vulnerable.

At Carlos Franqui's suggestion I got in touch with Cortázar, Fuentes, Vargas Llosa, Semprún, and García Márquez. I also tried to reach Heberto by telephone. No one answered. So, we decided that we had to send a telegram to Haydée Santamaría — director of Casa de las Américas. We cabled our dismay over the slanderous accusations made against Padilla and, at the same time, expressed our continued support for "all actions taken by Casa de las Américas in defense of intellectual freedom." When we received Haydée's reply several days later, we were taken by surprise. "Inexplicable that from such a distance you are able to determine that an accusation against Padilla is slander rather than an accusation against him. Stop. The cultural line of Casa de las Américas is the line of our Revolution, the Cuban Revolution, and the attitude of Casa de las Américas will continue to be what Che wanted: with the guns ready and shooting all around."

After that, we heard little about Padilla. Once Carlos Franqui had defected and the number of my friends visiting Cuba had diminished, contacts became far more remote. Those messages and coded letters I did occasionally receive now concentrated on describing the climate of paranoid distrust described so eloquently by the Chilean writer, Jorge Edwards (Allende's first envoy to Cuba), in *Persona Non Grata.* By the time we had decided to publish *Libre,* a good part of our group had recognized that the fraternal and just society described by Marx had been replaced by an Orwellian nightmare.

When I came back to Paris after a fall teaching stint at Boston University, I went ahead with our plans to get an office. In December 1970 we found the miniscule quarters on rue de Bièvre in the building that later became the site of the cous-cous restaurant. The place was so cramped that years later García Márquez recalled: "It was so small, the only thing there was room for was fucking."

García Márquez, at that time, suggested I meet a friend of his, Plinio Apuleyo Mendoza, to discuss his joining the *Libre* staff. Informally we talked about what *Libre*'s general orientation would be: critical support of the Cuban Revolution, moral support for Allende, opposition to the Franco regime and other military dictatorships, a joint condemnation of North American imperialism in Vietnam and Soviet aggression in Czechoslovakia, support for the democratic struggle of countries in the Eastern Socialist bloc whose independence seemed threatened, and freedom of artistic, sexual, and moral expression. Because of García Márquez's high opinion of Plinio, and because of Plinio's close link with MAS, a Venezuelan group which at the time was the most dynamic dissident political force in Latin America, we rapidly decided that he would be our editor in chief.

In 1971 Cortázar and Vargas Llosa went to Cuba for the annual reunion of Casa de las Américas in order to get the participation of the Cuban writers in *Libre*. But the Cubans were frosty toward their proposal. After their return to Europe, hostile, alarming rumors emanating from Cuba began to circulate about *Libre*. We immediately decided to publish a statement in *Libre*'s first issue outlining the points we had already informally agreed to and pointing out that we were an independently financed magazine. Our decision was supported by Cortázar as well as by the group of Latin American writers, so many of whom were now living in Barcelona.

In our first issue we published Mario Vargas Llosa, Julio Cortázar, Octavio Paz, José Donoso, my brother, Luis Goytisolo, Carlos Fuentes, and several previously unpublished pieces of Che Guevara. Suddenly, many Latin American writers dropped by to see us. The wives of several of the writers helped us run the office, and we began to make plans for the Latin American distribution of *Libre*. Meanwhile, Severo Sarduy — through his connections at Seuil — was arranging for our European distribution. My fears and anxieties about embarking on such a project had been allayed; we all felt optimistic. Then Albina suddenly was attacked for being the granddaughter of Patiño and having inherited the "ugly Patiño fortune." *Libre* was put on the defensive for receiving her modest support — a matter which shouldn't have needed any justification at all. The next bomb exploded when Plinio telephoned me: greatly alarmed, he told me that Padilla had been arrested in Cuba.

Our worst fears had been verified. We felt a terrible sense of impotence despite the many telephone calls from friends in Spain, England, and Italy offering us their help.

Carlos Franqui suggested that I get in touch with Cortázar, in whose apartment on Place du Général Beuret we composed a discreet letter to Fidel Castro: we respectfully maintained our belief in the principles of the Revolution while expressing our concern at arrests of intellectuals who had openly criticized the regime; we pointed out that such repressive measures would have a negative effect on the artistic and intellectual world for whom the Cuban Revolution had been an important symbol. Among the fifty who signed our letter were Sartre, de Beauvoir, Claudín, Calvino, Fuentes, Moravia, Nono, Paz, Sontag, Semprún, and Vargas Llosa. Plinio hadn't been able to locate García Márquez in Barranquilla and, erroneously assuming he shared our point of view, included his name on the list.

García Márquez indeed was to show a certain political adroitness at avoiding a potentially delicate situation. Now becoming known throughout the world as the author of *One Hundred Years Of Solitude,* his personal friendships were being dealt with in a more sophisticated way. He chose to keep a discreet distance from our position while, at the same time, avoiding any real confrontation with us. Without our recognizing the changes taking place, the international García Márquez who was to become the intimate friend of political heads of state and espouser of presumed "advanced causes" was about to be born.

Several days after we had written our first letter to Mario Vargas Llosa, who was one of the Latin American writers living then in Barcelona. His Chilean friend, Jorge Edwards, was leaving his diplomatic post in Cuba to join Allende's Paris Embassy staff and wanted to give Cortázar and me a firsthand account of what was going on in Cuba. From what Edwards later told me, I realized that Heberto's arrest wasn't an isolated instance; rather, it represented Fidel's personal policy decision to eliminate all dissidence and firmly establish his single-minded "monolithic ideology."

I was traveling through the Sahara and Morocco when our letter to Castro was published. When I read a brief piece in the *Herald Tribune* referring to Padilla's "confession" I immediately telephoned Plinio in Paris to find out what this was all about. I then decided to stop in Barcelona to discuss it with Vargas Llosa. Mario had Padilla's complete confession. It was obvious to those of us who knew Heberto that he had used a grotesque mockery of the language of the Soviet trials of the 1930s. As his coded references weren't that coded, I was amazed that the Cuban cultural *caciques* hadn't been able to spot his ruse. Heberto's personality was extraordinarily complex: at times the frivolous *enfant terrible,* he relished impulsive and imprudent acts putting him at the edge of a precipice. His intelligence was

both cynical and corrosive, and he knew the Soviet bloc languages
and mentalities, having spent a year in the Soviet Union working as
a proofreader for the weekly magazine, *Novedades*. That experience
in Russia had tramautized him. I remember Heberto's remarks to
me during a Gallimard garden cocktail party. He stared at the literary crowd lolling about the well-kept turf, balancing the customary
glasses of champagne while chattering confidently. Laughing, he sardonically muttered, "Ah — if they only knew!" Having just returned
from the "society of the future," he had found most of the people at
the party politically inane. But it was also like Heberto to place
himself squarely in the jaws of the lion and return to Cuba. Clearly
he hadn't taken even the minimum of precautions, but kept openly
voicing his opinions until, like other independent souls in Cuba at
that time, he was arrested.

As Mario Vargas Llosa had the whole text of Padilla's confession, I was able to read about the complete proceedings of Heberto's
"self-criticism." The shocking and ridiculous ritual enacted at UNEAC
(Cuban National Council for Education and Culture) has made that
memorable evening one of the worst moments in the history of the
Cuban Revolution. And all those involved in the Padilla "confession,"
whether as witnesses or judges, have come out of that event stained
permanently and morally. There, in Mario's apartment, I was also
able to read Castro's diatribe against "bourgeois intellectuals, shame-
less pseudo-leftists living gloriously in Paris, Rome, or London instead of fighting in the front lines . . . CIA agents and libelists," homosexuality, extravagant dress, exotic African religions, "intellectual
rats," and "agents of imperialism." His housecleaning shopping list
began to resemble the ravings usually mouthed by fascist dictators.

Obviously Padilla's tragic, humiliating position, coupled with
Castro's attack on our letter, needed a reply. In Mario's apartment
Hans Magnus Enzenberger, my brother Luis, Castellet, Carlos Barral, Mario and I, drafted a second letter to Fidel Castro. Instead
of addressing ourselves to specific failures of the Cuban Revolution,
we decided to limit our answer to the UNEAC confession show. At
the last minute we realized our focus had been too narrow, and we
added the following paragraph which, probably, should have been
made the main issue:

> The contempt for human dignity involved in forcing a man to
> ridiculously accuse himself of the worst sorts of crimes and be-
> trayals isn't shocking to us because it has involved a fellow

writer, but, rather, because any Cuban—peasant, worker, technican or intellectual—is also in danger of being victimized by this sort of violence and debasement.

We had few illusions about our ability to change conditions in Cuba, but, nonetheless, resolved to collect as many signatures as possible before sending a copy of our letter to *Le Monde*. The next morning Mario wrote his resignation to the Casa de las Américas, and I took the plane back to Paris.

The *Libre* office was immediately deluged by those who wanted to know more about our position in the Padilla case. Most of those who had signed our first letter supported the second one. In addition, we also had the support of many people who didn't have a chance actually to sign the letter such as Alain Resnais, Pasolini, and the Mexican writer, Juan Rulfo. But we also had defections. The most important was Cortázar. In looking back I realize that he had also been ambivalent about the first letter, which he had helped draft. Now, after a cursory glance at the second letter, Cortázar abruptly informed me that he wasn't signing it. Carlos Barral, the Barcelona editor (and close friend of Padilla's), also called to remove his name.

After *Le Monde* published our text there was an enormous reaction. In Cuba, Chile, Mexico, Peru, Uruguay, Argentina, and Spain an avalanche of accusatory letters and articles were published against us. Luigi Nono, who had dropped into our place at rue de Bièvre just several weeks before with a message from Franqui, now made a quick reversal. He wired from Chile asking "to suspend publication of *Libre* backed by Patiño. Truly mortal offense to Bolivian miners and to all comrades in the Latin American struggle."

The campaign against us rapidly mounted. Castro was livid that the signers of the letter had included the most prestigious intellectuals in Europe and Ibero America, and his fury opened the door for every method of attack; photographers even came to Rue de Bièvre to take pictures of the *Libre* "palace." Our besieged situation was nothing new: the annals of the last fifty years of political history are filled with such stories.

As Maxime Rodinson in describing his own experiences as a militant in the Third World pointed out: "To criticize means to attack. . . . Your past, origins, personal habits are used, when necessary, to discredit your ideas. Your sources will be doubted. Who has written the book you are quoting? A Trotskyite? A Bukharinite? A

bourgeois? Published by whom? Paid by whom? Why now? In connection with what kind of political manipulation?" During those days
we had all sorts of disappointments. One day I ran into Régis Debray — who, himself, had just been freed from a Bolivian prison due
to the intervention of Western intellectuals. As Debray had just
returned from Cuba, I inquired after Heberto. Debray, who previously had lauded Padilla in print as being the ideal example of the
intellectual revolutionary, replied that the Cuban poet was a CIA
agent and deserved his fate. Right after that the Cubans started a
rumor that Sartre also was a member of the CIA. Simone de Beauvoir told me with chagrin that when she and Sartre had bumped into
the Cuban writer Alejo Carpentier on Boulevard Raspail, he abruptly
turned away in order to avoid greeting them.

   During this tense period the first issue of *Libre* was due for publication. We decided to postpone it until fall when we could include a
complete dossier of documents vis-à-vis Cuba which, we felt, would
present a more objective perspective than that which thus far had appeared in the European and Latin American press. The dossier had
in it the entire UNEAC "confession" text, Castro's closing speech to
the Cuban National Council for Education and Culture, our two letters to Castro, Vargas Llosa's correspondence with the head of Casa
de las Américas and, with Cortázar's assent, an editorial statement
pointing out that *Libre* was made up of writers with diverse political
tendencies and that we considered a debate on the Padilla case an
absolute necessity.

   Suddenly Julio, however, took us all by surprise by sending us
a long, odd political verse about the Padilla affair in which he complained against hothouse liberals who so generously translate "the in-
structions of the Jackal with headquarters in Washington." Even
worse than his diatribe against us was his sugary pro-revolutionary
sentiment, as he described the "Bright Tomorrow that awaits us . . ."
There were lines which read: "Good morning, Fidel, good morning
Haydée, good morning my Casa de las Américas . . ." And his
former friends and collaborators were scornfully referred to as "virtuous signers of letters." Nonplussed, one of the editors remarked
that the poem sounded like a tango with lyrics by Vichinsky. Sadly,
this author, who had formerly dazzled us with his fine style, had
made a tardy — and absolute — political conversion which was to change
him profoundly. Even his insistent presence at every political rally
thereafter could not conceal the abrupt decline of his former and exceptional literary grace.

But to demonstrate the existence of a certain semblance of unity at *Libre* we felt obliged to keep up with Cortázar and his circle, who had taken a stand diametrically opposed to our own. Looking back now, I feel we made too many concessions. The British Hispanist, J. M. Cohen, gave us a letter from the Cuban writer, Lisandro Otero, which was a reply to one Cohen had written protesting the humiliations inflicted on Padilla. Otero's letter — an extraordinary melange of insult, invective, and scatological references — struck me as worth publishing because of its real reflection of the hysteria prevalent in the Cuban bureaucracy over this case, but because of Cortázar's dissent we didn't publish it. Little by little, my physical distance from Paris made my ties with *Libre* increasingly remote. The final four issues of the magazine were so obviously articles published by compromise, I am very much ashamed when I think about it now.

Of course many of us early sympathizers with the Cuban Revolution, who saw in it the perfect model for the future already were familiar with the sad voyage of Barbusse, Romain Rolland, Aragon, Alberti, and Neruda. When confronted with the mock trials of the 1930s, they remained silent a very long time and, indeed, continued to make "revolutionary tourist" trips to the Soviet Union, enjoying all kinds of privileges — accomplished practitioners of what Enzenberger points out is an "old habit of lying knowing that one is lying." Still, in the early 1960s when we first visited Cuba, the idea that such an experience could repeat itself seemed remote, and we were shocked and embittered when the Cubans adopted the repressive methods used by the Soviet Union. These brand-new emulators of "socialism" quickly showed their indifference to the fate of a Biely, Pasternak, or Akhamatova. Their rationalization for remaining quiet and their absolute defense of "real socialism" were the same as in the thirties: don't discourage the morale of other comrades, don't give fuel to the enemy.

In examining the deplorable consequences of such a Manichean attitude, Vargas Llosa has pointed out: "Latin American intellectuals have been the biggest agents in the preservation of Latin American underdevelopment." These sorts of intellectuals, constantly looking outside, never permit self-examination of their way of life. Why do the bloody and reactionary dictatorships of Central and South America support Castro? In this odd Alice-in-Wonderland morality one reads statements such as: "The crimes and errors committed in a socialist country are not on the same level as those com-

mitted in an imperialist country." Why not? Latin America's conspicuous absence from the Russell Stockholm tribunal which had
gathered to condemn Soviet aggression in Afghanistan — though in
previous years they had come there to condemn American crimes in
Southeast Asia and Central America — was publicly censured by the
tribunal's president, Vladimir Dedidjir, and is a direct consequence
of this peculiar floating metaphysics. But my experience at *Libre*
taught me that a high degree of artistic ability doesn't necessarily im-
ply a corresponding intellectual and moral rigor.

Camus' *The Plague* starts: "On the 16th of April Doctor Bernard
Rieux left his office and stumbled across a dead rat lying on the staircase landing." And a lot of water has flowed through the Seine at
whose banks the rue de Bièvre ends since those days in the early
1960s when I saw my first "rat." There was the expulsion then of
many of my friends in the liberal wing of the Spanish Communist
Party who were allowed to flounder by themselves in Franco's Spain;
my own eye-opening trip to the Soviet Union, then to Czechoslovakia, my brief 1967 visit to Cuba, and, finally, the frustrated adventures of *Libre* magazine. With the advent of the Padilla case the ro-
dent's invasion turned into a plague.

In a very curious way, though, reality can be symbolic. After
my several friends and I left the cheap cous-cous restaurant on rue
de Bièvre that had made me recall so much of the old days, I suddenly
saw an authenic memento: there on the street in front of twenty-six
rue de Bièvre was the corpse of a real mouse.

*Juan Goytisolo, the Spanish novelist and essayist, is at work on his mem-
oirs. Among his works available in English are* Count Julian *and* Makbara,
published by Viking Press.

Sidney Hook

THE COMMUNIST PEACE OFFENSIVE

Another episode in which I was involved was of major significance compared to previous experiences in which I discovered systematic efforts by the Communists to control, and failing that, to undermine democratic movements and organizations. I no longer recall the exact date early in 1949 that I saw the announcement of the convening of the Cultural and Scientific Conference for World Peace at the swank Waldorf Astoria Hotel in New York City, under the auspices of the National Council of the Arts, Sciences and Professions, on March 25 to 27. I was vaguely aware that the predecessor of the National Council was the Independent Citizens Committee of the Arts, Sciences, and Professions which had endorsed and actively campaigned for Henry Wallace in the presidential election of the previous year. But I was definitely unaware at the time of the ramifications of the conference, the details of which came to light in the exciting weeks before its convocation.

The full text of the call for the conference was not available to me but, according to the news story, after detailing some considerations critical of current American foreign policy, it invited American artists, scientists, and professionals to come together "to discuss and seek a basis for common action on the central question of peace." It concluded with the following sentence: "We call upon those of no one party but of all parties, on all men of good will, to join with us."

Although naturally suspicious that this was just window dressing for another ambitious propaganda event to further the Soviet cause, I resolved to take the organizers of the conference at their word. Since I was a devotee of peace and considered myself a man of good will, I wrote to three members of the Program Committee among those listed who, I had reason to believe, were not Communist sympathizers, offering to read a paper on "Science, Culture and Peace," a topic that had an obvious bearing on the central theme of the Conference. I proposed to establish three theses which I spelled out in brief detail in the summary that I submitted:

1. There are no 'national truths' in science, and that it is only by its deficiencies that a science can ever become the science of

Editor's Note: This is a chapter excerpted from a forthcoming autobiography tentatively titled, *Out of Step: A Life in the Twentieth Century.* © Sidney Hook.

one nation or another. Illustrations: 'German Science,' 'Jewish Science.'

2. There are no 'class truths' or 'party truths' in science. The belief that there are confuses the objective evidence for a theory which, if warranted, is universally valid with the *uses*, good, bad, or indifferent that are made of it. Illustrations: 'proletarian science,' 'bourgeois physics,' *Partinost*.

3. The cause of international scientific cooperation and peace has been very seriously undermined by the influence of doctrines which uphold the doctrine that there are 'national' or 'class' or 'party' truths."

The members of the Program Committee to whom I wrote were Dr. Herbert John Davis, President of Smith College, Dr. Guy Emory Shipler, editor of *The Churchman*, and Dr. Sarah Gibson Blanding, President of Vassar College. The Chairman of the Program Committee was Dr. Harlow Shapley of Harvard University, but at the time I wrote he was listed only as Chairman of the conference. I heard from Dr. Davis and Dr. Shipler. The first wrote that he was glad to support my request to present a paper and that he was writing to Shapley "with my request that you should be given a full opportunity to present your views at a suitable plenary session of the Congress." Dr. Shipler also wrote to Shapley saying "it would be well if Dr. Hook were given an opportunity to present his paper." Upon receipt of Dr. Davis's letter I wrote to Shapley asking the time and place of the session at which I was scheduled to present my paper. Instead of a response from Shapley, I received a letter from a Mrs. Dorner, of the conference office, Suite 71, 49 West 44th Street, New York City, informing me that Shapley had telephoned that there was no place for me on the program. I could not reach Shapley on the telephone either at Cambridge or New York to confirm this. Nor would Mrs. Dorner answer the phone when I identified myself. When by a ruse she finally came on the phone, she brusquely repeated Shapley's message. To my request that I be permitted to open the discussion in the plenary session on science she flatly refused and said I would have to take my chances with everyone else on the floor of the conference, and that my speaking depended on whether or not I was recognized by the chairman of the session. She was not even sure that there would be time for a question and discussion period because of the number of speakers. Since I was an old hand at organizing and attending conferences, I knew what that meant.

I then telephoned Dr. Sarah Blanding of Vassar College and to my astonishment was told that there had never been a meeting of the

Program Committee! She made public announcement of this fact when she withdrew as a sponsor of the conference, as did Dr. Davis. It was now clear to me what the conference was. To make doubly sure I made extensive inquiries among friends and acquaintances in radical circles in New York, and telephoned individuals in a half dozen universities and colleges in the East. I discovered that not a single person openly critical of Soviet foreign policy or of the Communist Party line in any field of the arts and sciences had been invited. The program of speakers, to the extent that it could be discovered, indicated that the conference was to be a family affair among Communists and "honest liberals," the quaint expression used by the Communist Party to designate formally unaffiliated individuals who were willing to echo the party line or go along with it in uncritical complicity. My normal indignation with the deceptions practiced by the Communists reached a pitch of anger at the crudity and gall with which they were conducting this operation and the publicity it was receiving. They were posing as champions of peace at a time when the Soviet Union was threatening the peace of Europe with their blockade of Berlin, and as advocates of a free culture at the height of the Zhdanov purges and the imposition of Lysenkoism on Soviet scientists.

Resolved to counter this ambitious grandiose fraud on the American public with its pretensions to defend the cause of peace by concentrated attacks against American policies at home and abroad, I called a meeting consisting of as many local members I could reach of the Committee for Cultural Freedom, organized in 1939, which had become dormant during World War II, and some of its erstwhile revolutionary critics who had been sobered by the postwar experience. The meeting was held at the home of Dwight Macdonald, who made up in enthusiasm for the Spartan simplicity of his hospitality. There were about thirty persons present — Counts, Childs and one or two others from Teachers College, Kallen from The New School, Norman Thomas, James Farrell, Arnold Beichman, Bertram Wolfe, the editors of *The New Leader*, *Partisan Review*, and *Commentary*, and others whom I do not now recall. I explained the situation to them, cited the details of my own case as compelling evidence of the dishonesty of the proceedings, and proposed that we launch an educational countercampaign to expose the true auspices and purposes of the conference. By this time the conference had become controversial. The State Department had charged that it would become primarily "a sounding board for Communist propaganda," and its refusal to issue visas to some well-known European Communists who had been invited to attend disturbed the civil rights community. My proposal was unanimously approved. We took up a collection which amounted, if memory serves me correctly, to $280.00. With that and with a force of volunteers whose sacrificial labors reached heroic proportions, we launched the Ad Hoc Committee for Intellectual Freedom. I myself initially held out for calling our group the Committee for Cultural Freedom in order to stress our continuity with the earlier embodiment of our position, but in view of the fact that there were so many fresh accessions to our ranks I yielded on that point.

Meanwhile the organizers of the Waldorf Conference had not been idle. With vast resources at their disposal, they issued a stream of releases of the names of distinguished Communists and left-wingers from foreign countries scheduled to attend. The contingent from the Soviet Union, which included Dmitri Shostakovitch, was particularly impressive. (In a recent book purporting to be Shostakovitch's *Memoirs* it is alleged that Shostakovitch attended the Waldorf Conference at Stalin's personal behest.) An intensive campaign was undertaken to solicit sponsorship for the conference's program among leading figures in American cultural life.

The strategy we adopted in our countercampaign was a principled one. We proclaimed that we had no objection to the Communists or anyone else holding their meeting. We defended their right to do so. We made no demands that we be given a place on their program, although we were prepared to accept invitations if they were offered. We announced we would hold our own meeting and invited Dr. Shapley to speak or send a representative. We protested the selective policy of the State Department in refusing to issue visas to some of the Communist delegates from foreign countries like Bernal and Crowther. We also issued statements condemning the noisy picketing of the Waldorf Conference by militant pickets of the American Legion and other right-wing groups, on the ground that their antics prevented reasonable discussion. What we objected to were the false pretenses under which the conference was soliciting support, its declared objectives, in advance of the meeting, to hold the United States solely responsible for the cold war and to condemn its alleged domestic, political, and cultural repressions, while remaining silent about, and in effect condoning, the Kremlin's aggressions in Eastern Europe, Czechoslovakia, and West Berlin, and the merciless Zhdanov purges in the Soviet Union and satellite countries that were destroying thousands of innocent men and women by exile, imprisonment in concentration camps, and execution, for heresies in thought and style.

We did a little research and discovered the origins of the conference in the organization of the Cominform — the Communist Information Bureau — which replaced the Communist International
that had nominally been dissolved in 1943. The Cominform had
been set up to further the foreign policy goals of the Kremlin as soon
as Western resistance to post-war Soviet aggression developed. In
September 1947 at the first formal meeting of the Cominform in
Poland under the leadership of Zhdanov, the directives and strategy
of the world campaign against the democratic West were laid down.
Soon in various countries of the West, committees approved ostensibly in defense of peace against the machinations of American imperialism, in actuality in furtherance of the aggressions of the Soviet
Union. The distinctive feature of this round of "nonpartisan" peace
front activities was the concentration of their appeals to the intellectuals of the West — "to men of letters, men of art, culture and science,"
to rally to the defense of peace and to the exposure of the American
warmongers.

Among the first steps in this campaign was an Open Letter to
Writers and Men of Culture in the United States by a group of Soviet writers calling upon American intellectuals to raise their voices
against "the new threat of Fascism," equated with the threat of recently defeated Nazism, and "against the instigators of war" in the
West. Signed by some of the leading standbys of official Soviet literature like Fadayev, Sholokhov, Fedin, Katayev, and others, it elic-
ited a response only from functionaries and members of the American
Communist Party in *Masses and Mainstream*, May 1948, the official
organ of the Party in the field of culture. Shortly after this a World
Congress of Intellectuals was convened at Wroclaw (formerly Breslau)
in Poland, August 25 to 28, 1948. Its keynote speaker was Fadayev,
the Secretary of the Union of Soviet Writers. He directed a furious
attack against American imperialists and monopolists, and "the
beasts [who were] indispensable for their plans for world dominion."
These beasts were literary men characterized as "jackals who learned
to use the typewriter" and "hyenas who mastered the fountain pen" —
the writers and intellectuals who were in any way critical of the Soviet Union. They had lost their human estate since the days when
Stalin called them "gangsters of the pen." They were contrasted with
the heroic American writers who were resisting "the cold terror" being waged by the United States government against dissenters. "A
writer who writes anything dissenting from the official policy of the
Government of the United States," he declared, "is threatened with
ten years in prison." Neither he nor anyone else present at that Con-

gress of Intellectuals mentioned the fate of dissenters in the Soviet Union not only in politics but in any field of the arts and sciences.

Among the participants were some thirty Americans, most of them members of the Communist Party or notorious fellow travellers like Albert E. Kahn, William Gropper, Donald Ogden Stuart, Joe Davidson, and Howard Fast, all of whom were staunch sponsors of the Waldorf Conference. Also at Wroclaw were Harlow Shapley, Colston Warne, and other activists in the campaign for Henry Wallace. Fortunately for us there was one genuine innocent at the Congress, Bryn J. Hovde of the New School. When he realized what the tenor and real purposes of the Congress were, he made a spirited but totally ignored defense of "democracy as the only basis for peace." As soon as news got out of our countercampaign, he joined us and provided the documentary details that established that the Waldorf Conference was largely the work of the Continuations Committee of the Wroclaw Congress — one of several "peace" conferences scheduled to follow up the meetings of the Congress. Had I known the details of the Wroclaw Congress meeting revealed by Hovde, I doubt whether I would have offered to present a paper at the Waldorf Conference, since I would have taken it as a foregone conclusion that I would be automatically excluded from any of its sessions, but at the time the Congress was being held, I was in West Berlin acting as an educational advisor to the Office of Military Government of the United States at the height of the Communist blockade, after having attended the International Congress of Philosophy at Amsterdam from August 11 to 18, 1948. My ignorance of the connection between the Congress at Wroclaw, the Waldorf Conference in New York, and (a month later) the World Congress of Partisans of Peace at Paris, was fortunate but hard to explain in view of my intense interest in the ideological struggle between the Communist and free world. I do not know how to account for the lapse, since there was nothing I now recall to have diverted me. When I returned to New York from Europe in the fall, the electoral campaign was in full flood. Everyone I knew took the victory of Governor Thomas Dewey for granted. I was not active in the campaign, restricting myself to a debate with Mark van Doren who, under the influence of Scott Buchanan, was a naive and uncritical supporter of Henry Wallace, and to several forays against Communist Party stalwarts masquerading as Progressives. John Dewey was trying to rally American educators for Truman, but at that time I had little admiration for Truman, a judgment revised in the light of his successors. I was surprised and somewhat flattered by a phone call from a senior staff member of Republican Senator Keating of New York inquiring whether in the event of Thomas Dewey's election, about which the caller was completely sanguine, I would be willing to serve in some capacity as a foreign policy advisor in Washington. I made a noncommittal response because of my disagreements with the Republican Party platform on domestic issues. Besides, I was not prepared to give up the life of the academy. The pursuit of philosophical activity still seemed to me to be the most important thing in the world. Little did I realize the extent to which in the next few months I was to be diverted from it.

With the knowledge of the Waldorf Conference's antecedents, we threw ourselves into the educational struggle. A war of mimeograph machines and public relations releases began between the mammoth propaganda facilities of the Conference and our handful of volunteers. But we had two experienced newsmen working for us — Arnold Beichman and Melvin J. Pitzele, who were more than a match for the opposition, although they kept on complaining about fellow-travelling reporters on the *New York Times* and clamoring for more money to meet mounting expenses. These were incurred by our decision to rent a single room at the enemy's stronghold, the Waldorf Astoria Hotel, in whose luxurious suites most of the foreign and native participants of the conference were lodged. Pearl Kluger, a genius at organization and experienced in operating shoestring left-wing causes, was in charge of a clerical staff that worked day and night. No one was paid or dreamed of asking for pay. Since there was not time for leisurely meals in restaurants, food was supplied by room service and, despite my protests, justified in the interests of time and efficiency. I was dismayed at these costs, not to mention the extra tariffs we paid for emergency printing, rent of machines, telephone and telegram charges. The money we had initially raised, together with supplementary contributions from visitors, vanished quickly, but a personal appeal to David Dubinsky, the President of the International Ladies Garment Workers Union, brought the funds that gave us our momentum after we were launched. A heartening aspect of our enterprise was a constant stream of unsolicited contributions from the public after the news of our existence and purpose was published. But at one crucial point Arnold Beichman informed me that if we couldn't pony up more money we would have to shut down. In desperation I appealed to Dubinsky again, who gave us a "final" five hundred dollars. Louis Marx, the toy manufacturer, who had attended my lectures at The New School, sent us an equal amount which I matched from my own savings.

Our task was quite formidable, not merely because our material resources were comparatively pitiful. Lingering memories of Soviet-American wartime cooperating were still strong in some liberal centers, especially the universities. Despite the defeat of the Communist-backed Wallace ticket in the fall of 1948, the graphic evidence of Soviet aggression in Czechoslovakia, West Berlin, and elsewhere, the Gouzenko revelations of the pervasiveness of the Kremlin's espionage apparatus, the demagogic appeal of the Communist peace slogans snared a considerable number of outstanding figures in American cultural life. Criticisms of British and French imperalism, of Chinese domestic repression, were accepted as a matter of course application of liberal principles, but in certain quarters fundamental criticism of Soviet policies at home and abroad were denounced as invocations to war. We circularized the hundreds of sponsors of the Waldorf Conference who could be differentiated from Party members like John Howard Lawson or A. B. Magill or from hardened professional fellow travellers like Corliss Lamont or Frederick L. Schuman. Of the approximately six hundred fifty sponsors, about one hundred fifty clearly did not belong there. We pointed out to them that the main interest of the conference was in furthering the foreign policy of the Soviet Union, that the genuine defense of peace would be strengthened by their dissociation from the list of sponsors. Failing that, we requested that in the interests of fair play, they bring pressure on the organizers of the conference to permit another point of view to be expressed on the program. We cited my case in point as evidence of the chicanery of the organizers.

Only a few of the non-Communist sponsors were induced to resign as sponsors. Among them was Irwin Edman, one of my former teachers at Columbia University, news of whose defection was suppressed by the organizers of the conference. Edman revealed the chief technique by which some genuine liberals were ensnared. A prominent individual like Harlow Shapley who exploited his association with Harvard University and claimed to be speaking with the authority and permission of Albert Einstein, another sponsor, would telephone the prospective signer. Prestige by association is even easier to acquire than guilt by association. Who could suspect an astronomer whose profession had the aura of the remoteness and purity of the stars, supported by Einstein, to play the role of anchorman or rather, barker, at a Communist carnival?

There were other liberal figures whose resentment of the bullying pickets and aggressive newspaper campaign surpassed any regrets or doubts we raised in their minds about the auspices of the conference. Their resentment of the noisy picketing was justified, and we shared it, but it was not a sufficient ground to permit their names to be used as a cover-up of the purposes of the conference. Somewhat to my surprise, some of the sponsors maintained that not Communism but Catholicism, not the Kremlin but the Vatican, threatened peace and freedom in the world, a bizarre judgment that had no relevance to the issues and anti-American orientation of the conference. But the chief rejoinder to our protests was the assertion we had heard in the thirties, and which was repeated many years later, that the concern of American liberals was primarily with "the sins of our own country. We live here and not abroad. Whatever the actions of Stalin we cannot affect them." This came from men and women who had on dozens of occasions protested the actions of British and French imperialism, of Hitler, Franco, and Mussolini, of dictators in Southern and Central America, of Chiang Kai-shek in distant China. It seems only yesterday that Lillian Hellman, in replying to Dan Rather's question, on a CBS interview, of why she remained silent about Stalin's Gulag Archipelago and other infamous crimes while passionately denouncing the excesses of the McCarthy investigation, replied, "I don't really know what one thing has to do with another. I was not a Russian, I was an American." (She was not a German yet she blasted Hitler, not a Spaniard but attacked Franco.) Finally, there were the impressive German exiles, Einstein, Thomas Mann, Irwin Panofsky, whose hatred of the Germans was so profound that they felt greater gratitude towards than fear of the Russians, despite what was occurring in Eastern and Central Europe and within the Soviet Union itself. (The case of Einstein I shall discuss in a separate chapter.)

It was undoubtedly Harlow Shapley who played the leading role in involving the non-Communist sponsors. He was especially effective with scientists who lacked sophistication. It was he who had approached A. J. Carlson, the brilliant and temperamental physiologist at the University of Chicago. I had known Carlson in the mid-thirties. I was then a member of the Council of the American Association of University Professors when Carlson was president and Ralph Himstead executive secretary. At one of the Council meetings a communication had been received from the College Teachers Union, Local Five, then under the control of the Communist Party, proposing a program of joint action with the AAUP. The words were honeyed and inoffensive. In the discussion I read from an internal bulletin of the Union, revealing that its strategy was first to collaborate with the AAUP and then bore from within, ultimately to take it over or destroy it. After convincing itself of the authenticity of the document from which I read, the Council naturally rejected the overtures from the College Teachers Union. In the course of the discussion, however, Colston C. Warne, of Amherst College, had heatedly arisen to take issue with me. In his rather incoherent speech trying to explain away the official document from which I had read as "sectarian," and not representative of the true statements of the College Teachers Union of which he was a proud member, he alluded to me as a "Trotskyist." Most of the Council members didn't understand the meaning or the relevance of the term. I shall never forget, however, the retort of A. J. Carlson, speaking in his thick unmistakable Swedish accent: "Excuse me Professor Warne, the only persons I know who call others Trotskyists are Stalinists!" That silenced Colston Warne who, almost needless to say, was a leading sponsor of the Waldorf Conference, a speaker at one of its sessions, and a participant at the Wroclaw Congress.

After I telephoned Carlson and sent him the relevant documents, he sent a strong letter of protest to Shapley with a carbon copy to Thomas Mann (See Appendix). The conference officials denied ever receiving it and to the bitter end listed Carlson as a sponsor. Carlson was only one of the many sponsors to whom I had written, and although most of them refused to take a public stand against the conference, they forwarded my letter to Shapley with strong recommendations that a place be made for me on the program. Whereupon Shapley wrote me a letter dated March 18, 1949, the first paragraph of which read:

> Several of the sponsors and participants in our coming Cultural and Scientific Conference for World Peace have sent me the letters you have written them. In some of these communications I regret to see that you have made plain mis-statements of fact. For example, neither President Davis or Dr. Shipler have written me any instruction or request or communication whatever with regard to your demand (*sic!*) that you be placed on the Conference program.

Addressed to me at New York University, I received it on Monday, March 21. That afternoon a reporter from the *New York Times* telephoned me and in belligerent tones asked me what I had to say about Dr. Shapley's statement that I was "a downright liar." Either Shapley had made a copy of his letter to me available to the press or someone from the conference's office had leaked it. I told the reporter that I was prepared to make the letters of President Davis and Dr. Shipler public and that if Shapley was telling the truth about his not having received these letters, this was additional evidence that he was not really in charge of the conference and that it was being run behind his back. Once more, after writing to Shapley giving the dates and details of the communications from Davis and Shipler, I tried to reach him on the phone, to make sure he received my letter. It was to no avail. I was now convinced that Shapley was going to repeat his serious charge that I was guilty of a malicious fabrication at the opening session of the conference in order to discredit the only responsible opposition that had been organized against it. My own integrity had been impugned. I decided to confront Shapley with the evidence of the letters he denied and before a public witness.

On the evening of the day the Waldorf Conference was scheduled to begin, actually at the cocktail hour before the gala banquet, I summoned the newspaper reporter from the *Herald Tribune* who was covering the events at the conference, and went to Shapley's room at the Waldorf Astoria. I knocked at the door and was invited in. Shapley and another man, both in formal dress, and their wives were sipping drinks. Shapley had never met me. He rose from his chair with a startled look when I introduced myself and the reporter from the *Herald Tribune.* He introduced the other man, Martin Popper, and the wives. "Please excuse my visit," I began, "but I have been unable to reach you in any other way since Monday. You have impugned my integrity, Dr. Shapley, by denying that my offer to read a paper at the conference was ever accepted by any members of the Program Committee. You have specifically claimed that President Davis and Dr. Shipler never wrote you. Well, here's the evidence — letters from Davis and Shipler." And I plumped down copies before him.

Shapley didn't seem disconcerted a bit. "Oh!" he replied, "I know about the existence of these letters." "Then why did you issue your statement accusing me of deceiving the public?" I demanded. "Well," he responded, "it's a long story and we can't go into it here before the ladies who are getting ready to go down to the banquet soon. Let us leave them, and go outside to talk about it." He put his glass down, went to the door, opened it, and stepped into the hall where I thought he would lead us to a table and a few upholstered chairs clustered around it just a few yards away. But no sooner had the reporter and I left the room and turned to the table, than he jumped back into the room, slammed the door and snapped the lock. From the hubbub of voices within I heard Popper say: "Call the desk. Call Security." My purpose accomplished, the delivery before a reputable witness of the evidence that it was not I who was deceiving the public, I left.

The *Herald Tribune* ran an exclusive front-page story of the incident the next day. The *New York Times* ran a boxed item reporting a hearsay account of the incident, probably relayed by Shapley or one of his assistants, in which the whole point of my visit was suppressed and in which I was portrayed as a wild man bursting in on an innocent Shapley. To cover himself the reporter added that an attempt to confirm the details by a phone call to my home was unsuccessful. No one answered the phone! It so happened, however, that I went immediately home after the encounter with Shapley to prepare my talk at the counterdemonstration meeting we were holding at Freedom House the afternoon of the next day. The simple truth was that the reporter, who presumably was the same one who was writing slanted stories against our Ad Hoc Committee, now rechristened Americans for Intellectual Freedom, never telephoned.

I never learned the details of Shapley's collaboration with the Communist Party and how he had become involved. He had been a very active participant in the World Congress of Intellectuals at Wroclaw the previous year. He was known as an ardent supporter of Henry Wallace's campaign. To his credit he had helped line up American scientists before the Nazi-Soviet Pact in denouncing Nazi persecution of Jewish and non-conforming scientists, even though this involved collaboration with the Boas Committee which studiously avoided any mention of the ideological purges of scientists in the Soviet Union. But he was now playing the role not only of master of ceremonies at the Waldorf intellectual circus but of extenuator, if not outright apologist, of Soviet scientific repression. The Waldorf Conference followed hard on the brutal purge of Soviet geneticists after Stalin had decided that Lysenko's views were in accordance with the principles of dialectical materialism. When questioned about the fate of Vavilov, the eminent Soviet geneticist who perished in a concentration camp, and other Soviet biologists, Shapley claimed that they had merely suffered "demotions." In a letter to one of the sponsors (Dr. Lengyel) who had requested that I be permitted to speak at the conference, he again referred to the "demotions" of these victims and compared them to the uncertain fate of Jewish applicants to medical schools in America. "The admission of Jews to medical schools and the demotions of Russian geneticists are not too distantly related." In answer to our criticisms, he did declare a few days before the conference met: "Science has to be free — in our Southern states as well as Russia" (*New York Times*, March 20, 1949). This coupling of reference to the silly unenforced laws against evolution in three Southern states with the horrendous and widespread persecutions that led to exile and sentences to concentration camps that were often sentences of death, this equation between the farfetched possibility of United States repression with the actuality of Soviet persecution became standard procedure whenever Shapley was compelled to acknowledge the true state of affairs in Russia. When asked to explain why, when he denounced Nazi persecution of scientists on racial grounds, he never coupled them with reference to Southern racism or to the silly laws against the teaching of evolution, still on the books, or to the discriminatory practices against Jewish applicants to medical schools that were much more severe in the thirties than in the late forties, he vouchsafed no answer. Nor did he ever acknowledge the scope and depth of the Soviet purges in areas other than genetics from astronomy to zoology, in the arts, music, and literature, as attested by the Resolutions of the Central Committee of the All-Union Communist Party.

Shapley never forgave me for my role in exposing the Communist bias and control of the conference. He exercised considerable influence in American intellectual life. I have been told on excellent authority that until he died he was an important power in determining the membership of the American Institute of Arts and Sciences. In one colloquy with Curt Ducasse, he vowed that so long as he could help it I would never become a member of the Institute. And from 1949 on until his death he consistently blackballed my election. His colleagues seemed indifferent to or unaware of his political bias. I remember how incredulous the Nobelist Harvard physicist, Percy Bridgman, was when I tried to tell him the story of the Waldorf. "I can't believe that is true of the man I know," he protested. One hardly expected W. Ernest Hocking, the Harvard philosopher who joined clerical reactionaries in opposing Bertrand Russell's appointment to the College of the City of New York on grounds of his radicalism, to be a sponsor of a Conference that was stage-managed to further the foreign policy of the Soviet Union. He was. But in his correspondence with me he dismissed all the seeming evidence and denied that this could be because of the presence of Shapley. Undoubtedly Shapley was a complex character, for the previous year he had written another sponsor of the conference (Robert Lynd) pointing out the danger of compromising liberal causes by too close an association with Communists. However, there was soon to surface public evidence of his strong authoritarian streak. He was the editor of an extremely profitable series of scientific texts published by Macmillan. When he learned that Macmillan was about to publish one of Velikovsky's heretical books, he threatened to organize a boycott of Macmillan among the scientific community. Under his pressure Macmillan withdrew the book and dismissed its editor, James Putnam. I am under the impression that Einstein, to whom Velikovsky had complained, rebuked Shapley for his intolerance, not that Einstein put any stock in Velikovsky's bizarre theories.

Probably every non-Communist sponsor of the conference had some reason that appeared good and sufficient to him to remain steadfast in his sponsorship. The case of Rudolf Carnap, whose philosophy was antipodal to that of Hocking's, is interesting because Carnap was aware that anyone holding views even remotely suggesting his would get extremely short shrift in the Soviet Union or any country in which Communist orthodoxy prevailed. Nonetheless, like several others, he wrote me that he regarded the preservation of peace in the world as a consideration outweighing everything else. He seemed utterly oblivious to the fact that if we had been guided by the same consideration when Hitler was professing peace as the be-all and end-all of his foreign policy, the world he was living in would not exist.

*   *   *

The real triumph of our cause was achieved in the counter-demonstration we held at Freedom House far away from the Waldorf. The crowd was so large that the street had to be blocked off and loudspeakers set up to reach the audience. We had invited Oparin to meet Muller, the Soviet writers to meet the American writers they had denounced as "jackals" and "hyenas," Shapley himself to discuss the *bona fides* of his Conference with its critics. I chaired the meeting and read strong telegrams of support from individuals of such diverse views as Bertrand Russell, T. S. Eliot, Arthur Koestler, and Senator Paul Douglas. There were many speakers, but because of the diverse themes the audience remained attentive. Among them were Bryn Hovde who had been at Wroclaw, George Counts, who was co-chairman with me of the American Committee for Intellectual Freedom, Max Eastman, who had vast knowledge of the details of Soviet suppression of dissident Russian writers, Max Yergan, the black publicist who, although sharply critical of American racialism, exposed the hypocrisy of Soviet professions of cultural autonomy for its ethnic minorities, Morris Ernst of the American Civil Liberties Union, who compared the state of civil liberties in the United States and the

Soviet Union, Arthur Schlesinger, Jr., who defended the vital center against political extremists of every coloration, H. J. Muller, the renowned Nobelist in genetics, who had flown in from Indiana to relate the story of Soviet repression in biology to enforce a theory that actually had different social implications from those they feared, Bertram Wolfe, who traced the varieties of ways in which the Kremlin had violated its pledges at Yalta and Teheran. We also gave the platform to A. J. Muste, militant pacifist and erstwhile revolutionist, who denounced the American government as equally responsible for the cold war as the Soviet Union. Begun in the early afternoon, night had already fallen when we concluded.

We shared the headlines in the Sunday press the next day. That the cause of peace was furthered is extremely doubtful, but our point that the Waldorf Conference was convoked not to further peace but to propagandize for Soviet foreign policy was sustained. The conference terminated the day after our meeting with a typical Communist rally at Madison Square Garden in which the domestic and foreign policy of the United States was roundly denounced. We had frustrated one of the most ambitious undertakings of the Kremlin whose next act was scheduled to be performed in Paris the subsequent month. I myself had scrupulously refrained from attending any of the sessions at the Waldorf, but several of our members did visit some sessions where they sought to ask questions that were turned aside. There was no discussion whatsoever. The few questions asked to which no follow-up was permitted were later cited as evidence by some apologists for the conference that a genuine give-and-take had occurred. William Barrett, who probably attended more sessions than anyone else, described them in detail in an article he published in *Commentary* in May 1949. What depressed him was not only the low level of the proceedings but that despite the international situation, so many non-Communist intellectuals had been snared. There is reason to believe that even they had learned something from the experience. Until the rise of the New Left in the sixties there was very little fellow-travelling, primarily due not so much to our efforts as to the change of climate in the country and the appearance on the scene of Senator McCarthy and the Congressional investigating committees.

After the event an effort was made by some of the sponsors of the Waldorf Conference who clung to the label of "liberal," although they had over the previous years denied the truth of allegations of intellectual and cultural repression in the Soviet Union, to justify their sponsorship. They claimed that they were interested in encouraging "a fair and free exchange of ideas" — that we were not; and sought to pin on us responsibility for the raucous picketing of the Conference we had publicly condemned. For example, see Theodore Brameld, an educator then at Long Island University, in a letter to the *New York Times*, April 3, 1949. The sincerity of this claim can be judged from the fact that neither Brameld nor any of the sponsors for whom he presumed to speak made the slightest effort to open up the program to open and honest discussion of different points of view. He was not among those who wrote to Shapley. He remained conspicuously silent at the public meetings and together with his colleagues, they became accomplices in the perpetuation of an intellectual fraud. In his letter he belatedly acknowledges that the Soviet dictatorship "deserved severe criticism" but at the conference he did not offer it. He cites the delivery of one critical speech — one was permitted at Wroclaw, too — and a few desultory questions from the floor as evidence that there was actually "free interchange of ideas" at the Waldorf. It is also noteworthy that indignant as Brameld was with the anti-Communist picketing, he never before or since ever uttered a word in condemnation of Communist picketing every whit as disorderly, if not more so, than the picketing he deplored.

There is a natural tendency in writing about events of the past to reconstruct them so as to support or express present attitudes that are judged to be acceptable to regnant public opinion. No one is immune from this tendency, including the present writer. Consciousness of the danger is a source of restraint; the public record, when it is available, is a better one, even allowing for the selective bias and distortions that creep into contemporary accounts.

I regret to note that in his treatment of the incidents treated in this chapter, Nicolas Nabakov in his *Bagázh-Memoirs of a Russian Cosmopolitan* has let his fancy roam, and given a very misleading description of the origin, nature, personnel, and development of the opposition movement to the Waldorf Conference — a movement in which he played a very subordinate role. Because he was a modernist Russian musician he was asked to speak briefly at our meeting at Freedom House. He is mistaken about there being any policy, or differences about policy, concerning the desirability of individual members of our committee participating in the panel sessions of the Waldorf meeting. He pictures himself as urging peaceful and civilized discourse rather than violent disruption — something no one proposed. According to him the meetings and plans of the opposition were worked out at his flat. How reliable that account is may be judged from the following: "We agreed," he writes, "that whatever we did should have public appeal and the support of the press, but at the same time should be authentic. It should not look as if it were government-sponsored or—as Mary [McCarthy] said—'staged by Joe McCarthy'."

Mary McCarthy could not have said it nor Nabakov heard it in the spring of 1949 when we organized our Committee. For Senator Joseph McCarthy did not go on the anti-Communist warpath until 1950! None of us had even heard of him at that time.

*   *   *

Appendix

The following letters are referred to in the text of the article:

March 14, 1949

Mr. Thomas Mann
Palisades, California

Dear Mr. Mann:

I am writing to you once more about the Cultural and Scientific Conference for World Peace which is meeting at the Waldorf Astoria, New York City, March 25th and 26th. I have been refused permission to present a paper by the controlling group of the Conference. In this paper I wished to defend three theses which seemed to me of the greatest importance to-day.

1. There are no "national truths" in science, and that it is only by its deficiencies that a science can ever become the science of one nation or another.
2. There are no "class truths" or "party truths" in science. The belief that there is confuses the objective evidence for a theory which, if warranted, is universally valid with the *uses*, good, bad or indifferent, that are made of it.
3. The cause of international scientific cooperation and peace has been very seriously undermined by the influence of doctrines which uphold the notion that there are "national" or "class" or "party" truths in science.

Not only have I been refused permission to present a paper at any of the sessions, but I have also been refused permission to lead the discussion at the plenary session. I requested at least fifteen minutes. And this despite the fact that some members of the Program Committee, including Drs. Herbert Davis and Guy Emory Shipler, requested Professor Shapley that I be given an opportunity to be heard.

Since your name is listed as a sponsor of this Congress, I am appealing to you to support my request that I be permitted to read a paper at the plenary session. No arrangements have been made, apparently, by the Program Committee to have the point of view which I represent presented to the Congress. Further, no person who has in recent years ever spoken a critical word against all varieties of totalitarianism, including Stalin's, has been invited to participate in the actual program of the Congress. Neither John Dewey nor Ernest Nagel nor Horace Kallen nor James T. Farrell nor Dos Passos nor Edmund Wilson nor Meyer Schapiro nor scores of others have been invited to this Congress for World Peace.

Professor H. Muller, American geneticist and Nobel Prize winner, has *not* been invited but A. Oparin, Acting Secretary of the Biological Section of the Soviet Academy of Science who moved to expel Prof. Muller from the Soviet Academy of Science because of his criticisms of Lysenko *has been invited.*

The *New York Times* of March 4th reports the resignation of Professor Edman of Columbia University from the sponsoring committee of the Congress on grounds that it is designed to promote "the Communist point of view or one closely approximating to it." I sincerely hope that this is not true. But the way this Congress has been organized and my experience with it suggests that it is on the order of Wroclaw-Breslan.

Sincerely yours,

Sidney Hook

P.S. Since writing the above I have discovered that the Americans who were appointed to the Continuations Committee of the Wroclaw-Breslau Communist peace conference last summer were Dr. Harlow Shapley, Howard Fast, Joe Davidson, and Albert E. Kahn, a notorious card-holding Communist and member of the Executive Committee of the New York State Communist Party. All except Dr. Shapley accepted; all including Dr. Shapley are organizers and sponsors of the Cultural and Scientific Conference for World Peace. Further, I have identified by actual count more than ninety well known fellow-travellers of the Communist Party line, of the order of Corliss Lamont and Harry Ward, in the list of sponsors as published on the official stationery of the Conference.

I am confident that although you are listed as a sponsor of the Conference, your name was procured under false pretenses. At any rate, it seems to me highly desirable for the sake of your own good name to insist that the point of view I have expressed in my paper be presented at the Conference and that a place be made for me on the program. I shall appreciate it if you will send me a copy of your communication to Dr. Shapley. I am asking you to send me a copy of any telegrams or letters you address to the Conference because Professor Edman's letter of resignation was suppressed by the Organizing Committee and he was compelled to make it public himself.

It seems to me that the cause of peace would be better served if independent persons like yourself make the sharpest dissociation from any individuals or groups whose main interest is in furthering the interests of Soviet foreign policy.

March 23, 1949

Dr. Harlow Shapley
Cultural and Scientific Conference for World Peace
49 West 44th Street
New York, N.Y.

Dear Dr. Shapley:

In a communication to me dated March 18 — the first direct word I have had from you since the announcement of your Conference — you claim that in my letter to some of the sponsors of the Conference I have been guilty of "plain misstatements of fact." You go on to say:

> For example, neither President Davis nor Dr. Shipler have written me any instruction or request or communication whatsoever with regard to your demand that you be placed on the Conference program.

I have in my possession the following letter which President Davis sent me dated February 24th, 1949, which I reproduce in its entirety. Please note the sentences I have underlined.

> Dear Mr. Hook:
>
> Many thanks for your kind letter of February 23rd. As I should myself agree with the theses which you put forward, I should be very glad to support your request that you should read a paper before one of the sessions of the Congress on the theme you suggest. I have been concerned with the program for only one of the meetings on Education, and I find that the general program has already gone to print. I assume that you have probably written also to Dr. Shapley but I will send him a copy of this letter with my request that you should be given a full opportunity to present your views at a suitable plenary session of the Congress.
> Yours very sincerely,
>
> Herbert Davis

On February 25th, I wrote you as follows and I quote the opening and concluding paragraph from the carbon copy of my letter:

> President Davis of Smith College has informed me that he has requested you to make provision at a plenary session of the Cultural and Scientific Conference for World Peace for the reading of my paper on "Science, Culture, and Peace."
>
> Will you please let me know the time and place of the plenary session at which my address will be scheduled?
> Sincerely,
>
> Sidney Hook

I have also in my possession a carbon copy, sent to me by Dr. Shipler, of the letter he wrote you on March 7, 1949. I quote the opening paragraphs:

My dear Dr. Shapley:

I am enclosing a letter I received sometime ago from Dr. Sidney Hook. I am sorry for the delay in bringing the matter to your attention, but as you may imagine, I was swamped by arrangements for the dinner to Bishop Ornam.

As you know, my only function as a member of the program committee of the Cultural and Scientific Conference for World Peace is in helping with the religious panel. I know nothing as to how speakers on the other panels, or at the plenary sessions, are chosen. I suggest, however, that it would be well if Dr. Hook were given an opportunity to present his paper. . . .

Very cordially yours,

Guy Emery Shipler
Editor

Dr. Shipler confirmed his request to you in his statement to the press on March 20th, cf. *N.Y. Herald Tribune* of that date, page 19, column 4.

What am I to think, Dr. Shapley: As an astronomer you know that the probability of three independently written letters, mailed at different times about the same subject to the same person, being lost in the mails is indeterminately if not infinitely small. At the same time I am loath to conclude that you are deliberately telling an untruth although you have not scrupled to slander my integrity in charging me with plain and persistent misstatement of fact.

There is only one alternative explanation which plausibly accounts for your conduct, unexampled in scientific and academic circles. It is that you do not know what is going on within your own organization, that the inner Communist group are deceiving you to the point of suppressing letters sent to you which they do not wish to come to your attention, and that you have become the willing dupe of enemies of your own country as well as of the ideals of moral decency and scientific truth you profess.

Since you probably sent copies of your letter to the sponsors of the Conference who forwarded my communication to you, I demand either a public apology or the names and addresses of all the persons to whom you have sent your untruthful charges against me.

Needless to say I regard your conduct in this matter as unbecoming a teacher, scholar and scientist.

Yours very truly,

Sidney Hook

* * *

Sidney Hook is Professor of Philosophy Emeritus at New York University and Senior Research Fellow at the Hoover Institution on War, Revolution, and Peace.

Alfred Kazin

FEAR OF THE AGE:
AN ESSAY IN CULTURAL CRITICISM

Art is a child of pain.
Stephen Crane

A despairing literature is a contradiction in terms.
Albert Camus

There are people for whom reading is nothing but a form
of relaxation and even a narcotic or escape. I wish I were one of
them, as of course I am one on occasion — say at three in the morning, when the real world is too much for my heart and mind and the
sleepless self wants, as they say, to escape. What I am going to talk
about is what I read and think about in the middle of the night,
when the external world is no longer a distraction from my real
thoughts and I recognize that the world is nowhere but in my "real
thoughts."

Let me begin with a poem from the nineteenth century — a century in which literature was still the capital of discourse, a necessity
before specialization took over even for scientists like Darwin,
philosophers like Nietzsche and William James, doctors to the soul
like Freud. The poem is Matthew Arnold's early sonnet "To A
Friend" (1848), and the opening is one of the worst lines ever written
by a good poet. But since this opening asks the question that I shall
be asking, I have to quote it —

Who prop, thou ask'st, in these bad days, my mind?

The "bad days" to Arnold may have been the revolutionary outbreak of 1848. *I* think of them as life in the closing decades in the
twentieth century, when more than twenty towns in Missouri have
been poisoned by dioxin; when millions, being unemployed, have lost
their health insurance, are swiftly coming to the end of their unem-
ployment compensation, and hundreds of thousands among them have
in this freest and most buoyant of countries given up looking for

work. While the threat of war and world destruction hangs over our heads, our leaders assure us in the same breath that we are the most God-fearing people in the world, but that peace can be assured only by accepting every social hardship, every cutback in education and health, the erosion of our cities, roads, bridges, in favor of a massive rearmament at the cost of almost two trillions. No one dare question. Even experienced battleship admirals protested the outlay of $383 million to put the *New Jersey* back into service, but to no avail. A hundred million, not just sixty, will soon be sent down to shore up the Salvadoran government, but this same government derides the noble example of priests and nuns still trying to defend landless peasants against a government whose military and security services have committed thirty thousand unpunished murders, are responsible for over ten thousand "disappearances" of civilians in custody.

There was a time when a Pope, like Pius XII, was so haughty and secluded that he took all his meals alone. John Paul II, a native of one of the most grievously wounded and suffering of all European countries, rushes from country to country pleading for peace and reconciliation. And the daily terror and outrage are made worse by communications. In Alabama a desperate unemployed man sets fire to himself, and the television cameramen allow him to burn for eighty-two seconds so that the television viewers can get their evening cocktail of shock, horror, terror, surprise. The New York *Post,* a vile tabloid, headlines a murder every day, and for some reason it gets more readers every day, either because people don't know *what* they are reading, or can't take it in, or perhaps don't believe any of it. The media have a bad reputation now with everyone, but fascinate even those scornful of it; it is impossible *not* to know what is going on.

Now what has this to do with the reading of books, literary study, education itself in an age like ours? For most people, nothing at all, for to read seriously nowadays, to take reading seriously, is to believe that there is some necessary relation between literature and the disorder in our age, the disorder in our hearts. It is to proclaim one's membership in a so-called elite and adherence to discarded culture. Everyone in a university knows nowadays that the sense of tradition on which literature depends no longer exists, that certain difficult modernist texts in the English Department curriculum are never enjoyed as works of art but have to be elucidated, often word for word. The greatest works of literature in English have become foreign to many students. They can read a computer more easily than a great political thriller by Conrad, like *The Secret Agent,* that requires knowing when the Russian Revolution occurred and what the anarchist movement was all about.

Still, that makes teaching, which is my life and my love, possible. But Matthew Arnold's question *Who prop, thou ask'st, in these bad days, my mind?* is a question I ask myself day and night, even if it is addressed to nobody but myself. After praising Homer as "the clearest-soul'd of men," and Epictetus, Arnold ends with his famous tribute to Sophocles:

> But be his
> My special thanks, whose even-balanced soul,
> From first youth tested up to extreme old age,
> Business could not make dull, nor passion wild;
> Who saw life steadily, and saw it whole.

Ah, that nineteenth-century faith in the book, especially a book not of your own century! Matthew Arnold so much believed in the classics that on his many journeys as a school inspector to the grim state schools of industrial England he cheered himself up with his famous touchstones, examples of what, he confidently believed, embodied another of his lasting phrases—"the best that has been thought and said in the world."

The most exquisite lines that stayed in Arnold's beautifully cultivated mind—from Homer, Dante, Shakespeare, Milton, etc., etc.—their tone, their extension into and from the mind, their "high seriousness," "the high seriousness which comes from absolute sincerity"—these gave him not only, he was assured, a standard by which to test the poetry "on burning ground as we approach the poetry of times so near to us," but obviously great comfort in the face of modern illiteracy. In the essay "Literature and Science," he sadly notes:

> I once mentioned in a school-report how a young man in one of our English training colleges having to paraphrase the passage in *Macbeth* beginning,
>
> *Cans't thou not minister to a mind diseased?*
>
> turned this line into *Can you not wait upon the lunatic?* And I remarked what a curious state of things it would be, if every pupil of our national schools knew, let us say, that the moon is

two thousand one hundred and sixty miles in diameter, and thought at the same time that a good paraphrase for *Cans't thou not minister to a mind diseas'd* was *Can you not wait upon the lunatic?*

Arnold was born and died in the last century to believe that reading maketh a full man, a complete man — that literature is the queen of the arts — that the great writer is not just a hero but, as Arnold said of Emerson, "the friend and aider of those who would live in the spirit . . . One can scarcely overrate the importance of thus holding fast to happiness and hope. It gives to Emerson's work an invaluable virtue." Henry Adams in his *Education* relates an anecdote told him by an English friend about Victor Hugo in the 1870s. "I was shown into a large room with women and men seated in chairs against the walls, and Hugo at one end throned. No one spoke. At last Hugo raised his voice solemnly and uttered the words: 'Quant à moi, je crois en Dieu!' Silence followed. Then a woman responded as if in deep meditation: 'Chose sublime! Un Dieu qui croit en Dieu!'"

Lest you think that Victor Hugo merely thought himself as great as he looked, let me remind you of how, after Dostoevsky's great speech of 1880 at the Pushkin monument, the audience was so "transported with enthusiasm" that old enemies were reconciled; how Turgenev begged Tolstoy — "O great writer of the Russian land!" — to cease and desist his foolish moralistic practices and go back to writing fiction; how Melville, who was inspired to revise *Moby-Dick* by his meetings with Hawthorne, wrote those amazingly still rapturous letters from Pittsfield to Tanglewood unable to contain himself for enthusiasm and gratitude that the great Hawthorne had inspired him, the sailor-hack, with a sense of his own greatness. "And when the big hearts strike together, the Concussion is a little stunning." What Thoreau and Whitman owed to Emerson, Baudelaire to Poe, James to Turgenev, Hemingway to *Huckleberry Finn,* Eliot to Laforgue and the Jacobean dramatists, in our day Ellison to Faulkner (even though, as he once said, the word "nigger" seemed to be on every page) — these belong to the nineteenth-century belief which writers as *readers* shared. It inspired many an intellectual, like George Eliot, to become a novelist. Nothing itself could be so valuable, so bracing, so life-enhancing, and above all so *lasting,* as a certain book, a particular passage, even one of those great lines, like Dante's *In la sua volontade è nostra pace,* which consoled Arnold for his lack of religion and so impressed T. S. Eliot that he seems quite seriously to have believed that you could not fully appropriate this line unless you had a religion something like Dante's.

Who prop, thou ask'st, in these bad days, my mind? Well, in these bad days, I have to tell you, not many. And why do I call them bad days at all when every morning as I pick up my *Times* I can see on the front page my charming, utterly courteous president smiling, smiling—when neither I nor my children need stand in that long long queue for stale bread outside the bakery on Broadway and 99th Street that reminds me so much of the 1930s? When there is so much ready intelligence around to work computers, get men to the moon, explain schizophrenia, extricate and picture DNA that I truly believe, as H. G. Wells did at the confident beginning of the century, that whereas literature is the work of the exceptional and isolated individual, science, taking in all its steady progress, is "the mind of the race?"

I call these "bad days" *not* because science and technology are now greater myth-makers than literature, and have a deservedly wider resonance and appeal. Darwin was a far more patient and luminous writer than many literary people today. The propositions laid down in *The Origin of Species* and *The Descent of Man* became irresistible to educated people because Darwin's sense of plot, his mastery of detail, his concern for man in our friendless universe have not been equalled since the great nineteenth-century novelists. I call them "bad days" not just because of the obvious contempt in high places for the poor and their suffering, but because they and their like, even in low places, add up to what Nathalie Sarraute called "the Age of Suspicion," and what Solzhenitsyn graphically and indeed heartbrokenly emphasized in the last volume of *The Gulag Archipelago*. He noted that where in Czarist times a prisoner escaping from confinement in Siberia was usually given shelter by the peasants (who felt themselves equally at the mercy of the Czar and the tundra in winter), under Soviet rule the escaping prisoner was routinely returned by the craven populace.

The days are bad, the times are bad and will get worse because our old belief in the unity of the human race now hardly exists. Of course the Elizabethan slave traders, like Sir Francis Drake, favorites of the court who chose as their emblem a manacled Negro, did not believe in this unity. Those who were regularly burned at the stake for their religious differences were no great testimony to this unity. But the slave trade and even slavery more or less yielded, over excruciatingly long periods of time, to the still potent ecumenicism of Christianity. And a significant number of Catholics troubled over colonialist oppression—see only Robert Stone's *A Flag for Sunrise*—

have learned to make personal problems out of their moral anxiety. Conscience based on the original and historic claim to human solidarity does work its way to the surface, even to self-sacrificing political rebellion, despite every seemingly prior claim of authority.

Nevertheless, the idea of this solidarity, no matter how often violated and profaned, was not challenged intellectually until the nineteenth century, when the seeds of communism and fascism were planted in the idea of the necessary extermination, on a total basis, of people belonging to the wrong race or class. Marx and Engels were children of the Enlightenment. Marx believed that "the mission of German philosophy" would be carried out by the proletariat — a class he hardly knew at first hand and one on which his immense powers of myth bestowed all the attributes of his favorite hero, Prometheus. His overabundant confidence that every rational man must believe in the necessary progression of history — this will make you free — became something else in Russia, China, Vietnam, Cambodia, Cuba. These are areas with a political history exclusively despotic. They have become prolonged experiences in manipulation of the average man and of terror not even against actual opponents but against people too "intellectual" for the thought police themselves. The Yugoslav dissident Djilas saw Stalin's confidants laughingly passing around death warrants in the midst of their all-night banquets. A sodden commisar could add any name to the list.

The enduring horror of the Holocaust is that whole peoples may now be considered excessive. In Brazil I heard a government official say, quite seriously, "We have a hundred million people here, most of whom we don't need." This is not the old-fashioned crudity of the slave trader. We live in a period when more and more people, too many of them intellectuals, have learned to deny human appeals in the name of nineteenth-century postures. Malraux was right to predict that the end of our century would see religious wars. The French writer Roger Caillois, a refugee in Brazil during World War II, met a group of ethnic Germans as the war was ending who had not been able to follow the progress of the war. After Caillois described the defeat of Germany, they replied: "At least we've made others suffer."

The American Spectator, a neoconservative magazine that claims inspiration from Mencken, derides the sending of reading matter into American prisons. In Los Angeles a survivor of Auschwitz has to sue a rightist in order to prove that Auschwitz and its horrors actually existed. Ezra Pound said that literature is news that stays news. This is the harshest criticism that can be made of much contemporary literature; even the attested horrors of Naziland may not always stay "news." A radical feminist poet, already notorious for excluding men from her lectures and readings, publishes a bitter attack on Beethoven's Ninth Symphony — now *there* was human solidarity for you! — as nothing but the noise put out by an impotent man.

There are more and more local examples. At a time of increasing social pain, especially for people out of sight, I am struck by the principled coldness and rejection on the part of so many social theorists. At least in the Great Depression there was desperate camaraderie and mutual aid. A leading theorist of the New Right, Professor Irving Kristol, recently protested that to discuss school lunches "is to make politics squalid." Of course Professor Kristol grew up under the intellectual influence of Trotsky's grand, sweeping historical equations. The great man told the Russian democratic Left in 1917, "Now you belong to the dustbin of history!" It is exactly such suicidal as well as homicidal grandiloquence that left Trotsky in the dustbin of history. But there is a moral poison in so much contempt for losers that affects twentieth-century intellectual as well as political life.

And what has all this to do with literature — especially with criticism, literary thinking and judgment? One essential fact of our age is the steady destruction of the past in our relentlessly revolutionary epoch — of man's real memory, his unconscious loyalty and belief. This is violated when we refuse our sympathy, our curiosity, to certain subjects and people. A more obvious danger is the lack of common values. Of course literature is no longer expected to change very much. Criticism, which is inherently an educative activity, a way of establishing standards and correcting taste, has become a form of grandstand play, an exercise in personal assertion. The Yale critic Geoffrey Hartman, who obviously believes that if he says often enough that criticism is "creative" he will be taken for another Nietzsche, is contemptuous of the English Department's "service activity."

I have never in years of teaching literature and writing criticism been so conscious of the gap between the educated and the non-educated — between genuine interest and knowledge on the one hand and the yawning contempt for literature, as a body of knowledge and a criticism of life, that is now concealed behind academic trivia as well as by professionalism in law, medicine, computer science, and the like. Of course intellectual and anti-intellectual groups are traditional adversaries in middle-class society. But until recently criticism in general, whether cultural, social, or strictly literary, was geared to a public whom the critic, like Mencken or Edmund Wilson, felt he could actually create.

The more professionalized life becomes, the more specialists of every sort come to see themselves as an elite, the less they are intellectuals in any traditional sense as bearers of ideas, forces for change and renovation; they more and more come to despise the untrained mass. Very few critics now seem interested in changing their audience, even in arguing with them. Mencken constantly assailed mass taste, mass religion, because like a good Victorian, like his adored Nietzsche, Ibsen, Shaw, he wanted to bring his benighted countryman up to his level. The critic of the international style in architecture, of the deplorable taste in wine of corporation executives, of the lettering on East Hampton tombstones, is occupied with fashion, not taste; with the moneyed elite of our society, not with the general level of information and taste. Professor Marvin Mudrick in his California State University, which looks like a Howard Johnson's and intellectually is just as demanding, tells *his* captive audience that Shakespeare is overrated, that Jane Austen and Lady Murasaki are the only novelists of the last twelve centuries worth considering. But if you think there is a run on Austen and the *Tales of Genji* in the Santa Barbara Library, guess again. There are academic critics in this country who in their native preserve have the aura of a Baryshnikov and spellbind their grateful audience with a verve and erudition similarly remote from the audience's ability to participate. So in the great bazaar of contemporary criticism, the key word is significantly *performance.* While the performance is generally bright, there is no agreement on the issues being discussed because there is no common knowledge. One reviewer writes that Doctorow's *Loon Lake* reads like Dreiser without Dreiser's faults. *Sister Carrie* has never been more alive eighty-three years since its own publisher Frank Doubleday tried to kill it. But there is no place in a great metropolitan newspaper or book review, no accessible forum in the great city, in which to make the essential point that externally Dreiser and Doctorow may have "tragic America" in common, but as artists nothing whatever.

The ghost of Vladimir Nabokov, as lively and wonderfully independent as the great man was in life, is present with a book of lectures on Russian writers. And of course Nabokov very properly said that the Bolshies totally misrepresented the amount of liberal intellect under Czarism. Obvious, in view of the great Russian novel!

But Nabokov was also genially unmindful of the wretchedness and suppression under Czarism. Dostoevsky's "melodramas" were the actual melodramas of millions of victims, rebels and prisoners like himself.

Nabokov sneers that Dostoevsky's favorite theme was the misadventures of human dignity. Such "misadventures" were the theme of Gogol's great story "The Overcoat." Nabokov approved of Gogol, not least because Gogol apologized to the authorities for even being suspected of lampooning their sacred importance. Nabokov himself, who thought art just a game, or a feat of magic, never understood deprivation rather than mere exile like his own. He was an aristocratic liberal, from a culture in which few aristocrats were anything but primitive landowners. The Nabokov hero, who seems mad to us, is in his own eyes simply nostalgic for his lost paradise — and especially as in *Lolita* for his first love affair. This is what Freud thought, too — we are always looking back to lost paradises. But Nabokov could not spell Freud without deriding him, and he could not do justice to Dostoevsky for the same reason. They were too *conscious of the irrational in man*. Nabokov's lost paradise was the perfect liberalism of his childhood and his family. It is chilling to read in his *Lectures on Russian Literature* that when Dostoevsky was awaiting trial for his interest in utopian socialism, the commander of the prison was a General Nabokov, "an ancestor of mine. The correspondence which passed between this General Nabokov and Tsar Nicholas in regard to their prisoner makes rather amusing reading."

Nabokov lived longer in America than he did in Russia, and he certainly endured more privations in America. He wrote his masterpieces — *Lolita, Pnin, Pale Fire* — in America. Unable to appreciate Dostoevsky any more than he could Freud, Conrad, or Faulkner, Nabokov put Dostoevsky down to Cornell undergraduates who could no more have argued with the lordly and always sparkling Vladimir Vladimirovitch than they could have rocketed themselves to the moon. And where were the reviewers to argue with Nabokov's dismissal of Dostoevsky? Leon Edel in *The New Republic*, Joel Agee in *Harper's* were the only ones to rebut the great man.

There is no arguing about taste? Criticism is nothing but argument about taste; arguing seeks a common measure of understanding, not of agreement. So why don't we see the likes of a Mencken battling it out for Dreiser, of a Wilson who patiently and elaborately explained fifty years ago in *Axel's Castle* what Proust, *Ulysses,* and late Yeats were all about? Randall Jarrell in the 1950s still had to fight it out for Whitman and Frost in the teeth of all the old-new critics who were ashamed of Whitman's exuberance. Because dogmatists like Yvor Winters had authoritatively put it down that Frost was a "hedonist," one had to explain, so patiently, that Frost is in fact one of our great tragic writers — with examples, many examples, and illustrations from the history of English poetry. And there's the rub, since just as all it needs to be a television critic these days is an eccentric moustache, so all it needs to make your mark in certain magazines is the ability to recite one's own prejudices with insolence and if possible a white suit in all seasons.

In truth, there have never been so many intelligent critics working at the same time, so much opinion informed by the *tradition of modernism* in all its particular emphasis on sophistication and style. When I think of the crude moralizing and propagandizing of general reviewing in the thirties, when I began in this trade, and the professional stuffiness of academic opinion, still resolutely opposed to everything of the twenties that was already history, I note a distinct rise in literary intelligence. But modernism has not really existed since the twenties; there are only students of modernism, museums of modernism. The once banned and exiled Joyce, victim of many a philistine's book fire, is now the academy's favorite pedant. Hemingway, Eliot, Joyce, Pound, Cummings, Djuna Barnes have had no continuation in the century of the common man that began with the thirties. The liveliest fictionalists of our time and place are not experimentalists but social novelists of a period when the moral order is not meaningless, as it was for the twenties, but plainly disintegrating.

"Can you describe this?" a woman said to the great Russian lyric poet Akhmatova as the women stood in line before one of Stalin's prisons in the hope of obtaining some communication with their menfolk. "Yes!" said Akhmatova, and in *Requiem* she did. But the freezing terror had taken over, the subject had taken over after so much talk in the twenties about "the revolution of the word." In our day *events* dominate. Literature must share "reality" with journalism, often turns to journalism in order to do justice to such a vast dislocation.

So all this abundant critical intelligence does not have the old resonance, the influence on the private reader in his solitude. No one takes criticism so seriously as a critic, but there are fewer and fewer critics now, much as I may admire the general performance, who influence my reading and thinking as did Eliot on Pascal, D. H.

Lawrence on Hardy, Auden on A. E. Housman, Randall Jarrell on Whitman, Conrad Aiken on Faulkner, Edmund Wilson on Flaubert, Richard Chase on American romanticism, Erich Auerbach on mimesis, E. M. Forster in *Aspects of the Novel.*

Who prop, thou ask'st, in these bad days, my mind? These days, Matthew, not many, not many. And like the protagonist of Saul Bellow's *The Dean's December,* who in the freezing human moral climate of East Europe recognizes that a lifetime of reading is no help to him now, that he has in fact read far too much, I feel that I have too often carried vast libraries on my back, and that all the humanist professions of the nineteenth century in which I grew up—Literature maketh the full man, Literature is *Bildung*—are of no avail: just another way of making a living, like being a medical examiner.

But this isn't the whole story either. For though I may very well have wasted my life in reading, reading in certain texts is such an arduous and physical experience for me that the contrasts are often comic, as good as a play. I knew I was fated to become a critic when, on completing Dostoevsky's *The Idiot* one summer day long ago, I fell out of my chair in a kind of happy trance at the scene in which Rogózhin goes mad and saintly Myshkin pitifully strokes his hair. I have known the bliss of sailing in a balloon whenever I turn to Chapter 111 of *Moby-Dick,* "The Pacific," and read that "The same waves wash the moles of the new-built California towns, but yesterday planted by the recentest race of men, and lave the faded but still gorgeous skirts of Asiatic lands, older than Abraham; while all between float milky-ways of coral isles, and low-lying, endless, unknown Archipelagoes, and impenetrable Japans."

Whenever the night gets tough and I try to read myself to sleep, I find that one plays critic despite all one's longing to let go and read Sherlock Holmes over and over, as I did as a boy. The consecutiveness of thought, all that we really mean by the narrative line that is central to every piece of writing, makes itself known, amidst my yawns, the minute I peer at a page.

The line is of course strictest in good poetry, where the thought is not only *most* consecutive but where the thinking is most unexpected, for the images and associations fly in from every direction. But there is most famously the tight line of a really good novel—not as in the short story, which is often just a one-act play, where form is demonstrative rather than innate in the development—but in a sustained fiction where the palpable act of thought, line by line, item by item, is so centralized, it reminds me of everything a blind man has to carry in his head.

At difficult times I long for the mish-mash of the usual movie and especially the television, which works like a drug by disconnecting all the usual lines of logic. What with the commercials and the indifferent violence of the story, there is such a jumble of appetites on the lower frequencies that I can forget my fear of the age. That is my problem: fear of the age. But despite this, there is in the end nothing like the satisfaction of narrative, terror-stricken as it may leave me, where nothing can be taken out, nothing need be added. Perfection can be of a loneliness, said Rilke, that takes it beyond criticism:

> I now perceived clearly that he was supposed to seize the knife himself, as it travelled from hand to hand above him, and plunge it into his own breast. But he did not do so, he merely turned his head, which was still free to move, and gazed around him. He could not completely rise to the occasion, he could not relieve the officials of all their tasks; the responsibility for this last failure of his lay with him who had not left him the remnant of strength necessary for the deed. His glance fell on the top storey of the house adjoining the quarry. With a flicker as of a light going up, the casements of a window there suddenly flew open; a human figure, faint and insubstantial at that distance and that height, leaned abruptly far forward and stretched both arms still farther. Who was it? A friend? A good man? Someone who sympathized? Someone who wanted to help? Was it one person only? Or were they all there? Was help at hand? Were there some arguments in his favor that had been overlooked? Of course there must be. Logic is doubtless unshakable, but it cannot withstand a man who wants to go on living. Where was the Judge whom he had never seen? Where was the High Court, to which he had never penetrated? He raised his hands and spread out all his fingers.

> But the hands of the partners were already at K.'s throat, while the other thrust the knife into his heart and turned it there twice. With failing eyes, K. could still see the two of them, cheek leaning against cheek, immediately before his face, watching the final act. "Like a dog!" he said: It was as if he meant the shame of it to outlive him.

>   (Franz Kafka, *The Trial*)

Alfred Kazin is Distinguished Professor of English at the Graduate Center, City University of New York. His book An American Procession *was recently published by Alfred A. Knopf.*

Mary McCarthy

HANNAH ARENDT AND POLITICS

Politics was the engrossing occupation of Hannah's life. At least fifty percent of her conversation was devoted to it. That was a constant, no matter whom she was talking with; it could not drop below fifty percent. Depending on whom she was talking with, music might be ten percent, art and architecture ten percent, philosophy up to twenty percent, poetry and fiction up to fifteen percent. That leaves little space for personalities, but people as a subject could usually be fitted into one of the other headings, often under "politics"; there you would find magazine editors, writers, her colleagues, friends, and enemies.

Yet she was not very active politically, in the sense of going to meetings, signing petitions and manifestos, or marching in demonstrations. "*Ohne mich.*" It always came as a slight surprise to me that she voted. I think she considered voting a requirement for an American citizen, at any rate a naturalized one. I don't know whether she contributed often to the campaign chests of office seekers, or to help defray the cost of an ad in *The New York Times*. I somehow doubt it. She was an extremely generous, concerned, and warm-hearted person, but her philanthropy was usually directed toward persons rather than toward organizations and entities. I know that she gave money to help dissidents in Czechoslovakia and Chile, but contributing sums of money to try to save desperate and hunted people is a basic act like those natural duties of brotherhood — feeding the hungry and so on — imposed on us by just about every religion; compared to paying for an ad in the *Times*, all that is almost prepolitical.

She also contributed regularly to an organization called Spanish Refugee Aid and for a while served as its chairman. But, though the recipients of sewing machines, warm clothing, small amounts of money were anti-Franco to a man, woman, and child, they were old, disabled, tubercular; in other words, through bodily incapacity they were outside the political arena, having long ago been driven to the sidelines. Helping them furthered no political aim. It could not

Editor's Note: This essay was first presented at a conference sponsored by Bard College, Empire State College, the New School for Social Research, and New York University, in October 1981.

change anything, except in a marginal way in these refugees' lonely and quite miserable lives in southern France. They were grateful to be remembered by what they called "Spanish." "Today Spanish came to see us." This was very much in Hannah Arendt's vein, and what appealed to her especially about "Spanish" was the fantastically low operating costs. Less than twenty-five percent, if I'm not mistaken, went towards administration. And this pleased her, not only as a former social worker — Youth Aliyah — but in her political nature. One of her great fears and detestations was bureaucracy, which she called the "rule of nobody," as contrasted with the rule of the few represented by oligarchy or the rule of one represented by autocracy. She considered bureaucracy a more dangerous phenomenon than these others, because creeping and impossible to fix responsibility on, and also perhaps because it is less well diagnosed, being omnipresent.

In any case, she was somewhat inactive politically, above all when her physical participation is compared to the hyperactive state of her mind. For her, the reading of a newspaper was a political experience of a galvanic kind, calling forth violent reactions of eye, hand, entire body, nods of confirmation, sudden chuckles, gasps. To her, a newspaper was a political document, to be interpreted, read between the lines, thrown aside as devoid of interest once the marrow had been swiftly extracted. She never let old newspapers pile up as I do.

I do not know how active politically she had been in Europe before the Nazi occupation of France drove her here. Certainly she and her mother while still in Germany had engaged in sufficient anti-Nazi activity to have the daughter held in jail for a time. In France, as foreigners, no doubt they did less or were less overt. What is interesting about her career of political involvement in this country is that she was fully engaged shortly after her arrival, joining the *Aufbau* group in New York and not only writing in that German-language Jewish newspaper on political issues, hotly debated ones, like the proposal for a Jewish army, but going regularly to meetings, where she supported her views — something she was never to do again, even in an academic forum, and perhaps had never done before.

Possibly the war and Hitler were sufficient reason for this frenzy of commitment in a new country. But Hitler had been present all along, very much so since 1932, and war had seemed clearly foreordained at least from the Saar time, from the Sudeten time, the Anschluss, without enlisting the passions of the young Hannah Arendt in what amounted (with the *Aufbau* group) to an activist campaign of

articles, meetings, letter-writing—I am surprised there were no leaf-
lets—aimed at recruiting the Jewish community to a kind of war effort. When the European war ended, Hannah Arendt's direct commitment ended. Yet it was not that she lost interest; far from it. It
was as though, having been freed by the fall of the Third Reich from
the duties of militancy, i.e., advocacy of a single, determined, "fighting" view, she was able, finally, to indulge her real interest in politics, which was that of a spectator and judge, never of an actor and
doer—the terms of course are hers.

    I think that she developed a certain trust in the protection of the
United States (those were the Truman years) to give that interest of
hers free rein, but always within the limits of writing and theoretical
discussion. Out of this came *The Origins of Totalitarianism*, which was
produced over a period of years in her (so to speak) spare time. Her
participation in panels and round tables, like her teaching activity,
began a bit later. In a sense one could say that her truest political engagement was her teaching, which should be taken to include her
contributions to panels and symposia. In her teaching she was concerned, I feel, with forming citizens just as much as young Ph.D.s in
Political Philosophy—more so surely. Her distaste for professionals
in that field can be inferred from *The Life of the Mind*, where she repeatedly cites Kant's disparaging "*Denker von Gewerbe*," professional
thinkers.

    Certainly she had a deep vocation for teaching, which, like the
call heard by Socrates, was in essence political. She was an educator.
But it may also be that teaching was, to some slight degree, a diver-
sionary channel for her political energies, which otherwise might
have overflowed the banks she quite strictly set for them and poured
into the public arena. The truth is that after the first years—the *Aufbau*
years—she became wary. With her, as with her whole generation of
refugees, one must remember that she was gun-shy. Having experienced the malignant transformation of a republic (Weimar) into the
National Socialist monstrosity, they sensed the Nazi potential everywhere and lived in half- or fully conscious horror of a repetition, as
though Nazism, once invented, were subject to eternal recurrence.
The McCarthy years were more frightening to German Jewish refugees than a native American could imagine.

    Neither Hannah Arendt nor her husband nor (I believe) any
close friend suffered the slightest persecution from McCarthy,
McCarran, Cohn, Shine, the House Un-American Activities Committee; but that is not the point. The phenomenon of recurrence was

no less fearful in their eyes for failing to affect their personal destinies. It might have been *more* alarming, like a sword of Damocles still
not deigning to descend. I used to tell Hannah Arendt that McCarthy
could not last on the American political scene, but she did not believe
me. Her expressed fear, then and later, was for our State Department, which she expected to be emasculated by the McCarthy campaign. She was right about that, positively prescient, but in reality
that was only the visible, admissible part of her fear for our country;
at the same time, quietly, she was looking for signs that concentration camps were opening. Well, when you remember Nixon, that is
not such a joke.

In fact, though, it did not happen, or has not yet happened —
whichever you prefer. But for Hannah Arendt and many of her
friends, the original trust she had had in the protection of this country for her right of free thought vanished on the spot and was never
fully restored. Once again, under Nixon, in the last years of the
Vietnamese war, she became apprehensive. She actually talked about
emigrating back to Europe *fast*, while there was still time. That she
was willing to accept the prospect of being a refugee twice, two times
over, made me understand finally the absence of assurance she had
been living in for roughly thirty years without my taking note of it.
She was not prudent or "careful" in what she wrote — think of *Eichmann*
— but in the practical sphere, the sphere of daily life, she exercised
what was sometimes an extreme prudence — a prime political virtue
according to Aristotle. Though she knew herself to be an outstanding, even inspiring teacher, I cannot imagine her having taken part
in any of the teach-ins about the war in Vietnam. It was not that she
hid her opinion about that conflict — she simply steered clear of en-
listment in the political process that seemed inevitable to so many
opponents of the war. And yet when I became impassioned about
finding a means of resisting the war for people like ourselves too old
to practice draft resistance in any of its forms, she was the *only* person willing to listen attentively to the argument I put forward. I had
worked out a formula for tax resistance. When I had finished, she
nodded, "You are right, of course. It would be the way." And there-
upon she sighed. What the sigh meant, I think, was complex: first,
that I would never get the original nucleus I needed for twenty-five
prominent people to start the movement; and, second, that, if contrary to her expectations and her judgment of prominent people, I
did round up twenty-five, she might feel compelled to join us, contrary to all dictates of prudence. Friendship and intellectual convic-

tion ("You are right. It would be the way.") would enjoin her to defy
a lifetime policy. As you can imagine, it was never put to the test.

Some of her reluctance to involve herself must have sprung
from her reticence. She was shy. She disliked exposing herself to
public curiosity. That was why she was almost never on radio and
only once that I know of on television—in *French*, possibly as a further safeguard. She was heard once on a West German program,
but that, I think, was radio, and it was in the context of a panel discussion. There must be very few recordings of her voice in existence;
the BBC, which did a radio program on her a year or two ago, was
unable to get hold of a single tape of her speaking, which was too
bad, since her voice, more than most people's, seemed to contain the
very essence and fiber of her. Hoarse, deep, guttural, cutting, it was
her political organ, just as her dark, deep eye was her aesthetic organ.

But we are approaching a mystery. Given her shyness, her reticence, her extreme prudence, what was it that drew her to politics?
Where was the fascination? It cannot have been a simple attraction
to power, for, so far as I could observe, she did not especially care to
have power, still less to exercise it when she could not avoid awareness of being in command. As for manipulating the people around
her, a pastime dear to politicians and statesmen, nothing could have
been more foreign to her nature.

It occurs to me that her being Jewish may have had something
to do with the passionate interest she took in political affairs. To be a
Jew is to constitute a problem, for others, and hence for oneself. It is
to be born an issue, like a disputed frontier. In the past, the problem
the Jew presented was chiefly administrative: where and how to contain him, as a foreign element, within the framework of Christian society. The institution of the ghetto, the definition of the Pale were
regulatory measures, involving curfews, the opening and closing of
gates, which mirrored the continuous closing and opening of certain
activities and professions to Jews. Other measures sought to *eliminate*
the problem: the periodic expulsions, forced conversions, pogroms.
In modern times, the Jew remained a problem, albeit a social one,
for a world that was no longer Christian but secularized. Unbelieving Christians and unbelieving Jews, though no longer separated by
a religion, were still held not to mix—in schools, clubs, buildings,
and neighborhoods. But with this development, the Jew, who, if not
practicing, might be no more than a special history, became even
more of an issue, more problematic to himself and others, than the
Jew of the Middle Ages contained within regulations had been.

Thus to be Jewish, especially if one was highly intelligent, was to be doomed to an interest in politics, even if Hitler had been a mere *posse* rather than an *esse*.

With Zionism, I suspect, and the eventual creation of Israel, the problematical issue of being a Jew became personified in a national entity, a state, inescapably political, as the Vatican State, for example, is. It is relevant, then, that the first (and last) commitment of a young woman more drawn to philosophy, the *vita contemplativa*, than to the *vita activa*, in fact was to Zionism. Unlike so many of her generation, unlike her husband, Heinrich Bluecher, who was in the German Communist Party in the thirties, she was not much attracted to Marxism. Her study of Marx's thought came later in her life and responded, obviously, to the interest in politics first quickened in her by Zionism and the Jewish question. I would go even further and say this: insofar as Hannah Arendt was a practicing political animal, with a keen nose for power plays, strategic alignments, risks, the reason was always Israel.

This may seem paradoxical to those who want to think that she was a disloyal Jew, anti-Zionist or anti-Israel (because of the Eichmann book), but of course the Eichmann book was a *product* of her almost maternal concern for Israel — a concern that literally kept her awake worrying at the slightest sign of danger to the survival of what its enemies call "the Zionist entity." It is true that after her early years she was never a Zionist, may have seen Zionism, as it materialized in the national state, to be a mistaken, potentially perilous answer to the complicated problem it pretended to solve. But that could not turn her "against" Israel; almost the reverse — it sharpened her concern.

Meanwhile she did become an American citizen in more than the passport sense. She identified herself with America especially in its bad times; she had an admiration for its political institutions to the point of being somberly concerned for their wellbeing; she would much rather live in New York, certainly, than in Tel Aviv or even Paris. And yet it was not the same, as her *Eichmann in Jerusalem* showed. In the *Eichmann* she stuck her neck out, disregarded all her own counsels of prudence, invited vilification; she may even — who knows? — have shortened her life by it; certainly thanks to the attacks on her, she lost a year, maybe more, of work on what she hoped would be her crowning achievement, *The Life of the Mind*.

Much as she was attached to the United States, she would never have behaved with such blunt recklessness and candor to set us straight when she felt we were going wrong. No. Had we gone too far down Mr. Nixon's road, rather than denounce, she would have silently packed her bags and left us. As I said just now, it was in her mind. Meanwhile she had uttered grave warnings, in the essays collected under the title *Crises of the Republic*; she had celebrated the American "way" in *On Revolution*, but both blame and praise evidenced a thoughtful care and moderation. Whatever the danger she imagined for us, she would never have murmured, as if to herself, "I am so worried about this country." One of the last times she took me in a taxi to the airport the driver's radio was on, too low for me to catch what it was saying, but *she* heard the name "Israel," and abruptly told the driver to turn it on full. Then she apologized to me. "I am so worried about Israel," she confessed, shaking her head.

But if this is so, if Israel was the prime source of her political concern, that still leaves a good deal to wonder about — idiosyncrasies of her thought, as well as idiosyncrasies of behavior. I would locate my own wonder in the region of her concept of "the public space," the space she assigned to action as distinguished from labor and work in *The Human Condition*, whose first title was *The Vita Activa*. As you know, within the *vita activa* there was a hierarchy of values — a ladder ascending from labor at the bottom to action, which is none other than our friend, politics, at the top.

The public space, where action takes place, is the same as the public stage of classical metaphor. The actor, or doer, on that stage, raised platform, or scene, is usually an orator (Trotsky in the Russian Revolution haranguing his troops from the train, as she used to point out) as well as a doer, pronouncing immortal, soul-swaying words. The concept, no doubt, is universal. The extension of the old Latin word "tribune" to denote not just a magistrate but also the space or raised platform he occupies when giving judgment shows how the function tends to be perceived in distinct spatial terms. Some height is important; the dais may be equated with a pedestal on which the actor, turned into his own statue of bronze or marble, will stand. Hannah Arendt was less concerned with height than with the aspect of visibility: she sees the man of action emerging from the darkness of the household, or private life, onto the brilliantly lit public scene. But the aspect of permanence conveyed by bronze or marble is important for her, too: a statue, when not of a god, is a man of action turned to stone. And for her, the function of the historian — and poet — is to cast the deed in time-defying bronze or, working in stone, to cut away the superfluous material to reveal the "speaking" form.

Just to show how widespread such images of public life are, I will cite a conversation I had with Pham Van Dong, the Vietnamese Prime Minister, in Hanoi in late March 1968 while the bombs were still falling—there was an alert during our conversation that Pham Van Dong, with an elegant irritable gesture, dismissed like a childish interruption: nobody, not even the tea-pourers, went to the shelter. Elegance, in a sense, is the point. Pham Van Dong was speaking of Kennedy. Kennedy, he said, enemy or not, had been a figure on the world political stage, a great actor on that scene, while Johnson, he went on contemptuously, was nobody, a trivial clown. "He is speaking Hannah's language," I said to myself with delight.

Public life, so conceived, is evidently a classic drama modernized by Corneille. And this perhaps explains the fascination it had for Hannah Arendt. During a panel on her work I once asked her a question that had long been bothering me: what was supposed to happen in the political realm, if such matters as housing, school lunches, welfare payments, were considered to be mere problems of administration, too "low" to be imported onto the public scene? Questions of mass unhappiness, she declared—the point is made most decisively in *On Revolution*—had no place on the political agenda, the roster of the laws; it was the mistake of the French Revolution to attempt to legislate these questions and promise relief from misery as if that could be enacted in a code. But if such "social" matters (as she termed them) were to be excluded from the public space, what was left? After the act of foundation—the constitution of the Republic—all I could see (using Thucydides as a reference aid) for the *polis* to decide on was war, the declaration and waging of it; beyond that there seemed to be nothing that was a *political* concern for the state but, precisely, foreign relations, leading up to war or avoiding it. The public space, then, would be occupied by war, diplomacy, and oratory. If I remember rightly, she agreed but did not seem concerned by the limitation: my restriction of that space to its proper concerns was correct, however queer it might seem to an American liberal like myself.

In practice she was not quite so rigid. I remember a conversation, perhaps several, in which she maintained that a hot breakfast was the solution to all New York's school problems: the children were unruly and could not learn because they went to school on empty stomachs. I think there was a lot of truth in that, but a politician who introduced a hot-breakfast program into his campaign platform would be moving outside what she defined as the proper concern of politics. Or have I misunderstood something?

It was one of the delights of Hannah Arendt's mind that it had a strong practical streak that at the same time was quirky, far out, sometimes almost like a witty summing-up. She was always hitting on eminently sensible remedies that no common-sensible person would ever entertain. The school hot breakfasts were an example, and I remember, too, her solution for the Berlin crisis of late 1961, when Kennedy was in power. The Russians had cut off access to West Berlin (this was the dramatic moment of the Wall), and the air lift to supply the old capital had not yet been instituted, partly for fear that it would lead to air battles and hence to war. For a few tense days or weeks nobody knew what to do. Hannah's solution, eminently peaceful, was to move West Berlin to a better location, outside the Russian zone. Not just nominally or symbolically move it but pick it up, building by building, street by street, landmark by landmark. American technology was perfectly fitted, she said, to do the job, which could not possibly be construed as "an act of war." The Russians might even be happy to have that "showcase of democracy" removed from view.

Of course it was not done. I tried to get Arthur Schlesinger to propose it to Kennedy, but I think the commission embarrassed him — too "far out" for a presidential counselor to be identified with. Indeed, now that I think back on it and on the hot breakfasts, I see that they smack of housekeeping. In Miss Arendt's phraseology they are administrative rather than political ways of coping with a crisis. I suppose that in some lights they would appear *too* practical, hence ignoble, evasive of central issues. And thinking of this, remembering other "brain waves" of hers — on Little Rock, for instance — I finally see what I missed in her schema of politics during her lifetime. Moving West Berlin would not have been perceived by her as a political act but rather as a dramatic feat of engineering having no more to do with the *polis* in a true sense than Caesar's bridge across the Rhine. And to Caesar as to her, politics was "above" or beyond the ingenuities of bridge-building, which belonged to his generalship rather than to his proconsular role. For him, in his campaigns, local politics (i.e., foreign and colonial policy) would have consisted of the harangues he addressed to the various chieftains, among them the insolent German, Ariovistus (that was *before* the bridge) — pieces of oratory, the music, you could call it, of politics, that he carefully recorded. Serious politics, of course, was in the City, that is, Rome.

She was drawn to politics by its enduring, noble aspect and was particularly drawn to what she called the act of foundation, the setting of the stage, with its columns and great proscenium arch. What is curious here is that, despite her shyness, her reticence and sense of privacy, she was a dramatic, even theatrical personality. I have spoken of her before as resembling a great actress, the magnificent Sarah Bernhardt, and anyone who ever heard her speak from a public stage cannot have failed to sense this. It's as if in mounting the platform she stepped into the public space, acquiring visibility, which in normal life she shunned. This transformation, this shedding of the privative, was within the reach of every citizen who consented to be raised to a political dimension if only for a few moments.

If she loved the act of foundation, the well-laid cornerstones of republics that constitute their constitutions (she seems to have had no interest in monarchies), it may be that for her the Founders are the only true *dramatis personae*. The early, authentic soviets of the Russian October survive barely as a memory in most minds; for her the drama ends with that eroded foundation, that false prelude, the hollow name "Soviet Union." Her zest for the Hungarian Revolution of 1956, evident in the late editions of her *Totalitarianism*, shows her hope of a brave new foundation arising there, its contours just emerging — she loved workers' councils, romantically, like a girl. She had a great liking for our own Founding Fathers, above all for Madison and the authors of *The Federalist*: I cannot recall her ever speaking of Lincoln. Her fondness for the art of foundation and for the political geniuses who framed new sets of laws perhaps reflects the importance she gave in her general thinking to beginning and beginners, to man as the animal capable of incessant novelty, of being born new each time as unique individual, in the repetitive pattern of species life.

Mary McCarthy has just received the Edward MacDowell Award for Literature. She is at work on an intellectual memoir.

Daphne Merkin

THE PLIGHT OF READING:
IN SEARCH OF THE NEW FICTION

This is how it is in the word within the world: I am having dinner with my father, a businessman with an ancillary interest in culture. We are sitting at a restaurant table covered with crisp linen, gleaming with glasses and silver. If this were a story by a certain kind of writer, a Saul Bellow or a Philip Roth, my father would probably be described — in the interests of clarity as well as of hostility — as a mogul. So, my father the mogul wants to know what my novel is going to be about. I fidget with the menu, a large calligraphically rendered object. My father, like many men who don't either write or teach them, doesn't read novels. He does, however, savor book reviews; he knows who is well or badly received and will bring home expensive hardcovers, the latest Iris Murdoch, and once in a while an odd, literary choice. "I don't know," I finally say, "I'm having trouble beginning. But it will probably be," I add, as though this weren't the obvious irritant in the oyster of the novice's imagination, "about me." I settle back in my upholstered chair. I've said it all: The Daughter is planning to write about Herself. At this point my father the mogul peers over his half-glasses and says with a conviction I find dazzling: "If I could write, which I can't, I'd write about *issues.*"

"If I could write . . ." But doesn't everyone in America believe that, given the inclination, he or she could "write" — string a bunch of words together? Issues . . . Of course I know about them, I read the paper like any watchful citizen, but I had never thought to bog my novel — that embryonic, fleeting vision behind my eyes — down in *them.*

There are many things I suppose I could have said in my own, and literature's, defense: Issues aren't novels. (Although some of the more artistically successful books of the past few years have been those in which "real life" pulses at the edge of the page: the biography-cum-novel, such as *Edie* or, more recently, Joyce Johnson's novelistic memoir of her affair with Jack Kerouac, *Minor Characters.*) Art rises beyond the everyday. I might have quoted Ford Madox Ford, who went so far as to suggest that it was best for writers not to have any views at all: "Your business with the world," he pronounced to Conrad, "is rendering, not alteration." But for a moment, in this well-appointed spot filled with the murmurings of coiffed women

and successful men — lawyers, doctors, perhaps a publisher or two —
I am not so sure of myself or my novel. In truth I have, as Dorothy
Braude wisely remarks in *Becoming a Writer*, "no impressive paraphernalia to impose respect on the layman" — no musical instrument
or paintbrushes I can point to in evidence. During the main course I
toy quite seriously with writing a novel about a cadre of American
businessmen who take over the Israeli government. That's issues for
you! But it is hopeless: I can see that by the time the dessert wagon is
rolled around. I am constitutionally indebted to the interior, what
pulses behind words and actions. Don't we, after all, live in our
minds as much as we live in the world? Even if those minds are perilous frigates to venture entire novels on? For as William Gass has
pointed out, "No one really believes in any other feelings than his
own." And what is one to do with the acid indictment of the writer
soi-disant that Mary McCarthy offers in her essay on Nathalie Sarraute's novel about the act of writing a novel, *Between Life and Death*:
"Most people have had an unhappy childhood, an erratic ancestor.
Who does he think he is?"

This is how it is in the world within the word: I am talking to a
literary critic, a man with a slightly jaded sense of his own purpose,
who might not take my father up on his proposal (politics, the critic
says with not a trace of apology, bore him) but who reads too many
books too quickly to be much smitten. We are talking about a psychologist friend of his who is finishing a book — one of those distinctly
contemporary books about men and women, intimacy and the lack
thereof, affection versus desire, that appear regularly and to an avid
audience, the way travel books did in the nineteenth century. I am
listening, but only just, when suddenly the critic says, alluding to a
concluding paragraph in the book that he has reservations about,
"Writers love the dying fall." The sentence — its sheer suggestiveness
— makes us both happy, and for a while we walk on in a companionable silence. I see: White swans, feathers fluttering, *a sudden blow*.
What does the critic see inside his head? Perhaps he envisions something altogether different — his own fate, a ballerina folding over on
stage — but it doesn't matter: The sonorousness of the image has
brought us, however temporarily, together. The critic appears newly
vital to me, a man able to spruce up the mental horizon with leafy
plantings.

Days later I remember the remark and think how nice it would
be to be able to live *in* quotations — a goal which the systematic quo-
tation-gatherer Walter Benjamin, more than anyone else, seems to
have come closest to attaining. Among the jottings and musings that

comprise *Montauk*, a novel about the ways in which "issues" ("In 1972 I had been preoccupied with the world") vie with private agendas ("In 1972 I knew no woman called Lynn"), Max Frisch observes: "He wishes there did not always have to be memories." Pages later, he also remarks, without benefit of addenda: "Living in quotations." Perhaps it is a literary dreamer's dream: Imagine if one's memories were only *of* quotations — the sounding rather than the impact itself — so that a disastrous marriage could be cancelled by a brittle but supremely knowing phrase: "She was a girl who for a ringing phone dropped exactly nothing." If "I can fall in love with *a sentence spoken to me*," as Roland Barthes admitted in his book, *A Lover's Discourse: Fragments*, isn't there a possibility of falling *out* of love the same way? Or, at the very least, a way of forestalling the entire process, as the narrator in Mary McCarthy's "Portrait of the Intellectual as a Yale Man" tries to do by observing, self-preservingly, of the belle of the ball that "she was the kind of girl who was having too good of a time." Except that "See more glass," as the little girl looking for bananafish calls him in Salinger's famous story, shoots himself in the head while in the very same room as his wife, that craven girl who ignores ringing phones. The perils of emotion transformed into the pleasures of phrasing can salve wounds, it seems, but not spare one wounds.

This is how it is in the world: According to a survey quoted by a biographer of Barbara Cartland and reported by Steven Aronson in his swashbucklingly meretricious book, *Hype*, "39 percent of American women had never read a book in their lives," although "18 percent of American women had read at least one Barbara Cartland novel." (Is this 18 percent part of the 39, which would raise a very tiny cheer for literacy, or in addition to? All is unclear in this book of sodden revelations.) These statistics stirred me, however unfounded, because I had always thought it was women who carried the burden of reading, who responded to its message of interiority. As to serious reading — well, that, as we know, is done by graduate students and a resilient few. Among the latter I include myself and a youngish man who works part-time on the staff of an excellent bookstore on Madison Avenue. He has blonde hair which falls over one eye, like Veronica Lake's, and he wears tortoiseshell glasses. He is not fey but he certainly knows *where it's at*.

When I enter the store late one afternoon, I look over the books on the center table: a reissued memoir, nearly a century old, of a housekeeper who ran a grand English home (a cross between Samuel Pepys and "Upstairs, Downstairs"); biographies of the great and near-great and might-have-been-great; shiny, large "coffee-table" books filled with photographs of beauteous brunches or haughty faces; also several "art books" exploring the mystique of female body-building. I move on to the shelves containing new fiction. All the glistening covers. There seems to be a trend in book jackets for first or "literary" novels: lots of white space and blues, the design figurative rather than abstract, Magritte- or Hockney-like. A chair stands in the middle of an empty room on one cover; a tightly made up hospital bed angles off the corner of another: *The White Hotel* started it. I pick up a novel and riffle the pages, trying to get a whiff: lots of dialogue, "line spaces," compression is the name of the game. I glance at another novel which seems almost antiquated in its density: long paragraphs printed tightly together and so many names—the real, Dickensian cast of characters. I put it down, at a loss. The blonde salesman who has advised me well in the past comes over. Matrons in this neighborhood, who don't wait for the paperback, fall for him. He has helped to sell, he informs me proudly, seven thousand copies of a first novel he liked, from this store alone. "Anything good?" I ask, hoping to be swamped in someone else's consciousness. "I cannot bear myself," Max Frisch writes, again in *Montauk*. "But I cannot wake up, as one can when one's dreams become too unbearable." In lieu of waking up, I've always thought, there is fiction: other people's lives, more or less bearable, under whose sway we willingly cede our own sovereignty for a while. "Nothing," says the bookseller. "Really?" I ask. "I'm looking for something to read," I add, as though my presence needs clarification. "Nope," he repeats, "it's been a bad year. No one's reading these days. No one I know." "That's true," I say, a bit desperately. "Everyone's writing screenplays," he says, firmly. "Seen any good movies lately?"

NO ONE'S READING THESE DAYS? Could it be because there isn't a character in a recent novel or short story that you, the reader, can hold an imaginery conversation with—which was Orwell's "test" for characters in fiction? Or could it be that we have tired of the new fiction's refusal to provide us with what Ernst Becker called "the suction of the infinite"? If we are simply reading about other men and women who, as one critic put it, "rarely see things through" then perhaps we, like Bartleby, would rather not: How well, after all, we do that ourselves. The critic Frank McShane, in a recent article in the *New York Times*, attempted to attribute the popularity of Italo Calvino's books to just that quality of indeterminacy I consider to be a deterrent to reader responsiveness: "If love fails, they begin again; their lives are a series of new beginnings, where complications have not yet begun to show themselves. Unlike the great Russian and French novelists, who follow their characters through the long and winding caverns of their lives, Calvino just turns off the set after the easy beginning and switches to another channel." This explanation may account for the kind of fiction we find ourselves getting, but it seems to me to beg the question of what people read *for*. And Calvino is popular, if at all, among theorists, consumers of "texts" rather than of novels and stories. . . . I buy a book anyway, a small act of defiance: *Look at Me*, a novel which will prove to be in the great English tradition of Henry James and Elizabeth Bowen, where corrupted innocence is conveyed by the raising of a brow. But Anita Brookner, its author, is British, and they, it might be noted, continue to write fiction as though the movies never happened. The blonde pessimist is pleased, contradicting himself: "Tell me what you think. I hear she's interesting."

Some years ago, an anthology of short stories that had first appeared in *Esquire* was published under the title *All Our Secrets Are the Same*. I remember being struck by the aptness of that title, for I am most clear on what it is that is dear to me about fiction when I am engaged in a routine, in what Benjamin called "the drudgery of usefulness" — brushing my teeth, say, in the morning — and fantasizing about disappearing into a warm country or murdering a former lover or being any person I am not: a country singer, a brain surgeon, anything but what the day ahead presents as my fate accompli. What is also clear to me is that most adults lead courageously Walter Mitty-like lives, doing what's expected of them while daydreams of liberation proliferate. Few of us are blessed with the existences we think are owed us. And if all our secrets are the same, or pretty nearly — that we want to be rich, famous, and loved for ourselves alone rather than our yellow hair — then the service that the reading of fiction provides is an *enabling* one; we uncover our own willful longings through Madame Bovary's or Portnoy's. What good fiction gives us is the gossip on our desires, the chaotic promptings and unreasonable wishes; it allows us to wonder who and where we would be if the drift of our lives hadn't hemmed us in. This imaginatively subversive aspect must have been, I suppose, what the novelist Caroline Gordon had in mind when she cautioned that "the writing of fiction is almost too dangerous an occupation for women."

Listen, for instance, to John Gardner, who wrote in his admirably straight-shooting if very partisan *On Becoming a Novelist*: "In nearly all good fiction, the basic — all but inescapable — plot form is this: *A central character wants something, goes after it despite opposition (per-*

haps including his own doubts), and so arrives at a win, lose or draw." It is right here, I propose, that we arrive at the heart of the problem, the lack of excitement generated by our new writers. In most recent fiction, no one seems to want much of anything; even the secrets are nerveless. Here is what one character reveals of another in a prototypical short story, "Keats," from the collection, *In Constant Flight,* by a heralded newcomer, Elizabeth Tallent: "'My intuition told me I should never have tried to drive through Wyoming on the way to Cincinnati,' he said. 'But I have always had this nameless longing to see antelope.' That was his word, 'longing.'" It is hard to know what to make of such a declaration, placed rather strategically at a point in the story where the abandoned lover, Luke, has just suffered a head fracture. Are we to understand that he is appealing—mutely, via someone else's "nameless longing to see antelope"—to the narrator for a sympathy convergent with love? The effect is striking, certainly, but wholly oblique, and it may well require too much filling-in for most readers. Gardner again: "One of the most common mistakes among young writers . . . is the idea that a story gets its power from withheld information—that is, from the writer's setting the reader up and then bushwacking him." Tallent rarely bushwacks, I'll say that for her; she just withholds. Children and lovers come and go, seemingly beyond inspiration. There is often a dog or cat who ignites a flicker of passion (the Keats in "Keats" whose custody is at issue, thereby connecting Luke and his ex-girlfriend, is a dog), but it is still a far cry from the leap into the lyric which Jupiter, the abidingly high-spirited retriever, evokes at the end of John Cheever's "The Country Husband": "Then it is dark; it is a night where kings in golden suits ride elephants over the mountains."

The men and women in Tallent's honed but oddly tangential stories are beyond inspiration, even the inspiration of images. All is steadfastly ironic, her characters' wishes as washed-out as old blue jeans. There is, of course, an established lineage from which this style of cool obliquity descends. Renata Adler tried to pin together a novel, *Speedboat*, with scraps of hip observation—"I don't know what it means. I am in this brownstone."—some years ago. Donald Barthelme and Robert Coover were among the earliest, and best, practitioners of the form in what is probably its natural habitat, the short story. Ann Beattie has been its most visible exemplar for a while now, although her talent is such that she does manage, some of the time, to suggest a genuine poignancy. But this school—and once an influence becomes enshrined it becomes just that—advocating the tireless use of brandnames and deadpan dialogue, has its inherent dangers. For a demonstration of them at their most serious, one need only take a look at *Moon Deluxe*, a collection of stories by Frederick Barthelme (brother of Donald).

Many of these stories, like Beattie's and Tallent's and the other Barthelme's, first appeared in *The New Yorker*, and there is a certain shared aspect of glossy inertness to them. Frederick Barthelme has sensibility in abundance, but never has so much been expended on so little; it is as though a very acute observer had decided to take up residence in a motel off a highway for several years and record his impressions. Barthelme's stories are set in anonymous locations— shopping malls, supermarkets, and, most often, apartment condo- miniums—where the living is transient and conversation is fleeting. Again, there are no secrets here, not even when a guy named Milby explains why he has hit Lois, the friend of a woman named Cherry in a story named "Lumber": "She deserved it," he tells Frank, the narrator, "you know what I'm saying? I mean, bitch, bitch, bitch— you got to do something. . . . The thing is, they take advantage of everything—all the differences—but you can't. You get pissed after a while." "I wonder," Frank muses, "why I don't tell him what I want to tell him, why he scares me." The reader might well wonder too. If Frank actually bothered to explain why Milby's misogyny passed off as regular-guy machismo (and this effect Barthelme handles ex- pertly) frightens him, we might get really interested. But that revela- tion, in turn, would give the story a focus, a gravitational pull, and this Barthelme won't or can't do.

What he does instead is provide incidentals, slightly awry clues: "The waitress, a pudgy woman wearing a purple satin-look bowling shirt with 'GlueSlingers' in gold script across the back. . . ." ("Gila Flambé") "The girl is six feet tall. As I look at her standing beside the couch, dialing numbers on the telephone, I realize that the pants are too big by design, a way to simultaneously disguise and exploit her thinness." ("Violet") "Near the stationery, you face a shelf of ceramic coin banks shaped and painted like trays of big crinkle French fries smothered in ketchup." ("Moon Deluxe") Some- times a T-shirt-with-slogan seems to be worn by a character in lieu of personality—or just to give Barthelme the chance to describe it: "She answered Lily's abbreviated knock wearing khaki shorts and a white T-shirt with 'So many men, so little time' silk-screened in two lines across the chest. 'Irony,' Lily says, pointing at the shirt." If God is in the details, surely there has also to be at least the semblance of a master plan? So consummate a designer as Flaubert was detail- obsessed, documenting his fiction constantly, but when he writes in

a letter to a friend, "I'm baffled by the psychology of my characters,"
I don't think he has in mind the sort of radical authorial confounded-
ness that Barthelme evinces, indeed cultivates. This is photo-realist baf-
flement and, as with a certain kind of painting, one can be struck by
the precision of the verisimilitude: "'Just a beer for me,' Amos says.
He is in the corner of the room, looking at the zither, which is bal-
anced on top of one of the natural-finish stereo speakers. He plucks a
few strings, then looks at himself in a mirror mounted on the wall.
'This reminds me of something,' he says." ("Box Step")

The stories in *Moon Deluxe* have, undoubtedly, a campy appeal;
there is humor of sorts ("Mrs. Scree," goes the conclusion of "Pool
Lights," "wags her arms like an explorer in a jungle and introduces
you as the king of the crawl.") and an amiable looseness. Midway
through reading them I found myself absently composing Barthelme-
like openings in my mind: "'I've forgotten what the primary colors
are,' a redhead in a silver tank-top says over her shoulder to Sylvia,
her friend. 'Is it red, green, and blue?' Sylvia leans forward from the
back seat, cracking her gum, and says 'Who knows?'" I may not have
been conducting imaginary conversations with any of Barthelme's
characters (that would be difficult, since there aren't any), to return
to Orwell's criterion, but I did seem to be having a dialogue with the
stories, instead. What Barthelme's readers settle for, I think, are the
pleasures of the void—and the contagion.

There are other, dissimilar figures on the scene: Bette Howland
(*Blue in Chicago*) has come out with a "collection" of three stories,
Things to Come and Go, that doesn't lack for vitality. She has, on the
other hand, an almost ruinous tendency to write out of the corner of
her mouth, the way gangsters are supposed to talk: "It was in the
high-school corridors at lunchtime, and everyone was fetching up
brown paper bags that smelled of tuna fish and bananas and slam-
ming tin lockers, and there was Donny—tall and dark and built like
a statue. No kidding. His shoulders and chest were as muscular as
armor—a breastplate. His jaw was hinged. He had that kind of curly
grapecluster hair that statues have, and his nose was like a statue's
too; smashed. Flattened in a fight. I wouldn't say it spoiled his looks,
but it made them moody." Leonard Michaels's earlier stories are
brilliant examples of this tone, and Bruce Jay Friedman's novel,
Stern, before him, but Michaels had the habit of every once in a
while sprinkling a little tenderizer over the tough parts, just so that
the reader could go soft, relax. Howland never lets up, and although
she can be striking in her unsentimental approach to the sentiments
of family life ("The Life You Gave Me" is especially good in this

way), there is something too sinewy about her perceptions: It keeps the reader, as well as any false emotions, at bay.

One can't survey the fictional scene without noting, in a shower of acclaim, the presence of Raymond Carver. Carver took the flat, working-class tonal landscape and made of it an original, unpretty blossom in his first collection of stories, *Will You Please Be Quiet, Please?* The effort seemed, to me, a bit less fresh in *What We Talk About When We Talk About Love* and now, in his most recent collection, *Cathedral*, he appears to have walled himself off in the driest of fictional terrains, where the weeds of hopes and desires spring up lushly — as though greenness itself were a fantasy. I begin to find a strain of the hokum in Carver's style, a touch of the earnest writing-class approach to how "real people" feel and talk. Here is the opening of "Feathers": "This friend of mine from work, Bud, he asked Fran and me for supper. I didn't know his wife and he didn't know Fran. That made us even." Or consider this patch of dialogue from a story called "Chef's House": "Then I started talking about the kids. Wes said he wished he could do it over again and do it right this time. They love you, I said. No, they don't, he said. I said, Someday, they'll understand things. Maybe, Wes said. But it won't matter then. . . ." There is, arguably, a grayness of vision that is a form of wisdom — endemic despair, so to speak, the kind you can't get out of books — but I find something intensely literary and synthetic about Carver's presentation of it all the same. He is writing in the American grain, with Hemingway's the clearest influence, but he may not yet have made his territory totally his own. It seems, at least some of the time, to be on loan to him by his characters — who reclaim it the minute the story is over and thereby disappear into a vast grimness. If it is true, as Flaubert wrote, that a writer "does not choose his subject," it seems to me equally true that at some point a writer must hold his subject, especially if it has served him well, up to scrutiny.

There are two stories in *Cathedral*, however, which recall the ways in which Carver — as he did more frequently in the earlier volumes — lifts the most banal of people and situations and makes them soar. The title story, in spite of its obligatory thumb-in-mouth opening (signalling, I guess, that Carver knows his folk too well to grant them linguistic grace, although in this story he will grant a grace of a larger order), is a beauty: "This blind man," the narrator begins, "an old friend of my wife's, he was on his way to spend the night." Sounds like the same guy from "Feathers," doesn't it, but only a couple of sentences later he opens up, and you know you're in for something different, that the tone is under Carver's control rather than he under its: "I wasn't enthusiastic about his visit. He was no one I knew. And his being blind bothered me. My idea of blindness came from the movies. In the movies, the blind moved slowly and never laughed. Sometimes they were led by seeing-eye dogs. A blind man in my house was not something I looked forward to." The story spirals, by the most gossamer of strokes, into an epiphany — a moment of vision so subtle you could almost miss it. The blind guest aides his reluctant host, whom he insists on calling "bub" (one of those strokes), in the drawing of a cathedral, which he has never seen, on an emptied shopping bag: "I put in windows with arches. I drew flying buttresses. I hung great doors, I couldn't stop. . . ."

"A Small, Good Thing," although expert, is a little more contrived; I didn't quite believe in one of the characters, a baker who transcends his own malevolent hostility and becomes a life-giving benefactor. (What I doubted was the extent of the original hostility, which is integral to the plot; why would a baker, even a tormented one in a Raymond Carver story, harass a customer for failing to pick up a birthday cake she has ordered for her son? Don't bakers have better things to do?) But this is a mere quibble, not a full-fledged grievance. The story works, and it imparts a strange, awkward radiance.

And this, finally, is how it looks to be in the world of words, where novels and volumes of short stories keep tumbling out pell-mell — defying, like "the amorous subject" itself, "the thousand forces of the world which are, all of them," Roland Barthes confirmed, "disparaging forces." There is, with all my misgivings about some of the new writing, no dearth of talent. Some of the most interesting novels seem to take as their starting point that lovely, penetrating line of Auden's: "The desires of the heart are as crooked as cork-screws." Mary Morris, for instance, has written a novel, *Crossroads*, which is a quietly acute examination of a contemporary woman who is caught between what she genuinely wants from men and her notions of what she should choose in men. Some months back there was Gwyneth Craven's *Love and Work*, which described the clamor and eventual longeurs of an office romance with unfailing intelligence.

Two of the more resonant of recent novels have had exotic settings. *My Old Sweetheart* (that's the one my blonde book-seller sold with his heart), a first novel by Susannah Moore, uses its locale, Hawaii, to great effect. Although uneven, the novel is most moving in its depiction of that first and most fixated of obsessions, mother-love. And Wendy Law-Yone's *The Coffin Tree* is a dark gem of a novel, about a Burmese brother and sister who are deposited and abandoned to their own resources in New York City. The ferocity of much of the material—living in a welfare hotel, subsisting on menial jobs and the odd kindness, while all the while there are memories of a brutal soldier-father and the colorful culture left behind—is belied, startlingly, by the matter-of-factness of the narrator's tone. There was also Louise Shiver's *Come to Get My Baby Out of Jail*, a Southern novel with an unflagging sense of storytelling.

Why, then, does there seem to be a lack of energy within the literature itself and an absent audience outside it? To start with, one must take into account those "disparaging forces," forces within a particular society that do or don't encourage the exhibition of work. At the most basic level, there is the fact that books—hardcover novels and collections—are increasingly expensive. According to an October 1982 issue of *Publisher's Weekly*, the average price of a hardcover book is $19.06. For that price, you can go to three or four movies.

Ah, yes, the movies: They may well be the strongest anti-force this generation of writers has to contend with. Although the film industry has drawn creative people and generated excitement from the very beginning, it seems to me that the cumulative effect of this new medium was slow in coming, so that the writers of the fifties and sixties could afford to go on as though the traditional pull of fiction— its slow but steady seduction of the reader—presented a valid alternative to the "quick fix" offered by the movies. But it is possible that by this date the center of energy has shifted irrevocably. The reading of fiction, after all, presupposes not only leisure, but a certain *quality* of leisure: attentive and isolated. Perhaps the movies give us all our secrets which are the same in a more amenable fashion, collectively, for one thing, and instantaneously: the camera shot that sweeps over a whole room compared to a plodding, line-by-line description of the same room and its artifacts—the mohair-covered couch, the brown-leafed rhododendron, the pipe still smoking in an ashtray on a desk. "Preliminary good advice," concedes John Gardner in *Becoming a Novelist*, "might be: Write as if you were a movie camera. Get exactly what is there. . . . Getting it down precisely is all that is meant by the 'accuracy of the writer's eye.'"

I am in a darkened balcony, next to a friend, watching Cary Grant lean over a poisoned Ingrid Bergman and loosen his upper lip. The parrying is over, not a moment too soon, and he wants her: "I was a fat-headed guy full of pain," he declares. "It tore me up not having you." My friend and I have both seen "Notorious" several times and we both know, or assume, she will live: She has too beautiful a mouth not to. We are at the movies, where certain thrills are never gone, even if you've seen the climax before. The audience stirs around us, collects their belongings. We leave misty-eyed, swollenchested. In our hearts we are all daring spies, all beautiful and hand-some, all worthy of romantic outpourings from Cary Grant and Ingrid Bergman.

But when all is said and done, such explanations won't suffice. The distribution of blame is too one-sided. One has to turn to the writers of fiction themselves. What is missing among them, almost uniformly, is the sense of literature as a vocation, and a vigorous one, at that. Bellow, Roth, Malamud, Updike, Cheever—they all had it; you could point to them and say, confidently, these are the dominant voices of the age. But of whom can you say that in this generation? The voices are disparate and irregular; they call out feebly and then subside. In order to collar an audience, writers today may have to use greater force than ever. Instead, many of them write with an almost throwaway casualness, unsure of their own entitlement. Can it be that the enterprise of fiction has lost its ambi-tion, its—if I may borrow a phrase from the realm of issues, of poli-tics—will to power?

I am alone in a room, rereading Malcolm Lowry's *Under the Volcano*, rediscovering the drunken Consul who is "homesick for being homesick." All our secrets are there, in this most powerful and thin-skinned of twentieth-century novels. The secrets are not the happy but the tortuous kind: Geoffrey Firmin, the Consul, is bent on self-destruction and by novel's end will get, quite literally, thrown to the dogs. In the extremity of his suffering, we catch glimpses of our own taste for poison, the paths we set on to impede ourselves.

I have gone back to *Under the Volcano* (make of this what you will) because it has been made into a movie. John Huston is direc-tor, so the chances are good. But how to catch its astonishingly pri-vate impact—you, while you read it, are the Consul, there's no es-caping it—the juggernaut of language, its *love of literature*? Lowry's ingestion of countless books that he in turn alludes to gives the novel its thickness. The Consul is adrift on a sea of half-remembered quo-tations from sources great and small.

"I am," wrote Lowry, himself an alcoholic, in a letter to his mentor Conrad Aiken, "a small boy chased by furies." The state of contemporary fiction is an eviscerated one; the furies have been chastened. Irony reigns. It is time to reclaim them, those furies that engage us and that should engage the fiction we read: love, hate, despair, greed, desire, envy, sloth—the whole mixed lot. Who knows? We may win over a few readers.

Daphne Merkin is a contributing editor of Partisan Review *and is working on a novel to be published by Harcourt Brace Jovanovich.*

Robert Motherwell

KAFKA'S VISUAL RECOIL: A NOTE

A general reader cannot help but be aware of the numerous authorities on the life and works of Franz Kafka, let alone the horde of major novelists, poets, playwrights, critics, psychologists, and intellectuals who have commented on him, briefly or at length, from broad generalities to detailed and sometimes arcane analyses. As a mere painter, I will not venture where angels fear to tread. What I can contribute to this occasion—or any other, for that matter—is personal experience, for whatever it is worth, as one human being to others, each with our own uniqueness that in some way overlaps, or we could not speak to each other at all. . . . Besides, painters sometimes see things that word-purveyors do not.

I first encountered the work of Kafka while a student, aged twenty-two, at the Graduate School of Philosophy at Harvard University during the academic year of 1937–38. I liked my brilliant professors (more brilliant then than now) and my school work, but found myself depressingly lonely—it was my first year on the Atlantic Coast after being on the Pacific Coast, where I grew up. My chief avocation became browsing in the secondhand bookstores around Harvard Square. In those days before paperbacks, scholarly and other esoteric books were rarely reprinted. It was a modest little triumph to find a longed-for, out-of-print book, say, the two volumes of the nineteenth-century Wilhelm Windelband's *History of Philosophy* in translation. Just off the Square was a rather small, highly selective bookstore whose name I forget, which dealt in new and often elitist books. It was there, as a recognized browser, that I was persuaded to buy *The Metamorphosis,* that shatteringly poignant story. If I remember correctly, the book was printed unusually nicely and, of all places, in Dublin. I used to wonder how and why. . . . At any rate, after moving on to Paris, and at the onset of the Second World War, to New York, I had my first show at Peggy Guggenheim's, in which one of the watercolors was entitled *Kafka's Room.* I did not have such an idea in mind. The picture simply demanded that title when it was

Editor's Note: This essay was first presented as a speech at the "Kafka Unorthodox" Commemoration at the Cooper Union, New York City, in March 1983.

finished, though I did worry a bit about it being taken too literally, rather than as an analogous visual metaphor. But obviously Kafka was deeply imbedded in my preconscious, like a thrown apple that had hit its mark.

It so happens that I was born on January 24, 1915, which means that I was conceived some weeks after my parents' marriage in March 1914; and somewhat more significantly, all of peaceful Europe at my conception was at war at the time of my birth. (I spent my kindergarten years for the most part drawing and painting war planes.) It recently occurred to me to look up in Allen Blunden's excellent chronology of Kafka's life what *he* was doing in 1915. On January 23 and 24, Kafka and Felice are meeting at Bodenbach on the Czech-German border and find that "their aims remain incompatible: he wants a life shaped around his writing, while she has conventional middle-class aspirations." The next month Kafka leaves his suffocating home for his first rented room. Restless, the next month he takes another room, noisy, but "with a fine view of the Old Town of Prague." He then travels to Vienna and Budapest but returns, writing of himself, "incapable of living with people, talking to people. Totally absorbed in myself, thinking about myself. Dull, mindless, fearful." He tries to enlist in the army but is turned down (like my own father, who was very close to Kafka in age) two years later, when America also enters the First World War.

In October of 1915, two important things happen to Kafka. Carl Sternheim, who has won the Fontane Prize for literature, passes the prize on to Kafka. And *The Metamorphosis* is published in a literary review, and then in book form a month later by the famed and estimable publisher, Kurt Wolff. Then something trivial on the surface, but profoundly interesting to a painter of my abstract expressionist generation, happens. Wolff throughout his career cared not only about fine writing, but also about a fine physical appearance to his books. Wolff informs Kafka that he has commissioned an artist to do a frontispiece for *The Metamorphosis*. Kafka is horrified and writes to Wolff: "It occurred to me . . . that [the artist] might want to draw the insect itself. Please, not that — anything, but that! The insect itself cannot be drawn. It cannot even be shown in the distance!" Blunden comments astutely that "Kafka knows that the ambiguities of his fiction can only be accommodated in the mind, in the imagination: to *draw* his images is to resolve their ambiguity, 'take them literally' — and hence destroy them." Dare I assert that this recoil of Franz Kafka's to the benign intention of Kurt Wolff to illustrate his insect is identical in its reasons to the principal, and certainly principled, major preoccupation of my generation of abstract expressionist painters thirty years later in the mid-1940s—Gorky, Kline, de Kooning, Pollock, Rothko, David Smith, and the others. The subject matter was at once too "real" as felt and too ultimate in its existential concerns not to be betrayed by the domesticized beauty of the School of Paris, or by the graphic design tradition of constructivism, or by the obviousness and pathos of the socially varied forms of realism, or by the fantasies and black humor of the surrealists. No, in the 1940s, with the Second World War, the atomic bomb, and the beginnings of the electronic era now exploding, only a monumental ambiguity would do. . . . When we were sardonically asked in those days, "What does *that* represent?" we learned to reply, "What do *you* represent?"

Part of Kafka's tragedy was that he dared not ask that question — not even of his father, especially not of his father, nor of his fatherland. His genius is not artfulness, but truth. He could not lie. In this he was matched in modern Germany—to my limited knowledge—in a relentless and unflinching fidelity to his truth only by another Jew in the Hapsburg Empire writing at the same time, Sigmund Freud. Supreme artfulness belonged instead to self-chosen and cunning exiles during the first third of our century, to James Joyce, to Pablo Picasso, to Igor Stravinsky. In this sense, Kafka cannot instruct us as artists; he instead moves us to the depths of our being by his own doom, which was to be unable to lie. He had no conception of art in Picasso's sense that "art is a lie that makes us see the truth." Kafka lived his truth. He dared not share the living of it. The old-fashioned women of Kafka's day, with their highly developed sense that their survival depended on their man — in German there is no word for husband, simply "my man"—must have sensed this about Kafka, that so much truth could not be lived with in harmony or, probably, at all.

And if his friend Max Brod had not gone against Kafka's posthumous wishes, neither could we, the general public, share his lived truth. His writings were to be destroyed. True, *we* have the advantage of sharing them from a psychic distance, like Dante led by Virgil through Hell, so that Kafka's images become less personally hurtful. They are subjects for meditation and awe, but lack the awesomeness of Dante, for whom the punishments of hell are justified by his conception of the universe. Kafka's ultimate leitmotif is that there is no justification or, if there is, asks *what* that justification is.

As André Breton put it beautifully in his anthology of black humor, Kafka raises "the question of all time: where are we going, to what do we owe allegiance, what is the law?" For my own part, from lived experience, an eternal optimist emotionally if not intellectually, and tonal in contrast to such starkness, it seems that emotional pleasure from the world as sensed, plus emotional empathy and social respect for the beingness of other human beings, counterbalances the empty space left by not knowing "the law." Any painter knows that empty space is his most powerful artistic weapon, *if* he can adequately animate it. The void need not be terrifying. It can indeed vivify, when contrasted as an image with the fragility of human life — as centuries of Oriental painting and calligraphic poetry, not to mention our own century's essays in modernism, reveal. Think of *Guernica*.

Kafka's sense of emptiness is mainly but not only personal. His middle Europe was an empty shell. He himself described Vienna as "an enormous village dying on its feet." When I was there several years ago, my museum-official hosts described it as a capital city without a country. My point in relation to Kafka is that, in some curious way, the more subjective and the more faithful to one's own truth that one becomes, the more objective one becomes as a witness to historical truth. Here I think Kafka has been underestimated. But no one can forget him. To read him is to be marked for life — as he was — marked by the reality of inwardness, that most sacred of modern domains of which he is a vivid witness.

Robert Motherwell's major retrospective will finish its tour of six museums at the Guggenheim Museum, from December 1984 through February 1985.

Cynthia Ozick

THE QUESTION OF OUR SPEECH: THE RETURN TO AURAL CULTURE

Visiting from England after a considerable period away, Henry James took fresh notice of American styles of speech, particularly of the pervasively conquering *r*:

> . . . the letter, I grant, gets terribly little rest among those great masses of our population that strike us, in the boundless West especially, as, under some strange impulse received toward consonantal recovery of balance, making it present even in words from which it is absent, bringing it in everywhere as with the small vulgar effect of a sort of morose grinding of the back teeth. There are, you see, sounds of a mysterious intrinsic meanness, and there are sounds of a mysterious intrinsic frankness and sweetness; and I think the recurrent note I have indicated — fatherr and motherr and otherr, waterr and matterr and scatterr, harrd and barrd, parrt, starrt, and (dreadful to say) arrt (the repetition it is that drives home the ugliness), are signal specimens of what becomes of a custom of utterance out of which the principle of taste has dropped.

In 1905, when James made these observations, to drop the *r* was to drop, for the cultivated ear, a principle of taste; yet only four decades on, exactly the opposite was true. By the forties of this century radio had accomplished its leveling effect, and Midwest speech, colonizing by means of "announcers," had ascended to the rank of "standard" speech. The history and sociolinguistics governing this reversal of the prestige of the *r* is less pressing to examine than the question of standard speech itself. James's New York/Boston expectations, reinforced by southern England, assumed that Eastern American speech, tied as it was to the cultural reign of London, had a right to rule and to rule out. James claimed that "the voice *plus* the way it is employed" determined "positively the history of the national character, almost the history of the people." His views on all this, his alarms and anxieties, he compressed into a fluid little talk — "The Question of Our Speech" — he gave at the Bryn Mawr College Commencement of June 8, 1905, exactly one year and two days before my mother, nine years old, having passed through Castle Garden, stood on the corner of Battery Park, waiting to board the horse-car for Madison Street on the Lower East Side.

James was in great fear of the child waiting for the horse-car. "Keep in sight," he warned, "the so interesting historical truth that no language, so far back as our acquaintance with history goes, has known any such ordeal, any such stress or strain, as was to await the English in this huge new community it was to help, at first, to father and mother. It came *over*, as the phrase is, came over originally without fear and without guile — but to find itself transplanted to spaces it had never dreamed, in its comparative humility, of covering, to conditions it had never dreamed, in its comparative innnocence, of meeting." He spoke of English as an "unfriended heroine," "our transported medium, our unrescued Andromeda, our medium of utterance . . . disjoined from all the associations, the other presences, that had attended her, that had watched for her and with her, that had helped to form her manners and her voice, her taste and her genius."

And if English, orphaned as it was and cut off from its "ancestral circle," did not have enough to contend with in its own immigrant situation, arriving "without fear and without guile" only to be ambushed by "a social and political order that was both without previous precedent and example and incalculably expansive," including also the expansiveness of a diligent public school network and "the mighty maniac" of journalism — if all this was not threatening enough, there was the special danger my nine-year-old mother posed. She represented an unstable new ingredient. She represented violation, a kind of linguistic Armageddon. She stood for disorder and promiscuity. "I am perfectly aware," James said at Bryn Mawr,

> that the common school and the newspaper are influences that shall often have been named to you, exactly, as favorable, as positively and actively contributive, to the prosperity of our idiom; the answer to which is that the matter depends, distinctively, on what is meant by prosperity. It is prosperity, of a sort, that a hundred million people, a few years hence, will be unanimously, loudly — above all loudly, I think! — speaking it, and that, moreover, many of these millions will have been artfully wooed and weaned from the Dutch, from the Spanish, from the German, from the Italian, from the Norse, from the Finnish, from the Yiddish even, strange to say, and (stranger still to say), even from the English, for the sweet sake, or the sublime consciousness, as we may perhaps put it, of speaking, of talking, for the first time in their lives, *really* at their ease. There are many

things our now so profusely important and, as is claimed, quickly
assimilated foreign brothers and sisters may do at their ease in
this country, and at two minutes' notice, and without asking any
one else's leave or taking any circumstance whatever into account
— any save an infinite uplifting sense of freedom and facility; but
the thing they may best do is play, to their heart's content, with
the English language, or, in other words, dump their mountain
of promiscuous material into the foundation of the American.

"All the while we sleep," he continued, "the vast contingent of aliens
whom we make welcome, and whose main contention, as I say, is
that, from the moment of their arrival, they have just as much property in our speech as we have, and just as good a right to do what
they choose with it . . . all the while we sleep the innumerable aliens
are sitting up (*they* don't sleep!) to work their will on their new inheritance." And he compared the immigrants' use of English to oilcloth — "highly convenient . . . durable, tough, cheap."

James's thesis in his address to his audience of young aristocrats
was not precisely focused. On the one hand, in describing the dep-
redations of the innumerable sleepless aliens, in protesting "the common schools and the 'daily paper,'" he appeared to admit defeat —
"the forces of looseness are in possession of the field." Yet in asking
the graduates to see to the perfection of their own speech, he had, he
confessed, no models to offer them. Imitate, he advised — but whom?
Parents and teachers were themselves not watchful. "I am at a loss to
name you particular and unmistakable, edifying and illuminating
groups or classes," he said, and recommended, in the most general
way, the hope of "encountering, blessedly, here and there, articulate
individuals, torch-bearers, as we may rightly describe them, guardians of the sacred flame."

As it turned out, James not only had no solution; he had not
even put the right question. These young women of good family
whom he was exhorting to excellence were all situated in society to
do exactly what James had described the immigrants as doing:
speaking "*really* at their ease," playing, "to their heart's content, with
the English language" in "an infinite uplifting sense of freedom and
facility." Whereas the "aliens," hard-pressed by the scramblings of
poverty and cultural confusions, had no notion at all of linguistic
"freedom and facility," took no witting license with the English
tongue, and felt no remotest ownership in the language they hoped
merely to earn their wretched bread by. If they did not sleep, it was

because of long hours in the sweatshops and similar places of employment; they were no more in a position to "play" with English than they were to acquire bona fide Mayflower ancestry. Ease, content, facility—these were not the lot of the unsleeping aliens.

To the young people of Bryn Mawr James could offer nothing more sanguine, nothing less gossamer, than the merest metaphor— "guardians of the sacred flame." Whom then should they imitate but himself, the most "articulate individual" of them all? We have no record of the graduates' response to James's extravagant "later style" as profusely exhibited in this address: whatever it was, they could not have accepted it for standard American. James's English had become, by this time, an invention of his own fashioning, so shaded, so leafy, so imbricated, so brachiate, so filigreed, as to cast a thousand momentary ornamental obscurities, like the effect of the drill-holes in the spiraled stone hair of an imperial Roman portrait-bust. He was the most eminent torchbearer in sight, the purest of all possible guardians of the flame—but a model he could not have been for anyone's everyday speech, no more than the Romans talked like the Odes of Horace. Not that he failed to recognize the exigencies of an active language, "a living organism, fed by the very breath of those who employ it, whoever these may happen to be," a language able "to respond, from its core, to the constant appeal of time, perpetually demanding new tricks, new experiments, new amusements." He saw American English as the flexible servant "of those who carry it with them, on their long road, as their specific experience grows larger and more complex, and who need it to help them to meet this expansion." And at the same time he excluded from these widened possibilities its slangy young native speakers and the very immigrants whose educated children would enrich and reanimate the American language (eight decades later we may judge how vividly), as well as master and augment its literature.

Its literature. It is striking beyond anything that James left out, in the course of this lecture, any reference to reading. Certainly it was not overtly his subject. He was concerned with enunciation and with idiom, with syllables, with vowels and consonants, with tone and inflection, with *sound*—but he linked the American voice to such "underlying things" as "proprieties and values, perfect possessions of the educated spirit, clear humanities," as well as "the imparting of a coherent culture." Implicit was his conviction that speech affects literature, as, in the case of native speakers, it inevitably does: naturalism in the dialogue of a novel, say, is itself always a kind of dialect of a particular place and time. But in a newly roiling society of immigrant speakers, James could not see ahead (and why should we have seen ahead? Castle Garden was unprecedented in all of human history) to the idea that a national literature can create a national speech. The immigrants who learned to read learned to speak. Those who only learned to speak did not, in effect, learn to speak.

In supposing the overriding opposite — that quality of speech creates culture, rather than culture quality of speech — James in "The Question of Our Speech" slighted the one formulation most pertinent to his complaints: the uses of literature. Pressing for "civility of utterance," warning against "influences round about us that make for . . . the confused, the ugly, the flat, the thin, the mean, the helpless, that reduce articulation to an easy and ignoble minimum, and so keep it as little distinct as possible from the grunting, the squealing, the barking or roaring of animals," James thought it overwhelmingly an issue of the imitation of oral models, an issue of "the influence of *observation*," above all an issue of manners — "for that," he insisted, "is indissolubly involved." "At first dimly, but then more and more distinctively, you will find yourselves noting, comparing, preferring, at last positively emulating and imitating." Bryn Mawr, of course, was the knowing occasion, not the guilty target, of this admonition — he was speaking of the young voices he had been hearing in the street and in the parlors of friends, and he ended with a sacred charge for the graduates themselves: "You may, sounding the clearer note of intercourse as only women can, become yourselves models and missionaries, perhaps even a little martyrs, of the good cause."

But why did he address himself to this thesis exclusively in America? Could he not, even more emphatically, have made the same declarations, uttered the same dooms, in his adopted England? No doubt it would not have been seemly; no doubt he would have condemned any appearance of ingratitude toward his welcoming hosts. All true, but this was hardly the reason the lecture at Bryn Mawr would not have done for Girton College. In Britain, regionalisms are the soul of ordinary English speech, and in James's time more than in our own. Even now one can move from hamlet to hamlet and hear the vowels chime charmingly with a different tone in each village. Hull, England, is a city farther from London in speech — though in distance only 140 miles to the north — than Hull, Massachusetts, is from San Francisco, 3000 miles to the west. Of England, it is clear, James had only the expectations of class, and a single class set the standard for cultivated speech. Back home in America, diversity was without enchantment, and James demanded a uniform sound. He would not have dreamed of requiring a uniform British sound: English diversity was *English* diversity, earned, native, beaten out through centuries of the "ancestral circle" — while American diversity meant a proliferating concatenation of the innumerable sleepless aliens and the half-educated slangy young. With regard to England, James knew whence the standard derived. It was a quality — an emanation, even — of those who, for generations, had been privileged in their education. As Virginia Woolf acknowledged in connection with another complaint, the standard was Oxbridge. To raise the question of "our" speech in England would have been a superfluity: both the question and the answer were self-evident. In England the question, if anyone bothered to put it at all, was: Who sets the standard? And the answer, if anyone bothered to give it at all, was: those who have been through the great public schools, those who have been through either of the great pair of ancient universities — in short, those who run things.

This was perhaps what led James, in his American reflections, to trip over the issues, and to miss getting at the better question, the right and pertinent question: *the* question, in fact, concerning American speech. In Britain, and in the smaller America of his boyhood that strained to be a mirror of the cousinly English culture, it remained to the point to ask who sets the standard. And the rejoinder was simple enough: the people at the top. To risk the identical question in the America of 1905, with my mother about to emerge from Castle Garden to stand waiting for the horse-car on the corner of Battery Park, was unavoidably to hurtle to the very answer James most dreaded and then desperately conceded: the people at the bottom.

The right and pertinent question for America was something else. If, in politics, America's Enlightenment cry before the world was to be "a nation of laws, not of men," then it was natural for culture to apply in its own jurisdiction the same measure: unassailable institutions are preferable to models or heroes. To look for aristocratic models for common speech in the America of 1905 was to end exactly where James *did* end: "I am at a loss to name you particular and unmistakably edifying and illuminating groups or classes." It could not be done. As long as James believed in the premise of "edifying and illuminating" models, his analysis could go nowhere. Or, rather, it could go only into the rhapsody of vaporous

hope that is the conclusion of "The Question of Our Speech"
—"become yourselves models and missionaries, even a little martyrs, of the good cause."

No, it was the wrong question for America, this emphasis on
who, the wrong note for a campus (however homogeneous, however
elite) just outside Philadelphia, that Enlightenment citadel, whose
cracked though mighty Bell was engraved, in Hebrew, with the majestic word *dror*: a word my nine-year-old mother, on her way to
Madison Street, would have been able to read in the original, though
presumably James could not—a deprivation of literacy my mother
might have marked him down for. "All life," James asserted on that
brilliant June day (my mother's life was that day still under the yoke
of the Czar; the Kishinev pogrom, with its massacre and its maim-
ings, had occurred only two years earlier), "all life comes back to the
question of our speech, the medium through which we communicate
with each other; for all life comes back to the question of our relations with each other." And: "A care for tone is part of a care for
many things besides; for the fact, for the value, of good breeding,
above all, as to which tone unites with various other personal, social
signs to bear testimony. The idea of good breeding . . . is one of the
most precious conquests of civilization, the very core of our social
heritage."

Speech, then, was *who*; it was breeding; it was "relations"; it
was manners; and manners, in this view, make culture. As a novelist, and particularly as a celebrated practitioner of "the novel of manners" (though to reduce James merely to this is to diminish him
radically as a recorder of evil and to silence his full moral genius), it
was requisite, it was the soul of vitality itself, for James to analyze in
the mode of *who*. But for a social theorist—and in his lecture social
theory was what James was pressing toward—it was a failing and an
error. The absence of models was not simply an embarrasment; it
should have been a hint. It should have hinted at the necessary relin-
quishment of *who* in favor of *what*: not who appoints the national
speech, but what creates the standard.

If, still sticking to his formulation, James had dared to give his
private answer, he might have announced: "Young women, I,
Henry James, am that august Who who fixes the firmament of our
national speech. Follow me, and you follow excellence." But how
had this vast substantial Who that was Henry James come to be
fashioned? It was no Who *he* followed. It was instead a great
cumulative corporeal What, the voluminous and manifold heritage

of Literature he had been saturated in since childhood. In short, he *read*: he was a reader, he had always read, reading was not so much his passion or his possession as it was his bread, and not so much his bread as it was the primordial fountain of his life. Ludicrous it is to say of Henry James that he read, he was a reader! As much say of Vesuvius that it erupted, or of Olympus that it kept the gods. But reading—just that, *what is read*— is the whole, the intricate, secret of his exemplum.

The vulgarity of the low press James could see for himself. On the other hand, he had never set foot in an American public school (his education was, to say the least, Americanly untypical), and he had no inkling of any representative curriculum. Nevertheless it was this public but meticulous curriculum that was to set the standard; and it was a curriculum not far different from what James might have found for himself, exploring on his own among his father's shelves.

A year or so after my mother stepped off the horse-car into Madison Street, she was given Sir Walter Scott's "The Lady of the Lake" to read as a school assignment. She never forgot it. She spoke of it all her life. Mastering it was the triumph of her childhood, and though, like every little girl of her generation, she read *Pollyanna*, and in the last months of her eighty-third year every word of Willa Cather, it was "The Lady of the Lake" that enduringly typified achievement, education, culture.

Some seventy-odd years after my mother studied it at P.S. 131 on the Lower East Side, I open "The Lady of the Lake" and take in lines I have never looked on before:

Not thus, in ancient days of Caledon,
    Was thy voice mute amid the festal crowd,
When lay of hopeless love, or glory won,
    Aroused the fearful, or subdued the proud.
At each according pause was heard aloud
    Thine ardent symphony sublime and high!
Fair dames and crested chiefs attention bowed;
    For still the burden of thy minstrelsy
Was Knighthood's dauntless deed, and Beauty's matchless eye.

O wake once more! how rude soe'er the hand
    That ventures o'er thy magic maze to stray;
O wake once more! though scarce my skill command
    Some feeble echoing of thine earlier lay;

Though harsh and faint, and soon to die away,
   And all unworthy of thy nobler strain,
Yet if one heart throb higher at its sway,
   The wizard note has not been touched in vain.
Then silent to be no more! Enchantress, wake again!

My mother was an immigrant child, the poorest of the poor. She had come in steerage; she knew not a word of English when she stepped off the horse-car into Madison Street; she was one of the innumerable unsleeping aliens. Her teachers were the entirely ordinary daughters of the Irish immigration (as my own teachers still were, a generation on), and had no special genius, and assuredly no special training (a certain Miss Walsh was in fact ferociously hostile), for the initiation of a Russian Jewish child into the astoundingly distant and incomprehensible premises of such poetry. And yet it was accomplished, and within the briefest period after the voyage in steerage.

What was accomplished was not merely that my mother "learned" this sort of poetry — i.e., could read and understand it. She learned what it represented in the widest sense — not only the legendary heritage implicit in each and every word and phrase (to a child from Hlusk, where the wooden sidewalks sank into mud and the peasants carried water-buckets dangling from shoulder-yokes, what was "minstrelsy," what was "Knighthood's dauntless deed," what on earth was a "wizard note"?), but what it represented in the American social and tribal code. The quickest means of stitching all this down is to say that what "The Lady of the Lake" stood for, in the robes and tapestries of its particular English, was the received tradition exemplified by Bryn Mawr in 1905, including James's presence there as commencement speaker.

The American standard derived from an American institution: the public school, free, democratic, open, urgent, pressing on the young a program of reading not so much for its "literary value," though this counted too, as for the stamp of Heritage. All this James overlooked. He had no first-hand sense of it. He was himself the grandson of an ambitiously money-making Irish immigrant; but his father, arranging his affluent life as a metaphysician, had separated himself from public institutions — from any practical idea, in fact, of institutions *per se* — and dunked his numerous children in and out of school on two continents, like a nomad in search of the wettest oasis of all. It was hardly a wonder that James, raised in a self-enclosed clan, asserted the ascendancy of manners over institutions, or that he ascribed to personal speech "positively the history of the national character, almost the history of the people," or that he spoke of the "ancestral circle" as if kinship were the only means to transmit that national character and history.

It was as if James, who could imagine nearly everything, had in this instance neglected imagination itself: kinship as construct and covenant, kinship imagined—and what are institutions if not invented kinship circles: society as contract? In the self-generating Enlightenment society of the American founding philosophers, it was uniquely the power of institutions to imagine, to create, kinship and community. The Constitution, itself a kind of covenant or imaginatively established "ancestral circle," created peoplehood out of an idea, and the public schools, begotten and proliferated by that idea, implemented the Constitution; and more than the Constitution. They, implemented and transmitted the old cultural mesh. Where there was so much diversity, the institution substituted for the clan, and discovered—through a kind of civic magnetism—that it could transmit, almost as effectively as the kinship clan itself, "the very core of our social heritage."

To name all this the principle of the Melting Pot is not quite right, and overwhelmingly insufficient. The Melting Pot called for imitation. Imagination, which is at the heart of institutionalized covenants, promotes what is intrinsic. I find on my shelves two old textbooks used widely in the "common schools" James deplored. The first is *A Practical English Grammar*, dated 1880, the work of one Albert N. Raub, A.M., Ph.D. ("Author of 'Raub's Readers,' 'Raub's Arithmetics,' 'Plain Educational Talks, Etc.'"). It is a relentless volume, thorough, determined, with no loopholes; every permutation of the language is scrutinized, analyzed, accounted for. It is also a commonplace book replete with morally instructive quotations, some splendidly familiar. Each explanatory chapter is followed by "Remarks," "Cautions," and "Exercises," and every Exercise includes a high-minded hoard of literary Remarks and Cautions. For instance, under Personal Pronouns:

> Though the mills of God grind slowly, yet they
>   grind exceedingly small;
> Though with patience He stands waiting, with
>   exactness grinds He all.

This above all, to thine own self be true,
And it must follow, as the night the day,
Thou canst not then be false to any man.

These are thy glorious works, Parent of good,
    Almighty! Thine this universal frame.

Alas! they had been friends in youth,
But whispering tongues can poison truth;
And constancy lives in realms above,
    And life is thorny, and youth is vain;
And to be wroth with one we love
    Doth work like madness on the brain.

So much for Longfellow, Shakespeare, Milton, and Coleridge. But also Addison, Cowper, Pope, Ossian, Scott, Ruskin, Thomson, Wordsworth, Trollope, Gray, Byron, Whittier, Lowell, Holmes, Moore, Collins, Hood, Goldsmith, Bryant, Dickens, Bacon, Franklin, Locke, the Bible—these appear throughout, in the form of addenda to Participles, Parsing, Irregular Verbs, and the rule of the Nominative Independent; in addition, a handful of lost presences, Bushnell, H. Wise, Wayland, Dwight, Blair, Mrs. Welby, and Anon. The *content* of this volume is not its subject matter, neither its syntactic lessons nor its poetic maxims. It is the voice of a language; rather, of language itself, language as texture, gesture, innateness. To read from beginning to end of a schoolbook of this sort is to recognize at once that James had it backwards and upside down: it is not that manners lead culture; it is culture that leads manners. What shapes culture—this is not a tautology or a redundancy—is culture. "Who makes the country?" was the latent question James was prodding and poking, all gingerly; and it was the wrong—because unanswerable—one. "What kind of country shall we have?" was Albert N. Raub's question, and it *was* answerable. The answer lay in the reading given to the children in the schoolhouse: the institutionalization, so to say, of our common speech at its noblest.

My second text is even more striking: *The Etymological Reader,* edited by Epes Sargent and Amasa May, dated 1872. "We here offer to the schools of the United States," begins the Preface, "the first systematic attempt to associate the study of etymology with exercises in reading." What follows is a blitz of "vocabulary," Latin roots, Saxon roots, prefixes and suffixes, but these quickly subside, and nine-tenths of this inventive book is an anthology engaging in its richness, range, and ambition. "Lochinvar" is here; so are the Declaration of Independence and selections from Shakespeare; so is Shelley's "To a Skylark"; so is the whole "Star-Spangled Banner." But also: "Description of a Bee Hunt," "Creation a Continuous Work," "The Sahara," "Anglo-Saxon and Norman French," "Conversation," "Progress of Civilization," "Effects of Machinery," "On the Choice of Books," "Our Indebtedness to the Greeks," "Animal Heat," "Corruptions of Language," "Jerusalem from the Mount of Olives," "On the Act of Habeas Corpus," "Individual Character," "Going Up in a Balloon," and dozens of other essays. Among the writers: Dickens, Macaulay, Wordsworth, Irving, Mark Twain, Emerson, Channing, John Stuart Mill, Carlyle, De Quincey, Tennyson, Mirabeau, and so on and so on.

It would be foolish to consider *The Etymological Reader* merely charming, a period piece, "Americana" — it is too immediately useful, too uncompromising, and, for the most part, too enduring to be dismissed with condescension.

> It was one of those heads which Guido has often painted — mild, pale, penetrating, free from all commonplace ideas of fat, contented ignorance, looking downward upon the earth; it looked forward, but looked as if it looked at something beyond this world. How one of his order came by it, Heaven above, who let it fall upon a monk's shoulders, best knows; but it would have suited a Brahmin, and had I met it upon the plains of Hindostan, I had reverenced it.

To come upon Sterne, just like this, all of a sudden, for the first time, pressed between Southey's sigh ("How beautiful is night!") and Byron's "And the might of the Gentile, unsmote by the sword,/ Hath melted like snow in the glance of the Lord" — to come upon Sterne, just like that, is to come upon an unexpected human fact. Such textbooks filled vessels more fundamental than the Melting Pot — blood vessels, one might venture. Virtuous, elevated, striving and stirring, the best that has been thought and said: thus the voice of the common schools. A fraction of their offerings had a heroic, or monumental, quality, on the style perhaps of George Washington's head. They stood for the power of civics. But the rest were the purest belles-lettres: and it was belles-lettres that were expected to be the fountainhead of American civilization, including civility. Belles-lettres provided style, vocabulary, speech itself; and also the themes of Vic-

torian seriousness: conscience and work. Elevated literature was the
model for an educated tongue. Sentences, like conscience and work,
were demanding.

What did these demanding sentences do in and for society?
First, they demanded to be studied. Second, they demanded sharp-
ness and cadence in writing. They promoted, in short, literacy — and
not merely literacy, but a vigorous and manifold recognition of literature as a *force*. They promoted an educated class. Not a hereditarily
educated class, but one that had been introduced to the initiating
and shaping texts early in life, almost like the hereditarily educated
class itself.

All that, we know, is gone. Where once the *Odyssey* was read in
the schools, in a jeweled and mandarin translation, Holden Caul-
field takes his stand. He is winning and truthful, but he is not
demanding. His sentences reach no higher than his gaze. The idea
of belles-lettres, when we knock our unaccustomed knees against it,
looks archaic and bizarre: rusted away, like an old car chassis. The
content of belles-lettres is the property of a segregated caste or the
dissipated recollections of the very old.

Belles-lettres in the schools fashioned both speech and the art of
punctuation — the sound and the look of nuance. Who spoke well
pointed well; who pointed well spoke well. One was the skill of the
other. No one now punctuates for nuance — or, rather, whoever punctuates for nuance is "corrected." Copy editors do not know the whole
stippled range of the colon or the semicolon, do not know that "O" is
not "oh," do not know that not all juxtaposed adjectives are coor-
dinate adjectives; and so forth. The degeneration of punctuation and
word-by-word literacy is pandemic among English speakers: this includes most poets and novelists. To glimpse a typical original manuscript undoctored by a copy editor is to suffer a shock at the sight of
ignorant imprecision; and to examine a densely literate manuscript
after it has passed through the leveling hands of a copy editor is
again to suffer a shock at the sight of ignorant imprecision.

In 1930 none of this was so. The relentlessly gradual return of
aural culture, beginning with the telephone (a farewell to letter-
writing), the radio, the motion picture, and the phonograph, speeded
up by the television set, the tape-recorder, and lately the video-
recorder, has by now, after half a century's worth of technology, restored us to the pre-literate status of face-to-face speech. And mass
literacy itself is the fixity of no more than a century, starting with the
advancing reforms following the industrial revolution — reforms in-

troducing, in England, the notion of severely limited leisure to the classes that formerly had labored with no leisure at all. Into that small new recreational space fell what we call the "nineteenth-century novel," both in its supreme and lesser versions. The act of reading—the *work*, in fact, of the act of reading—appeared to complicate and intensify the most ordinary intelligence. The silent physiological translation of letters into sounds, the leaping eye encoding, the transmigration of blotches on a page into the story of, say, Dorothea Brooke, must surely count among the most intricate of biological and transcendent designs. In 1930 the so-called shopgirl, with her pulp romance, is habitually engaged in this electrifying webwork of eye and mind. In 1980 she reverts, via electronics, to the simple speaking face. And then it is all over, by and large, for mass literacy. High literacy has been the province of an elite class since Sumer; there is nothing novel in having a caste of princely readers. But the culture of mass literacy, in its narrow period from 1830 to 1930, was something else: Gutenberg's revolution did not take effect in a popular sense—did not properly begin—until the rise of the middle class at the time, approximately, of the English Reform Act of 1832. Addison's *Spectator*, with its Latin epigraphs, was read by gentlemen, but Dickens was read by nearly everyone. The almost universal habit of reading for recreation or excitement conferred the greatest complexity on the greatest number, and the thinnest sliver of history expressed it: no more than a single century. It flashed by between aural culture and aural culture, no longer-lived than a lightning bug. The world of the Betamax is closer to the pre-literate society of traveling mummers than it is to that of the young Scott Fitzgerald's readership in 1920.

When James read out "The Question of Our Speech" in 1905, the era of print-supremacy was still in force, unquestioned; the typewriter and the electric light had arrived to strengthen it, and the telephone was greeted only as a convenience, not a substitute. The telephone was particularly welcome—not much was lost that ought not to have been lost in the omission of letters agreeing to meet the 8:42 on Tuesday night on the east platform. Since then, the telephone has abetted more serious losses: exchanges between artists and thinkers; documents of family and business relations; quarrels and cabals among politicians; everything that in the past tended to be preserved for biographers and cultural historians. The advent of the computer used as word-processor similarly points toward the wiping-out of any *progressive* record of thought; the grain of a life can lie in the illumination of the crossed-out word.

But James, in the remoteness of post-Victorian technology, spoke unshadowed by these threatened disintegrations among the community of the literate; he spoke in the very interior of what seemed then to be a permanently post-aural culture. He read from a manuscript; his talk was not recorded until later that year when Houghton Mifflin bound it in one volume together with another lecture, this one far more famous, "The Lesson of Balzac." We cannot hear his voice on a phonograph record, as we can hear his fellow self-exile T. S. Eliot's; and this, it might be said, is another kind of loss. If we cherish photographs of Henry James's extraordinarily striking head with its lantern eyes, we can regret the loss of a filmed interview of the kind that nowadays captures and delivers into the future Norman Mailer and John Updike. The return to an aural culture is, obviously, not *all* a question of loss; only of the most significant loss of all: the widespread nurture by portable print; print as water, and sometimes wine. It was, in its small heyday (we must now begin to say *was*), the most glorious work of the eye-linked brain.

And in the heyday of that glorious work, James made a false analysis. In asking for living models, his analysis belonged to the old aural culture, and he did not imagine its risks. In the old aural culture, speech *was* manner, manner *was* manners, manners *did* teach the tone of the civilized world. In the new aural culture, speech remains manner, manner becomes manners, manners go on teaching the tone of the world. The difference is that the new aural culture, based, as James urged, on emulation, is governed from below. Emulation as a principle cannot control its sources. To seize on only two blatancies: the guerrilla toy of the urban underclass, the huge and hugely loud portable radio — the "ghetto blaster" — is adopted by affluent middle-class white adolescents; so is the locution "Hey, man," which now crosses both class and gender. James worried about the replacement in America of "Yes" by "Yeah" (and further by the comedic "Yep"); its source was the drawl endemic to the gilt-and-plush parlors of the upper middle class. "Yeah" did not come out of the street; it went into the street. But it is also fairly certain that the "Yeah"-sayers, whatever their place in society, could not have been strong readers, even given the fissure that lies between reading and the style of one's talk. The more attached one is to the community of readers, the narrower the fissure. In a society where belles-lettres are central to education of the young, what controls speech is the degree of absorption in print. Reading governs speech, governs tone, governs manner and manners and civilization. "It is easier to overlook any question of speech than to trouble about it," James complained, "but then it is also easier to snort or neigh, to growl or 'meaow,' than to articulate and intonate."

And yet he overlooked the primacy of the high act of reading. No one who, in the age of conscience and work, submitted to "The Lady of the Lake," or parsed under the aegis of Albert N. Raub, or sent down a bucket into *The Etymological Reader*, was likely to snort or neigh or emit the cry of the tabby. Agreed, it was a more publicly formal and socially encrusted age than ours, and James was more publicly formal and socially encrusted than many of his contemporaries: he was an old-fashioned gentleman. He had come of age during the Civil War. His clothes were laid out by a manservant. His standard was uncompromising. All the same, he missed how and where his own standard ruled. He failed to discover it in the schoolhouses, to which it had migrated after the attenuation of the old aural culture. To be sure, the school texts, however aspiring, could not promise to the children of the poor, or to the children of the immigrants, or to the children of working men, any hope of a manservant; but they *did* promise a habit of speech, more mobilizing and organizing, even, than a valet. The key to American speech was under James's nose. It was at that very moment being turned in a thousand locks. It was opening gate after gate. Those who could read according to an elevated standard could write sufficiently accomplished sentences, and those who could write such sentences could "articulate and intonate."

"Read, read! Read yourself through all the stages of the masters of the language," James might have exhorted the graduates. Instead he told them to seek "contact and communication, a beneficent contagion," in order to "bring about the happy state — the state of sensibility to tone." It offended him, he confessed, that there were "forces assembled to make you believe that no form of speech is provably better than another." How *is* any form of speech "provably better than another"? In a relativist era, the forces representing relativism in enunciation have for the moment won the argument, it seems; yet James has had his way all the same. With the exception of the South and parts of the East Coast, there is very nearly a uniform *vox Americana*. And we have everywhere a uniform "tone." It is in the streets and in the supermarkets, on the radio and on television; and it is low, low, low. In music, in speech, in manner, the upper has learned to imitate the lower. Cheapened imprecise speech is the triumph of James's tribute to emulation. A maleficent contagion is the only possible legacy that could have come of the principle of emulation.

Then why did James plead for vocal imitation instead of reading? He lived in a sea of reading, at the highest tide of literacy, in the time of the crashing of its billows. He did not dream that the sea would shrink, that it was impermanent, that we would return, through the most refined technologies, to the aural culture. He had had his own dealings with a continuing branch of the aural culture — the theater. He had written for it as if for a body of accomplished readers and it turned on him with contempt. "Forget not," he warned in the wake of his humiliation as a playwright, "that you write for the stupid — that is, your maximum of refinement must meet the minimum of intelligence of the audience — the intelligence, in other words, of the biggest ass it may conceivably contain. It is a most unholy trade!" He was judging, in this outcry, all those forms that arrange for the verbal to bypass the eye and enter chiefly through the ear. The ear is, for subtlety of interpretation, a coarser organ than the eye; it follows that nearly all verbal culture designed for the ear is broader, brighter, larger, louder, simpler, less intimate, more insistent — more *theatrical* — than any page of any book.

For the population in general, the unholy trades — they are now tremendously in the plural — have rendered reading nearly obsolete, except as a source of data and as a means of record-keeping — "warehousing information." For this the computer is an admittedly startling advance over Pharoah's indefatigably meticulous scribes, notwithstanding the lofty liturgical poetry that adorned the ancient records, offering a tendril of beauty among the granary lists. Pragmatic reading cannot die, of course, but as the experience that feeds *homo ridens,* reading is already close to moribund. In the new aural culture of America, intellectuals habitually define "film" as "art" in the most solemn sense, as a counterpart of the literary novel, and ridicule survivors of the age of "movies" as naïfs incapable of making the transition from an old form of popular entertainment to a new form of serious expression meriting a sober equation with written art — as if the issue had anything to do with what is inherently complex in the medium, rather than with what is inherently complex in the recipient of the medium. Undoubtedly any movie is more "complicated" than any book; and also more limited by the apparatus of the "real." As James noted, the maker of aural culture brings to his medium a "maximum of refinement" — i.e., he does the best he can with what he has to work with; sometimes he is even Shakespeare. But the job of sitting in a theater or in a movie house or at home in front of a television set is not so reciprocally complex as the wheels-within-wheels job of reading almost anything at all (including the comics). Reading is an act of imaginative conversion. That specks on a paper can turn into tale or philosophy is as deep a marvel as alchemy or wizardry. A secret brush construes phantom portraits. In the proscenium or the Betamax everything is imagined *for* one: there is nothing to do but see and hear, and what's there is what is literally there. When film is "poetic," it is almost never because of language, but rather because of the resemblance to paintings or engravings—one thinks of the knight on a horse in a field of flowers in Bergman's *The Virgin Spring*. Where film is most art, it is least a novelty.

The new aural culture is prone to appliance-novelty—a while ago who could have predicted the video-recorder or the hand-held miniature television set, and who now knows what variations and inventions lie ahead? At the same time there is a rigidity to the products of the aural culture—like those static Egyptian sculptures, stylistically unaltered for three millennia, that are brilliantly executed but limited in imaginative intent.

In the new aural culture there is no prevalent belles-lettres curriculum to stimulate novel imaginative intent, that "wizard note" of the awakened Enchantress; what there is is replication—not a reverberation or an echo, but a copy. The Back to Basics movement in education, which on the surface looks as if it is calling for revivification of a belles-lettres syllabus, is not so much reactionary as lost in literalism, or *trompe l'oeil:* another example of the replication-impulse of the new aural culture, the culture of theater. Only in a *trompe l'oeil* society would it occur to anyone to "bring back the old values" through bringing back the McGuffey Reader—a scenic designer's idea, and still another instance of the muddle encouraged by the notion of "emulation." The celebration of the McGuffey Reader can happen only in an atmosphere where "film," a copyist's medium, is taken as seriously as a book.

A book is not a "medium" at all; it is far spookier than that, one of the few things-in-themselves that we can be sure of, a Platonic form that can inhabit a virtual infinity of experimental incarnations: any idea, any story, any body of poetry, any incantation, in any language. Above all, a book is the riverbank for the river of language. Language without the riverbank is only television-talk—a free fall, a loose splash, a spill. And that is what an aural society, following a time of complex literacy, finally admits to: spill and more spill. James had nothing to complain of: he flourished in a period when whoever read well could speak well; the rest was provincialism—or call it, in kindness, regional exclusiveness. Still, the river of language—to cling to the old metaphor—ran most forcefully when confined to the banks that governed its course. But we who come after the hundred-year hegemony of the ordinary reader, we who see around us, in all these heaps of appliances (each one a plausible "electronic miracle"), the dying heaves of the caste-free passion for letters, should know how profoundly—and possibly how irreversibly—the mummers have claimed us.

Cynthia Ozick's latest book is Art and Ardor: Essays, *recently published by E. P. Dutton.*

William Phillips

OUR COUNTRY AND OUR CULTURE

The purpose of the original symposium on "Our Country and Our Culture" was quite precise, and the problems we addressed were concrete. The questions in 1952 were specific. Essentially, we wanted to know whether it was our country and culture or theirs. That is, whether writers and intellectuals generally do, or should, feel identified with their country and their culture—not that this is a unidimensional culture—or think of themselves as outsiders, as internationalists rather than nationalists, more concerned with abstract or ideal principles and causes, with the fate of other peoples or of humanity as a whole, than with the survival of their own country and the democratic values associated with it. The adversary view

Editor's Note: This is a revised version of a talk given at the Y.M.H.A. in a series of symposia on Our Country and Our Culture, in January 1984.

was put forcefully by Eugene Debs in a speech in 1941: "I have no country to fight for; my country is the earth, and I am a citizen of the world;" and personally by E. M. Forster in his famous remark about finding it easier to betray his country than a friend. The cultural side of the question is also whether one feels at home in the culture or alienated from it.

The 1952 symposium was led off by an editorial statement, written by Delmore Schwartz and myself, and a number of writers were invited to comment on it. The issues seemed clear at the time, but in the recent revival of the subject, a part of the Left and some of the neoconservatives have misconstrued the meaning of the symposium and the questions it raised.

These questions are complex and cannot be reduced to the clichéd Left-Right formulations. Nor are the concepts of country and culture the same thing. If they have been coupled, it is because the shift in attitude toward one sometimes has been coupled by a shift in attitude toward the other.

In the thirties and forties, many intellectuals felt they had to reject America as a "land of capitalist reaction" and to regard its culture as politically and esthetically alien. The mystique of Marxism, which then was at its height, lay in its power to transform man into mankind, national experience into an international utopia. If you were a Marxist, it was possible to hate your neighbor, but to love humanity. As Ignazio Silone put it, somewhat cynically, a fascist had to be deaf, a communist had to lack a sense of smell. The uplift of Marxism was reinforced by a theoretical definition of America as capitalist, imperialist, reactionary, and repressive. Its freedom was bourgeois freedom. It was, as Anatole France said, the freedom to starve.

But the radical view of the country and, particularly, its culture was planted in fertile soil. America had had a long tradition of dissent and a feeling by writers of being disinherited by a spiritually barren culture. One has only to think of Thoreau in an earlier period, and of Henry James, T. S. Eliot, Gertrude Stein, Ezra Pound, who exiled themselves from the "crude and garish climate," as Henry James put it, to immerse themselves in the ripe culture of Europe. Of those who did not take to exile, one thinks of Mencken's characterization of the country as the land of the "Booboisie" and of Sinclair Lewis's portraits of middle American philistinism.

The adversary ethos of Marxism absorbed the native critical tradition. But the Marxists took it a step further, advocating a "proletarian" literature and dismissing existing culture as bourgeois. And like most ideologues, the communists carried their doctrines to absurd extremes. I remember a meeting at the John Reed Club of Writers — noted more for their militancy than for their talent — at the time of the Scottsboro case, in which several illiterate black boys were accused of raping some white girls. Some letters from those boys protesting their innocence were read — the gist of which was a repetition of the phrase, "I ain't jazzed nobody. I ain't jazzed no girls. Nobody jazzed nobody." Right after the reading, one member of the club jumped up and announced, "*This* is proletarian literature."

Europe, too, was flooded with proletarian, antibourgeois slogans, but there, most serious writers did not have contempt for their own literary heritage. America, unlike Europe, was the land of cultural self-hatred. One of the constant laments was the absence of a long intellectual tradition of the kind Europe enjoyed. American culture often was thought of as colonial. Its past was in Europe. And Americans played hide-and-seek with Europe, both envying and rejecting the European lineage, like children reacting against accomplished parents. On the other hand, there was a positive side to having no past. The individual strains of writers like Thoreau, Emerson, Melville, and Whitman, for example, came out of a maverick, freewheeling sensibility that took more from experience than from national memory. More recently, the pendulum has swung the other way and has been turned into an asset by the apologists for the cult of novelty.

But, though the earlier antipathy to American society had political overtones and consequences, it was primarily cultural. Except for Pound, whose motives were pathological as well as literary, writers who were dissenters or were critical of the culture were not politically anti-American. They were not indifferent to America's political fate. They did not take the side of some other country or people or some cause that was in conflict with American interest — assuming there is some acceptable definition of these interests. They did not favor the victory of the other side, as some intellectuals did during the Vietnam War. In this respect, the Marxism of the thirties brought a new component into the cultural-political scene.

By the fifties, Marxism had lost much of its attraction for American intellectuals. The process of disillusionment that had begun in the early thirties had become quite widespread by the fifties. But illusions die slowly, and beliefs linger, particularly among intellectuals looking for something to believe in. Even among anti-communists, who did not become conservatives, there were residues of earlier ideas about socialism and capitalism. Nevertheless, as writers and intellectuals became aware that existing democracy was preferable not only to communist regimes but also to the socialism of some distant and questionable future, they began to revive their attitude to America. This was what our editorial statement went on to note.

Partisan Review was at the center of this evolution, which was marked by violent polemics, crises of conscience, splits, and unresolved contradictions. We were divided about supporting World War II. Though the barbaric nature of fascism was becoming evident, we were not fully aware of the extent of the Holocaust, at least at the beginning, partly because our minds were on the old question about the nature of fascism and its relation to capitalism. Dwight Macdonald and Clement Greenberg, on one side, argued that the war would not solve any problems any more than World War I had. Philip Rahv argued that Hitler had to be defeated. I was in conflict, which I now see to have been wrong. But everyone's feelings were in conflict with their thinking. We lived in the unreality created by the shuffling of abstract theories. Macdonald, as I recall, while thinking this was an old-fashioned imperialist war, was frightened by the power of Germany. One day, in the office, he thought he heard some air raid sirens and started to run to save his wife and children. I couldn't convince him that German planes could not reach America.

These issues led to the split with Macdonald, who resigned from *Partisan Review* to start *Politics*. He felt we were becoming less political, less radical, more literary. His own publication was more anarchist in content and style.

The 1952 statement, in addition to noting the swing, also pointed to new problems and contradictions. It warned that if the swing went too far it would lead, as it had in some cases, to cultural and political chauvinism. It emphasized the need for maintaining a spirit of "critical non-conformism," as we put it. It assumed there was no contradiction between loyalty to one's society and a critical attitude toward particular administrations, institutions, and social forces. It also assumed we cannot be loyal without being critical. Non-critical loyalty, which was about as common then as now, is knee-jerk conservatism. This position was stated quite succinctly by Mark Twain, of all people, who wrote in 1889 in *A Connecticut Yankee in King Arthur's Court* that his "kind of loyalty was to one's country not to its institutions or office holders." Such a stand, by the way, is taken for granted in most West European countries, where criticism — or dissidence when it is not in the service of another country — is not considered subversive.

We also went on to talk about the cultural implications of the shift. One of the topics discussed was mass culture, which is a complex problem. At that time, many of us thought of it as the enemy of traditional culture. In 1952, we said that mass culture separated the artist from his natural audience. As we put it, "It satisfies demands that it creates." Today mass — or media or commercial — culture has created a counterculture, a pop culture that is reborn every minute. The need of pop culture for constant novelty is substituted for the more genuine kind of novelty and innovation that traditional art and criticism develop more organically. The result has been a lowering and confusion of critical standards.

But the effect of this critical chaos on art is more difficult to determine. It does not mean that individual talents have not been blossoming, or that first-rate work has not been produced. However, the effect on criticism is clearer. There has been a certain amount of socially and esthetically informed criticism by such writers as Trilling, Howe, Kazin, and some others. But there has also been a good deal of superficial journalistic criticism, abstract theoretical criticism, flourishing mostly in the universities, that has its head, so to speak, in the sand, and recently, a new kind of criticism, obviously adapting to the current situation, that amalgamates *Kojak* with Proust, the Beatles with Eliot, entertainment with theater, and that advocates the application of the same kind of criticism to all these diverse objects.

A few years ago *Partisan Review* received a manuscript about the television show *Kojak,* from a critic who taught at an Ivy League school. The piece argued that only snobs failed to see that *Kojak* was a work of art to be treated as seriously as Bellow or Malamud or Mailer. It failed to mention that the rise and fall of *Kojak* had something to do with the Nielson ratings. Or that the inflation of *Kojak* into art is to deflate it as entertainment.

The effect of the media on art is difficult to pin down, since there is no way of measuring it or comparing it with art produced in a society without mass or pop culture. The only advanced countries without mass culture have mass politics, and the French solve the problem with conferences to debate how bad *Dallas* is for French culture.

What can one do about it — other than to emphasize the importance of distinctions and standards—given that mass culture is an outgrowth of modern political democracy and the commercial considerations of a free market, and that history is not reversible? As might be expected, some writers have adapted to the situation with ingenious theories about "elitism" and the death of "high culture," rationalizing what they can't change. If, as Orwell once said, there is a kind of nonsense one can learn only in college, then we might add that there is a kind of apologetics only intellectuals can invent.

Another difficult question is the relation of art to power. Edmund Wilson, in 1947, in *Europe without Baedeker*, linked American growth with an advance in the arts. "My optimistic opinion," he wrote, "is that the United States is politically more advanced than any other part of the world. . . . It has been accompanied by a remarkable renascence of American arts and letters." And just recently, a leftist French critic has claimed that abstract expressionism flourished because of the rise of American power and the flexing of American muscles in the cold war. Interestingly, this point also was made by Hilton Kramer some time ago, when he said that the reproduction of a Pollock painting in *Time* magazine, upside down, reflected American imperialist strength and fit in with Henry Luce's thesis that this was the American century.

An even more complex question is that of alienation, which has been a dominant theme in the literature of modernism. Though its political and philosophical roots are in Hegel and Marx, for whom it involved alienation from the products of one's own labor, it has been converted into a feeling of alienation from contemporary capitalist society. But the idea of alienation in art, which has been influenced to some extent by political forces, is more complicated. In figures like Joyce and Kafka, for example, or in such esthetically subversive movements as surrealism and Dadaism, alienation amounted to a discomfort with the quality of life in modern industrial and commercial society. And it was often associated with a pathology of aloneness and suffering, or psychology turned into itself. But it was not necessarily political, nor always on the Left. It was also an adjunct of aristocracy and conservatism, as in such writers as Eliot, Wyndham Lewis, Pound, T. E. Hulme, and Celine. And its emphasis was not on the radical rejection of one's country or of an entire national culture, but on its own cultural tradition, rooted in certain moral and esthetic values and in the history and the problems of a particular medium.

This brings us back to our relation to our country and our culture. In the realm of culture, as I have suggested, the necessities of the mass production of art, of critical opinion, of entertainment, of endless talk about politics and culture, all intertwined, produced a new kind of kitsch. Kitsch in the past, as Clement Greenberg pointed out, was simply the imitation of high art for more popular consumption. We now have a constant flow of books, movies, television shows, art objects, that fit into a new world of predigested cultural assumptions for large masses of people. We have instant opinions, instant knowledge, instant art. (I am not talking about genuine folk art or culture, which, for polemical reasons or because of ignorance, often has been confused with mass or popular culture.)

Our age, which is nothing if not innovative, also has produced what might be called "kitsch politics" — a politics that looks like Marxist — or socialist — politics, but is actually a patchwork of seemingly radical and moral stances and popular causes that is not revolutionary or communist but echoes the most fashionable clichés about the Third World, Israel, liberation movements, peace, and so on. It is this "kitsch politics" that is largely responsible for the undiscriminating anti-Americanism and total rejection of our culture as bourgeois, or masculine, or racist. It is this "kitsch politics" that fails to distinguish between the kind of critical nonconformism essential to all serious art and thought and politics, and the political and cultural self-hatred that unfortunately has become chic in many enlightened circles.

We also have a kitsch politics of the Right by neoconservatives who mix up abortion, homosexuality, affirmative action, and national security, and who abuse anyone an inch to the left of them. This is not the politics of earlier genuine conservatives, such as Burke, or Toqueville, or more recent figures such as Popper, or Schumpeter, or Churchill. If, to paraphrase Dr. Johnson, chauvinism is the last refuge of a reconstructed radical, anti-Americanism is the last refuge of an unreconstructed one.

Culture, we must remember, is not one thing, like a party or a movement. It has many levels and facets, and one has to look at each one separately. But taken as a whole, one has to be as ambivalent toward it as it is towards us. I remember in the thirties when I was teaching at New York University, the dean declared that a Jew could not teach English literature, only a Gentile could. He did not know that writers are both nationalist and internationalist. I, myself, have been drawn more to the great Russian and European novelists than to the English writers, and, as I wrote in a 1949 *Commentary* symposium, *The Jewish Writer and the English Literary Tradition*, the Holocaust forced us to recognize that the Anglo-Saxon literary tradition was not necessarily our own. We belong to the larger Western tradition.

William Phillips has edited Partisan Review *since its inception. His memoir,* A Partisan View, *has recently been published by Stein and Day.*

Muriel Spark

ON LOVE

There are many types of love. In ancient Greece from whence all ideas flow, there were seven main words for love. Maternal love is like, but not the same as, love of country or love between friends. And love of fellow men and women, which the old Bible called charity, is also something akin to these but different.

What I'm writing about here is exclusively the love we mean when we are "in love"; and it includes a certain amount of passion and desire, a certain amount of madness while it lasts. Its main feature is that you cannot argue about it. The most unlikely people may fall in love with each other; their friends, amazed, look for the reason. This is useless; there is no reason. The lovers themselves may try to explain it: "her beautiful eyes," "his lovely manners, his brains," and so on. But these claims never fit the case comprehensively. For love is inexplicable. It is something like poetry. Certainly, you can analyze it and expound its various senses and intentions, but there is always something left over, mysteriously hovering between music and meaning.

It is said that love is blind. I don't agree. I think that, on the contrary, love sharpens the perceptions. The lovers see especially clearly, but often irrationally; they like what they perceive even if, in anyone else, they wouldn't. They see the reality and something extra. Proust, one of the greatest writers on the subject of love, shows in his love story of Swann and Odette how Swann, civilized, well-bred and artistic, saw perfectly clearly that Odette was vulgar, promiscuous, and not at all a suitable partner for him in the Parisian world of his time. Right at the end of a section of the book, Swann even resigned himself to the loss of Odette: "After all, she was not my style." Nevertheless, at the beginning of the next chapter, Swann is already married to Odette, because he adored her and couldn't resist her, even while unhappily knowing and loving the worst about her.

Falling in love is by nature an unforeseen and chance affair, but it is limited by the factor of opportunity. The number of people in the world any one person can meet is comparatively few, and this is usually further limited by occasions of meeting. In *The Tempest,* Miranda exclaims when she first sees Ferdinand:

> I might call him
> A thing divine, for nothing natural
> I ever saw so noble.

But if she had never seen Ferdinand — if there had been no storm, no shipwreck, to bring him into her life? Undoubtedly this nubile maiden would eventually have become infatuated with Caliban. Even though she has said of him:

> 'Tis a villain, sir,
> I do not love to look on.

Miranda would inevitably have become enamored of the monster, knowing him, by comparison with her father (who was taboo), to be hideous, because Caliban was the only available male within her range of opportunity. Prospero, of course, was aware of this danger.

Today there is an English aristocratic family, of which the four daughters have all married dukes and earls. And, goes the apochryphal story, when the mother is asked how she managed to marry her daughters "so well," she replies, "They never got to meet anyone else but dukes and earls." If the story isn't true, it's to the point.

Love is not blind, and it is also not deaf. It is possible to fall in love with a voice, a timbre, a certain way of talking, a charming accent. Many inexplicable love affairs, especially those of the long past where we have only photographs or paintings to go by, would probably be better understood if we could hear the lovers speak. Many a warped-looking and ill-favored Caliban has been endowed with a winning, mellow and irresistible voice. Many a shapely and gorgeous Ferdinand caws like an adenoidal crow. And the same with women. One often sees how a husky, sexy voice takes a raddled face further in love than does a little-girl twang issuing from a smooth-cheeked nymph.

The first time I was aware of two people in love was when an English master and an art mistress at my school got engaged. They observed the utmost discretion in front of the girls, but we registered their every move and glance when they happened to meet in the corridors. We exchanged endless information on this subject. These two teachers were not at all loverlike. Both were already middle-aged (and alas must now be dead, or else aged ninety-nine). He was tall and gawky with a long horselike face and eyes, too, not unhorse-like. She was dumpy, with the same shape over and under her waist, which was more or less tied-in around the middle. They were both pleasant characters. I liked him better, because he was fond of English literature; she, on the other hand, was inclined to stick her fore-finger onto my painting and say, "What does it mean? It doesn't mean anything." Which of course was true, and I didn't take it amiss.

The only puzzling thing about this love affair was what he, or anybody, could see in her. What she could see in him was also difficult to place, but still, he had something you could call "personality." She, none. We pondered on this at the same time as we noted how he followed her with his eyes—they were dark and vertically long—and how she, apparently oblivious of his enamored long-eyed look, would stump off upon her stodgy way, on her little peglike legs, with never a smile nor a light in her eyes. One thing we learned: love is incomprehensible. He saw the same person as we saw, but he saw something extra. It never occurred to us to think that perhaps she was an excellent cook, which might very likely have been the magic element in the love affair. It might also have been the case that neither of them had really had time to meet anybody else.

Observing people in love has a certain charm and, sometimes, entertainment value. But to my mind watching them actually making love is something different. I find it most unappealing to walk through a London park on a mild spring day and find the grass littered with couples making love. It turns me up, it turns me off. I don't understand how voyeurism turns people on.

With animals, strangely enough, I feel the opposite. I live most of the time in the Italian countryside, and nothing is more attractive and moving than to look out of the window on a sunny morning, as I did recently, and see a couple of young hares making love. He hopped towards her, she hopped away. He hopped and she hopped through the long grass, till at last he hopped on. Then too, not long ago, driving with a friend down a country road, we had to stop while a horse mated with a mare. There were a number of cars, but we all lined up respectfully and with deep interest, for it was known that the owner of the horses, who was standing by, depended for his living on events like this and was delighted that the horse had at last arrived at his decision, even in the middle of the road. The horse mounted the mare slowly, laid his nose dreamily along her flank, entered her precisely, and performed without bungle. The horse-coper radiated joy and success. The horse and mare moved off casually into a field, and the caravan of cars went its way.

The aspects of love that one could discuss are endless. But certainly, as the old songs say, love is the sweetest thing, and it makes the world go round.

Muriel Spark's latest book is a novel, The Only Problem, *recently published by G. P. Putnam's Sons.*

INTERVIEWS

Barbaralee Diamonstein

AN INTERVIEW WITH PHILIP JOHNSON

BLDD: In 1932, you and Henry Russell Hitchcock were the curators of an exhibition at the Museum of Modern Art entitled "The International Style." The exhibit defined a new movement in architecture. How did you come up with the idea for the show?

PJ: The International Style was a very severe type of design such as we haven't seen since the Gothic. It was a discipline of architecture that avoided ornament, used flat roofs, and lots of ribbons of glass, and stucco, or plain materials, and castigated the beaux arts. It was almost a moral movement. We thought we'd saved the world.

BLDD: So, in addition to being a discipline of architecture, it was also a philosophy. You really believed that architecture would make a difference.

PJ: We did believe it. Le Corbusier once said people will be better people if they live behind glass. Of course, that's an absurdity. In the 1920s, when the International Style work was at its greatest in Europe, the rules were very strict, and the hopes for the future were endless. It was the old socialist dream that everybody was going to be happy. We don't have those illusions anymore.

BLDD: What has replaced them?

PJ: A perfectly delightful sense of living in a real world.

BLDD: Have you enjoyed your roles as a teacher and as a curator? Have you ever really abandoned them?

PJ: No, I'm still doing it. I still tell everybody what to do. Just ask me.

BLDD: When did you first become a practicing architect, and under what circumstances?

PJ: I was practicing long before I was allowed to. I couldn't wait

Editor's Note: This interview is excerpted from the forthcoming book, *American Architecture Now: Part II* by Barbaralee Diamonstein, to be published in the spring of 1985 by Rizolli International Publications, Inc.

for a little thing like a license; that meant I'd have to go to school and write a thesis and draw. So I started building buildings.

BLDD: Did you practice without a license?

PJ: Yes, and they threw me out of New York. A man came around and tapped me on the shoulder and said, you're going to have to close this office and leave New York State.

BLDD: Where did you go?

PJ: I went to New Canaan, Connecticut, where they didn't have any silly laws, and went right on building until they passed a law there, and then I had to do something. So I went to school. I was thirty-four, and my classmates looked all of fifteen to me. I suppose they were a little older.

BLDD: Who was the dean of the school then?

PJ: Dean Hudnutt from Columbia, but the leading man, of course, was Walter Gropius, the leading spirit of the Bauhaus and one of the creators of the International Style.

BLDD: To whose work did you essentially respond then, and by whom were you most influenced?

PJ: I disliked Mr. Gropius so much that I had no trouble getting inspiration from other places. The man who influenced me most was Miës van der Rohe, my guru, who was the head of the school in Chicago.

BLDD: Most architects today reject Miës van der Rohe's austerity. What do you see as his most lasting contribution to architecture?

PJ: To me, the most significant quality of his work was his classicism. Naturally, we see that a lot more now that we're all classicists — we slice the butter differently every time, and right now it's sliced that way. We don't consider him an austere, monotonous man. We consider him a productionist-classicist — a "contaminated classicist."

BLDD: A contaminated classicist?

PJ: A marvelous new term.

BLDD: What does it mean?

PJ: The term was invented by Peter Eisenman. It's my present philosophy and describes what Miës did. His very careful balancing of parts in the Seagram Building, for example, was almost thrown out of the canon of the International Style because it was too symmetrical. Our sense of balance in the International Style came from Mondrian and the cubist spatial lapping, whereas Miës's came from Schinkel, the great Prussian classicist, and from his own historic sense. Miës was an historian. He and I always

spent our vacations looking at classical architecture, never bothered with modern. Now, we see him as the leader of the anti-
modern, protoclassical revolution.

BLDD: You are noted as a kind of patron of younger architects. You
send work their way, and follow their careers closely. Who are
some of your favorites?

PJ: Robert Venturi seems to me the most important architect in the
world today. You'll notice I use the word *important.* I don't care so
much for his work as I do for his thinking. He revolutionized
architecture with his book in 1966.

BLDD: Complexity and Contradiction?

PJ: That is right. It was a very seminal book. It freed architects,
untying all the chains with one brief stroke. Another favorite of
mine is, of course, Michael Graves, who's also a "classicist."

BLDD: You were helpful in getting Michael Graves the commission
to do the new Portland Municipal Building in Oregon, a building
that is almost as controversial as your own AT&T building. What
do you think of that building now that it's finished?

PJ: Don't forget another building that I was the cause of—the Beau-
bourg in Paris. I was the man who picked that one, so I've had my
troubles. I think he was up against it. That building was a hopeless endeavor from the beginning, but a very important one,
because it signals the first public building in the after-modern
period, after-International Style period. And it's a very important
building, but Michael Graves didn't have a chance.

BLDD: Why? Was the architectural community as well as the general public opposed to that notion?

PJ: Everybody was opposed to it. Except me. But the point is that
he was given a squat cubic building with much too much to go
in it and a budget with which no one could build a building. And
because the building had to be built for so little money, there was
no chance of using any decent materials, or of designing a de-
cently shaped building. But Graves is building lots of buildings.
In the next five years he will be the leading architect.

BLDD: What other architects do you consider major today?

PJ: I also like the work of Richard Meier, Frank Gehry, and Peter
Eisenman. There's a whole slew of them. I would name any of
these children that I talk about—they're over fifty years old now!
—as potentials. I don't think any of them think of themselves that
way. Miës was convinced that he was the greatest architect in the

world, and Frank Lloyd Wright, when he was young, believed that there were only two architects that ever lived—Michelangelo and himself—which he wasn't at all hesitant to tell you.

BLDD: And you did not hesitate to argue that point with him once in your career.

PJ: That was embarrassing. I told him he was the greatest architect of the nineteenth century, and it was way into the twentieth when I said that. That was very unfair, because he did a lot of his best work after that, but as I told you before, the International Style was a moral movement as well as an intellectual one, and Wright didn't fit. We were very mean to him. I apologize, Frankie.

BLDD: During 1948 and 1949, you designed the famous "glass house" for yourself in Connecticut. How does that look to you today?

PJ: It's marvelous. I wouldn't want to live anywhere else, but I also wouldn't build another like it now. It isn't interesting enough. I spent all my time thinking, "How do you hold up glass? With a piece that size by that size." It took months, years, to do every one of those little details. It wasn't one of your broad-brush interesting shapes.

BLDD: What was the most important aspect of that design for you at the time that you were creating it?

PJ: The siting; if you have a glass box without any character, and without any interesting details, then it damned well better look well placed. So, I found a glorious site in Connecticut that I've never tired of.

BLDD: After building that glass box, you continued to expand that environment. How many houses are there now?

PJ: I forget—five or six. Every time I get an idea, I build it there for myself. There's only one good client, and that's oneself!

BLDD: A concern of every architect is the initial perception of a space in a room or a building, and I wondered if you would tell us what you think about when you plan that entrance. How are your designs different in the design of a building and that of a room?

PJ: A room is the opposite of a building. We always talk in our office of our "inside buildings" and our "outside buildings." Some of our buildings are very successful outside, but the interiors are not exciting, while others have great rooms, but we just tacked the outside onto the great room. The great trick in architecture, and I don't think I've ever totally succeeded at it, is the combination.

The Parthenon, for example, is an outside building. It hasn't any inside. On the other hand, some of the cathedrals of the Middle Ages have no exterior.

BLDD: Did you ever expect the public furor that erupted when the design for the AT&T building was announced several years ago?

PJ: No. I was given the job because I had worked on the Seagram Building twenty years before. We promised AT&T, "We're going to give you the most important building in the city of New York, which is only your due as the biggest company in the world." We designed it, and they loved it. We started the building and, suddenly, all hell broke loose. Ada Louise Huxtable hated it. If Ada Louise hated a building, you were in deep trouble.

BLDD: It certainly became the most notorious unbuilt building in America. What were you trying to do there, and do you think you succeeded?

PJ: I was trying to recall the great periods of New York architecture. For instance, the colonnade is the same as the Municipal Building, which was built by McKim, Mead & White in 1911. There was nothing unusual or new about a colonnade of that kind. There's nothing unusual about windows cut in a hole. The top is unusual but that was an old classical theme.

BLDD: You have also done something in that building that is either revisionist or a very fresh idea: instead of overhead, fluorescent lighting, you plan to rely on incandescent desk lamps. Why did you decide to do that?

PJ: To reduce the glare of fluorescent light ceilings, the bad color of fluorescent tubes, the boredom of the office world.

BLDD: What other innovations have you developed in response to either financial or technological constraints?

PJ: The best thing we did was that we got rid of the elevators. At the end of that great room on the ground level are four "shuttle cars," as we call them. They go up to the lobby, which is up on top of that great, big arch. That's why the great, big arch is such a great, big arch. When you get up to the real lobby, you're still under the arch itself. The lobby of the building is ten stories high.

BLDD: What prompted you to design that monumental space on the ground level?

PJ: The public. We had a big building to construct on a tight site. We wanted to give as much of the ground back to the public as we could, so we took the elevators, that would have taken up the whole ground floor on a small site like that, and just lifted them up. We left the whole ground floor open. What people object to

today, and they're right, is the shadowing of the street, the feeling
that you are moving around in canyons and shouldn't have to.
They're trying to pass laws to alleviate that and I don't know how
it can be done.

BLDD: In your opinion, is architecture too important to be left to
the bankers, the developers, the planning officials, and government agencies?

PJ: Of course.

BLDD: But in the end, how much of a building is designed by each
of the above?

PJ: That's an interesting question. I think the architect is gradually
gaining importance. Twenty years ago we didn't have a chance.

BLDD: But I've heard you describe architects as the employees of
the developers. That isn't a very flattering description of the architect's role.

PJ: A more flattering one may be "whore." I don't think that's a very
nice word either, but it's apt. Employees—I wish we were, because we don't get paid as well as most employees. Developers
know they can get architectural work done quite cheaply, because
we're dying to build and would do it for nothing, if we could still
eat. They don't like to have us starve to death, but, as employees,
we're on the lower echelon.

BLDD: You've said, however, that there are commissions that an
architect can and should refuse. What would be an example of
this from your own experience?

PJ: My own experience is Lever House, and it's going to be redone.
They haven't used their air rights, so they can build on top of the
existing structure. But in another two months, the Landmarks
Preservation Commission will make it a landmark, and the air
rights will be gone.

BLDD: But they could go across the street to St. Bartholomew's
Church. Now, there's a commission that you refused.

PJ: Yes, I refused St. Bart's.

BLDD: Why?

PJ: Because I didn't want to hurt Bertram Goodhue's great building.
To me, great architecture is something that has to be preserved at
all costs. There are very rich people in that church, and they owe
it to New York to preserve that building because it's an open
space, and Goodhue is a great architect, unrecognized now, but
you wait five years. I wouldn't want to overshadow his building or
tear part of it down. I refused still more important jobs—the
tower over Grand Central Station, for example. That was my first

statement of principle, because I felt it would have defaced Grand Central.

BLDD: You've said that you do not know of any great period in architecture that paid no attention to detail. To what details should the architect be most attentive today?

PJ: That changes with the period. The details that Miës paid most attention to were the frames of the windows, the spandrels, and the doors. Miës was a bear on corners, which, of course, he learned from Schinkel. I don't worry about window details so much. In my latest building, I'm worrying about the relation of a circle to a cylinder and a rectangular thing. They bump into each other, and it leaves a scar in the sky. I leave the scar and make it a different material. The scar above the Fort Hill building in Boston is mirror glass. I'm very proud of it. It's based on a village concept. There are six buildings, all different types, and two kinds, round ones and rectangular ones, and they bump together, making only two buildings with a garden in between. In Boston, the sites downtown are laid out in medieval patterns. We just designed around them with these six buildings all bumping each other. It's the tallest building in Boston, as tall as the Hancock!

BLDD: Who has commissioned that village?

PJ: The Elman Company from Pittsburgh.

BLDD: In Pittsburgh, you are building a structure that is in many ways different from AT&T in New York, in its proportions, its scale, and its use of materials. Can you describe that building?

PJ: You mean the Pittsburgh Plate Glass building? That's the opposite of AT&T. AT&T is a classical building, built of granite, with little windows in it. PPG is built of glass, but the details are Gothic. It has delicious four-corner spires.

BLDD: You've designed buildings in glass before. In fact, one of them is the world's first drive-in church, and it's longer and wider and higher than Notre-Dame—the Crystal Cathedral in Garden Grove, California. The patron, Dr. Robert Schuller, requested you to tie the religious experience to nature. How did you manage to do that?

PJ: Over protests. We designed a perfectly sensible church, with a nice roof and solid walls and with a nice, mysterious feeling that made you feel that you were in a church. When he said he wanted it to be all glass, I said, "Dr. Schuller, you certainly don't want to sit here and look at all the parked cars." He said, "Yes. What is wrong with cars? You live in your car all day long. Are you ashamed of it? Is God not in the car?" It's an entirely different way of looking at religion from the way I look at it in the Gothic cathedral.

BLDD: How do you think that type of building works as a place of worship, as contrasted to more traditional form?

PJ: It works marvelously. We used almost opaque glass. It's like being under water. If you've been under water long enough, you know that lovely feeling. . . .

BLDD: Do you ever set out to design a building in a particular style?

PJ: Yes, I designed the Dade County Cultural Center in Miami. It's right in the middle of the city, and we decided to build a little Acropolis at the square, heavily influenced by the Tuscan. It looks like a de Chirico, they tell me, and maybe I hope it does. De Chirico is a much maligned, undervalued influence on architects. He had more influence on architects than Picasso did. It isn't counted, but it should be.

BLDD: I wonder if you would talk for a moment about one of your recent generous acts, that is, as a member of the Board of Trustees of the Museum of Modern Art, you served on the architecture committee that commissioned another architect to design the new museum tower. In addition to approving the work of another architect, you sacrificed a building that you had co-designed in an earlier period.

PJ: No, I got fired. That's why I didn't do that building. I wanted to build it.

BLDD: How did you get fired?

PJ: They wanted to go outside the Board of Trustees and get an objective view, and I don't blame them.

BLDD: At the age of seventy-six you are as active as most people half your age.

PJ: I think we've got to mention here that it isn't all me. I was very clever and, about sixteen years ago, got a man, John Burgee, who's a good deal brighter than I am in many ways, to be my partner. We even changed the name of the firm to Johnson Burgee. There's no point at all in a middle-aged man who does half the work always calling it "Johnson's AT&T building, Johnson's Transco Building." That isn't fair. I couldn't get the jobs, and carry them out, or design them, without sitting down with John on every single detail. There was no way to give him credit. No journalist will ever give the plural credit line. It's the same problem with Scott-Brown and Venturi. Everyone says, "Venturi's house, Venturi's plan, Venturi's West Way." It isn't. It's Venturi and Scott-Brown, but who's going to swallow all those words?

BLDD: What do you think of as your greatest contribution? Is it a particular building, or an idea or theory, or even an attitude?

PJ: It infuriates me to believe it, but probably my major influence is that I talk so much, and that I favor the young, so, naturally, they reciprocate by thinking I must be good. I have five or six young architects whom I like a lot, and we have a mutual admiration society. If they become good architects, then my reputation will be perfectly safe, because that will mean good architects will say I'm good.

BLDD: For what would you like to be best known?

PJ: For my buildings, naturally.

BLDD: Are there any that you would cite especially?

PJ: I guess I can't help but be known for the glass house, but I always feel that my newest building will be the best — the one in Boston, for example, or the project that's coming up in Times Square.

BLDD: What *is* coming up in Times Square? Can you describe it briefly?

PJ: Times Square is in very bad shape. The city and the state of New York, mainly through the brilliance of Richard Kahan, a former head of the Urban Development Corporation, have laid out the edges around Times Square and let it out to a developer. We're building four buildings that will be more or less the same — sort of a Rockefeller Center for that part of town, only somewhat larger. We're putting up some four million square feet there that should be a new center for New York.

BLDD: Is there a particular type of building that you haven't designed yet and would like to?

PJ: Yes, I had hoped to get the commission to do an architectural school. I did the design, but I guess we aren't going to get the job. But I would like to do something like that. I'd also like to do a museum. I haven't been asked to do a museum for twenty years. I'd also like to do a house.

BLDD: You say that both historians and architects make very bad prophets, but if there were a prophecy you'd care or dare to make, what would it be?

PJ: It would be that we are entering an unbelievably glorious age of mélange, eclecticism of random choices and leadership that should be the greatest period architecture has ever seen.

Barbaralee Diamonstein is a commissioner of the New York Landmarks Preservation Commission.

Deborah Solomon

AN INTERVIEW WITH
HELEN FRANKENTHALER

DS: You first visited the Pollocks at their home in Springs, East
Hampton, in the spring of 1951. Lee Krasner was then preparing
for her first one-man show, which was held at the Betty Parsons
Gallery the following fall. You were accompanied by Clement
Greenberg. Do you remember whether Lee talked about her paint-
ings or took you up to the bedroom that she used as her studio?

HF: Yes. I think the feeling out there was much more . . . her concern with Jackson's work. And what he was up to. His mood permeated the ménage. But one was fully aware of Lee's interest and
seriousness in relation to her own work, and I would say that after
full attention had been given to Jackson's paintings, his being the
main emphasis, then we would almost always look at Lee's studio
upstairs. I remember, one of the associations with her work then,
among others, was that of Tobey.

DS: You're referring to her *Little Images*?

HF: Yes. She was serious. But I think she herself felt that she was
married to a great artist who needed more than the usual tender
loving care.

DS: You didn't see Jackson paint. Is that correct?

HF: Correct.

DS: But he would come into the house and invite you into the studio.

HF: Well, it was assumed that we would be going out there [to the
studio] soon after we arrived . . . the main interest was in seeing
a new body of work in his studio. We all knew that's what was going to happen. The actual process of his work I had only known
about from something like *Life* magazine.

DS: He was sullen. Did you ever attempt to talk to Pollock about his
work when you first met him?

HF: He was sullen, often seemingly shy, humble. But I think his
sullenness was out of a real inability to relate soberly. And therefore one had to read it as the pain of his shyness. In retrospect, he
was probably suffering terribly himself. Eventually, being out

Editor's Note: This interview was conducted on March 5, 1984, at the artist's studio
in New York City in preparation for the forthcoming biography of Jackson Pollock
by Deborah Solomon.

there for a weekend, I was able, for example, at the breakfast table, to talk to him and feel there was somewhat of a dialogue. But it was never what one would call manifestations of a close friendship, or rapport. You felt it was very difficult for this person to have an exchange.

DS: Did you spend any time doing typical weekend activities, such as swimming, or walking on the beach?

HF: Yes, it was usually very pleasant. And Lee had made a very lovely home. Mealtime was nice. There were often others around, Alfonso [Ossorio] and Ted [Dragon]. . . . In those days, the art world in New York around Tenth Street and Fifty-seventh Street was a relative capsule compared to what it is now. There was an early East Hampton-Springs core that was part of that capsule. Lee and Jackson were quite close to [Wilfrid] Zogbaum and the [James] Brooks, for example.

DS: Did Lee do all the cooking on those weekends?

HF: I think so. Very often the cooking was determined by the kind of treatment Jackson was in. For a while they were into homeopathy or certain other related diets and attitudes and therapies. Not that everyone else had to follow it, but that permeated the house. . . . They both were trying everything to rein in his destructive raging beast.

DS: Did Jackson see any of your shows, or your work, in the fifties?

HF: I think he did. He would probably see my shows or the group shows we all might be in. I vaguely remember him coming to my studio. I don't remember conversations about my painting with him. One felt that he registered the painting, but that something in him prevented him from either showing interest or concern about what one might have been about. I think he took it seriously and he looked, but I don't think it meant terribly much to him. Even though he helped spawn me. Like most great painters, he was more or less obsessed by his own painting.

DS: He wasn't very encouraging to younger artists. But it doesn't sound as if he insulted you, either.

HF: No. I'd say he was a silent hero.

DS: What about Greenberg's apartment at 90 Bank Street? Was it a scene of any sort? Was it a gathering place for the art crowd?

HF: Yes. From every facet. People would be in town. Painters, collectors, critics, students, museum people. They were offered a drink in the late afternoon and very often there would be a mélange of people who didn't know each other or who only half knew each other. It could be two or twelve.

DS: Did Jackson feel comfortable at such gatherings?

HF: No. Either he was sullen and silent and suffering because he wasn't drinking, or else he was drinking and he was an impossible bull in the room. And neither was something one learned to cherish socially. One couldn't entertain a dialogue with him about life or art. One experienced the man quiet or the man wild. I would guess he was his true self when painting. That's where he lived. Living in other modes was very difficult. I think he was extremely lonely. He probably felt a huge lack of support; along with his gift and conviction, he was probably in part unsure of what he had to make as an artist. I think Lee was a great support to him. Along with Clem, there was Betty Parsons, Alfonso, a handful.

DS: When you first started spending time with Pollock, he was taking risks with his work; he was beginning his black on white period, which was a departure from earlier work. Did he express any doubts to you about the work?

HF: No. I think he respected Clem's judgment enormously. But he always showed the picture *fait accompli*. He wasn't asking how to make that picture, but Clem's reaction and encouragement or questioning were very important to him. He related to me because I was along, and eventually very familiar with the pattern of the visits. A lot of it was extremely pleasant. Very sweetly done. With care.

DS: Do you think Jackson felt an obligation to be sober—or a need to be drunk—when he was around Greenberg? Was he usually one way or the other?

HF: Generally, being on home territory, it was easier for him to be sober. Unless we were in a pack of people, all of them drinking; when he couldn't stand the strain, he joined in. But I think New York was a very difficult place for him to maintain sobriety.

DS: Then most of the weekends in Springs were sober weekends?

HF: Frequently. I think to most of the art world Jackson was boring when he was sober. And an event such as dreadful drunkenness becomes a kind of theater for a lot of people. But for others who care, it can be a terrible, suffering nightmare to endure. Both in terms of his horror, and how terrible it was for everybody else in the room . . . and he was extremely intelligent. He was capable of a sense of humor. He was certainly very opinionated on many subjects. All these things I seldom saw because his anxiety took over.

DS: Since you mentioned Jackson's drunkenness as a source of entertainment for the art crowd, let's talk about the Cedar Street Tavern.

HF: The Cedar bar was another side of the New York art world, a center, a gathering place. Other than Tenth Street lofts and the Club, there was the Cedar bar where you could get a terrible hamburger and something to drink and sit in a booth and see who was standing at the bar and what cliques were banded together in what booths, and who was in town, and what youngsters were next to what first generation painters . . . you got a general potpourri and lineup of the then-market of the art world. And certain collectors would be brought down there by artists or dealers. The bar had its own inner sanctum and hierarchy and regulars. I used to go for fun. We would be out in the evening and often check in to see what was going on at the Cedar bar. It was the only place to "fall in." I wasn't one of the ones who would stay late. I was . . .

DS: Working.

HF: Yes, working. But there was a whole gang that made it through the night. And into the morning. And there was a lot of drinking. And lots of love life exchanges there. Franz [Kline], Bill [de Kooning] and the twins [Joan and Nancy Ward]. That became an entertainment for everybody. That can be sort of boring. Gossip . . . it's debilitating.

DS: What about Pollock and the Cedar?

HF: It's axiomatic that if he was in the Cedar he was probably drinking. On the wagon, it wouldn't be easy. The bar rippled with excitement when Jackson was in town, and with guesses as to when he would appear. There was an aura. Along with the detachment and lack of support he felt, he was also a star. I'm sure he knew both sides of the coin. Stars are often hated, envied, or resented stars, yet very desirable, needed stars. When they fall, there's a reverberation of unconscious or conscious delight. The star, the king, the hero, the outsider, the brilliant shiner, the light-giver has failed. I think someplace he felt that. I think he wanted the camaraderie, but he knew it was impossible. I think he felt that he could paint them all solid. That he was a better painter. That he made a greater contribution. His pictures were more radiant and

more beautiful. They were harder to take. He was probably very
lonely, and that's part of the terrible price.

DS: What about the Club, the Friday night lectures; did they mean
a lot to you? Did you consider them a source of support for yourself and other artists?

HF: It was a meeting place. All of us with some common denomina-
tor in the early fifties had a place to recognize each other as a
force. You might have felt that some of the panels were ridiculous
or infuriating or shouldn't have happened at all, but it was a wonderful event. We would huff and puff up those steep stairs and,
somehow, everybody showed up, and everybody had a voice, and
you know I can remember [Frederick] Kiesler and John Ferren
and all kinds of visitors, steadies, and strangers. It's the first place
I saw the art world in full force, other than gallery openings. Zogbaum, Mercedes Matter, Joop Sanders, [Milton]̄Resnick, [Paul]
Resika, [Giorgio] Cavallon, all of them. I think the Club and the
Cedar were the glue, the check-in spots. I participated often, but I
never wanted it to be my university. I participated from the
periphery.

DS: Did you have the feeling by the mid-fifties that an aesthetic or
personal rift existed between de Kooning and Pollock, and that
the art world was taking sides? Or did that come only in retrospect?

HF: The schism was felt before the mid-fifties. There were de Kooning, Harold Rosenberg, Tom Hess, and many satellites, many,
many, many. And then there were Clem and Jackson and very
few immediate satellites. I think of myself. And Friedel Dzubas.
There were also a number of artists of the first generation who
didn't seem to take sides at all. Rothko, Newman, Motherwell,
Still were all independent islands and related to — depending on
the season — the critics of both sides and to the satellites of both
sides. At the hard core, there were those who made it clear they
were divided into camps . . . for example, I certainly think Joan
Mitchell and Alfred Leslie and Grace Hartigan all admired
Jackson very much, but their painting, I think, and their aesthetic
identity and their camaraderie were centered on Bill.

DS: Was that partly because he was the more charismatic of the two?

HF: Probably. I think it was his personality as well as the appeal of
his wrist and aesthetic message. He seemed much easier to learn
from or to imitate than Pollock, more facile and more pick-upable
to acquire a de Kooning action-painting gesture and make a pic-

ture that looked and felt de Kooning. Pollock was another ball game. It was a totally different gestalt and offered things that were much more difficult, more rewarding, something to learn from and to develop in oneself. If you had it in yourself, you could go from there.

DS: He was much harder to improve on than de Kooning.

HF: Much more, and therefore much more exciting, vital. For me, there was more of the history and future of art in Pollock than. . . .

Helen Frankenthaler is having a retrospective of her works on paper, 1949–84, at the Guggenheim Museum in February 1985.

Diana Trilling

AN INTERVIEW WITH DWIGHT MACDONALD

DT: Will you tell us a little about your background, Dwight: where you were born, what your parents did, where you went to school, the jobs you have held.

DM: Well, I was born on March 24th in 1906 in New York City, and I've always lived there. My father was a lawyer. My mother was from a rather rich family, and there was great objection on her family's part to her marrying my father—he went to Exeter and Yale but he was penniless. At that time, he ran a tutoring school and was getting his law degree. But she did marry him, and in general it was an extremely happy marriage. I was very fond of my father but I didn't take to my mother so much. She was very fond of *me*. I was never disciplined because I was a very good boy. I was fond of my father because he was interested in me. In fact, he should have been the woman, and she should have been the man, because he wasn't a very successful lawyer and left nothing at his death, and she had all the qualities that a businesswoman should have. That's one of the reasons I liked my father better.

DT: You went to Exeter?

DM: First to Barnard School, a private school at 122nd Street in New York, then to Exeter for four years, Yale for my B.A. I didn't like Yale at all, but Exeter was a great place in those days. I got a very good education, especially in Greek and English. At Yale I just felt I was churning water, even though I was the editor of everything: the head of the *Yale Record,* managing editor of the *Lit,* a columnist on the Yale *News.*

DT: Was Fred Dupee at Yale with you?

DM: Yes, he was.

DT: Were you friends?

DM: Very close friends the last two years he was there. He was a couple of years ahead of me. I graduated in 1928.

Editor's Note: This is excerpted from two interviews conducted in the spring of 1979 as part of a series on the literary culture of New York.

DT: And after that?

DM: Well, first I was on *Fortune* magazine, working for Henry Luce from 1929 through 1936. Then I resigned because I felt I'd gotten enough out of it. I should have resigned a couple of years earlier. I was making ten thousand bucks a year, which was quite a lot for then. My mother thought I was crazy. Then I immediately became involved in trying to write a history of the steel industry in the United States, which I spent at least half a year on; it never came to anything. Then the Moscow Trials came along, and I joined the Trotsky Defense Committee. Then I got involved in *Partisan Review.*

DT: What year was that, 1937?

DM: The end of 1937, when Dupee and George Morris, both of whom were Yale friends of mine, joined with Philip Rahv and William Phillips to take it away from the Communists. It had really been suspended for a year. Rahv and Phillips had a mailing list which, after all, is all that matters in such a magazine. Morris financed the magazine. I left in 1943 because I was the only one of the editors who was so against the war.

DT: You went on to found *Politics* in '44? You stayed with that until 1949?

DM: Yes. That was a one-man thing.

DT: Then what?

DM: I became a staff writer for *The New Yorker* although in the first issue of *Partisan Review* I had had an article satirizing and analyzing the first articles in *The New Yorker,* called "Laugh and Lie Down." Precisely for that reason, I discovered later, Shawn was delighted to offer me a job as staff writer. My period of real productivity there was from '50 to '60. I wanted to be the movie critic, but for some reason they wouldn't let me do it. So I became the movie critic at *Esquire.*

DT: What year was that?

DM: '60 to '66. Then I did the political column: that lasted about a year and a half. After that, since I couldn't write —

DT: You had a writing block for a while?

DM: I had a writing block then and turned to teaching. I did a great deal of teaching: Buffalo, Texas, California, Santa Cruz, and New York.

DT: Did you teach English literature or literature and politics?

DM: I had three courses that I managed well. I taught a sort of general course in Masterpieces of the Film. And I invented two

courses: one was called American Political Novels, from
Hawthorne to Mailer; the other was a course in Edgar Allan Poe.
He's always been my favorite American writer. I think he's much
underestimated.

DT: Looking back over your career, Dwight, would you think of
yourself as primarily a political person, or as someone comment-
ing on society and culture, or as a literary person?

DM: Actually, I would consider myself all three, at different times.
For instance, when I was at Yale, I had absolutely no interest in
politics at all. I considered myself a literary person; a literary
critic, by the way. I wrote a few poems and stories for the *Lit,* but
that's something that everybody else did. But I had no illusions; I
had no interest in anything except criticism. The job on *Fortune*
taught me a great deal about journalism: how to organize and
research. I was still not at all interested in politics then. My political pèriod began with the Moscow trials.

DT: The Depression didn't hit you?

DM: Well, you know, *Fortune* radicalized me, so to speak. I saw what
idiots and coarse and stupid people these big captains of industry
were and how scared they were and how Roosevelt had saved
their bacon and yet they were always grumbling about him. They
were inferior people. I saw that, and so I turned naturally to the
only party I'd heard of—I hadn't heard of anarchism and Trotskyism in those days—and I became a mild fellow-traveller.

DT: You're talking about the early or mid-thirties?

DM: The mid-thirties: about 1932 to 1936.

DT: If I look back on your career, I'm struck by the contradiction
between your work as a literary critic or journalist—

DM: Yes, I always thought of myself as what Edmund Wilson called
himself, a literary journalist.

DT: —and your work or positions as a political writer and thinker.
In literary criticism, I was almost always wholly in accord with
you, but in politics, while we shared some general grounds of
agreement, we were almost always battling each other throughout
our acquaintance. I don't mean that these were major battles in
your life or even in mine, but whenever we came up against each
other, it was in controversy. It's always seemed to me that you
were best in your literary journalism: your wonderful incisive
style, so swift and precise, in addition to your sound judgment.
Yet this same intelligence, when it operated in the field of politics,
raised large questions in my mind. In 1957, for instance, you ran

the first installment of *Politics Past,* the two-part memoir of your experience of radical politics in the thirties and forties, in *Encounter*; you called it "Reminiscence of Politics Past" and gave it the rather arch subtitle, "A Backward Glance at Roads Once Travelled More than Now." I reviewed it in *The New Leader* when it came out as a book and I remarked that archness was not what I expected of Dwight Macdonald. I also didn't expect this kind of frivolousness about his past from a serious man.

DM: I remember that review. If I might say so, I thought it showed a certain lack of humor on your part. I was making fun of myself all the way through because you know, it was called *Memoirs of a Revolutionary,* the book was, and I was constantly making fun of the pretenses of these little groups, including the Trotskyists. Yet I had been part of it. But that doesn't mean I didn't learn a lot and that I wasn't perfectly serious.

DT: Well, it was followed by a long letter from you and a rebuttal by me. I said you seemed embarrassed by your recollection of yourself as a Marxist and could treat that period of your life only with irony or humor.

DM: But I wasn't embarrassed at all. On the contrary, I learned a great deal in those years as a Trotskyist. That was my second big intellectual weapon. The first was Exeter and the other school was the Marxist school, and I wasn't at all embarrassed about it.

DT: You yourself said I should go on and read the second part of your memoir, that that was when life became serious. You said that it wasn't until the forties that politics actually became serious — that's the chief point I want to raise here. We all did many things in the radical movement that are hilariously funny when we look back on them. But it was a very serious time, the period of the Depression. And we came to our Marxism in the Depression.

DM: But I wasn't at all involved until 1936. I had no interest in politics at all when I was on *Fortune* from '29 to '36. I said I became *radicalized*—

DT: Isn't that what we're talking about?

DM: Well yes, I suppose I did become a *mild* fellow-traveller. But it didn't amount to anything. In fact, I remember that they [the Communists] tried to recruit me and they let me into a branch meeting, which was a big honor in a very secret time, and when I left I said to myself, my God, these people, they're just simply wobbits, they don't have any brains and they're scared to death of each other and they have no sense of humor, no *life*! How could

anybody live in this airless atmosphere? Of course, I had no intention of joining them. What I did was the usual kind of liberal
things like—they gave a pay party for Angelo Herndon and for
the silicosis business—that kind of stuff.

DT: The fact is, though, that it was in that period in the thirties that
you got your grounding in Marxism, wasn't it?

DM: No, not until '37.

DT: You mean that you sprang full-blown into the Trotskyite movement?

DM: Yes. I first read Marx on a summer vacation abroad in 1935.
But it was quite boring. Not my style at all. It was the Moscow
trials that awakened the old moralist in me. My attitude, by the
way, toward politics has always been extremely moralistic. I'm a
very moralistic guy. So I was appalled by what I soon learned
about Trotsky and the Moscow trials.

DT: So as soon as you were really learning about the Soviet Union
you were learning it in the spirit of dissent from it?

DM: Yes, sure.

DT: That was of course not the common experience. The common
experience was that one became a fellow traveller, one went along
with it, and then became disillusioned.

DM: Well, you can read an article I wrote about the Communist
Party in *Fortune* around 1934 with illustrations by Walker Evans.
We went up to Camp—it was a camp for the families of Com-
munists. Don't-give-a-care Camp . . .

DT: It was called *Camp Nicht gedaiget,* Camp Not-to-Worry. (Laughter.)

DM: Anyway, this article was on the Communist Party and the
faction parties: the Trotskyists and the Gitlowites and the Weis-
bordites. Some of those. And my attitude towards all of them was
certainly not respectful. I mean, it's not Communist-baiting—I
wasn't even interested enough to be against it. If anything, I suppose I thought, well, they must have something if they have all
that country and so on. Well, read it. It certainly wasn't enthusiastic, it was ironical. The second time I read Marx was when
I was trying to decide whether to join the Trotskyist Party in the
fall of 1939 and finally I decided that I *really,* on the whole, was
not a Marxist. I didn't like their rather arrogant, know-it-all tone.
I hated the whole scientific pretensions of the thing. I joined the
Trotskyist Party, typically, characteristically, after the pact and
when war had broken out. The British had declared war. I joined

the Party for purely moral reasons. This is typical of me. Because I said, if I really do have this view of the world, which I do, my place is there too. You know, I have to suffer with them. Of course, I didn't suffer anything.

DT: But didn't Trotsky follow the Soviet line about war: if the Soviet Union was involved in a war, then one had to be on the side of the Soviet Union?

DM: Right. I joined the Trotskyist Party just when this split was beginning; a faction fight did break out over exactly that point, the invasion of Finland. And of course I was on the side against Trotsky. Trotsky said it was a revolutionary army that was invading Finland, and we said, it's not a revolutionary army that invades a country, it's an imperialist army, and even the cats and dogs don't stay to be liberated. Oh, it drove Trotsky wild.

DT: But before the split in the Trotskyists you went down to Mexico, didn't you, for the hearings of the Trotsky Defense Committee?

DM: No, I didn't go down. As usual. I never do anything; I miss everything.

DT: But you were a member of the Trotsky Defense Committee.

DM: Oh sure, I joined the Committee.

DT: When did you first meet Trotsky?

DM: I never met him. I always miss everything.

DT: Dwight, you came very substantially from the middle class—

DM: My mother was upper middle. My father too.

DT: And as far back as what—Exeter? Yale?—you began to feel some kind of separation from the class in which you were bred—

DM: No, not with the class. Just as an intellectual. But that's natural, of course.

DT: Was this a separation from the bourgeois ethic?

DM: No, not at all. If anything, I daresay I was rather a priggish conservative. Certainly at Exeter and Yale, I despised my classmates.

DT: You felt they were stupid?

DM: Not stupid but they were just ordinary guys and I was quite a bright fellow. I just had the biggest contempt for them.

DT: And certainly when you went to *Fortune* you couldn't have had a very active principle of opposition to the bourgeois world or you wouldn't have been able to take that job?

DM: Well, first of all, that wouldn't be possible. I got the job in 1929, at the depth of the Depression. I would have taken any job. I had no money and I had to support my mother.

DT: Well, at what point did you become conscious of the middle-class world not representing your moral position in society?

DM: I told you, when I met all those big captains of industry. I did all of those industry stories: U.S. Steel and Republic Steel and the great A&P. All that stuff.

DT: What I'm trying to find out is, were you always a rebel or did you become—

DM: Yes, I was always a rebel.

DT: How did it show itself?

DM: Okay. At Exeter it showed itself by the fact that we founded a club of three members called the Hedonists and we used to go out walking with canes and we wore batik neckties. It was called the Genius Club, of course, by the hoi polloi. And at Yale—What I really finally got fired for from Yale was when I wrote an editorial for the *Record* calling on William Lyon Phelps not to teach Shakespeare on the grounds that if he really thought it over he wasn't competent to do it. I was very reasonable about it. I said, you know, you really just don't show much competence. He was the god of all those athletes and so on. The Dean called me in and said, "Did you write this?" I said, "You certainly aren't going to suppress that, are you? It's free speech," and so on, and he said, "Of course I'm not going to suppress it but if you print it, you leave Yale."

DT: What happened?

DM: You know what happened.

DT: You graduated.

DM: As usual I made the compromise sensible decision. Everybody thinks I'm a wild man, but I'm always in the middle.

DT: You don't see yourself as being absolutely, finally, the sturdiest, most principled, unimpeachable character going?

DM: No. I'm not of the stuff of martyrs. It would never have occurred to *me* to go to Spain in 1939, the way it occurred to Orwell and all those others. I'm absolutely squarely in the middle. The Arab-Israeli issue, for instance. My one son is a violent Zionist, the other son is a violent Arabist. But I'm always in this middle position, it seems to me. Israel should have been a biracial state. And also they should have let back the refugees. They shouldn't have stolen their vineyards and so on. I was called an anti-Semite by my old pals, William Phillips and Clement Greenberg and Philip Rahv and so on, because I said, "Why the hell don't you Jews do something about this? You shouldn't give all your money to Jewish relief. Give some to those Arabs."

DT: You say you became a Trotskyite after the war began; you had stayed on at *Partisan Review* for another few years after the beginning of the war. What in general was the attitude toward the war of the New York literary intellectuals?

DM: Rahv and Phillips had exactly the same position that I had. It was the official position of the magazine, which was that it was an imperialist war, et cetera. But it changed the day of Pearl Harbor when the United States got into it.

DT: As soon as the United States was involved, they were in favor of it?

DM: Sure.

DT: What was Delmore Schwartz's position?

DM: Delmore had no position. None whatsoever.

DT: What about Clem Greenberg?

DM: Well, Greenberg and I—I got Greenberg on the magazine. In fact, I invented Clem Greenberg. As follows. He was a clerk in the Customs House in New York City and apparently had no contact with literary circles and I wrote an article in *PR*, a three-part series on the Soviet cinema. In the last part I made the daring speculation that the Soviet cinema was very popular with the peasants of Russia. I don't know where I ever got such a weird idea. And then I said, look at what wonderful things the Africans do. Well, Greenberg wrote an absolutely brilliant letter to the editor refuting this whole position, called "Avant Garde and Kitsch."

DT: His most famous piece.

DM: But it began as a letter to the editor and he was absolutely right. He pointed out that the first thing that these marvelous native tribesmen in Africa and Australia, who do such wonderful abstract work, demand of the explorer is not the works of Picasso but picture postcards, gaudy, horrible. So I said, listen, you're right, this is too good for a letter to the editor. And that's how it all began. Now, as for his suddenly bursting into the *Nation* as the art critic, I'm not so sure that he did know anything about art. But he had something that was very important: a moralistic approach to everything. He made people feel guilty if they didn't like Jackson Pollock, that's what it amounts to. And that's very powerful medicine with all this worried, jumped-up, wartime-educated public.

DT: But you said that you always had a moral base for all your thinking. Wasn't that a moral base that Clem had?

DM: No, of course not. He uses morality as a way to make people

feel guilty. I don't want to make people feel guilty. I'm serious.
(Laughter.) I'm moral.

DT: Let's just go on free-associating, Dwight. What about Fred
Dupee? He came later than the rest of you, didn't he?

DM: No, he didn't. He was the link between Rahv and Phillips and
me and George Morris. Fred was my best friend, of course, practically all of our lives. We had terrible rows and long periods,
sometimes lasting years, in which we practically didn't speak to
each other. Yet even then we had some sort of communication.

DT: He was a very lovable person. And always appropriate to himself. He never violated his own style.

DM: No. He was completely honest and also extremely intelligent.
One of the few people I've known in my life that I really considered absolutely my—I could talk to him about anything and he
would get it, you know.

DT: I remember when I was about to make my first speech in public
and I told Fred how nervous I was. He asked me if I had my
speech written and when I said I had, he told me to come and
read it to him. He rehearsed me for more than an hour, made me
stand up straight, speak slowly.

DM: He was a sweetie.

DT: What about Mary McCarthy? At what point did she come into
the picture?

DM: Mary came in pretty much at the beginning, I think. She used
to do drama for us. And she wrote those stories: *The Company She
Keeps.* She wasn't on the magazine very long for the simple reason
that she ran off with Edmund Wilson. It was a crushing blow to
Rahv. I remember Rahv saying, my God, why did I ever intro-
duce her to that guy? Of course Wilson was a very eminent guy,
and so on. Also she might have had an instinct that she needed
him as a kind of, you know, a guide.

DT: As the years went on, the magazine became just Rahv and
Phillips, and a rather fierce tug-of-war developed between them,
didn't it?

DM: Oh boy, I'll say. I made a good crack about that period when
they were together on *Partisan Review* and yet fighting like hell. I
said, they're staying together for the sake of the child, which was
actually true. Rahv was a big bear, you know, and a pretty brutal
guy in many ways. For some reason or other, women loved him.
My wife thought he was adorable. He was quite a womanizer but
also quite avuncular with women. But boy, with his equals and

with men he could be pretty damn tough. And he had a power complex too. He thought power was a big thing. He was very paranoiac, very suspicious, as power people are.

DT: Tell me about the other people you knew around *PR.* Isaac Rosenfeld? His *Passage from Home* was one of the most talented first novels of the period. He was very crazy and very gifted.

DM: Very crazy, yes. The one thing I remember distinctly about him is the phase when he was an orgone box guy.

DT: Did you ever get into an orgone box?

DM: Oh sure. I sat there for an hour and when I came out, he said, how do you feel? And I said, just the same, I feel sort of hot. After all, it's hot sitting in a telephone booth. And his face fell and he said, why I thought you looked as if your whole vitality was revived.

DT: Who else believed in the orgone box? Did Saul Bellow? Wasn't Saul more rationalistic than that?

DM: Yes. But there were a lot of Reichians around. Of course, Reich was a lot more than the orgone box. He was brilliant.

DT: Brilliant and crazy.

DM: He wasn't crazy in his earlier books; he became crazy when he got to this country. But his analysis of repressed sex and fascism was an extremely interesting book.

DT: Did you know Saul Bellow?

DM: I knew him slightly. We published his first stuff, you know. "The Mexican General," I think, was one of his first published things. Of course, the most outstanding thing about Saul Bellow is his sensitivity to criticism. I remember a time at some party; I'd been reading *Augie March* and I made some criticism, but *surrounding* it with garlands of praise. He said, well, so that's what you think of me, that's the gratitude I get for publishing in your magazine!

DT: You had quite a bit in the earliest issues of *Politics* about this new third form of state power which is not socialism but also not democracy.

DM: Bureaucratic collectivism. I had a long piece in *Partisan Review* about it which came from material I did for the Trotskyists. The Trotskyists would only publish a quarter of it, and they said, it was really so dull and I didn't know my stuff, and I said, "I'm the only professional writer you've ever had, and I couldn't possibly write an article as dull as everybody else on this goddamn magazine."

DT: And that was the break?

DM: Yes. It showed something very serious, that they were not willing, as I thought they were, to go all the way in breaking with the Old Man [Trotsky] and with Marxism.

DT: Where did you get the money for *Politics*?

DM: Partly from the remnants of my savings from my *Fortune* job. Partly, perhaps mostly, from a small income, a trust fund, that Nancy [Macdonald] had. In those days, it didn't cost much. Our deficit in some years was under a thousand dollars.

DT: But you and Nancy did all the work.

DM: Yes, of course, and we didn't have any salaries. But we paid five dollars a page. Not very much. One of the reasons I gave it up, outside of being tired of it and realizing that no magazine can go on forever — you know, they have lives just like people do — is that I was just fagged out.

DT: Dwight, what did you feel about Yalta?

DM: I felt disgusted. That was a sell-out. We just delivered it over — they didn't have to do it, you know. Stalin was leading from weakness. He just bluffed them. We didn't have to stop at the Elbe, and Berlin didn't have to be divided. During the war everybody began again to love Stalin.

DT: Do you believe that the Soviet Union and America, when they have detente, have something that has significance? Isn't it simply a momentary strategy and tomorrow it can change?

DM: Of course, but I don't think it's a one-sided thing. I don't think it's a plot on the part of the Soviets against this country or vice versa. I think that detente is useful just as I thought it was useful for Nixon to go to China and bring it back into the community of nations, recognize the fact that there is such a thing as China. And I'm delighted by what's happening in China now [1979] because, as you know, it's completely counterrevolutionary. I discover, every time I hear the word revolution, that everything revolutionary is lousy.

DT: Don't you want a revolution?

DM: Of course not. I mean, yes, I want a revolution but an anarchist revolution, which will never happen in this country.

DT: Dwight, you wrote about the 1949 Waldorf Conference —

DM: You mean the conference of the Stalinists? I wrote about it in *Politics*.

DT: Who was the moving spirit in the plan to break it up? Was it Sidney Hook?

DM: On the contrary. First of all, it wasn't a plan to break up the conference. There was one section of the conference that three or four of us, and some others we didn't expect, Mary McCarthy and myself and Cal Lowell, decided to attend. We found out that Jean Malaquais, I think it was, and George Counts were also there to make trouble. Malaquais was a French novelist, a friend of Norman Mailer. Hook, on the other hand, the Hookites, did everything possible to discourage us. They said that this was not a good idea at all; we would make fools of ourselves. We would also give the Stalinists a talking point; it was rude to go to their functions. And they, of course, held their own separate thing at Freedom House. But we thought that we were not humiliating or insulting Shostakovich but showing our solidarity with him. The poor guy was doing his best to be a good boy.

DT: Shostakovich was the star of that panel?

DM: The Russian star. Norman Mailer was the big American star. We didn't address any questions to Norman. We'd known him but we assumed that he still was what he was before, a loyal Wallace-ite. But we did ask a lot of questions about what had happened to various people. That was our aim, to ask embarrassing questions. We asked questions about the way things were being run, and at one point I remember that the chairman, Louis Untermeyer, made some crack about Hook being a four-letter word, and either I or Mary got up and said, "We object, Mr. Chairman, to such language from the chair. You're not supposed to use such language." But of course the sensation was Mailer's speech. He was the most highly applauded when he got up because he was the darling of the session. But when he sat down there was hardly any applause, and when he was talking there were audible rustlings of discontent among the mob because that's where he announced that there were two imperialisms, America's and Russia's. That was the first time anybody heard that. And then we were invited to a party by Howard Fast, given by the Stalinists. And what struck me was that they weren't so different from the Trotskyites and the other radicals that I'd known.

DT: In what sense?

DM: It was just that there was a river of blood between us. But otherwise they were just the same type. They were perfectly nice, amiable people and idealistic. They didn't behave like totalitarians.

DT: Did you expect them to have horns or fangs or something?

DM: Yes, something like that, or at least to be antagonistic. Of course, we were very careful to avoid the deadly subject of Stalin.

DT: At what session did Lillian Hellman make the remark attributed to her by Garry Wills in the introduction to *Scoundrel Time,* that you don't insult your host at the table?

DM: That was directed at us, of course. But she wasn't in this session at all and I never saw her there. She was in the big public session which we also attended but didn't say anything because we didn't have that much nerve. You know, they had a big dinner and so on, something like that. She wasn't at the critics' session.

DT: I take it that you've just re-read *Scoundrel Time.* Would you like to comment on it while you have it freshly in mind?

DM: I thought it was an absolutely disgusting book. And as a matter of fact, I've been quite friendly with Lillian for a long time, especially after she signed the protest I got up about Siniavski and Daniel in 1969, which I think was a turning point politically for her, because in three distinct places in this book you'll see, if you read it carefully, she's given up on Stalinism. She says in so many words, I was wrong about it. But she then goes on to say that the people who really were wrong and vicious and bad for America were *us,* you know. That's why I think it's a silly book and also a very dishonest book. The reason I think it's a dishonest book primarily is that she gives us this self-dramatizing impression that she was isolated, that the liberals didn't help her, that nobody helped her. The book itself makes clear that this isn't true, that even Arthur Krock wrote her a letter saying, I admire your stand but not your politics, et cetera, et cetera. I mean, if you read the book you'll see all through it that everybody is on her side. Not politically, but for civil liberties. But she has the gall to say, and the dishonesty to say, that she didn't get any support. What she means is that nobody was on her side as a Stalinist. And why the hell should we be? She was then still a Stalinist. [Dashiell] Hammett of course made no bones about being a Communist. She supported the whole Wallace business, she apologized for the rape of Czechoslovakia, and all that kind of stuff. That's why this book is so really disgusting. I don't understand why she writes this all up now and pretends that she's the Joan of Arc and so on—

DT: Because a new generation only knows that there was a phenomenon called McCarthyism. They take her to be a symbol of the forces that withstood McCarthy.

DM: Well, that's true to some extent, of course. And it's probably true that she was damaged and harrassed. Not by McCarthy, by the HUAC. But it certainly is not true that she didn't get plenty of support.

DT: What about Hannah Arendt: you haven't spoken about her yet. Did you know her well?

DM: I can't remember when I first met her. In my *Responsibility of Peoples* in 1945, I remember that's when I was first aware of Hannah. And then I reviewed the *Origins* at great length for *The New Leader.* We soon became very, very fast friends. And her husband, who was an anarchist like me, Heinrich Blücher, I liked him very, very much too. I think he had a very good effect on Hannah, by the way. I think Hannah's one trouble was that she had this Germanic scholastic training: people like Jaspers. Extremely vague, extremely abstract, and *general.* And I thought the great thing about that first book of hers was that it was historical, not philosophical. And I think that Heinrich's pressure was always in that direction. Well naturally, since an anarchist's view of things would be exactly the opposite of the Hegelian, German, Jaspers kind of view. She was my literary executor until her death.

DT: And you were a great admirer of *The Origins of Totalitarianism*?

DM: A great admirer also of *Eichmann in Jerusalem.* I wrote an article about it for *Partisan Review.*

DT: I thought Lionel Abel wrote the review in *Partisan Review.*

DM: Yes, right. He published a very vicious attack.

DT: And then William Phillips wrote an editorial exception to it. And then you did a piece.

DM: Well, Mary did a piece, and then I did a piece. Mary's piece, I guess, was directed entirely at Lionel Abel's piece. My piece came after Mary's, and I took up the broader question, including some nasty remarks about Lionel Abel she hadn't made. He wrote two of the most vicious articles against Hannah Arendt I've ever read. This was the second one. The first one was in some Jewish magazine. I don't know why he had such a down on Hannah, but he did. He was very personal and very insulting and, you know, saying she was a joke as a philosopher. All this kind of stuff. What interested me was that practically all of the people, the Jewish intellectuals, that I grew up with — you know, around *Partisan* and the Trotskyist movement and Irving Howe — all tended to line up against Hannah. They tended to think she was attacking in some way or other the Jewish people and saying that they were cowards, they should have risen up. Of course, she said nothing of the kind.

She was talking of their leadership and not the people. Daniel Bell was the only one who behaved with any common sense at all. As usual, Bell was in the middle, which perhaps isn't the most heroic position but it was perfectly intelligent. What was always strange to me was that all these people that were leftists and Marxists together with me suddenly turned out to be, you know, Jewish nationalists. We wouldn't have spit on that position when we were Marxists.

DT: I want to get back to your interest in films, Dwight. You said earlier that as far back as your connection with *The New Yorker* you wanted to do film criticism.

DM: Long before that; I *did* start in the very early thirties. I wrote several long articles on D. W. Griffith and on the Soviet cinema. And before that, in the magazine we had called *The Miscellany.*

DT: Well, for a long time you were best known, I think, for the distinction you had made between mass cult and mid-cult. In that period did you specifically have in mind the film as the medium that reached the widest audience?

DM: No, film didn't enter into it in any specific way because I was never interested in the movies sociologically. My interest was entirely aesthetic, as an art form.

DT: Are you still more interested in them as an art form than as social document?

DM: Not more than. But it wouldn't be the way that I would approach them. Only a tiny, tiny minority of films have some pretensions to be an art.

DT: You and Jim Agee both had this same view, as opposed to somebody like Robert Warshow who saw the film as a cultural commentary?

DM: Oh, sure. Warshow's approach was very brilliant and very interesting. That was a classic little book he wrote on some of the things in the movies, the Western and so on. But that's entirely different from our approach because Agee and I were absolutely convinced that movies were the most exciting and interesting art form of this century. We were much more interested in movies than in books. We wanted to make movies and we were bored with writing, and finally Agee did that. He never directed a movie but he wrote some scripts for movies. If he'd lived even another five years, he would undoubtedly have made movies. His luck was bad: he died just before it became possible to make a movie on practically nothing. Ultimately he would have made movies in

Hollywood too because Hollywood was becoming civilized just when he died. In my film book, I have a long thing on Agee and the movies, with a lot of correspondence. I have a letter that he wrote me when he was seventeen years old, and this letter gives a view of the movies and of what he wants to do with the movies, if he ever could make a movie, which is incredibly mature. Also in *Against the American Grain,* I have a long memoir on Agee with a lot of letters. We liked each other very much and we respected each other, which is perhaps equally important. He was pretty much of a bum in many ways. He didn't wash very much, his clothes were filthy, and he was very bad sexually, to say the least — you know, a loose liver. And he drank too much. But I must say, he's one of the few people that I've met that I would consider, without any question, a genius. Like Auden, Eliot, people like that. I don't think he's a critic. For one thing, he wildly exaggerated the merits of some of the movies that he wrote about, including Chaplin's *Monsieur Verdoux.* I wrote a long thing about that. I think he tended to be a creator and to see values in movies that only a guy that wanted to make a movie himself would see. He was consistently overrating movies. He wasn't a critic, he was a creator. His main achievement was only one book, really: *Let Us Now Praise Famous Men.* Lionel [Trilling] was one of the few people who really saw what a great book that was. It got very bad reviews.

DT: Yes, it sold only 600 copies. Dwight, you've said of yourself that you have a cultural conservatism existing side by side with a political radicalism and anarchism.

DM: Yes. I belong to various societies for keeping things as they are: the Victorian Society and the Sierra Club, things like that. And every time they do anything new in New York, I'm against it. Pull down things and put up other things. Also I've discovered that culturally I'm a snob. I'm an intellectual snob. But politically I've always been very radical and for the people. And this does present all kinds of problems, one of them, which I know you're going to bring up, about the sit-in at Columbia.

DT: It's our next subject.

DM: Right. But let me just go on about this. Almost my only big idea I've had in my life, that I exploited far too much perhaps, is this mass culture business — I was really the originator even of the phrase — I myself called it popular culture to begin with but then Meyer Schapiro said it should be called mass culture. Anyway, I wondered why it was that I was there taking a completely undemocratic position. For instance, I'm in favor of public libraries and in favor of public art museums but I'm against trying to get people to use public libraries or to use art museums. I'm against the whole technique of the Museum of Modern Art, the Metropolitan and so on, of trying to get people to come and see their pictures. My idea of a good museum is a warehouse: the Louvre or something like that. A place where everything is made as difficult as possible and the only people that go there are people that want to see the pictures. And the masses don't go there because the masses don't give a damn about art. My theory is that in any culture, including a High Renaissance, not more than twenty or twenty-five percent, at the most, give a goddamn about culture. This whole business is a kind of a cultural — a peculiar kind of democratic snobbism. It's everybody's right to be cultured, but it's not everybody's *duty* to be cultured. This King Tut exhibition is everything that I'm opposed to in the museum world today. People lining up. Applying for tickets. By the millions. And the Tut is bad Egyptian art; it's much too late to be any good at all; they have much better art from Egypt there which nobody pays any attention to, in the Middle East Department. But anyway, that always bothered me, and I solved it as follows. Everybody is an expert in politics. You have a right to have an opinion; it's a democratic thing. Whereas art is, to me, a completely snobbish thing. You have no right to crowd the museums if you don't know anything about art and if you just go because you think it's your democratic right. You have no right to do it because you make it hard for me to go and see the pictures, for one thing.

DT: All right then, how do you feel about universities?

DM: All for them. Of course. One of the things that bothered me about the SDS [Students for a Democratic Society], which I was all for too, because they were very anarchistic, you know, and I love anarchism — they weren't Marxists at all — was that they were ignoramuses. They had no respect for the past, no interest in the past. The Old Left considered that culture was the heritage of the working class and should therefore be preserved and paid respect to; the only trouble was that the working class was excluded from it. But when I read of the New Left attacking the libraries, it was as if I was religious and they were profaning a cathedral.

DT: Then you're not anarchist?

DM: I *am* anarchist. Kropotkin was an anarchist. Emma Goldman was anarchist. But they were very cultivated people. It would never have occurred to them to be anti-cultural. The SDS politically was anarchist and that was very good, because they didn't have any leadership and they got rid of all this Marxist junk and they really behaved towards each other much better than we Trotskyites ever did. They were very, very kind, supportive towards each other. And I was entirely for their contempt for bourgeois society and their thumbing their nose at it and so on. All that's fine. But I was not in favor of their anti-cultural stance.

DT: How did you feel about such things as their urinating on the President's carpets and defecating in the wastepaper baskets? You, with your fastidious feelings about these things?

DM: Are you kidding? I'm opposed — especially those acts, especially the defecating. I have a special horror of anything like that.

DT: Well, there you are. Those were the very things they were doing in the name of their freedom to do anything they wanted.

DM: That's not anarchism. That's just hoodlumism.

DT: You make a nice distinction.

DM: I do not make a nice distinction. Anarchism is a very idealistic philosophy and the great anarchists have been people — Emma Goldman was one of the most cultivated women of her day. She used to lecture on Ibsen and Strindberg. I mean, that's anarchism. I think anybody who would pee on anything or shit on anything is an animal and should be severely humiliated.

DT: But you believed that they could occupy the buildings: that was all right?

DM: I was all for that, yes. Because they didn't do any damage. And there were no bombs.

DT: But on what grounds is it all right to stop another person from pursuing his democratic right to have his education by blocking a building and making it inaccessible to him?

DM: Well, there were only four buildings involved.

DT: Yes, but those four.

DM: They had the majority of the students with them, didn't they?

DT: That was after the bust, not before. All you have to do is invite a police bust and then you'll get the masses of people. There's nothing like cracked heads to mobilize sympathy for a sit-in.

DM: We thought there should be no mixing up with the police, no violence. We should get permission from the college authorities. In my speech, I said, I do not agree with the idea of closing down universities or locking them up but I do agree with this particular thing. Because I think Columbia had become absolutely fossil-

ized. And Grayson Kirk, if anybody's windows can be peed out
of, it's his windows. He was a big stuffed shirt, and of course they
got rid of him, thank God. And also the Vietnam thing played a
big part too: Those war contracts should have been given up. The
gym, I think, was a fake issue. I thought that the campus was just
seething with discussions, and I saw jocks arguing with long-hairs
and I saw everybody giving out pamphlets and I thought this was
absolutely marvelous. This is what a university should be. It
should be something alive and something, you know, anarchistic
in a sense.

DT: Anarchism without violence. That's your slogan?

DM: Yes. Well —

DT: That'll be the day.

DM: There wasn't any violence there. They did put aside gently
a couple of aged guards that tried to say you can't go in there, but
they didn't beat them up.

DT: They just paralyzed a policeman.

DM: Oh, that was a mistake. It's true, somebody jumped out of a
window —

DT: And landed on him, and he's permanently paralyzed. And
some of the students picked up a tub in which a tree was planted
and dumped it over the railing of the bridge over Amsterdam
Avenue, onto a police car. Thank God, the car was empty; if
anybody had been in it, he would have been killed.

DM: Well, to play with such a chance I think is absolutely disgusting. I don't think they meant to kill anybody. If they did, then I
think they're pathological. And the guy that burned up the ten
years of research of that unpopular professor — that little business
I thought was absolutely disgusting and horrible, of course. But I
don't see what that has to do with it.

DT: What do you consider to be the results of the uprisings?

DM: Well, getting rid of Kirk, for one thing. And also getting a kind
of a [new] spirit into the university. And also I think it did liber-
alize and democratize — it gave the students more of a say in what
goes on, didn't it? Anyway, for a couple of weeks, at least, things
were sort of buzzing.

DT: Anything for a good buzz, right?

DM: No, no. No, Fred Dupee and I had just the same view about
the whole thing. He said, come up here, this is a revolution.

DT: I have no doubt he went over there with an old revolutionary's
receptivity to something that was spontaneously happening in the

student body. But after two or three days he began not to like what he was seeing—he saw some of the acts of violence or ugly disrespect that the students were indulging in and was very disgusted by them. Of all people he might have called, he called me and said he couldn't stand any more; he was leaving for the country, and I should phone him if anything happened that I thought required his return. I did call him very soon, in a day or two, for a sudden meeting of the faculty, and after he came back he indeed supported the uprising. There would have been a lot of pressure in his marriage for him to support it. But tell me, Dwight, in the period that you were up there, did you hear speeches against the Vietnam War?

DM: I suppose so. I don't know.

DT: I think I was on the campus every day and I never heard an anti-Vietnam word. That's another of the fallacies about the uprising, that it was a protest against the war. After all, similar university uprisings were taking place in Mexico City, in Japan, in Berlin. I think the university hasn't recovered from it and may never recover from it. Well, I think I've asked you everything I meant to. Perhaps there's something you want to say?

DM: Well, I want to make one confession—in a way, it's a confession. Two things that shocked me very much. One of them is the way that the whole student movement, not just the SDS, but the whole anti-Vietnam War radical student movement disappeared overnight, the minute they stopped conscripting college students and had a volunteer army. At Buffalo they had practically burned down a building, bombs and everything, but by the time I taught there, they were all off on some goddamn religious kick and there was no interest in politics at all.

DT: That's the difference in being a Marxist: a Marxist view of society at least produces a certain sense of responsibility because your judgments relate to a set of fixed premises. You don't just put your politics on and off like a hat. The students didn't have any responsibility to a position they'd held because they hadn't held a position; they'd held an attitude.

DM: Yes, exactly. That's what I liked about them, their primitive instinct. Anyway, that's one thing. The second thing is even more disturbing, and that is the large number of refugees from South Vietnam. When you think of the chances they take in those boats, it certainly shows that the regime is very unpopular.

DT: But look, Dwight, with your knowledge of communism, how could you foresee anything else? What was the nature of my debate with Mary McCarthy in the *New York Review of Books* except to say that of course the Americans had to get out of Vietnam, but it was a tragedy because of what was going to be left behind them? I didn't yet know about boat people but I was foreseeing just such a tragic outcome.

DM: Well, that's just a matter of words and so on.

DT: It's far more than words, Dwight. But I'm not going to argue with you anymore. It's your interview, after all. (Laughter.)

Diana Trilling's last book was Mrs. Harris, *published by Harcourt Brace Jovanovich. She is now working on a book that is both a personal memoir and a biography of her husband, Lionel Trilling, tentatively titled* Biography of a Marriage.

COMMENTS

Kathleen Agena

MAGICAL MOTIFS

Irving Howe's "Radical Questions and the American Intellectual" (2, 1966) was the lead article in the first issue of *Partisan Review* I read as an undergraduate in the Midwest. When I went back to the article again recently, I was struck by its prophetic power. The forces Howe defined as shaping the undercurrents of the intellectual climate almost two decades ago have emerged to dominate the cultural scene today.

The disintegration of Marxism, he wrote, was provoking confused efforts to patch together surrogate ideologies as a replacement for it, while a nostalgia for the revolutionary mystique had blinded many leading intellectuals to the realities of the current political scene. Now, with the collapse of nearly all the theoretical systems that have informed Western thought since the onset of the Industrial Age, the tendencies Howe defined in relation to the demise of Marxism have widened in influence. One scarcely blinks and yet another relic from the past has been propped up in either a "neo-" or "post-" form to create an illusory facade of coherence, while others have descended into the labyrinths of post-structuralism, tossing away the notion of coherence altogether, as well as the Ariadne thread that might lead them to reconnect thought with reality.

Moreover, many of our leading novelists also appear to have been influenced by these tendencies. Increasingly, they have turned to locating their narratives in a past or future never-never-land, where magic, not reason, rules reality. While this trend may be viewed as part of a broader anti-rationalist swing in Western thought, its distinguishing stylistic trait is not the manner in which irrational facets of the psyche or reality are portrayed—which were, in fact, probed with more verve and complexity by writers like Dostoevsky, Faulkner, and Joyce, for example—but rather the way in which magical paraphernalia and archaic symbols are hammered on as contrived obfuscations to evade penetrating the genuine chaos and irrationality of existence. Rather than amplifying the horizons of either the inner or outer world, the ultimate effect of these devices is that they reduce reality to facile abstractions—as, for example, when one of the be-deviled suburban shrews in Updike's recent novel, *The Witches of Eastwick,* somberly muses, "Any talk of money is magical."

A pernicious nihilism lurks behind the mask of magic in many of these recent representations that deflates the quixotic paradoxes of the human soul while simultaneously grinding down the contours of reality by patently dismissing its authentic ambiguity and irrationality off into a nether realm, as if these existed entirely in isolation from the texture of lived experience, or our own ambivalent desires.

The drift toward a magical vision of reality, which is increasingly evident in popular as well as high culture, parallels the closing of an epoch that began in the West with the Enlightenment. As such, it perhaps reflects the tendency toward submersion in archaic mysteries and a predeliction to elevate fairy tales to articles of belief that Goethe observed is typical at the end of an historical cycle, when the former cultural scaffolding has collapsed and nothing has yet crystallized to replace it.

Yet, given the peculiar nature of reality in this advanced-technological age, the appearance of magical motifs in the culture may foreshadow a more permanent shift, rather than a transient, cyclical phenomenon. We live, after all, in a reality that daily exposes us to electronic images and processes that function beyond the limits of our physical senses, encircled by an ever-expanding maze of technology that insidiously assaults traditional Western notions of self-determination and the uniqueness of the individual. It is a reality shaped by the truths of modern science and technology which, as Hannah Arendt observed in *The Human Condition,* have become so hermetically abstract that they can no longer be translated back into expression in normal speech and thought. This unprecedented situation, as Arendt argued, risks permanently rupturing the link between knowledge and thought, resulting in a collective schizoid state in which we will be unable to understand, to speak and think about the things which nevertheless we do, to evaluate our experience in any intelligible, particularly in any morally authentic, manner, or even fully to experience many of the activities that inform our daily lives.

It is an odd paradox that an unforeseen consequence of the prevailing technocratic rationality—which is entirely unlike the pursuit of rational inquiry envisioned during the Enlightenment—is that it is unhinging the legitimacy of the individual's rational powers, and revising

thus, radically revising the concept of the self upon which the democratic impetus evolved and seriously eroding traditional notions of the *polis*. It posits a rigid, strictly abstract mode of ordering reality that, in the extreme, results in a bizarre brand of mathematical narcissism—spinning out a world of its own that has no relationship to reality as it is personally experienced. Encoded in the new technology, it is able to perform with dazzling speed—producing results that seem almost "magical"—but the basis of its processes excludes, for the most part, critical analysis and judgment, reason as traditionally defined, as well as the more elusive category of perceptions related to emotional response and the senses. It places the locus of control and power—i.e., "authority"—beyond the individual in an impersonal realm, but remains emphatically utilitarian, usurping authority and homogenizing intrinsic diversities while violating the basic prerequisite of the human spirit for a sense of meaning and legitimacy that transcends banal pragmatism. (The apotheosis of the prevailing cult of technology is most clearly evident in the new breed of computerized, nuclear missiles that arouse fear not only because of the destructive force they embody, but because of the sense they provoke that the use of these weapons is beyond rational restraint, that they will go off unpredictably, erupting in a mad, psychotic apocalypse. As such, they reflect the loss of authority, the insignificance and futility of the individual's power that is insidiously eroding the viability of democratic values and infecting Western societies with an ominous, nihilistic pacifism.)

That the sterile, pseudo-rationality of our advanced-technological age should have its nemesis in a revival of the archaic tyranny of magical views of reality—which represent the individual as a pawn of inscrutable, supra-personal forces—is, on reflection, no surprise. But the implications of this contradiction in our culture, in particular the authoritarian implications inherent in such magical notions of reality, pose critical issues for liberal democracies.

Kathleen Agena is a contributing editor of Partisan Review.

accountability + consent

TV ads - a hearty egalitarian with erratic effect on actual politics and very corporate + government bureaucra, closer to direct expan...

Geoffrey H. Hartman

THE DUBIOUS CHARM OF M. TRUFFAUT

How difficult it is for the French to come to grips with the Occupation, even so long after the event! That is the first impression one receives from the aesthetic distance, the glassy, antiseptic touch, with which sensitive matters of collaboration and anti-Semitism were treated in Truffaut's *The Last Metro.* Though set in occupied Paris, and focusing on the plight of Jews trapped there by Vichy sympathizers and the Gestapo, the film remains curiously un-threatening and apolitical. One is tempted to raise the question of Truffaut's aestheticization of politics.

But as the film takes hold, one is obliged to modify that ques-tion. Truffaut's gift for lyric clarity seems almost a byproduct of the impermeable presence of Catherine Deneuve, who, as Marion Steiner, plays the role of the wife of a Jewish theater owner in danger of being deported. As the star of the film, Deneuve is a regis-ter separating by perceptible yet fine modulations a series of closely adjacent and vibrant emotions. There is, always, sexual attraction; there is fierce and loyal dedication to the Jewish husband whom she hides and looks after; there is the cold calculation that enables her to continue his Theatre de Montmartre under the nose of the Jew-hating Daxiat; there is, finally, her training as an actress which enables her to remain formal, even haughty, whatever she actually feels. Truffaut communicates a temperament at once passionate and inviolable. The entire movie participates in Deneuve's makeup; it is *porcelaine de Paris;* and the medium of film gives merely an extra gloss to the sense that everything in Paris is an extension of Deneuve and her kind of theater, despite the trivial "Norwegian" (i.e., Nordic, non-Jewish) or pseudo-Ibsenian play being rehearsed during the film.

As if by a magic wave of the wand, there are no victims. We know they exist, and a couple of scenes remind us of their suffering; yet the action is *determined* by people who are, or feel they are, on stage. Truffaut takes sides, of course, but he does not judge. The col-laborationist villains not only do not occupy center stage, they are overstylized. Yet the good people too are reduced by a silhouette-effect that either aestheticizes or eroticizes the action. It is as if the Homeric gods, who do look down occasionally, were still disposing of men's fate through the imperturbable sway of Eros. As viewers seeking to understand, we come to an impasse, or to its comic equivalent. It coincides with the film's ending, when Catherine Deneuve as Marion Steiner acknowledges the applause of the audience, linking hands with her husband, Lucas, who now comes out of the shadows as her director, not lover, *and* with the leading actor, who has replaced Lucas as her lover. It is a deliciously amoral moment in which the eternal triangle is deprived of emotional agony.

It is a bypass, then, rather than an impasse. This bypass exemplifies the seductive strength and danger of theater: Deneuve is all theater, spectacle personified. Her very stylishness, the cool resonating touch, the feeling that even in highly rhetorical speeches more is implied than said, harmonizes with Truffaut's own visual stenography. An example is the sequence in which Bernard Granger, the leading man, and a member of the Resistance, converts a record-player into an explosive device by a series of maneuvers whose meaning viewers cannot infer until the radio blares out the news of its successful detonation in an *attentat* against a Nazi admiral. Truffaut, of course, lets out the stops when he wishes: the same Bernard provokes and then assaults Daxiat in a posh Paris restaurant. But Bernard's fate, like that of the other men, rests in the hands of Deneuve. Truffaut appends the men to her, because they are clumsy and intemperate, because they cannot really bear to stay undercover (they must disclose the truth or lay bare the life-lie in Ibsenian fashion), and so would perish without a woman's dissemblance to protect them.

Perhaps that is enough of a message. Truffaut's link to Ibsen is real, after all; yet the women remain so undemystified that one suspects Truffaut of protecting *them.* This *amour courtois* of the cineast is a weakness, the indulgent flourish of his signature as filmmaker. Truffaut pays tribute to the power women have, who declare themselves when in love, and never in politics.

Truffaut's own power lies elsewhere, beyond the male/female split, even beyond the ability to create believable characters. He engages in an anarchic, nihilistic and by no means unjoyful exploration of the interchangeability or substitutability of destinies. *Jules and Jim* was a pure instance of this. And, in the present film, every attractive woman is like every other for Bernard, who himself moves with ease from Grand Guignol to Ibsenian theater. One actor or person can be replaced by another; and whether this or that Jew is betrayed, or this or that Resistance fighter is caught, or one is Daxiat or Granger, or homosexual or heterosexual—it all seems equally a card dealt by fate.

The human condition, in Truffaut's films, is shown to be absolutely duplicitous without becoming at all ambiguous. As Bernard is fond of repeating to the women he desires: There are two women in every woman. But the proposition of *The Last Metro* goes beyond duality to a more basic duplicity. As Marion ascends the circular staircase to see Dr. Dietrich in the Nazi *Kommandatur,* she sees her lower-class double descend the other side on the arm of a German officer. She is, or could be, that other, and no judgment is involved. The ultimate duplicity, however, is more subversive still. It is that between theater and life and leads to the question, "Which imitates which?"

Is Steiner really a Jew? Or is he an actor, who, by playing the part of a Jew, must undermine the part he so cunningly embodies? Is Daxiat really an anti-Semite fascist? Steiner, at one point, puts on a nose to imitate the Nazi caricature of what a Jew looks like; another episode shows him reading Marion anti-Semitic propaganda that claims the Jews take over everything, including beautiful non-Jewish women—as he begins to make love to her. Daxiat talks so earnestly to Marion about his esteem for Steiner's "Israelite" theater that one senses his envy or a rhetoric that could entrap him rather than his prey (Marion). Daxiat's influence through the notorious newspaper "Je Suis Partout" is, moreover, symmetrical with Steiner's covert presence as the souffleur-director of his theater. Steiner too is "everywhere." And so on.

No wonder an atmosphere of comedy prevails. The villain Daxiat is allowed to escape and die of an unspecified cancer, and Marion can hold hands with her lover and with her husband—her love having saved a husband who has led her into a great stage-career and the arms of the leading actor. The cool passion or strange duplicity of human nature, that *paradoxe du comédien* Diderot observed, saves a theater, as well as a Jew. And perhaps Truffaut intends it to save theater itself, by suggesting a fairytale marriage between Hellenic beauty, with its Gentile sangfroid, and that intense Hebrew or Puritan moral fervor which has always resisted the idolatrous charm of spectacle.

Geoffrey H. Hartman is Chairman of the Comparative Literature Department at Yale University and the author of The Fate of Reading: And Other Essays *(University of Chicago Press), among other works.*

Irving Howe

THINKING ABOUT SOCIALISM

Anyone writing a comprehensive study of modern socialism would have to put a heavy stress on the enormous damage that Stalinism has done to the socialist hope. Insofar as both right- and left-wing ideologues have found it convenient to identify the Russian state-party dictatorship with socialism, they have joined to discredit the entire socialist idea, since no humane person could want a "socialism" resembling either the Stalinist terror or the thuggish regimes that have come after it. What has followed from this identification has been an abandonment of radical politics, utopian visions, and often enough, any kind of politics.

Even before the rise of Stalinism there had become visible a deep crisis of socialist thought and practice, but with Stalinism that crisis became more acute, so that for the past several decades the socialist experience has often entailed a dislodgment of received persuasions, a melting-down of ideological structures, a search for new — or for cleansed and reaffirmed old — values that might again bring some moral luster to the cause. For the socialists themselves this was often a valuable, indeed, chastening experience; but for their movement it brought grave difficulties. Introspection seldom makes for public effectiveness.

It became customary for socialists of, for example, my generation to speak of their beliefs through what I'd call hygienic negatives: "We don't mean any sort of party-state dictatorship — the very thought appalls us. We don't mean the complete nationalization of industry; we want instead a democratization of ownership and control, or 'socialization.'"

After a time such responses came to be almost instinctive, with some of them constituting a deviation from previously-held premises and thereby a self-criticism. Serious socialists would describe the cooperative commonwealth in terms of its envisaged *qualities* — social, moral, esthetic. They would speak of sentiments of freedom, attitudes of fraternity, sometimes priorities of social allocation. They would propose to reaffirm socialism in the realm of values whereas, to simplify a little, the tradition in which a good many older

---

Editor's Note: This is excerpted from *Thinking about Socialism*, a work in progress.

socialists, especially those from the anti-Stalinist Marxist groups, had been raised was one that stressed institutional changes and transformations in the relations of power. In making this shift of emphasis, these socialists were doing something historically overdue, morally imperative, politically defensive, and tactically damaging. For unless plausible social mechanisms and agencies could be located for realizing the values that were now being placed at the center of socialist aspiration, we were finally left with good will.

Nevertheless, the clarification of socialist values was an essential task—a whole generation of the democratic Left had to expend itself in doing this. And if today such propositions as (a) there is no inevitable sequence from capitalism to socialism; (b) retrogressive societies can appear along the course of historical development; (c) the abolition of capitalism is not, in and of itself, necessarily a step toward liberation; (d) socialism cannot be "defined" simply as a society in which the means of production have been statified; (e) the idea of a total transformation of humanity under the guidance of a "vanguard" party is a corrupt fantasy; (f) the fundamental goal of socialists is the democratization of every area of social life, from politics to the workplace—if, as I say, these propositions are mostly accepted as truisms on the Left, that is because a not very large number of people fought for them bitterly, against a variety of dogmatisms, over the past several decades.

Several years ago Leszek Kolakowski succinctly described the present condition of reflective socialists:

> What we lack in our thinking about society in socialist terms is not [I'd say, no longer—I. H.] general values which we want to see materialized, but rather knowledge about how these values can be prevented from clashing with each other when put into practice and more knowledge of the forces preventing us from achieving our ideals . . .

During the past fifteen or so years, as Stalinism has gradually lost its influence in the industrialized nations, and the socialist movement, under pressure from its own awareness of crisis, has clarified its democratic commitment, there has occurred a significant shift in the direction of socialist thought. A clarification of values having, at least for the moment, been achieved, socialist writers like Alec Nove and Radoslav Selucky in Europe and Henry Pachter and Michael Harrington in the United States have turned to the study of social institutions and mechanisms through which these values might be brought into being. The task is far from completed, but there have been serious efforts to describe, by way of suggestive anticipation, what a feasible socialist society might look like, what its property forms and social relations might be, how investment decisions might be made, in which ways a market could work together with economic planning, how bureaucratism might be minimized, and so on. It would be foolhardy to expect that such efforts will soon lead to an increase of political effectiveness; in the short run, they may even prove to be somewhat disabling, since they disturb old pieties and slogans. But the work—surely requiring more than one generation—of socialist reconsideration goes on. Every end is a beginning.

Irving Howe is Distinguished Professor of English at the Graduate Center of the City University of New York. His latest book is A Margin of Hope, *published by Harcourt Brace Jovanovich.*

Edith Kurzweil

AN AMERICAN IN FRANKFURT

"I'm not an old leftist, but an old new leftist," said a participant at a recent meeting of left-oriented political psychologists. Such a fine differentiation, in America, would be understood by few, but in Frankfurt, while discussing "Identity Management in Our Society," everyone knew that old leftists mediate between cultural and political critique, that new leftists do so between political action and personal life, and that the particular participant was defending a more mature, or a post-New Left.

As it is, this was one of the easier theoretical assumptions by the participants, who easily moved from Kant's *Critique of Reason* to Hegel's phenomenology, discussed how their main tenets had been understood, by their teachers Horkheimer and Adorno, and who kept reminding each other that neither *mythos* nor *logos* was to gain the upper hand. This alone would have been heady stuff. But the unquestioning and unrelenting use of Marxist categories, of how the state apparatus dominates subjectivity, how capital determines it, or how the suspension of alienation into alienation as a given — (here Günther Anders was cited) — were clear indications that Marxism has become more than a worldview, or even a hoped-for salvation. Instead, as a method of inquiry, it has been turned into a security blanket, protecting these intelligent and dynamic individuals — against fascism, anti-Semitism, and the "collective narcissism" the Nazi period allegedly left behind.

In contrast to their parents' generation, and to their cohorts on the right, German leftists live with Nazi history (except for the few neo-fascist gangs mythologizing it) in order to avoid its repetition, and with the philosophical forebears who provide the solid tradition they affirm *and* reject. Horkheimer's *Dialectic of Enlightenment,* as both critique and perpetuation of this tradition, has become their bible. Whether references to Adorno's and Horkheimer's later works were missing, because these are less Marxist or do not deal directly with theoretical questions of subjectivity, was unclear. Still, the participants at this two-day meeting stuck closely to their theme, covering, thoroughly and theoretically, such diverse topics as the construction of subjectivity, how forms of subjectivity develop, the subject in social movements, the dimension of creativity in such movements, and neo-fascism. (Psychoanalysts, pedagogians, sociologists, and psychologists took part; and they were familiar with each others' intellectual premises.)

Undoubtedly, the conscience of this generation of Germans has changed; and, as Adorno already found, it is different (better) than that of Weimar. But, to paraphrase Adorno once more, they again fear opposing the East, insofar as its dynamic awakens the German past, not just ideologically, but because "the organic striking power of totalitarian systems forces something of their own essence onto their opponents." Or is there another explanation for the scant mention of this danger to the democracy Germans cherish, coupled to an ever more virulent anti-Americanism? Even the psychoanalysts who readily interpreted instances of projection by the neo-Nazis and other youth did not think of this — societal — sort of projection. Nor was this topic discussed in connection with issues of Marxist "totality" which seemed more urgent to the sociologists than the therapists.

Indeed, the media does its job. Ecological concerns, to Germans, are at least as important as questions of human rights are to Americans; and they are more tangible. Thus, the link between placing the Pershing IIs as a potential danger to the environment — part of the Greens' platform — was a natural one. The existence of the Greens itself (their criticism and antics elicit admiration even from Germans not voting for them) has upset predictable politics and has determined much of recent political discourse. In addition, "educational" films such as *Harlan County* or the German-produced "American" serial (in English) featuring "economic imperialists" who exploit the Third World, cut down woods, etc. (cassettes of it are sold), verify and expand on the anti-American cliches. That Germany has a conservative government only helps add credibility, since the population seems unaware that the media now is controlled by the Left. In fact, the amalgam of newscasts with Westerns and crime adventures has led sophisticated people to think of anti-American films as perfect presentations of day-by-day reality.

Anti-Americanism is not new. Even at a time when many older Germans ostensibly identified with the victors, they allegedly told their children to turn off the awful American music — rock and roll and jazz — which the latter played as a symbol of their own (generational) revolt. And they hated the American forces of occupation (today's NATO forces remain indistinguishable from them), because they reminded them of glorious visions turned sour and of defeat, though they recognized their greater fear and dislike of "the Bolsheviks." Extensive analyses of these contradictions, alongside which the complex Freudo-Marxist methodology to comprehend them evolved — certainly were decisive in creating the post-war German consciousness. At the same time, this new consciousness, acquired with the help of painful personal insights, became as attached to the Marxist vocabulary as to its liberating ideals. Although some older Germans were converted, by their children and occasionally with the help of psychoanalysis, on the whole, the German population was polarized. Thus it is important to recall that the new German Left was the sole sector of the population truly willing to face up to the Nazi evil and was the only trustworthy group. (In effect, the extensive cooptation of their ideas now leads them to state that there no longer exists a true Left.)

The events of 1968 and the Vietnam war allowed for the ambivalent anti-Americanism to lose its ambivalence and for alliances with guerilas in the Third World. Ironically, slogans against American economic imperialism, soon put on a par with fascism, began to mushroom just as Americans felt their political and economic power to be fading away. As John Vinocur put it, Watergate, the hostage crisis, the decline of the dollar and the car industry, the fourteen percent rate of inflation (Germany's was three percent) not only put Helmut Schmidt into a leadership role, but made his *Ostpolitik* plausible. By the time the American economy improved, the German public had become overtly hostile. Fantasizing about rapprochement with the East, while electing Chancellor Kohl, the ambivalences could be turned outward only. Still, even those who oppose this conservative government accept the "orderliness" they reject, and here too they can favorably compare Germany to the United States. (Garbage removal, public transportation, and social services function.) President Reagan's shrill and bombastic pronouncements at the beginning of his term, however, were most damaging: they were taken to be the tangible evidence of American bad intent, of our "warmongering," and it seemed to legitimate the already rampant anti-Americanism and the view of Kohl as Reagan's puppet. So, in a curious way, a great part of the chancellor's constituency as well began to feel justified in hating America. In this atmosphere of Left and Right cant, and in a newly revived "fear of fascism," no one recalls that American presidents are not *Führers,* that they are more or less responsible to Congress and the public, or that high interest rates may be the result of bungling rather than of malicious intent alone. Altogether, the hodgepodge of misinformation that has constructed a worldview where evil emanating from America must be demolished seems to have become impermeable. Love of clean air, of the Third World (but *not* in the form of guest workers), or hiking in the woods (expressed in high flown idealistic language) are counterposed to "high technology," another code word for American economic imperialism. And our unsuccessful Latin American policy (who knows that Reagan would not move in and out of Germany as he did in Grenada) has made the proverbial ugly American look uglier than ever. (As it is, no German believes that a number of Americans would just as gladly drop NATO and retreat into a retrograde isolationism.)

One person at the conference mentioned that anti-Americanism might have taken the place of anti-Semitism. Had this point been pursued, some of the myths helping to unite Germans of opposing persuasions conceivably might have been exploded: that the Marshall Plan was a conspiracy intended to turn Germany into a consumer

society led by Adenauer; that America is fascist; that its isolation as
a nuclear danger will assure Germany's peaceful future; or that free-
ing Europe of nuclear weapons "from Portugal to Poland" will assure
Soviet cooperation. One conference participant's comment that "the
French can do everything right except keep peace," however, was
challenged briefly. But here, and at other moments, anxiety was handled by a retreat to Marxist rhetoric. A new form of theory/-practice,
for instance, was called for, although no one knew how to "get out of
the old categories to avoid disaster." The taboo about mentioning the
Soviet threat appeared to be total, and positions about the Third
World as fixed as those about achieving disarmament. Just as in other
leftist gatherings American imperialist coups from Vietnam to Nica-
ragua, San Salvador, and Grenada were recited everywhere, and
Afghanistan, Cambodia, Poland, or repression in the Soviet bloc remained *hors du discours*. Even American suggestions of arms reduction have been called a "businessman's peace" dominated by "cold
warriors." What would happen, I kept asking myself, if a long-range
intelligent American foreign policy were forged? (Given our internal
political differences and ignorance about the rest of the world, this
appears unlikely.) Might it budge world opinion, and bridge the political polarization already in place? After all, we know that people
listen to views that confirm what they already believe. True, the
German Left takes note of the French socialists' determination to defend their country, but they write this off, as a rule, to an over-
developed French national identity.

Two conference participants, reporting on how they had in-
filtrated a number of neo-fascist groups, stated that they deliberately
told them that they were leftists (allegedly more acceptable to their
subjects than democrats — *Demokröten*), because they felt it necessary
to retain their own political identity. This need for political identity
— fostered by the Marxism innate to their Frankfurt School training,
and by their "updating" of Ernst Bloch, Gramsci, Lukacs, and, occasionally, Althusser — is, I believe, the most important reason why
German leftist critiques are unable to function outside rigid Marxist
categories.

Given my own malaise at having to take lonely political positions, I am sympathetic to their plight. That may be why conference
participants did not pursue the more provocative questions: why a
certain Hungarian had suggested that the mode of domination rather
than capitalism might determine individuals' subjectivity; whether
similar psychological mechanisms function in neo-fascist and left-

splinter groups; and what the unconscious mechanisms connecting anti-Semitism, philo-Semitism, and anti-Americanism might be. Still, near the end of the meeting, one man clearly asked what is to be done. "We need new categories of analysis, new theories," he stated, "because I don't want to wake up one morning and find out that it is too late." Although he was greeted by silence, we can only hope that he is not alone. For if he were heeded, the German Left again might take up its critical functions. Otherwise, it may well bring about the end of our liberal world and become the handmaiden of Soviet domination.

Edith Kurzweil, author of The Age of Structuralism *(Columbia University Press) and* Italian Entrepreneurs *(Praeger), teaches sociology at Rutgers University. She is Executive Editor of* Partisan Review.

The succeeding comments were written in response to the following statement: "The culture and the country have changed enormously over the past fifty years. How have you changed in your literary, political, or cultural views?"

Daniel Aaron

CAMBRIDGE 1936–39

Harvard University celebrated its tercentenary in 1936. Two events connected with that occasion stand out in my mind: a lecture by Carl Jung on the mandala and a presidential motorcade down Massachusetts Avenue.

I don't remember what Jung said, but at the end of his talk, I took a close look at him when I walked up to the platform with my companion, Charles Olson (then deep in his Melville book, *Call Me Ishmael*), and stood staring while Charlie asked Jung if he detected the mandala figure in the graphic symbolism of *Moby-Dick*. President Roosevelt's topless limousine — it might have been on the same day as Jung's lecture — passed a few yards from me, and I saw plainly the uptilted, smiling face. Impulsively I tossed my arms in the air and shouted. He was the first president I had ever seen in the flesh, and although I regarded myself then as considerably to the left of the New Deal, I still managed to square my disapproval of some of his policies with my admiration of the man.

Roosevelt's son Franklin Jr. was an undergraduate at the time of his father's visit. I once spotted him with a group of blue-shirted Hasty Pudding boys as they tried to hoot down a radical speaker who was addressing a crowd of students from the steps of Widener Library. There were lots of such gatherings then, and all manner of factions competed for attention. I heard the Reverend Gerald L. K. Smith, ally of the recently assassinated Huey Long, talk at a meeting sponsored by Harvard's Young Conservatives, a beleagured minority in those days. The audience was so noisily hostile that Smith ended his harangue by threatening with destruction Harvard and all it stood for. Exponents of Vilfredo Pareto's "elites" also had their moment in the university limelight, but generally speaking, what the Chicago *Tribune* and the Hearst papers referred to as Harvard's "Reds" and their fellow-traveling sympathizers made up the most determined and energetic segment of the social-minded in the Harvard community. They influenced the policies and tactics of the Harvard Teacher's Union to which I belonged. It pleased me that our union was an affiliate of the C.I.O., and although it exercised little real power, it served as a forum where its members could express their solidarity with the working class.

I'm sure I never tried to guess how many of my friends were actually communists, and not until the McCarthy investigations did I learn that several of them who attended the Marxist study group which met weekly at my apartment on Sumner Road were attached to the local Communist Party branch. It would have made no difference to me if I had known, for in this popular front period being a communist seemed scarcely more exotic than being a Republican or an Elk.

Thanks to its leadership in stirring up support for the Spanish Loyalists, the Party had reached the apogee of its popularity with the noncommunist intellectuals, and Harvard was aflame with fervor over Spain. Communists mingled harmoniously with other antifascist elements at the cocktail parties held to raise money for ambulances and medical supplies and at emotional gatherings like the one where the chain-smoking André Malraux, gaunt and holloweyed, and his American guide, the then communist journalist Louis

Fischer, held forth on the heroism of the Spanish people and the crimes of General Franco. Archibald MacLeish did too, and we savored his plangent words. The war in Spain foreshadowed greater wars to come, he told us. "How then can we refuse our help to those who fight our battles?"

Neither I nor my friends paid any attention to the stories or "lies" about the suppression of the Left opposition in Spain which were appearing in the "Trotskyite" or anti-Stalinist press (not until long after did I grasp the pejorative implication of that suffix, "ite"). But given our close-mindedness, it is doubtful if we would have touched those renegade sheets with a pair of tongs. Nor can I remember our being particularly aroused by the "show trials" in Moscow. The image of the Soviet Union taking shape in our minds derived largely from Soviet films like *Chapayev* or accounts by enraptured visitors to the Workers' State of strolls through parks of culture and rest. Among the so-called progressive nations, hadn't Russia alone, under the leadership of the sagacious Stalin, dared to challenge the legions of Mussolini and Hitler?

Granville Hicks, literary editor of the *New Masses,* was part of the Cambridge scene in 1938–39. He had been invited to Harvard as one of the half-dozen "counsellors" in American Civilization, and the hullabaloo in the "capitalist press" which followed the announcement of his appointment insured Harvard's welcome to its notorious alumnus. It was appropriate that the biographer of John Reed should be around when a portrait of the revolutionary martyr was presented to Adams House. He was good friends with the hard-drinking journalists who made up the first contingent of Nieman Fellows, and he guided the ad hoc Sumner Road seminar through the mysteries of the *Marxist Handbook.* Hicks proudly wore his Party label, but it was a point of honor with him not to proselytize students, a resolution to which he had always scrupulously adhered.

I think the most memorable episode of his Cambridge stay was his debate with Father Francis Curran, editor of the *Brooklyn Tablet,* held in Boston's Mechanic's Hall. Curran, a jovial and floridly rhetorical priest and the darling of the New England "Coughlinites," had featured horrific atrocity stories allegedly committed by the Spanish Republicans. Bus loads of Coughlin's followers from a wide area poured into the hall that night, raising their arms in what looked to us like the Nazi salute and screaming and hugging each other when their idol appeared on the platform. The few of us who had accompanied Hicks to the meeting were no match for Curran's intimidating group, and their howls drowned out our tentative cheers. Hicks would never have spoken at all had not Curran silenced the crowd with a wave of his arm and permitted Hicks to deliver a short and totally unpersuasive speech. This scary experience confirmed our belief in the sinister power of the Roman Catholic hierarchy and in what John Strachey called, in a much discussed book, the "coming struggle for power."

Yet despite my feelings about Spain and the Soviet Union, I felt no strong inclination to join a party whose programs and vocabulary made me uneasy. In retrospect, I attribute this reluctance to my sense that the Party, for all its celebration of Tom Paine, Walt Whitman, and Abraham Lincoln, was out of touch with the America whose history and culture were now my chief interest. I enjoyed the cartoons in the *New Masses,* the trips to New York to see *Waiting for Lefty* and *Awake and Sing,* and the Mercury Theater's production of *Julius Caesar* in which black-shirted and jack-booted Romans strutted across the stage, but no more, I think, than the Ballet Russe de Monte Carlo or the Old Howard. The Harvard atmosphere, in my case at least, was not conducive to the making of revolutionists. Rather it fostered irreverence. I memorized the poems of E. E. Cummings, read the novels of Nathanael West, made fun (as communists often did in private) of Party jargon, and composed and sung lugubriously a campaign song for the gubernatorial candidate of the Communist Party of Massachusetts, Otis Hood, to the tune of the "Volga Boatman." ("O-tis Hood, O-tis Hood/ He's good, he should/ Win your vote.") Moreover, I realized even then, for I was studying American church history, that to join the Party was the equivalent of joining a church. I felt no doctrinal commitment and wasn't prepared to make a metaphysical leap into faith. So when Granville Hicks hesitantly suggested I do just that, I declined.

He did not press me. In fact it seemed to me that he approved of my refusal, and I soon found out why. He himself was trembling on the edge of apostasy before the Soviet-German pact gave him the excuse he needed to resign.

Daniel Aaron is Victor Thomas Professor of English, Emeritus, at Harvard University, and has recently taught in the literature program of the University of Texas at Austin. He is the editor of American Men and Women of Letters *(Chelsea House, 1982), among other works.*

Lionel Abel

POSITIONS

Is anyone at all interested in how my view of our political scene has changed over the years? Then let me here state some of the positions I held formerly and the one I hold — or am trying to hold — today.

During the thirties, I supported the Trotskyists; in 1941, I broke with them because they did not support the war against Hitler. After the war, I was against McCarthyism, for civil rights, and against our policy in southeast Asia. I voted for the Democratic party candidate in 1960, 1964, and in 1968. But I did not support McGovern in 1972 or Jimmy Carter in 1976 or 1980. I shall vote for Ronald Reagan in the coming election.

But I do not consider myself to be a Republican or a right-winger for good and always. I was of the Left, but have strayed somewhat towards the Right. I cannot go into all the reasons for this. Let me just explain why I'm going to vote for a Republican in the coming election.

Morton Kondracke in the *Wall Street Journal* (June 28, 1984) has given five reasons for supporting Reagan for president and then a number of reasons for reserving judgment. I agree with the five reasons he has given for backing the president. I do not agree with his reservation, which I do not quite understand. So let me here summarize his reasons for backing the president.

Kondracke holds that (1) the president has reassured our allies about American resolve; (2) increased our defenses; (3) indicated that we are quite ready to use force; (4) out-maneuvered his domestic opponents; (5) and made much-objected-to cuts at one stroke in the beginning of his term. I find these reasons valid, but I want to add just another of my own.

I strongly object to the foreign policy notions held by the Democratic party's candidates. They follow the lead of President Carter who stressed "human rights" in foreign affairs, a policy which led to disaster for us and also for the people of Iran and of Iraq. On this matter of morals in foreign affairs, let me quote Raymond Aron:

> In international affairs, there are always elements of immorality because foreign policy is a conflict, to one degree or another.

> Also because there is no court in international relations. Within
> nations, there are rights, laws, and there are courts. But there is
> no international court.

The projection of "human rights" into foreign policy by President
Carter has shown that welfare state values, appropriate in domestic
affairs, can be disastrous when extended to international affairs. A
welfare state finds it difficult to frame a foreign policy; the Soviet
Union on the other hand finds it difficult to conduct a domestic policy; it treats internal problems as it treats foreign countries, which
means that the Soviet people are treated as foreigners by their own
government. I'm reminded here of the recent debate between Caspar
Weinberger, our secretary of defense, and E. P. Thompson, the intellectual leader of the British antinuclear movement. The subject of
the debate was the "morality" of American foreign policy as compared with Soviet foreign policy. I thought Caspar Weinberger won
the argument but I do not think he should have accepted the terms of
the argument so uncritically, for he did not distinguish between
domestic and foreign policy. What is objectionable about the Soviet
Union is that it does not restrict the "immoralism" inevitable in
foreign affairs; it extends this "immoralism" to all its domestic affairs, treating all of its people as foreigners. It is in this regard that
the American government may be said to be immensely superior,
morally speaking, to the Soviet state.

The harm done by projecting "human rights" into foreign
policy may be seen in the comparison made by most of the Democratic candidates of our problems in Central America with the problems we faced in Vietnam. Let me say at once that Central America
is not and cannot be another Vietnam. Here I would like to recall an
exchange I had with Zbigniew Brzezinski in *The New Leader* during
the sixties. He had written an article in support of our Vietnam War
policy, and I had written a letter to *The New Leader* objecting to his
views. My point was that we could not fight successfully in southeast Asia while we were at odds with the most powerful country in
Asia, China. His reply was that China was by no means the most
powerful country in Asia. I think events have proved that he was
wrong on this point, but what concerns me now is not his error at
that time but the present error of the Democratic party's candidates
and of the intellectuals who support them, when they express fear
that Central America may become another Vietnam. It can only be
another Vietnam for a power intruding in the Western hemisphere

but not for the United States, for we are the major military and political force in this part of the world.

And there is something else. André Malraux has said that politics is inevitably Manichean, but that this element in it ought not to be overemphasized. The Democrats and their supporters are overemphasizing the Manichean content of presidential politics; they have done this before, and they are doing it again. It is an error which may cost them the election. The difference between a moral and a political error is that for the first one can feel remorse, hardly for the second. A political mistake has little impact on conscience; thus it tends to be repeated. When the Democratic candidates say that the moral imperative for the people of this country is to defeat Ronald Reagan, they are overemphasizing the Manichean element in the contest.

Lionel Abel's memoir, The Intellectual Follies, *will be published by W. W. Norton this fall.*

Morris Dickstein

ORIGINS

Migration and resettlement are crucial features of so many modern lives, yet I'm surprised to discover how significantly they have figured in my own. As young adolescents my parents were wrenched out of small Yiddish-speaking towns in Russia and Poland, were brought to New York by distracted, heroic mothers amid a babble of elder siblings and strange languages. Their fathers had come many years earlier to try out the new world and drum up money for their passage, but a world war had intervened and cut them off. It was nine years before my mother saw her father again, a complete stranger who frightened her at the pier behind his full beard when he offered her a banana, a thing she had never seen.

The big city must have been terrifying too, but in the crowded ghetto, this new Pale of Settlement, the people and the language were soothingly familiar. Wildly different strands were braided together to create the amazing immigrant culture of the Lower East Side — part Europe and part American hurly-burly, part piety — with twenty tiny synagogues to a block — and part socialist ideology, part theaters and cafeterias and part sweatshop labor. Supposedly this culture was long past its glory days when I was growing up there in the 1940s, but when I read books like *The Downtown Jews* and *World of Our Fathers* there was much I recognized that had lingered on from forty years before.

What persisted for me especially was the religion. Unlike nearly everyone else on our block, who perhaps bought kosher meat and went to say *Yizkor* three or four times a year, and unlike the families that appear in most Jewish-American novels or memoirs, my parents were orthodox. That is to say, religion was less a "faith" than a way of life, a set of rules that colored everything they thought and did. For true believers more strict than my parents, it told them when to eat and when to wash, when to pray and when to make love. If their temperaments were more drawn to the forbidding side, it told them above all what *not* to do. Even in the *shtetl* this system needed to be defended against encroaching influences of modern life. To fortify me against America, but also to separate me from the street-kids who would never go anywhere, my parents sent me to a yeshiva, a Jewish day school, where I would be immersed in tradition, among Jews who would never assimilate, never yield.

When we moved to Queens at the end of the forties my parents' orthodoxy abated but their feeling for it did not. In a gentile neighborhood surrounded by temptation, I needed learning as a shield, a talisman, a life-line to the luminous past. Somehow it seemed a foregone conclusion that I would continue at the yeshiva, despite the long trip back and forth. So instead of walking a block to school as I had for years, I found myself, as a fifth-grader, taking a bus and three trains, leaving at 7:30 in the morning and getting back twelve hours later. Though I had no day left I don't recall I was ever fazed by these Dickensian hours or the endless ride from one corner of the city to another, which was exhilarating at first, then simply routine. Returning home on the very first day, instead of meeting my father at the place we had arranged, I retraced the course on my own and found the family mildly hysterical by the time I got home.

Fortunately for me the yeshiva was not one of those grim, dingy holes pictured by ghetto photographers at the turn of the century. But neither was it one of the spanky modern postwar schools that admitted girls and conducted classes in conversational Hebrew and taught its kids to dance in time to the new Zionist music. In my classes Hebrew was strictly a written language reserved for sacred texts and austere commentaries. The Bible, the Mishnah, the Talmud, and debates of later sages were analyzed for us in Yiddish, *mama-loshin,* the mother tongue of the European ghettoes that had just been savagely decimated. Hebrew was the language of the study, what the Almighty himself spoke — as distant as Sinai and revelation; Yiddish was the language of the street and the home, intimate and familial. For me, with Americanized parents who had come here young, this was an anachronism. I loved to listen to the racy gossip of my aunts and uncles, but Yiddish at school was a dry homiletic tongue that had no juice in it, a language of rote and proscription that was external to me and that hemmed me in.

As a rule Jews don't find orthodoxy confining except when they already are breaking away from it. Orthodox Judaism is a self-contained system irradiated by tradition and belief, sustained by habit, and enforced by communal and family sanctions. Eating kosher food or separating milk from meat is scarcely a burden to those who would never dream of doing otherwise. At school I dimly knew I could be chastened or ostracized for breaking the Sabbath or keeping my head uncovered. (Small knitted yarmulkas — an Israeli fashion — had not yet come in, and I must have worn my baseball cap eighteen hours a day.) In all my times at Yankee Stadium or the Polo Grounds I don't remember even *wanting* a hot dog; it was simply unthinkable; it lay outside the pale of my experience, and I didn't miss it. Yet just by being at all those games I showed that my Jewishness was less than a total system. A secular America had firmly laid its hand on me.

The structure of the school day was an emblem of my internal split: four hours of religious studies each morning, four hours of regular schoolwork in the afternoons. The yeshiva was really two parallel schools, and different people ran each half. Though the afternoon teachers abided by the forms of religion, their orthodoxy was never too closely examined. Many had jobs in the public schools earlier in the day; the pittance they were paid by the yeshiva could hardly support them. Some must have barely tolerated the orthodox environment; others no doubt were glad to be in a setting where they could be freely Jewish.

None resembled the bearded overseers who kept stern watch over our fidgety souls and bodies in the morning. The teachers who took a real interest wanted us to *do* something with our lives — to be good in math and English and history and go on to a good university. The principal of the high school, himself a math teacher at an elite public school, was inordinately proud of his Ivy League degree, and loved to steer two or three of the best students toward his alma mater. But many of the rabbis understood that the university, perhaps even Yeshiva University, was the road to perdition and assimilation, a one-way street from the world of our fathers into modern life.

It would be wrong to suggest that I ever felt imprisoned by Jewish orthodoxies. My parents were lax, tolerant, and loving. School and synagogue were places I could shine and be fussed over. My summers were spent in a small town on Long Island where sun and sand and a raucous extended family took precedence over everything. As an adolescent I had periods of real religious fervor, when the inertia of the familiar gave way to something more wildly emotional, when the words of the prayers and blessings suddenly took on meaning. But in my fifteenth year I suddenly found myself in total revolt.

I already was far along in Talmudical learning — many of my elders assumed I would go on to be ordained — when all at once the debates and legalisms went dead for me. I would steal away from the study hall to haunt the local public library. I would cut classes with friends on Wednesday afternoons to take in Broadway matinees. During Talmud lectures I was insolent or indifferent as long as I knew I could get away with it, but I was not exactly a candidate for reform school. Once the rabbi swooped down on something I had concealed beneath my huge *gemara*. He expected a comic book and planned to tear it to shreds as a lesson to the class. Instead, discomfited, he held up a volume of the Yale Shakespeare — significantly, *As You Like It* — which he laid aside in confusion. It was a book, after all, and he grudgingly respected it, though perhaps he knew what danger it held for me.

I was hungry for secular culture but also a wise-aleck who could be unthinkingly cruel. One of my rabbis, a painfully shy man, was no doubt a recent refugee from the Holocaust — an event almost

never mentioned at the yeshiva—for his English was not even rudi-
mentary. Even in Europe he would have been the epitome of the un-
worldly scholar, and here he was probably raising six small children
on a tiny salary. Once he looked up from his text and asked me
gruffly why I wasn't paying attention. Instead of answering in Yiddish I said, "Because it's spring, tra-la, and the birds are singing."
He understood hardly a word, but the rollicking laughter from the
class left him with a stricken look, and the brazen reply became a
legend that followed me to graduation and beyond.

And graduate I did, despite three years of iron resistance to
learning a single additional page of Talmud. Day after day I kept up
a stony wall of inner emigration while remaining the blue-eyed
favorite of my regular teachers. The links that bound me to Judaism
must still have been strong. Not only did I inexplicably remain at a
school where I was wasting half my day in passive rebellion, but
when I arrived at college this erstwhile radical looked like some kind
of religious throwback. I still kept kosher; I fell in at first with other
kids from vaguely religious backgrounds; and each weekend I went
back to my parents' synagogue to read the Torah, a skill I had per-
fected for my own bar mitzvah.

What I believed at that point I can scarcely fathom, but Judaism remained the anchor of my life even in opposition. I may have
been an atheist but I was a *Jewish* atheist, even a religious one. One
of my freshman roommates was a Catholic kid from Buffalo, as
eager and innocent as they come. While I donned my yarmulka to
rehearse for the weekend performance, he sat at his desk on the other
side of the room under a huge crucifix. We understood each other
perfectly. Our two other roommates, bleached-out Jews, thought us
both a little strange.

For me the double regimen of life at home and life in school
couldn't last. The split I had endured easily enough in high school
became a chasm. In the spring of my freshman year, as I headed
back home one Friday afternoon, I was overtaken by panic. My
heart was racing, my breathing grew shallow, and I became convinced that I would never get off the train alive. Somehow I stumbled home, and the family doctor gave me some tranquilizers, but in
the weeks that followed the same kind of anxiety would invade me
each time I began to read the Torah.

Some obscure conflict was tearing me apart and the cracks
were beginning to show. This time the doctor sternly ordered me to
"take it easy." This was just the license I needed to do as I pleased,

drop everything extraneous—the piano lessons, the pious remnants of my past—and burrow more deeply into the college world which, though it must have frightened me, was surely the place I really wanted to be. I began to spend all my weekends in the dorm, unimaginably free, cutting the umbilical cord that bound me to family and religion alike. The great books, the history of ideas, the culture of the West—these became the rock of my new faith, though, unlike many of my friends and teachers, I still remained caught up with the old one.

What I have described here may simply be a stereotype of the secularization of the Western—and Jewish—intellectual. An observer might question how much of a change was involved in my migration from one world to another. I went on being a student but studied different things. As a kind of temple of learning, the university saved me from the radical crisis of conscience and belief that afflicted so many Victorians and early moderns, to say nothing of *shtetl* philosophers. My immersion in The Book became a passion for books. The stress on right conduct, which Matthew Arnold called the essence of Hebraism, was gradually directed into a new framework—secular, moral, and political rather than religious. It never occurred to me that the politics of Jews—so long disenfranchised by their Christian brethren—could ever be anything but liberal, reformist, compassionate, and egalitarian.

In literature I've always been drawn without knowing why to writers impassioned by a strong moral vision: to poets like Blake and Wordsworth, novelists like James, George Eliot, and Dostoevsky, critics like Arnold, Leavis, Orwell, and Trilling. I dislike conservative polemicists (from Irving Babbitt to John Gardner) who use morality as an unwieldy club to beat imagination, but aesthetes, dandies, hack professionals, snobs, and practitioners of camp also leave me cold. This is hardly an idiosyncratic list. What has made me different from most other Jewish intellectuals, I suspect, was the persistence of a religious impulse and a spiritual hunger in all my dealings with the arts. Religion is untenable but profoundly human, the container of all man's fears and hopes, while atheism and scientism, those typical results of deconversion, seem merely reflexes of modernity, at once cerebral and unthinking.

Among most of the Jewish intellectuals I know or read, I'm struck by the thinness of the Jewish substratum, the feebleness of the culture they dismissed without really knowing. Their experience was strictly of the Jewish family and neighborhood, not of the richness of the cultural tradition or the astonishing complexity of Jewish law, with its pervasive effects on everyday life. The older generation of intellectuals was embarrassed by Judaism: they saw it through gentile eyes as a disability, a burden. They knew it in corrupted forms, robbed of all vitality. It reeked of poverty and the ghetto. It stank of provinciality, tribalism. Their very names seemed like impediments to worldly advancement and cultural universality. The barbarous anti-Semitism of the Nazis was a perplexing emphasis that few intellectuals in New York, Paris, or Frankfurt were ready to confront. "Why do you come with your special Jewish sorrows?" Rosa Luxemburg wrote to a friend in 1917. "I feel just as sorry for the wretched Indian victims in Putamayo, the negroes in Africa. . . . I cannot find a special corner in my heart for the ghetto." How typically Jewish!

As the past recedes it also looms larger, more insistent. We can never have done with our own origins. Year by year I find myself becoming more involved with the Holocaust, which was kept from me when I was growing up. I now read avidly about Weimar, about Hitler, about the death camps. The horror grows; the news, it seems, always gets worse — it can never be fully taken in; the insight into human nature unsettles all progressive truisms.

Whether out of fear or empathy I find myself brooding about the yellow star, the knock at the door in the dead of night, the cattle cars that held no cattle, the precious bowls that served human beings for both food and excrement. I know it's a weakness, if not actually ghoulish, for me to think too much about these images and worse. I sometimes wonder, do I see myself in their place, those victims with their "special Jewish sorrows"? Try as I may, I can't seem to get my mind around what happened: I always return to it with the same sense of disbelief. I now know why the rabbis at the yeshiva, themselves European, spoke so little of those recently slaughtered. They must have wondered in dark moments whether any sort of faith could survive such a catastrophe, as I wonder what moral calculus can encompass the murder of people just for who they were, not for anything they did — not even "accused of guilt," like Kafka's hero.

To maim and destroy people with cold calculation we must first dehumanize them — turn them into kikes or Japs or living skeletons who are physically repellent — categories of disposable things. Jews had already become vermin in the eyes of their exterminators. One justification for literature, and also an aim of liberal politics, is to enlarge the range of what we can identify with, the circle of what is human. No writer does this better than Wordsworth, whose blind beggars, maimed soldiers, and ancient leech-gatherers border on the inanimate yet also form a bedrock of suffering and endurance that commands our deepest feelings. In recent years this humanism has been under attack as a mask for privilege, a fictive construct, an ideology. But to imagine the humanity of others, and hence to know ourselves a little better, is a condition without which civilized life can hardly continue.

Morris Dickstein's most recent book was The Gates of Eden, *published by Basic Books in 1977. He is a member of the English Department of Queens College and a contributing editor of* Partisan Review.

Eugene Goodheart

IDEOLOGY PAST AND PRESENT

Growing up in Brooklyn, in a small world of Yiddishist "progressivism" in the forties and fifties, I did not choose my political or cultural views. They chose me. A child of immigrant parents, who had left Russia during the upheaval of 1917, I had identified the pro-gressivist conviction with the sentiment of being Jewish. The vanguard of progress was of course the Soviet Union, which had not only created a worker's state, but had emancipated the Jews from the Pale of Settlement. I remember May Day parades, summer camps, and theatrical spectacles in which we declaimed our twin beliefs in a socialist future and Yiddishkeit. Among my childhood heroes were Paul Robeson, Howard Fast, Theodore Dreiser, Pete Seeger, and Itzhik Pfeffer, the Soviet Yiddish poet who wrote a poem in which each of fifteen or twenty lines celebrated one of Stalin's virtues. (Pfeffer was killed by Stalin during a flare-up of anti-Semitic paranoia after the establishment of the State of Israel.)

I had a lot to live down when I entered Columbia College in 1949. The trial of Rudolph Slansky, the Jewish General Secretary of the Czech Communist party, for treason against socialism, made a deep impression on me. As with my elders who had witnessed the earlier travesties of justice in the purge trials of the thirties, scales fell from my eyes. My political conversion would have doubtless occurred if I had not been at Columbia, but it did occur there and in the presence of professors of the political experience and sophistication of Lionel Trilling, Fred Dupee, and Richard Hofstadter among others. I came to see not only the deceit and horror of Stalinism, but the cultural philistinism associated with it. This was particularly hard on me as a student of literature. I had much to unlearn as well as to learn. I recall being wounded by a remark made by a professor at Columbia, that my admiration of Dreiser might prevent me from experiencing the higher triumphs of imagination. (The remark in retrospect seems harsh and unjust to Dreiser, an expression of the cult of James at the time.)

Writers like Wordsworth, Stendhal, Dostoevsky, and Conrad confirmed my growing suspicion of all revolutionary ideologies, though I felt uncomfortable with the reactionary conclusions that some of the writers whom I admired seemed to have arrived at. I did not want to be defined by a hostility to a past to which I was still attached through old friendships. In my early years as teacher and critic, political concerns yielded to ideas of personal development and fulfillment. Lawrence's reactionary politics were irrelevant to my fascination with his exploration of personal relationships and states of consciousness.

The radicalism of the sixties caught me, like everyone else, by surprise, and it reawakened my anti-Stalinism. Though the ideologies of the sixties were decidedly un-Stalinist, even anti-Stalinist, I kept recognizing the Stalinist type in the arrogance and deceit of the new ideologues; I found the philistinism of the counterculture worse than anything I had experienced in my youth. What made the radical sixties possible was that it was a movement of the young, who had not experienced the ideological embitterments of those who were ten, fifteen, or twenty years older. I recall an argument in the sixties with a well-known young radical about ten years younger than I, who thought it absurd that he be made to suffer the guilt of Stalinism, since he had never had anything to do with it. He was unwilling to entertain the thought that there might be Stalinist tendencies in his own thinking and activity. I reacted strongly to the radicalism of the sixties, but I tried, as I had tried in my quarrel with my Stalinist upbringing, to keep my balance. I didn't want to be a case of the inverted ideologue, who is nourished by the passion of constant hostility to radical ideology.

This is the case of the neoconservatives, who emerged as an immediate reaction to the illusions of the sixties, but who represent a deeper tendency that began with the disillusionment with Stalinism and went underground in the sixties. As a conservatism without roots, it has a curious resemblance to the object of its revulsion. One has to listen or read for voice as well as sense, and I hear in the accents of neoconservatism some of the old ideological patterns from the past. While traditional conservatives have the equanimity of those who have nothing to exorcize, neoconservatives, or at least those of whom are embittered ex-leftists, recoil from their past with particular intensity. I find them stridently confident, predictable, and even fanatical in their opposition to every liberal or radical tendency (e.g., homosexual culture, feminism), in their habit of dividing the world too neatly between good and evil. They tend to be intolerant of softness, hesitation, equivocation, the contemptible faults of liberals. I recall the same scornful guilt inducing dismissal of liberals by Stalinists and sixties radicals. I think it a mark of strength in the liberal to scorn the scorners. The cultural corollary of the neoconservative position is, curiously enough, philistine in its cherishing of popular feeling and its mistrust of what it regards as avant-garde pretension. (In sketching a portrait of the neoconservative type I risk falling into the trap of ideological reduction. As with people on the Left, I know admirable people of neoconservative persuasion who do not fit the type. The first humanizing wisdom about ideology is that type and reality do not coincide. It is a wisdom that makes possible friendship across political lines, though these friendships are difficult to sustain in proportion to the intensity of ideological conflict.)

In comparison with the thirties and the sixties, the present time is, relatively speaking, devoid of ideological passion. The dominant conviction in most areas of thought is skepticism. I had been drawn to Matthew Arnold's idea of literature as a criticism of life and in particular of the political life. For all of his skepticism about the ideologies of his own time, he remained confident to a fault about the values of the literary imagination. But now for many of us whose

business is the study of literature, the confidence seems to be mis-
placed. An exemplary figure in contemporary literature is V. S.
Naipaul, whose sensitivity to ideological thinking is accompanied by
a disquieting skepticism, if not cynicism, about human possibility. A
radically skeptic disposition has recently overtaken the discipline of
literary study and has brought with it a loss of authority in the
literary intellectual to reflect on matters that are not strictly
linguistic. Not only is the critic uncertain about the objective meaning of the text, he is uncertain whether meaning inheres in the text.
Deconstruction, the most radical of literary skepticisms, holds the
view that written discourse is unreliable, that no matter how hard a
text may try to sustain the illusion of unity, coherence, meaning,
truth, it is incorrigibly prone to disunity, incoherence, mean-
inglessness, and error. For such skeptics, "reading" becomes a process of discovering the illusoriness of our knowledge of texts and of
the world. Who can complain against a healthy skepticism, but
skeptics should be modest and uncertain. The current breed strikes
me, as it strikes others, as often dogmatic and arrogant, engaged in a
power trip at the expense of literature. T. S. Eliot's caveat about
radical skepticism still seems persuasive. "Scepticism is a highly
civilized trait, though, when it declines into pyrrhonism, it is one of
which civilisation can die. Where scepticism is strength, pyrrhonism
is weakness: for we need not only the strength to defer a decision,
but the strength to make one."

It may be that what appears to be an internal development in
literary study represents another recoil from the illusions of the sixties, though its anti-authoritarianism may suggest an affinity with
the radical gestures of that decade. The skeptical sensibility prides
itself on its unblinking view of human reality. There is much that is
wrong-headed, pretentious, and even dogmatic in current skeptical
formulations, but it is not a challenge to be ignored. For someone
like myself who has spent much of life in a defensive position, reacting against ideological thinking, the new skeptical spirit is a challenge of another kind.

I find myself in sympathy with Alexander Herzen, the
nineteenth-century revolutionary and writer:

> Everyone [he writes] now plays with his cards on the table,
> and the game itself has become greatly simplified, it is impossible
> to make mistakes: in every corner of Europe there is the same
> struggle, the same two camps. You feel quite clearly which you

are against, but do you feel your tie with the other camp as clearly
as your hatred and disgust for that of the enemy.

In that uncertain place between rival camps and conflicting convictions, to maintain one's own convictions is to constantly resist a radical skepticism.

*Eugene Goodheart is Edytha Macy Gross Professor of Humanities at
Brandeis University. His book,* The Skeptic Disposition in Contemporary Criticism, *is forthcoming from Princeton University Press.*

Gerald Graff

TEACHING THE HUMANITIES

Until my late twenties — 1963 or 1964 — it's fair to say I had
no "literary, political, or cultural views." The cliches about apathy,
the Lonely Crowd, the uncommitted, may not describe the fifties as
a whole, but they describe my experience growing up in Chicago
quite well. I graduated from college in 1959 with an English major
that equipped me with a smattering of information, opinions, and
interpretive notions about literary works but hardly anything adding
up to any "views." About "politics and culture" I had little curiosity.
"Politics" meant boring electoral politics. "Culture" I associated with
gentility. Neither seemed to have much bearing on my experience.
    In 1959, I began graduate school in English at Stanford Uni-
versity and soon came under the influence of Yvor Winters, a critic
in the Samuel Johnson-Edmund Wilson-F. R. Leavis tradition.
Winters was a self-proclaimed "reactionary" in literature and a New
Deal Democrat in politics. He had joined the NAACP long before it
became acceptable for whites to espouse racial causes. But having
seen the literary leftism of the thirties at close quarters, Winters had

concluded that literature and politics don't mix. Literature stood for absolute values above time and place. At the same time, there were suggestive historical and cultural implications in Winters's critique of the anti-rationalism of Emerson, Whitman, and the European romantics and symbolists.

Winters provided something no teacher had given me, a challenging and worked-out point of view against which I could react and define myself. But for some time I didn't so much react against as adhere. Taking over Winters's critique of romantic and modernist ideas, I was suddenly able to have articulate views about subjects which previously I would never have assimilated. This was highly necessary in the competitive climate of graduate school in the early sixties, where it was important to be able to give at least the appearance of intellectual self-assurance.

I still saw little reason to incorporate politics into this program of intellectual self-manufacture. This aloofness lasted until about 1963, when I began my first teaching job at the University of New Mexico. By the time I moved to Northwestern University in 1966, I had become a convert to the new Left. My new leftism was more theoretical than activist, though I took part in the usual teach-ins and demonstrations and signed the usual protest petitions. I read Marx, Lukacs, and Noam Chomsky's articles in the *New York Review of Books,* and I started calling myself—when anybody asked—a democratic socialist. In matters of literature and culture I remained a student of Winters, except that I began to look for ways to unite politics with literature and teaching. I still think the sixties notion of "relevance" was basically a good idea; Morris Dickstein has rightly pointed out that it was actually an echo of Matthew Arnold's ideal of culture. But it was a notion that was quickly and fatally perverted by those who defined it too parochially.

My new leftism stopped abruptly at the portals of the counterculture and its new sensibility. I was too old, too Midwestern, and perhaps too square to want an "alternative lifestyle." But matters of temperament aside, I didn't see why the cause of peace and social justice needed to be linked with psychosexual nirvana. In fact, there seemed patently to be dangers in such a linkage: working-class Americans who might have been open to radical political arguments were left cold by the politics of ecstasy. Middle class people, on the other hand, were all too eager to take up swinging personal styles as a form of consumption while divorcing them from political commitments.

In any case, I found myself fumbling for a kind of synthesis of Winters and Marx. The combination is not so improbable as it sounds, especially if you borrow Lukacs's critique of "the ideology of modernism" as your intermediate link. Drawing on Winters's and Lukacs's critiques of romantic irrationalism and adding bits and pieces from Orwell and the "New York intellectual" critics, I started working out a kind of Left-conservative position (I borrow this term from my friend William Cain) as a corrective to the prevailing literary and cultural radicalisms. This may seem a depressingly negative way to describe one's role — it often seemed so to me. It can claim a constructive purpose, however, in a period when radicals have pursued programs which fatally undermine their own egalitarian goals and which tend to make the Left even more ineffectual politically than American society would make it anyway.

In the aftermath of the sixties, I continued to regard myself as a democratic socialist and, at moments, a heterodox Marxist. My book *Literature Against Itself* (1979) was praised and damned by some as a neoconservative tract, but its political orientation is basically old Left. The misreadings made a sort of sense in terms of the very confusions of Left and Right that I had attacked in the book: as cultural intellectuals have come to reduce political alignments to matters of style and epistemology, the rationalist old Left is seen as conservative while anti-Enlightenment reactionaries like Jung, Nietzsche, and Heidegger suddenly emerge as populists! But no doubt my being misread stemmed also from my failure to articulate a clear socialist view.

I now see that this failure reflected my nagging dissatisfaction at being theoretically committed to a politics I knew to be without hope of a future. On the one hand, I espoused a doctrine which said that only a full-scale dismantling of capitalism could address the root causes of contemporary problems. On the other, I couldn't help recognizing that this doctrine had no concrete application to the actual political situation in the West now or in the foreseeable future, which meant it was essentially a politics of play-acting. When adopting a socialist line of talk I occasionally wondered to myself if I would really be willing to give up my own middle-class comforts and privileges. I soon realized that I didn't need to consider such questions, since after about 1970, if not before, neither I nor any of my socialist friends had any real belief that a revolution could happen. As long as I knew there was no danger that any radical ideas I had would ever be put to a trial, my politics had reality only within the protected arena of university one-upmanship and careerism.

Barring an all-out takeover by the far Right, our choice figures to be not between capitalism and socialism but between different kinds of capitalism. This means choosing, at the extremes, between an egalitarian welfare-state capitalism (with socialist elements) aiming to make good on its democratic promises and the up-the-rich, screw-the-poor type of capitalism currently in favor among many of our leaders. What Marxists still sneeringly call liberal democratic "reformism" constitutes the effective limit of radical political action in the United States. Given the present conservative drift, however, "mere" reformist goals don't look quite so insignificant as they once did. As for the question of whether a socialist society could overcome the disastrous heritage of socialist experiments over the last half-century — it has become academic.

None of this is news to anybody, not even to Marxists, who often candidly concede these points in the late hours of cocktail parties. They are, after all, not stupid and can see as well as anybody that socialism in the United States, whether along Marxist or some other lines, is a dead issue. This is not to deny that as a methodology Marxism has much value for the investigation and analysis of culture. There is no coherent analysis of modern economic organization, communications, and culture that doesn't borrow heavily from Marx. Nor can we rule out using Marxism — despite its notorious disgraces — as a standpoint for measuring the corruptions of capitalism. But as a practical political philosophy, Marxism is little more than an academic fantasy — not a political philosophy at all so much as a professional "field."

I sometimes think the main "political" effect of American Marxism is on the politics of the university, where more-radical-than-thou positions are very effective in putting rival academic schools on the defensive. In the criticism of the arts, we currently see an interesting competition among deconstructionists, Marxists, feminists, and other "postmodern" revolutionaries in which each group tries to out-Left or out-radical the others. The effect is to raise the rhetorical ante to increasingly utopian and apocalyptic levels, less and less related to any actual or conceivable political situation.

But this is by no means to say that academic cultural radicalism has been without significant consequences in the real political world. On the contrary, it has been highly effective at discouraging the "mere" reformist liberalism which is all that stands in the way of the complete triumph of the Right. Liberal pluralism, which has kept the university open to a variety of dissenting ideologies, is still the philosophy that receives the most contemptuous abuse from the radicals it protects. Of course liberal pluralism is boring and middle class, lacking in the dramatic extravagance and charisma that the "literary" temperament traditionally craves.

Reading over what I've written, I see that this account of my views makes little reference to the concerns usually associated with the teaching of literature. This sort of thing angers some of my colleagues, who believe that the present crisis in literary studies can be attributed to literature professors' meddling with politics and culture instead of tending to their traditional critical business of producing interpretations of literary works. In response to this complaint, I would point out that it is only very recently that the interpretive function of literary criticism has been detached from broader moral, cultural, and political functions. The narrowing of criticism to textual explication is not "traditional" in any valid sense of the term, but a professional deviation from the tradition of Sidney, Dryden, Johnson, and Arnold. If I've developed any credo in the twenty years since I started having "literary, political, or cultural views," it is that the first of these terms is inseparable from the other two.

Gerald Graff, the author of Literature Against Itself *(University of Chicago Press, 1979), is Professor of English at Northwestern University.*

Clement Greenberg

ART AND CULTURE

Whether the country and its culture have changed "enormously" over the past fifty years, I wonder about. I'm not being captious. Continuity in this country has gotten to be underestimated.

I wouldn't say that my "literary" or "cultural" views have changed all that much during the same time. Maybe they've evolved or been revised—I hope so. I would also hope they've been expanded. But *changed:* no.

My political views have indeed changed enormously. I no longer "believe" in socialism, though I may still want it ideally. I've become something of a political agnostic (yet it still goes against the grain to vote Republican). At the same time I've turned more anti-Bolshevik than ever (I can't call Leninism, communism; communism, too, remains an ideal). My revulsion (a repentant sinner's) against leftist cant, leftist right-thinking, has become overriding. Consequences bear it out, and I've come to take actual consequences far more seriously than I used to. I read *Commentary* with relish for its own allergy to leftist cant (I don't take its "conservatism" seriously; it's not the same thing as reaction, which is the only thing I do take seriously in that direction).

Culture. I keep thinking, as I have for many years now, that Western high culture is in decline, Spenglerian decline. But I think I can isolate the decline: it's largely in point of cultivatedness and literature, on which cultivatedness depends most. I can't tell whether or not music is in decline; I suspect it, but distrust my suspicion; there are those who know better. Science thrives, of course; Spengler was so wrong in anticipating its decline in this century. More importantly, the world has become more humane in temper, despite all appearances to the contrary; I believe this because outrage has become more frequent and widespread. What awful things used to go on unnoticed in effect when I was young.

It may be my bias as an art critic that leads me to see visual art as a special case. (Visual art was a special case under decadence in late Rome too.) Yes, the very best new painting and sculpture remain in the background for the time being, but they've been there during each succeeding phase of modernism since Manet if not before. In the foreground everything philistines say, or used to say, about modern art is being borne out: in the museums that pay attention to contemporary art, in the market, in the art press, in official grants.

Some more canting of a sort, this time journalistic: about the postmodern or postmodernism. Modernism in the arts began and continues as a response to the threat of decadence. The visual arts have been by and large the most resolute in this response (painting is the "avant-garde" art above all others). If *major* visual art is going to keep on being made in foreseeable time, it won't be anything but modernist. And as valuable as minor art can be and still is, major has to be insisted on.

Much of Clement Greenberg's art criticism appeared in early issues of Partisan Review.

Irving Kristol

REFLECTIONS OF A NEOCONSERVATIVE

How have my literary, cultural, and political views changed over the past decades? My answer to that question is as clear to me as, I believe, it is to others: I have become more "conservative" in *all* of those views. The answer, however, gets rather more complicated when one tries to explain the nature of that change and the reasons for it.

Partisan Review had as its self-declared mission the union of "modern sensibility" in literature and the arts with the "radical consciousness" in politics. That mission was accomplished in the 1960s —though in a totally unforeseen way. It is a case, once again, of nothing having failed like success. For it turned out that this "modern sensibility" could be disengaged from the "highbrow" avant-garde tradition that *PR* celebrated and find a powerful, energetic, but—by *PR*'s original standards—debased existence in what was once contemptuously dismissed as the "middlebrow" and "popular" levels of culture.

It is both sad and ironic to observe the ways in which the original elite of *PR*'s *ancien régime* reacted to this new situation. Basically, they—at least most of them—decided that the "modern" they wished to be associated with ended about 1950. Clement Greenberg and Harold Rosenberg, those *enfants terribles* of "modern" art criticism, found themselves writing polemics against the very latest versions of modern sensibility in the arts. The avant-garde was now the old avant-garde, which is to say, the old guard. Meyer Schapiro, the leading academic expositor and defender of impressionism, cubism, expressionism, surrealism, and even abstract expressionism, retreated into his scholarly citadel. Lionel Trilling wrote some typically sensitive and thoughtful essays on the dilemma that he, the first to teach "modern" literature at Columbia University, had created for himself. William Barrett and Lionel Abel turned to the study of contemporary philosophy and ended up more or less "conservative." Along with secession, incrimination, and self-examination, there went co-optation. Mary McCarthy suddenly discovered that the infusion of the "modern sensibility" into the hitherto middlebrow realm of culture permitted her novels and stories to be quite popular and commercially successful. Similarly, a significant number of *PR* writers—McCarthy, Rosenberg, Edmund Wilson, Hannah Arendt

—began appearing regularly in the pages of the once-despised *New Yorker*.

Clearly, the new modernism was not anything like the ideal culture *PR* had had in mind. To begin with, it did (does) unquestionably involve a lowering of the entire cultural level. Norman Mailer, whatever his talent, is no James Joyce or William Faulkner, just as Susan Sontag, gifted though she is, is no Lionel Trilling. Moreover, it represented a significant shift from culture as something to be produced, to culture as a commodity to be consumed. Whereas "bohemianism" once meant a "life-style" organically associated with the presumed endeavor by a chosen few to produce art, it had now become nothing more than a mass "life-style" for millions who wished to declare themselves as potential consumers of art. Inevitably, too, "modernism" was thoroughly commercialized in the process. "Serious" writers took it for granted that they ought to be best-sellers, and most in fact now were. The distance between artists and writers on the one hand, and Madison Avenue and café society on the other, shrank into nothingness. The comparison of Andy Warhol with Jackson Pollock illustrates the point quite adequately.

Meanwhile, a parallel debasement was occurring in the area of radical thought. As more and more self-declared "socialist" societies emerged in the postwar world, and as they could be clearly perceived to be more or less totalitarian, ranging from the thoroughly disagreeable to the utterly hideous, the viability of the socialist idea itself came into question. Not so, however, with the newer generation of modernists of the 1960s, whose extreme individualism in culture was nicely complemented by an extraordinary tolerance of, even sympathy with, the totalitarian mode in politics. Primarily anticapitalist, antibourgeois, they would take their socialism as they found it, not as an older generation of socialists had once envisioned it. And in the course of the 1960s and 1970s, newer academic versions of Marxism, largely imported from France and Germany, provided a convenient rationalization for this posture. What most of these versions had in common was the belief that "socialism" could be imposed on society by a revolutionary movement of artists, intellectuals, and students—defining all these categories very loosely, of course—and that the evidently hopeless working class had lost the revolutionary charter which Marx had originally granted it. "*L'imagination au pouvoir*," as the Parisian students of 1968 proclaimed—a slogan subsequently put into practice by one student in Paris known to us as Pol Pot.

How did the original *PR* generation react to these developments? In all sorts of ways. Some, like Harold Rosenberg and Meyer Schapiro, kept their distance from the new "radical consciousness" while insisting on their loyalty to an increasingly wispy radical ideal. Others simply ceased to be radical. Some others tried to go with the trend, at least for a while, and to be youthfully radical once more. (Mary McCarthy was the most notable of these.) Philip Rahv made a heroic effort to meld the older radicalism with the new, but he ended up a pathetic, isolated, embittered partisan of a cause without followers. As in culture, so in politics: the new "radical consciousness," like the new "modernist" consciousness, left *Partisan Review* stranded in a time warp.

What went wrong? Or did anything go wrong? When Stalinist totalitarianism emerged out of the Bolshevik revolution, a great many radicals, including those around *Partisan Review,* became intensely interested in the question of whether the seeds of Stalinism were to be found in Bolshevism, or whether Stalinism could be explained (away?) as a creature of special Russian circumstances. The debate around this issue was lively and provocative of thought. And, in the end, the conclusion was inescapable: Stalinism did indeed have roots in Leninism and Bolshevism, so that a revision of the older "radical consciousness" was in order.

It seems to me to be time for another such discussion on the subject of "modernism" and the "radical consciousness." Just where and when did the seeds of eventual decay get planted? Trotsky used to argue that the Soviet Union under Stalin was a "degenerated" workers' state—but still a workers' state worth defending. Similarly, there are those who insist that, though today's "modernism" and today's "radical consciousness" may be "degenerative" specimens of modernism and the radical consciousness, the cultural and political modes themselves are worth defending. Is the second argument destined to go the way of the first?

Even to raise that question, of course, is to define oneself as some kind of conservative, if only an incipient kind of conservative. Just what "conservative" means, politically and culturally, in the last quarter of this turbulent twentieth century, it is not so easy to say. But, then, it is not so easy to say what "radical" or "modernist" means either. We do live, I am convinced, in one of those historic conjunctures when inherited categories of thought, dominant for some two hundred years now, have lost their creative vitality—though not, to be sure, their destructive energies. It is no accident, as one used to say, that there is an ever-growing interest among some of our bright-

est young people in *premodern* thinkers. This is a healthy, if still indeterminate, sign.

Meanwhile, for myself, I have reached certain conclusions:
that Jane Austen is a greater novelist than Proust or Joyce; that
Raphael is a greater painter than Picasso; that T. S. Eliot's later,
Christian poetry is much superior to his earlier; that C. S. Lewis is a
finer literary and cultural critic than Edmund Wilson; that Aristotle
is more worthy of careful study than Marx; that we have more to
learn from Tocqueville than from Max Weber; that Adam Smith
makes a lot more economic sense than any economist since; that the
Founding Fathers had a better understanding of democracy than
any political scientists since; that. . . . Well, enough. As I said at the
outset, I have become conservative, and whatever ambiguities at-
tach to that term, it should be obvious what it does *not* mean.

*Irving Kristol is Professor of Social Thought at the Graduate School of
Business at New York University and co-editor of* The Public Interest.

Harry Levin

A TEACHER AND WRITER AT HARVARD

Something must have changed, or I would not be writing
this response, since it happens to be my first contribution in forty-six
years to *Partisan Review*. I have continued to read it regularly during
those years, to feel respect and admiration for much that has appeared in its pages, and once or twice to write a mildly dissident letter which the editors have open-mindedly printed. But, never having
been a New Yorker, I simply did not feel at home in its earlier atmosphere; and, still believing — with Matthew Arnold — that criticism should maintain a certain disinterestedness, I was somewhat
put off by the more insistent watchwords of partisanship. I sym-

pathized, as I still do, with the broadly liberal-to-radical ideology; but my own political views, such as they were, had been shaped by a third-party movement originating in the Nonpartisan League; and, although any thinking person of my generation had to come to his own terms with Marx, I have been more strongly influenced by Veblen, whose paradigms had come a good deal closer to my own experience.

In retrospect it seems easier to realize that *Partisan Review* was finding its way out of the doctrinaire leftism of the thirties — not an intellectual retreat but a recognition of diversity and complexity. Others, terming themselves New Critics, prompted a sharp rebound to the opposite extreme: from social consciousness to esthetic formalism. This had some warrant in a reanimation of poetic texts too long obscured by pedantic contexts. But again I found myself an odd man out when, in a joint symposium on "Literature and the Professors" sponsored by *The Kenyon Review* and *The Southern Review*, I sought middle ground between New Criticism and historical scholarship. I gather that many other readers were troubled by such conflicts, since my essay attempting to reconcile them, "Literature as an Institution," has been more widely reprinted and translated than anything else I have written. The institutional concept made it possible to recognize the claims and pressures of society, while at the same time allowing for the semi-autonomous roles of convention, structure, and style.

It was at best a mere formula, a rough sketch, but tentative and flexible enough so that the operative idea could profit from the refinements and amplifications of ongoing critical thought, rather than be outdated by subsequent trends. My personal path — which may not be atypical for an academic critic — has led from a professional background in philology and old-fashioned literary history toward engagements with comparative literature and the history of ideas. But it has also provided me with stimulus from fellow travelers on the routes of Germanic stylistics, Russian formalism, and French structuralism. Insofar as I was a scholar or teacher, I was committed to keeping in touch with the past, to upholding cultural continuities, to handing on a humanistic tradition which has appreciably fallen off during the last half-century. Most of our own teachers would have considered it unprofessional to show a serious interest in the present: after all, I was a student of, and later an incongruous successor to, Irving Babbitt. Incongruous because we students were bound to become excited by writers who were then contemporary.

Joyce has since fitted so neatly into the curriculum and has become the staple of so bustling a Ph.D. industry, that those who have not been his junior contemporaries may find it hard to understand why he subsisted as "a banned writer" throughout the greater part of his career. *Ulysses* had been unbanned for no more than seven years when I started to teach his work in 1940, and that course would not have been approved by my seniors, had not the inclusion of Proust and Mann enabled us to hedge it with a language requirement. In a little book published on the occasion of Joyce's death in the following year, I tried to emphasize the watershed that it uniquely marked. On the one hand, he had carried naturalism farther than anyone else, through the unremitting description of detailed observation; it was that which had won him his notoriety. On the other hand, he had introduced — or reverted to — a mode of symbolism, by framing his commonplace episodes within the archetypal contours of heroic myth; and that had contributed to his earlier reputation for unintelligibility.

Our most notable critic, Edmund Wilson, even while elucidating the twentieth-century symbolists, had envisioned that movement coming to a dead end. Actually it was the naturalists who were reaching, if not a stalemate, then a point of diminishing returns. Meanwhile the symbolic vein of Joyce was reinforced by the belated influence of Kafka. Fictional experiment and critical method both were turning toward the mythical and the fabulous, the fantastic and the parabolic. Some of us who were interested in the reconsideration of American fiction undertook to point out that its traditional genre was not the novel but the romance, a compound of the moral allegory and the philosophical tale — which, in spite of more popular tendencies toward materialism and optimism, proved by no means incompatible with the dark introspection of our finest authors. Some of us also joined in the perennial quest for the archetype, as I did by joining my gifted colleague, the clinical psychologist Henry Murray, in a seminar on what we called thematics, subjecting the particulars of literature to the universals of psychology.

Living as we do today in a world where science fiction comes true, it is an increasing problem to discriminate fantasies from actualities. The underlying paradox of poetics (by which I mean literary theory) is the use of imagination to enlarge the sense of reality. Here a special challenge presents itself in the name of realism, since this has been the most deliberate, systematic, and comprehensive of such endeavors. Hence I was attracted to the main line of French novelists extending from Stendhal and Balzac through Flaubert and Zola to Proust. Their successive novels could be correlated with a sequence of revolutions, the emergence of middle-class democracy, and the spirit of scientific inquiry. My lengthy study convinced me that the cycle had run its course; our epoch did not breed such powerful individuality; our culture did not foster such incisive self-criticism. The recent "non-fiction novel" is more journalistic than realistic. The "media," while devising new modes of their own, have irreversibly undermined the old ones. Technology, while regimenting life, has augmented the odds against literature.

What a difference from the first three decades of the century! Whether we view ourselves as heirs of all the ages or as bearers of the burden of the past, we are likely to be self-conscious about chronology. In the eighties it seems quite natural that we should begin to think, as they did a hundred years before, of approaching a world-weary *fin du siècle*. But, for those who had been born into the bourgeois humanism of the late nineteenth century and had greeted the year 1900 as a landmark of their youth, the incoming twentieth century must have held a millennial promise. Many of them found a brilliant fulfilment in the high modernism that would attain its apogee during the twenties. This had a geographical as well as a historical dimension, which for American talents often meant an incubation in Europe, most often in Paris. America had drawn heavily on that source from the very beginning. But the intercultural tides were reversed when the great diaspora of leading European intellectuals, expatriated by the totalitarian regimes, boundlessly enriched the arts and sciences in the United States.

Ever since the Second World War we have ceased to live in a Eurocentric universe, which I am provincial enough to miss. As a fledgling middlewestern intellectual, moving east to Harvard and for a while abroad, I would have drawn modest encouragement from the illustrious precedent of T. S. Eliot, even if I had not heard him lecture and he had not accepted my first article for his *Criterion*. Admirers of his poetry could regard him as a revolutionary modernist. As a critic, he was deeply engaged in revising traditions. Later on, when I came to enjoy the privilege of his friendship, it was upon a basis which permitted us to joke about our differences in politics. Yet one could hardly look back at that elder persona, which he was creating for himself, as anything other than neoconservative — a word which, his example taught us, could be used without irony. Historically, to apply another neologism, one could look upon his traditionalism as a kind of prologue to postmodernism. Much of this was already prefigured in *The Waste Land,* with its reechoing quotations, its backward glances, its consciousness of aftermath.

We may well derive some sympathy for the postmodernists from our awareness that they were up against an exceptionally difficult act to follow, without merely consolidating the gains or assimilating the innovations of their modernistic predecessors. When my college friend James Laughlin founded his *New Directions* in 1936, he conceived it as a quasi-annual showcase for original talent and a publishing house for the avant-garde. But, admirably as it has performed its function, that has been more of a rearguard action, not to say a holding operation. If the pioneering skyscrapers loomed upward to symbolize modernity, there is no comparable statement to be discerned in the irresponsibly eclectic whimsies of Philip Johnson. Conversely, why should we talk about "the lost generation," when we have in mind the dynamic heyday of Hemingway, Fitzgerald, and Gertrude Stein? Would that poignant epithet not be better suited to such coevals as Delmore Schwartz, John Berryman, and Sylvia Plath? One of the distinctions between these generations is that so many of the later-born have taken shelter within the academy.

Speaking as a non-creative academician, I have welcomed this influx and believe in its leavening effect on pupils and even colleagues. I am less sure that it has turned out to be wholly salutary for the writers themselves, whose self-consciousness has been raised to an almost Alexandrian plane. Nor would I — at the risk of appearing sclerotic in my turn — agree that much of what is now contemporary writing needs or deserves classroom study, though it achieves this form of canonization far more readily than Eliot or Joyce did in their day. I do not share the feeling that literary studies are being jeopardized because of their present concern for methodological or theoretical problems, though I would not genuflect before the highly publicized French solutions to them. Anglo-American criticism, which had dealt so perceptively with the end products of literature, might indeed pay more attention to its basic processes. At all events, the follies we have survived encourage that collective search for wisdom in which *Partisan Review* has been so fully engaged, and it is a pleasure for me to revive the association.

Harry Levin is Irving Babbit Professor of Comparative Literature, Emeritus, at Harvard University. He is the author of Memories of the Moderns *(New Directions, 1980), among other works.*

Norman Podhoretz

THE FUTURE OF AMERICA

I am, frankly, at a loss in trying to answer your question about how my ideas have changed over the past few decades. About five years ago, in a political memoir called *Breaking Ranks, I tried to answer that very question in great detail. I gather from your own more recent political memoir, A Partisan View,* that you found my account less than fully convincing. So, as you say in that book, did "everyone" else. "Everyone" presumably means most of the people who will be reading this issue of *PR*. What can I do by way of clarification in two thousand words now that I was unable to do in a hundred thousand five years ago?

Nevertheless I have decided to accept the invitation to write this piece because in spite of everything (and "everyone"), I want to participate in commemorating the fiftieth anniversary of *PR*. I started reading *PR* in the late forties when I was still in my teens; I began writing for it in 1953 when I was in my early twenties; and I spent a goodly portion of my young adulthood in the company of people who were part of the intellectual community out of which *PR* came. For a brief period, I was one of the few members of that community who remained on equally good terms both with you and with Philip Rahv; at the same time, I was close to many others whose talent for backbiting was of course less highly developed than Rahv's, but only slightly. I wish I could say that I delighted in this brilliant company in spite of the backbiting, but the truth is that the backbiting was part of the fun; in many instances, it was inseparable from, and served as the driving force of, the brilliance. In any case, as the youngest member of the group, I took it all in with so large and eager an appetite that someone, I forget who, and not meaning it as a compliment, once called me the Boswell of *Partisan Review*.

Intellectually, politically, socially, *PR* was my world. And when, nearly twenty-five years ago, I became the editor of *Commentary*, I still considered myself, and was considered by "everyone" else, fully a part of that world. It wasn't until the late sixties that I found myself "breaking ranks"; and even then, enraged as I was by what I regarded, and still regard, as a betrayal by so many of my old friends and colleagues of so much of what had given honor and luster to their work in the past—even then it took several more years before the break was complete.

I can't go over the same ground here that I traveled in *Breaking Ranks,* but I do have to repeat something I said there. Whatever you and "everyone" else may have thought about my conversation to what has come to be called neoconservatism, what *I* thought I was doing was remaining loyal to the defining traditions of *Partisan Review.* In my eyes, it was you who were the apostates, not I. For what were the defining traditions of *Partisan Review?* The first, and most important, was anti-communism. Yet at a time when anti-anti-communism was sweeping through almost every parish of the intellectual world, *PR* itself, like its progeny the *New York Review,* threw in with it. Worse yet, such *PR* stalwarts as Philip Rahv, Mary McCarthy, and Susan Sontag all delivered themselves of apologetics for communist regimes (including most astonishingly, in the case of Rahv, the one in the Soviet Union!) so effusive that they would have made even the Stalinist enemies of the old *PR* blush. It is true that none of these disgraceful performances appeared in *PR* itself (that honor goes to the *New York Review*), but *PR* published its own share of pieces which differed mainly in being done by writers imported from the *Village Voice* and similarly elevated quarters who in the great days would not have been thought either intelligent enough or talented enough to write for a magazine of truly high standards. Opening itself to such writers represented a betrayal of the other defining tradition of *Partisan Review:* its stubborn intellectual distinction. And finally, there was a third betrayal, exemplified by the assault on high culture that was essential to the radical movement of the sixties and for which critics who were then or had in the past been associated with *PR* (Richard Poirier, Leslie Fiedler, and again Susan Sontag) provided supporting rationalizations.

Having in the late fififtes and early sixties done my own bit to plant these infections in the culture, I grew more and more appalled as I watched them spread and metastasize. In your new book, you tell the story of a heated argument we had in the late sixties about all this, but you get the details wrong. What we were actually arguing about that night was whether the radicals of that time were comparable to the Stalinists of the thirties. I said that for all practical purposes they were, and that my disaffection with the movement was similar to your break with the communists three decades earlier. You denied this: "They *aren't* like the communists," you insisted. I thought you were wrong then, and I still think so today. I broke, following the example he and the entire *PR* community had set for me in the thirties. Most of you, in one way or another and to one degree or another, decided (as I saw and see it) that *this* time the right thing to do was to stay within the fold; and so you went with, or at least failed to join the fight against, the spiritual children of the Stalinists it had once been your proudest boast to have opposed.

But now let me confess something. In the five years since *Breaking Ranks* was published, I have come to see that I was mistaken in claiming a greater loyalty to the defining traditions of *Partisan Review* than you yourself and a number of other intellectuals associated with the magazine have shown. I don't think I was mistaken about such members of the first *PR* generation as Philip Rahv and Mary McCarthy, or Leslie Fiedler of the second, or Susan Sontag and Richard Poirier of the third, or Morris Dickstein of the fourth. Surely nothing could have been more radically at odds with what *PR* stood for than the born-again Leninism of Rahv, or McCarthy's gushings over the Hanoi regime, or Fiedler's nihilistic celebrations of pop culture, not to mention the variations played on all these themes by Sontag, Poirier, and Dickstein. Nor did the fact that these traitors to the *PR* tradition were at odds with one another — Rahv, for example, supporting the New Left but attacking the counterculture — make them any the less culpable, each after his own kind.

As compared with all of them, I and a few others who had once been connected with *PR* (Sidney Hook, Lionel Abel, William Barrett, Hilton Kramer) *were* the true guardians of the magazine's legacy both in politics and in culture. But I now think that as compared with you in the first generation, Irving Howe in the second, Dennis Wrong in the third, and Leon Wieseltier in the fourth, it is we who were the apostates (or perhaps only heretics).

I say this because I now realize that neither *PR*'s anti-communism in the thirties nor its defense of "our country and our culture" in the fifties was powerful enough to overcome its unshakable commitment to the Left. *That*, it turns out, was what truly defined the tradition of *PR*: the struggle to maintain solidarity with the Left even when one recognized that the Soviet Union was (yes) an evil empire and that the United States was with all its faults a decent society. I for one have given up that struggle. I no longer see myself as a man of the Left and I no longer see the Left as a force for good in the world. At best it is relatively harmless, pushing for a little more redistribution of the wealth that only the capitalist system (for which the Left still cannot bring itself to say a good word) seems able to produce. At worst, it has, under the cover of nuclear hysteria and a historically baseless faith in disarmament negotiations, joined the clamor for appeasement of the Soviet Union in Europe and for acquiescence in the spread of communist regimes in Central America and other parts of the Third World.

Yes, I know that you and your current allies have reaffirmed your old anti-communist convictions and that you have distanced yourselves from the appeasers; I suspect that you in particular could even say a good word for capitalism without gagging. But on the evidence of your new book, you still believe in the dream of a Left that is democratic, that is anti-communist, that can find a proper balance between the values of freedom and equality, and that can set itself against the debasement of culture. Like the *Dissent* and the *New York Review* crowds, you believe in a Left that never was and that in my opinion never will be. The vision of this utopian Left is, it has now become clear, far more precious to all of you than the real civilization in which we live in the here and now and which I believe we are called upon to defend and preserve.

For a brief moment in the early fifties, when the United States had defeated the totalitarianism of the Right and was now taking on the responsibility for holding back the totalitarianism of the Left, *PR* recognized that there was something more to our formerly despised country and its culture than had met its eye in the thirties. Yet even then the recognition was grudging. As Hilton Kramer has so devastatingly put it: as between Auschwitz and the Gulag, on the whole most *PR* intellectuals preferred New York. And soon enough, even this faint recognition began to fade, with Philip Rahv going so far as to say that "there is more 'welfare' in the Soviet Union right now, with free education and free medical care guaranteed to all, than there is here. . . ," and with Mary McCarthy all but explicitly comparing the United States to Nazi Germany.

Still, even those like Irving Howe who protested against such smears did not go on to defend the United States. For example, Howe still preferred New York, but that certainly did not mean that New York was *good*. Only "democratic socialism" was good, "the name of our desire." But did that mean that Stockholm was the name of Irving Howe's desire? Not exactly. On the whole, he probably preferred New York even to Stockholm. But neither did *that* mean that New York—let alone the United States of America as a whole— was good, and anyone like myself who had the temerity to think so was sure to be sneered at and vilified.

In the end, as in the beginning—and except, to repeat, for a brief interlude in the middle—what *PR* has stood for is the refusal to choose between the actual alternatives offered by the real world, and a flight into the utopian dreams of the Left. I too was once mes-merized by those dreams, but I have come to see them as the breed-ing ground of a neutralism no less dangerous and immoral today than its counterpart was in the late thirties. Therefore, I have also come to see that I was wrong in the claim I once made to *PR*'s spiritual and political legacy. To commemorate *PR*'s fiftieth anni-versary by saying this brings no joy to my heart, and perhaps it will bring no joy to yours either. But there, alas, it is.

Norman Podhoretz, the editor of *Commentary,* is the author of *Why We Were in Vietnam* (Simon and Schuster, 1983) and other books of social criticism.

Arthur Schlesinger, Jr.

THE VITAL CENTER

Partisan Review asks how I have changed in my views over the past fifty years. Half a century ago I was in my seventeenth year, a New Dealer in politics and a traditionalist in literature. In the next dozen years, Hitler, Stalin, and Reinhold Niebuhr persuaded me of the reality of evil, and I came to see that original sin sets limits on human striving. *The Vital Center* registered those changes in 1949.

It is, I suppose, evidence of lack of imagination or of some other infirmity of character; but, I am rather embarrassed to say, I have not radically altered my views in the third of a century since. I took a look at *The Vital Center* the other day and would subscribe to most of it now. The writers I quote—Pascal, Dostoevsky, Yeats,

Proust, Niebuhr, Whitman—I cherish still. Today I would add Emerson, Tocqueville, Henry Adams, William James to the canon.

For the rest, if I were writing *The Vital Center* today, I would tone down the rhetoric, pay more attention than I did in 1949 to the question of racial justice, and modify my somewhat guileless faith in Keynesian management of the economy. I quite failed, for example, to identify inflation as the central weakness of the post-war economy. But I still believe that the diversification of ownership is the necessary foundation for individual freedom and civil liberty. I also still believe that ownership gives the men of business quite sufficient power and that they do not need to possess the political state as well; and that, when they do, greed inevitably leads them to adopt policies that undermine the free system. The little-brother-of-the-rich psychology that has consumed some ex-radicals—the ones who want to give business not only economic power but political power too—still seems pathetic. In short, I continue to believe that, if we would preserve a free democracy, we must rescue capitalism from the capitalists.

I also continue to believe that the national government is democracy's best instrument in keeping capitalism under control. I mentioned some limitations on affirmative government in *The Vital Center,* and I would add to the list today. But I have no doubt that the intervention of the national government has increased freedom, justice, and income for the average American. Nor do I believe that we can safely confide the problems of the future to a deregulated market controlled by great corporations, as the neoconservatives and neoliberals of the present day exhort us to do.

In foreign affairs I repent not a word of the anti-Stalinism that was a major theme of *The Vital Center.* There is much condemnatory talk these days about "cold-war liberalism." I did not then, and do not now, see how a person can claim to be a liberal and not understand that liberalism and communism have nothing in common, either as to means or as to ends. Nor would I greatly alter the analysis of the grounds of the totalitarian appeal.

I would, however, retreat from the mystical theory of totalitarianism popularized by George Orwell and Hannah Arendt. This theory must have been much in the air in the late 1940s, because *The Vital Center* came out before *1984* and *The Origins of Totalitarianism.* Now that we know far more about the inner workings of Nazism and Stalinism, it seems clear that totalitarian states are far less efficiently monolithic than Orwell and Arendt (and I) supposed; that the proj-

January 6, 1986.   A/A.

MAUREY GARBER

Partisan Review, 1940. Standing, from left: George Morris, Philip Rahv, Dwight Macdonald. Seated: Fred Dupee, William Phillips.